PAUL WITHIN PAGANISM

PAUL WITHIN PAGANISM

RESTORING THE MEDITERRANEAN CONTEXT TO THE APOSTLE

ALEXANDER CHANTZIANTONIOU
PAULA FREDRIKSEN
STEPHEN L. YOUNG

editors

FORTRESS PRESS
Minneapolis

PAUL WITHIN PAGANISM

Restoring the Mediterranean Context to the Apostle

30 29 28 27 26 2 3 4 5 6 7 8 9 10 11

Library of Congress Control Number: 2025933810 (print)

Cover image: Mosaic pavement of a 6th century synagogue at Beit Alpha, Jezreel Valley, northern Israel. The mosaic depicts the wheel of heaven, with Greco-Roman astral gods marking the signs of the zodiac, surrounding a central medallion of the sun god Helios driving his quadriga. Image from Wikimedia Commons.

Cover design: Josh Eller

Print ISBN: 979-8-8898-3426-7
eBook ISBN: 979-8-8898-3427-4

For Jonathan Z. Smith, whose *Drudgery Divine* cut a new pathway in the field of Pauline studies.

CONTENTS

Introduction ix
Paul within Paganism
Alexander Chantziantoniou, Paula Fredriksen, and Stephen L. Young

I
The Mediterranean Matrix

1. What Does It Mean to See Paul's Judaism "within Paganism"? 3
Alexander Chantziantoniou

2. Jews in a Pagan World 21
Erich S. Gruen

3. Paul and Roman Freelance Expertise 41
Heidi Wendt

II
A World Full of Gods

4. The Universal Polytheism and the Case of the Apostle Paul 59
Matthew V. Novenson

5. Pauline Polytheism and the Triumph of the Davidic Messiah 75
Paula Fredriksen

III
Deification and Spirit Possession

6. Paul among the Sons of God 93
Matthew Thiessen

7. Paul on Becoming (a) God 107
M. David Litwa

8. Paul among the Other Possessed 121
Giovanni B. Bazzana

IV
Divination, Magic, and Astrology

9. Paul among the Pagan Prophets 141
Matthew T. Sharp

10. Curses in the Pauline Letters 161
Laura Salah Nasrallah

11. Paul, the Moon, and Cosmic Philosophy 179
Robyn Faith Walsh

V
Authorizing Paul's Gospel

12. Paul, Epiphanies, and Social Formation 199
Sarah E. Rollens

13. Paul, Martial Imagery, and Adjuring Gentile Loyalty 219
Jennifer Eyl

14. Paul among Pagan Penises 235
Ryan D. Collman

15. Gendering Sin and Salvation in Paul 259
Stephen L. Young

Response 281
From Paul Beyond the Judaism/"Paganism" Divide to Paul as an Ancient Eastern Mediterranean Jew in the Early Roman Imperial Period
Troels Engberg-Pedersen

Contributors 303
Bibliography 305
Index of Subjects 333
Index of Scripture and Ancient Sources 337
Index of Authors 353

Introduction

Paul within Paganism

Alexander Chantziantoniou, Paula Fredriksen, and Stephen L. Young

Paul moved within the matrix of Mediterranean culture. Yet, though his indebtedness to contemporary rhetoric and philosophies has been extensively explored, Paul is still often conjured as standing over against everyday Greek and Roman practices involving gods: Both he, and late Second Temple Jews more generally, are imagined as living in a bell jar, separated from and consistently opposed to so-called Mediterranean "religion."[1] The old Judaism/Hellenism divide, denounced by scholars in theory, is once again reified in practice.

The effort to establish a perspective on Paul that reimagines him in his historical and cultural Jewish context by way of conformity rather than contrast began in 2010, when Mark Nanos and Magnus Zetterholm inaugurated the "Paul within Judaism" section of the Society of Biblical Literature.[2] This interpretive approach, and its eponymous seminar, remains alive and well to this day as one of the most productive approaches to Paul in recent times, with no signs of slowing. For well over a decade, scholars have produced monographs and collected essays devoted to the topic, to the point where many now take

---

1. Issues with the category of "religion" have been well explored, following the influential work of Jonathan Z. Smith, *Imagining Religion: From Babylon to Jonestown* (Chicago University Press, 1982). But see now, most recently, Stanley K. Stowers, *History and the Study of Religion* (Oxford University Press, 2024). Further on what is meant here by ancient Mediterranean religion and Paul's place within it, see Chantziantoniou's essay in this volume, in addition to the fuller discussion in Stanley K. Stowers, *Christian Beginnings: A Study in Ancient Mediterranean Religion* (Edinburgh University Press, 2024).

2. That initiative eventuated in their coedited anthology *Paul within Judaism: Restoring the First-Century Context to the Apostle* (Fortress Press, 2015), to which the current work is a companion volume.

for granted that Paul's religious program was but one of the many variegated expressions of Jewishness in the early Roman period.[3]

The more Paul's Jewish context came into focus, however, the more it brought with it an appreciation for the ways that forms of late Second Temple Judaism also fit within—not against—the broader culture of the Roman Mediterranean. Such a refocusing on Judaism itself as ancient Mediterranean religion naturally generated another vantage point for thinking about Paul. To what extent is Paul's particular brand of Jewish religious expertise also an example of Mediterranean religiosity? That is to say, to what extent is Paul, as a Jew "within Judaism," intelligible and recognizable within the wider world of gods and their images, of magic and divination, of deification and spirit possession, of ethnic reasoning and religious experts?

The heuristic designation of "Paul within paganism" was first officially coined as such at a small handful of seminars and symposia of the same name. In October 2021, the Enoch Seminar explored this scholarly perspective by convening a special seminar on "Paul within Paganism." Chaired by Paula Fredriksen, it offered papers by Jennifer Eyl, Matthew Sharp, Matthew Thiessen, and Stephen Young, with a response from Stanley Stowers. Due in large part to the positive response to and scholarly interest in that seminar, another was planned for the annual meeting of the Society of Biblical Literature, facilitated by the Pauline Epistles unit in November 2022. Chaired once again by Paula Fredriksen, this time together with Matthew Novenson, it offered papers by Giovanni Bazzana, Alexander Chantziantoniou, Jennifer Eyl, and Heidi Wendt. Seeing the need to discuss this burgeoning new approach to Paul within paganism, and to explore its relation to Paul within Judaism, March 2023 then saw an academic symposium on the topic at the University of

3. Some recent monographs: Paula Fredriksen, *Paul: The Pagans' Apostle* (Yale University Press, 2018); Matthew Thiessen, *A Jewish Paul: The Messiah's Herald to the Gentiles* (Baker, 2023); Matthew V. Novenson, *Paul and Judaism at the End of History* (Cambridge University Press, 2024). Some recent essay collections: Gabriele Boccaccini and Carlos A. Segovia, eds., *Paul the Jew: Rereading the Apostle as a Figure of Second Temple Judaism* (Fortress, 2016); Isaac W. Oliver and Gabriele Boccaccini, eds., *The Early Reception of Paul the Second Temple Jew: Text, Narrative, and Reception History* (T&T Clark, 2019); František Ábel, ed., *The Message of Paul the Apostle within Second Temple Judaism* (Lexington Books/Fortress Academic, 2020); Karin Hedner Zetterholm and Anders Runesson, eds., *Within Judaism? Interpretive Trajectories in Judaism, Christianity, and Islam from the First to the Twenty-First Century* (Lexington Books/Fortress Academic, 2024).

Cambridge, with papers by Paula Fredriksen and Alexander Chantziantoniou. Various publications and research projects now approach the apostle from this perspective, and future seminars and symposia are forthcoming.[4]

In short, "Paul within paganism" has established itself on the interpretive map. The current volume offers a florilegium of essays tracing the various ways in which Paul's Jewish religious program is native to the ancient Mediterranean. While providing a go-to introductory resource for teachers and scholars of Pauline studies, the essays are pitched to be accessible for students (both liberal arts and divinity), with modest notes and the most salient bibliography, in order to issue an invitation to think about Paul's letters within this paradigm. The anthology explores how Paul avails himself in positive ways of the ideas and activities constitutive of his own time and place—ideas and activities such as divination, deification, magic, astrology, "polytheism," and a host of other social practices traditionally attributed to pagans and so emphatically denied of Jews and Christians. At the same time, it interrogates how features of Paul's gospel traditionally categorized as exclusively "Jewish"—such as his visions of the risen Messiah, his claims about "faith," his focus on circumcision and foreskin, and his ideas of sin and salvation—are themselves evidence of Paul's participation in wider Mediterranean ways to engage with the numinous. Paul operated "within paganism" even at his "most Jewish" points.

In "Part I: The Mediterranean Matrix," Alexander Chantziantoniou introduces, in broad strokes, what it means to see Paul and his Judaism "within

---

4. See, for example, M. David Litwa, *We Are Being Transformed: Deification in Paul's Soteriology* (De Gruyter, 2012); Heidi Wendt, *At the Temple Gates: The Religion of Freelance Experts in the Roman Empire* (Oxford University Press, 2016); Jennifer Eyl, *Signs, Wonders, and Gifts: Divination in the Letters of Paul* (Oxford University Press, 2019); Giovanni Bazzana, *Having the Spirit of Christ: Spirit Possession and Exorcism in the Early Christ Groups* (Yale University Press, 2020); Paula Fredriksen, "What Does It Mean to See Paul 'within Judaism'?" *JBL* 141, no. 2 (2022): 359–80; Alexander Chantziantoniou, "Paul and the Politics of Idolatry: Ancient Mediterranean Cult Images and Iconic Ritual in the Letters of Paul" (PhD diss., University of Cambridge, 2023); Alexander Chantziantoniou, "Paul's Iconic Christ among Mediterranean Cult Statues: A Comparison of Divine Images," *JSNT* (forthcoming); Matthew Sharp, *Divination and Philosophy in the Letters of Paul* (Edinburgh University Press, 2023); Laura Salah Nasrallah, *Ancient Christians and the Power of Curses: Magic, Aesthetics, and Justice* (Cambridge University Press, 2024); Stephen L. Young, "Ethnic Ethics: Paul's Eschatological Myth of Jewish Sin," *NTS* 70 (2024): 235–48; Stephen L. Young, *Paul among the Mythmakers: Gods, Sins, Scriptures* (Edinburgh University Press, forthcoming).

paganism" as a new approach to the study of Paul ("What Does It Mean to See Paul's Judaism 'within Paganism'?"). Erich S. Gruen ("Jews in a Pagan World") then explores the ways that the lives of Greco-Roman Jews were embedded in majority culture, while Heidi Wendt ("Paul and Roman Freelance Expertise") contextualizes Paul within the particular early Roman phenomenon of traveling impresarios of religious esoterica.

"Part II: A World Full of Gods" offers investigations by Matthew V. Novenson, on the ways that Jews integrated and interpreted the gods of others into their own religious frameworks ("The Universal Polytheism and the Case of the Apostle Paul"), and by Paula Fredriksen, on the ways that Paul mobilized pagan gods to shape his vision of Jesus as the Davidic Messiah ("Pauline Polytheism and the Triumph of the Davidic Messiah").

"Part III: Deification and Spirit Possession" unpacks the ways that Paul envisages enfleshed humans transforming into divine bodies of *pneuma* or "spirit" (Matthew Thiessen, "Paul among the Sons of God"), and, indeed, how this process would itself multiply the cosmic population of posthuman divine beings at the eschaton (M. David Litwa, "Paul on Becoming (a) God"). Nonhuman powers in the meanwhile might inhabit human beings, as the Pauline practice of spirit possession and exorcism reveals (Giovanni B. Bazzana, "Paul among the Other Possessed").

In "Part IV: Divination, Magic, and Astrology," Matthew T. Sharp explores and explodes scholarly distinctions between "prophecy" and "divination," urging that Paul's interpretations of visions, signs, and texts precisely expresses his prowess in divinatory practices ("Paul among the Pagan Prophets"). Laura Salah Nasrallah looks at Paul's ritual practices, specifically cursing, as an instance of an ecumenical "magical" activity that attempts to mobilize special forces in the effort to seek justice ("Curses in the Pauline Letters"). Robin Faith Walsh ("Paul, the Moon, and Cosmic Philosophy") concludes this section with an examination of the ways in which Paul's use of technical terms like "spirit" (*pneuma*), "mind" (*nous*), and "word" or "reason" (*logos*) reveals his relation to broadband beliefs about the celestial cosmos, especially the moon, which in turn structures his ideas about human life and afterlife.

How did Paul persuade listeners of the authority of his views? "Part V: Authorizing Paul's Gospel" counts the ways. Sarah E. Rollens ("Paul, Epiphanies, and Social Formation") examines how epiphanies of the divine authorize the establishment of various types of civic associations and the ways that Paul claims exactly that numinous authorization when forming his *ekklēsiai* (traditionally, "churches"). Jennifer Eyl reinterprets Paul's language of *pistis* ("faith") as a mobilization of the language of Roman military fidelity ("Paul, Martial Imagery, and Adjuring Gentile Loyalty"). Are Paul's gentiles "uncircumcised" or "foreskinned"? Ryan D. Collman investigates this translation question by placing Paul's teachings on circumcision within contemporary medical and comedic literatures and artistic representations of male genitalia: This context reveals how Paul's ethnographical claims about circumcision/foreskin would have been intelligible to his gentile auditors ("Paul among Pagan Penises"). Finally, Stephen L. Young traces the ways that Paul's teachings on pagan moral degeneration express gendered binaries of vice (feminine or feminizing) and salvific virtue (masculine or masculinizing): Pauline salvation holds out the promise of postvice remasculinization ("Gendering Sin and Salvation in Paul").

Troels Engberg-Pederson has been at the forefront of important scholarly projects that challenge the old Judaism/Hellenism divide[5]—a divide that the current work calls into question specifically as it relates to ancient Mediterranean religion (so-called "paganism"). In his response essay, "From Paul beyond the Judaism/'Paganism' Divide to Paul as an Ancient Eastern Mediterranean Jew in the Early Roman Imperial Period," he offers a consideration and critique of the essays presented above, while conveying his own views on the state of the question and the contribution that "Paul within paganism" makes to it.

5. Both as the editor of collected volumes, such as Troels Engberg-Pedersen, ed., *Paul in His Hellenistic Context* (T&T Clark, 1994); Troels Engberg-Pedersen, ed., *Paul beyond the Judaism/Hellenism Divide* (Westminster John Knox Press, 2001), and in monographs of his own, such as Troels Engberg-Pedersen, *Cosmology and Self in the Apostle Paul: The Material Spirit* (Oxford University Press, 2010).

I

The Mediterranean Matrix

CHAPTER ONE

What Does It Mean to See Paul's Judaism "within Paganism"?

Alexander Chantziantoniou
Crandall University

Inclusion and the Problem of Insulation

In a recent journal article, titled "What Does It Mean to See Paul 'within Judaism'?," Paula Fredriksen set out "to explore what a Paul-within-Judaism would look like" through the lens of comparative religion.[1] This is, she notes, a historicizing project, one that proceeds as a strategy of defamiliarization: It makes the familiar strange.[2] The Protestant Christian Paul is, to put it mildly, an all-too-familiar figure. It takes effort to reimagine him within the porous and permeable boundaries of early Jewishness, apart from the theological mores that have long dominated biblical and theological scholarship since the Reformation.[3] Put slightly differently, there is a need to "make Paul weird again."[4] This is one key part of the scholarly project of situating Paul "within Judaism."

However, Fredriksen quickly qualifies that, to do just this, "we first have to consider Paul's larger contemporary context: 'Judaism' within 'paganism.'"[5]

1. Paula Fredriksen, "What Does It Mean to See Paul 'within Judaism'?" *JBL* 141, no. 2 (2022): 359–80, at 361.

2. Fredriksen, "What Does It Mean," 380.

3. On the issue of overfamiliarity and the challenges it poses for understanding the historical Paul, see Patrick Hart, *A Prolegomenon to the Study of Paul* (Brill, 2020), 1–12.

4. So Matthew V. Novenson, *Paul, Then and Now* (Eerdmans, 2022), 5–6; followed by Matthew Thiessen, *A Jewish Paul: The Messiah's Herald to the Gentiles* (Baker Academic, 2023), 11–22.

5. Fredriksen, "What Does It Mean," 362.

This, too, requires further defamiliarization, not only of Paul but also of his Judaism. Paul's Judaism must be reimagined not as an "abstract body of doctrines" (e.g., monotheism)—which the apostle may (or may not) redefine, reformulate, or abandon to his likings[6]—but as one of "many different styles of first-century Jewishness enacted within their own contemporary cultural matrix: Mediterranean 'paganisms.'"[7]

This clarification represents a critical corrective to a looming problem. Much recent scholarship has indeed come to conjure a Paul who operated *within* his native Judaism—to the point where scholars increasingly advocate (or else simply assume) the inclusion of Paul as primary evidence for the study of early Judaism.[8] In this way, Paul is treated as no "more" or "less" Jewish than, say, the Greek Pentateuch or Philo of Alexandria or the Dead Sea Scrolls or the Mishnah. To be sure, as Fredriksen puts it, "different Jews enacted Jewishness differently."[9] But to see Paul as one such enactment, rather than an exception to it, is "no longer a lonely position to take."[10] The problem emerges, however, as Jennifer Eyl aptly observes, when "Paul within Judaism" comes to look like "Paul *only* within Judaism."[11]

6. On which, see Matthew V. Novenson, "Did Paul Abandon Either Judaism or Monotheism?," in *The New Cambridge Companion to St. Paul*, ed. Bruce W. Longenecker (Cambridge University Press, 2020), 239–59.

7. Fredriksen, "What Does It Mean," 380. Further on "Paul's Judaism," "Pauline Judaism," or "apostolic Judaism," see Joshua Schwartz, "Methodological Remarks on 'Jewish' Identity: Jews, Jewish Christians, and Prolegomena on Pauline Judaism," in *Second Corinthians in the Perspective of Late Second Temple Judaism*, ed. Reimund Bieringer et al. (Brill, 2014), 36–58; Mark D. Nanos, "Paul and Judaism: Why Not Paul's Judaism?" in *Paul Unbound: Other Perspectives on the Apostle*, 2nd ed., ed. Mark D. Given(Society of Biblical Literature, 2022), 157–216; Anders Runesson, in collaboration with Rebecca Runesson, *Judaism for Gentiles: Reading Paul beyond the Parting of the Ways Paradigm* (Mohr Siebeck, 2022), 271–74, 288–91.

8. So Paula Fredriksen, *Paul: The Pagans' Apostle* (Yale University Press, 2018), 175. See, e.g., Stefan Larsson, "Just an Ordinary Jew: A Case for Why Paul Should Be Studied within Jewish Studies," *Nordisk judaistik/Scandinavian Jewish Studies* 29, no. 2 (2018): 2–16.

9. Fredriksen, "What Does It Mean," 368 (emphasis removed).

10. Fredriksen, *Paul*, 176.

11. Jennifer Eyl, "Putting the End Back into the Beginning: Paula Fredriksen, Eschatology, and *Paul: The Pagans' Apostle*," syndicate.network, https://syndicate.network/symposia/theology/paul-the-pagans-apostle/.

In the timely attempt to establish the Jewish pedigree of Paul's life and letters, scholars run the risk of insulating Paul within the complex varieties of early Judaism *to the exclusion of other ancient Mediterranean religion*. Such an approach subtly reinscribes the old Judaism/Hellenism divide through "habituated patterns of selectivity" that keep Paul once removed from non-Jewish comparanda.[12] That is to say, while Paul is rightly located alongside other early Jews as perhaps the most proximate comparanda of his own religious program, the historicizing project of defamiliarization should not end there. But too often it does. This highly selective methodological maneuver has been dubbed the "Hengel sidestep," whereby "any possible influence of Greco-Roman culture on the New Testament is systematically filtered through Hellenistic Judaism, which, presumably, renders it non-toxic for Christianity."[13] Even more forcefully, the influential comparativist Jonathan Z. Smith denounced this "duplicitous use" of early Jewish sources as an *insulating device*: It keeps Paul "pure" and "protected" from the charge of "pagan imprinting" or "pagan perversions," by shielding him within the more palatable boundaries of early Judaism.[14] By all means, Paul should be included within the body of evidence that comprises the study of early Judaism. But he should not be insulated within it.

In this essay, I explore what a Paul-within-"paganism" would look like through the lens of comparative religion.[15] But this is by no means to exclude Paul's Judaism from the picture. Due in large part to the work of

12. Annette Yoshiko Reed, "Writing Jewish Astronomy in the Early Hellenistic Age: The Enochic *Astronomical Book* as Aramaic Wisdom and Archival Impulse," *DSD* 24 (2017): 1–37, at 5: "Despite decades of critiques, this old contrast remains re-inscribed by habituated patterns of selectivity in scholarly training and practice." See the examples discussed in Laura B. Dingeldein, "Gaining Virtue, Gaining Christ: Moral Development in the Letters of Paul" (PhD diss., Brown University, 2014), 63–73; Stephen L. Young, "'Let's Take the Text Seriously': The Protectionist *Doxa* of Mainline New Testament Studies," *MTSR* 32 (2020): 328–63, at 345–54.

13. Luke Timothy Johnson, review of *No One Seeks for God*, by Richard H. Bell, *RBL* (1999).

14. Jonathan Z. Smith, *Drudgery Divine: On the Comparison of Early Christianities and the Religions of the Late Antiquity* (School of Oriental and African Studies, 1990), 117.

15. I return to the nomenclature of "paganism" below, which remains in scare quotes until then. For now, I note that the category itself is anachronistic and irreparably broken. No attempt is made here, or anywhere else in this volume, to defend it, reclaim it, or minimize its troubling history. Quite to the contrary, by applying "paganism" to Paul, it can be seen for what it is: a colonialist category that simply does not and cannot work, even on its own

Fredriksen herself, I take for granted Paul's place within the porous and permeable boundaries of early Jewishness, and I defer readers to her article as a helpful point of reference, in addition to the many other fine treatments on offer.[16] But I intend to build further on her insistence on placing Paul's Judaism within its wider ancient Mediterranean religious context. I aim to do so by outlining, in broad strokes, the research agenda of a burgeoning new approach to the study of Paul "within paganism," including its wider scholarly context, the contribution it makes to that context, how it does it, and why we need it.[17]

The Judaism/Paganism Divide

In the latter half of the twentieth century, a "small revolution" took place in the study of early Judaism.[18] Following the publication of Erwin Goodenough's thirteen-volume opus, *Jewish Symbols in the Greco-Roman Period*, and Martin Hengel's monumental monograph, *Judaism and Hellenism*,[19] a slew of studies emerged to explore the complex relation between early Jews, on the one hand, and the cultural processes of

terms, because the very practices it labels as "non-Jewish" or "non-Christian" can in fact be found among Jews and Christians, including Paul himself.

16. See Mark D. Nanos and Magnus Zetterholm, eds., *Paul within Judaism: Restoring the First-Century Context to the Apostle* (Fortress, 2015); Gabriele Boccaccini and Carlos A. Segovia, eds., *Paul the Jew: Rereading the Apostle as a Figure of Second Temple Judaism* (Fortress, 2016); František Ábel, ed., *The Message of Paul the Apostle within Second Temple Judaism* (Lexington Books/Fortress Academic, 2020).

17. The heuristic designation of "Paul within paganism" was first officially coined as such at panel discussions of the same name, facilitated by Paula Fredriksen—first at a virtual meeting of the Enoch Seminar in 2021, again at the Annual Meeting of the Society of Biblical Literature in 2022, and once more at a symposium at the University of Cambridge in 2023. The designation, then, properly speaking, is Fredriksen's. While I was thinking with the phrase in my own doctoral research prior to and independent of discovering its use by Fredriksen, I came to develop it most fully in ongoing collaboration with her.

18. James K. Aitken, "Hengel's *Judentum und Hellenismus*," *JBL* 123 (2004): 331–41, at 331.

19. Erwin R. Goodenough, *Jewish Symbols in the Greco-Roman Period*, 13 vols. (Princeton University Press, 1953–68); Martin Hengel, *Judentum und Hellenismus: Studien zu ihrer Begegnung unter Berücksichtigung Palästinas bis zur Mitte des 2 Jh.s v. Chr.* (Mohr Siebeck, 1969), revised and expanded edition in 1973, and eventually translated into English as

assimilation, acculturation, accommodation to ancient Greek culture—in a word, "Hellenization"—on the other.[20] These studies reexamined a dizzying array of literary, documentary, artistic, and archaeological evidence, not least including the letters of Paul. The overwhelming majority of scholars now near unanimously denounce what has come to be called "the Judaism/Hellenism divide."[21] What scholars once argued in painstaking detail is now more or less taken for granted as a scholarly truism: Each of the variegated enactments of early Jewishness was already "Hellenistic" or "Hellenized" by the time of Paul.[22]

In the past twenty years, however, scholars have increasingly suggested that Hengel and company did not go far enough. The very utility of "Hellenism," "Hellenization," and even "Hellenistic Judaism" as analytical categories in the study of Mediterranean antiquity has been called into question. James Aitken points out, for instance, that the assumption that Jews would need to "assimilate," "acculturate," or "accommodate" to dominant Greek culture itself contradicts a central thesis of Hengel's work.[23] It essentializes what counts as "Judaism" and "Hellenism," despite the irreducible diversity of both, and subtly reinforces an implicit dichotomy between them as self-contained rival entities that can resist or subsume one another.

Moreover, scholars have come to look through an ever-widening lens in comparative studies, moving away from a narrow focus on "Hellenism" as

---

Judaism and Hellenism: Studies in Their Encounter in Palestine during the Early Hellenistic Period, trans. John Bowden, 2 vols. (Fortress, 1974).

20. See, e.g., John J. Collins, *Between Athens and Jerusalem: Jewish Identity in the Hellenistic Diaspora* (Crossroad, 1986); John M. G. Barclay, *Jews in the Mediterranean Diaspora from Alexander to Trajan (323 BCE–117 CE)* (T&T Clark, 1996); Erich S. Gruen, *Heritage and Hellenism: The Reinvention of Jewish Tradition* (University of California Press, 1998); Lee I. Levine, *Judaism and Hellenism in Antiquity: Conflict or Confluence?* (University of Washington Press, 1998); Seth Schwartz, *Imperialism and Jewish Society, 200 BCE to 640 CE* (Princeton University Press, 2001).

21. See especially Troels Engberg-Pedersen, ed., *Paul beyond the Judaism/Hellenism Divide* (Westminster John Knox, 2001).

22. So Hengel, *Judaism and Hellenism*, 1:104: "From about the middle of the third century, all Judaism must really be designated 'Hellenistic Judaism' in the strict sense."

23. Aitken, "Hengel's *Judentum und Hellenismus*," 334, 339, 341.

the default frame of reference to a broader appreciation for what historians have called "Mediterraneanism."[24] This larger category refers to a set of globalizing cultural processes that pervaded the ancient Mediterranean basin, intelligible and recognizable among Jews and Greeks, no less than Romans, Persians, Egyptians, Gauls, Germans, Phoenicians, and a host of others, notwithstanding their regional variations. In a recent article that draws from globalization theory, Benjamin Wright put it thus:

> If we shift our focus away from cultures as self-contained entities, as is assumed when we talk about "Judaism" or "Hellenism," to understand them as permeable and porous, the picture shifts from the clash or contestation between these cultural entities to the relationships between different groups within a larger cultural "container," which we might characterize in the Hellenistic and Roman periods as the Mediterranean *oikoumenē* [or "inhabitable world"].[25]

This is the general direction of a growing number of studies on early Judaism in the Hellenistic and Roman periods, which increasingly write not of "Hellenistic Jews" (as if there were "non-Hellenized Jews" to be found anywhere anyway) but simply of Jews "in"/"of" the ancient Mediterranean. Jews, such as Paul, participated in widely shared practices of cultural production, which played out in regionally specific ways but which nevertheless remained recognizable in the process.

However, even in recent scholarship that otherwise decries the Judaism/Hellenism divide, lingering exceptions are still sometimes made specifically

24. The classic studies are Fernand Braudel, *La Méditerranée et la Monde Méditerranéen à l'Époque de Philippe II* (Colin, 1949), translated into English as *The Mediterranean and the Mediterranean World in the Age of Philip II*, trans. Siân Reynolds, 2 vols. (Collins, 1972–1973), and Peregrine Horden and Nicholas Purcell, *The Corrupting Sea: A Study of Mediterranean History* (Blackwell, 2000). But see also the discussions in W. V. Harris, ed., *Rethinking the Mediterranean* (Oxford University Press, 2005); Irad Malkin, ed., *Mediterranean Paradigms and Classical Antiquity* (Routledge, 2005); Cavan Concannon and Lindsay A. Mazurek, eds., *Across the Corrupting Sea: Post-Braudelian Approaches to the Ancient Eastern Mediterranean* (Routledge, 2016).

25. Benjamin G. Wright III, "Globalization and the 'Hellenization' of Jews in the Second Temple Period," *JSJ* 53 (2022): 1–20, at 5.

for social practices involving gods or other nonobvious divine beings, such as daimons, deceased ancestors, deified heroes, distant rulers, and the like. In a word, "religion" continues to be privileged as a sui generis category marked out from other ordinary modes of cultural production. It is one of the sole survivors of energetic scholarly attempts to dismantle the divide between Jews and non-Jews in the ancient Mediterranean.

So, for instance, in an otherwise excellent article that points in the globalizing direction gestured by Wright, Philip Alexander acknowledges that "it is now clear from archaeology that all the cultures of the eastern Mediterranean and Near East were in constant contact and interchange at both the material and intellectual levels from earliest antiquity."[26] This leads him to conclude that

> instead of thinking of the Levant and the ancient Near East in terms of a set of essentially self-contained cultures . . . we should think of a broadly uniform culture pervading the whole region, within which various groups adapted the dominant cultural patterns and structures in order to create subcultures and establish ethnic identities.[27]

But when it comes to "Jewish opposition to things Greek," he nevertheless makes an exception for what he calls "the idolatry of Greek popular religion." While Alexander argues that this approach "leaves huge swaths of Greek culture untouched," religion remains in a different category.[28]

Similarly, Seth Schwartz has moved even further in the direction of an all-encompassing Mediterranean. He unequivocally states, probably to the point of overstatement, that the "Roman imperial period is the only period in history when the Mediterranean basin (and adjacent areas) demonstrably shared elements of a single culture, and that culture had a recognizable affinity with ethnographic mediterraneanism."[29] As a result, he insists

---

26. Philip Alexander, "Hellenism and Hellenization as Problematic Historiographical Categories," in Engberg-Pedersen, *Paul beyond the Judaism/Hellenism Divide*, 64–80, at 69.

27. Alexander, "Hellenism and Hellenization," 70.

28. Alexander, "Hellenism and Hellenization," 66.

29. Seth Schwartz, *Were the Jews a Mediterranean Society? Reciprocity and Solidarity in Ancient Judaism* (Princeton University Press, 2009), 34–35.

that "for anyone working on the social and cultural history of the ancient Jews, mediterraneanism cannot be ignored."[30] But, even so, Schwartz ends up lending passing support to what he dubs "a religion-based hypothesis," which ultimately concedes the structural nonintegration of Jews in the Roman Empire specifically with respect to Jewish "religion," pointing to "monotheism" as one standout example.[31] Of the "demonstrably shared elements of a single culture" across the ancient Mediterranean, then, religion alone is once again left out of the package deal, at least so far as Jews are concerned.[32]

Perhaps the most straightforward attempt at arguing in full what others tend only to concede in passing was made by John Collins. In an essay that explicitly sets out to explore the limitations of "Hellenization" in early Judaism, Collins argues in no uncertain terms that the lines of social antagonism and cultural separatism should be drawn around "the conception and worship of God," or "what we would call religion."[33] But herein lies a problem. On the one hand, Collins wants to affirm that "in the Hellenistic world, religion was deeply imbedded in culture and politics."[34] But, on the other hand, he still wants to insist that Judaism and Hellenism were "neither competing systems nor incompatible concepts" within that world.[35] To do so, Collins must reject the possibility that Jewish antagonism to (and nonparticipation in) "pagan" *religion* be misconstrued as Jewish antagonism to (and nonparticipation in) Hellenistic *culture*. So he proposes that Jews in fact invented a categorical dichotomy between "religion" and "culture." The former could then be safety dismissed as "idolatry," "pagan worship," or "the worship of pagan gods" (in a word, "paganism"), while continuing to

30. Schwartz, *Were the Jews*, 22.

31. Schwartz, *Were the Jews*, 39.

32. For a lengthy critique along similar lines, see Michael L. Satlow, "A History of the Jews or Judaism? On Seth Schwartz's *Imperialism and Jewish Society, 200 BCE to 630 CE*," *JQR* 95, no. 1 (2005): 151–62.

33. John J. Collins, "Cult and Culture: The Limits of Hellenization in Judea," in *Jewish Cult and Hellenistic Culture: Essays on the Jewish Encounter with Hellenism and Roman Rule* (Brill, 2005), 21–43, at 23; on cultic separatism, see 25–26, 39–40, 41–43.

34. Collins, "Cult and Culture," 25.

35. Collins, "Cult and Culture," 21.

participate in the latter as an unproblematic phenomenon of "Hellenism" or "Hellenization."[36] Participation within ancient Greek culture ("Hellenism") has found its limits, for Jews at least, in those instances where religion is involved ("paganism").

Over half a century after Goodenough and Hengel gave rise to a generation of scholarly interest in the complex relation between early Jews and ancient Mediterranean cultural production, we find ourselves in a similar state. The Judaism/Hellenism divide has been effectively replaced by a Judaism/"paganism" divide, where "religion" is treated as a sui generis category marked out from other ordinary social kinds of cultural production, and therefore exempt from the cultural processes of "Hellenism" or "Mediterraneanism." In short, there is a new divide in the study of Paul and early Judaism, and there is once again a need for a small revolution to dismantle it.

Paul beyond the Judaism/Paganism Divide

And it has already begun. In the past fifteen years, a small but growing chorus in the academic study of religion has come to insist on redescribing Paul in terms of ancient Mediterranean cultural production, *including the many modes of religiosity*.[37] Many of these studies have followed Stanley Stowers's highly productive theory of Mediterranean religion, which proposes that "religion across the ancient Mediterranean shows common patterns so that it can with profit be analyzed into modes," that is, typological sets of social practices and cognitive processes involving gods or other nonobvious divine beings, which clustered

36. Collins, "Cult and Culture," 25–26.

37. Ron Cameron and Merril P. Miller ("Redescribing Paul and the Corinthians," in *Redescribing Paul and the Corinthians*, ed. Ron Cameron and Merril P. Miller [Society of Biblical Literature, 2011], 245–302, at 257) identify "experimentation with multiple modes of religion" as a central strategy of redescriptive approaches to Paul. Building on the insights of Jonathan Z. Smith, the concept of religion has been problematized in recent years as a descriptive, first-order concept in the study of antiquity, not least as it relates to Paul and early Judaism. See, e.g., Brent Nongbri, *Before Religion: A History of a Modern Concept* (Yale University Press, 2013); Carlin A. Barton and Daniel Boyarin, *Imagine No Religion: How Modern Abstractions Hide Ancient Realities* (Fordham University Press, 2016). Aware of these issues, many of the scholars discussed in this section draw from a polythetic theory of ancient Mediterranean religion developed by Stanley Stowers (see below).

together and interconnected.[38] "Religion," on this account, is a second-order, redescriptive category of social practices involving gods, which is understood to operate much like any other ordinary activity of cultural production.[39]

Such studies seek to contextualize Paul as both a *product of* and a *producer in* this wider religious environment. And they do so by comparing him to his "pagan" peers as "one among many."[40] He is not, then, isolated against any one particular "background," nor rooted in "origins" or "borrowings" derived from any one set of sources. Rather, he is taken as *an instance of* the ethnically coded evidence comprising freelance religious expertise in the wider world he inhabited.[41] Precisely as one such expert, Paul was "parasitic" upon the lived religion of everyday Greeks and Romans, no less than Jews, as the subject of philosophical reflection, counterintuitive interpretation, and the production of knowledge among his gentile followers. That is to say, Paul is situated firmly within the complex and comprehensive context of ancient Mediterranean religion, not as an exception to but an example of widely shared assumptions about the gods and variously linked social practices involving their presence

38. Stanley K. Stowers, "Why 'Common Judaism' Does Not Look Like Mediterranean Religion," in *Strength to Strength: Essays in Honor of Shaye J. D. Cohen*, ed. Michael L. Satlow (Brown Judaic Studies, 2018), 235–55, at 242. See further his *Christian Beginnings: A Study in Ancient Mediterranean Religion* (Edinburgh University Press, 2024); and *History and the Study of Religion: The Ancient Mediterranean as a Test Case* (New York: (Oxford University Press, 2024).

39. See Stanley K. Stowers, "The Ontology of Religion," in *Introducing Religion: Essays in Honor of Jonathan Z. Smith*, ed. Willi Braun and Russell T. McCutcheon (Equinox, 2008), 434–49, at 442: "Religion consists of variously linked social practices (involving arrangements of entities at sites) that carry understandings involving the existence and activity of gods, ancestors, and various normally unseen beings, and that shade off into other anthropomorphic interpretations of the world."

40. On decentering Paul as "one among many," see Melanie Johnson-DeBaufre and Laura S. Nasrallah, "Beyond the Heroic Paul: Toward a Feminist and Decolonizing Approach to the Letters of Paul," in *The Colonized Apostle: Paul through Postcolonial Eyes*, ed. Christopher D. Stanley (Fortress, 2011), 161–74; further developed in Cavan W. Concannon, *"When You Were Gentiles": Specters of Ethnicity in Roman Corinth and Paul's Corinthian Correspondence* (Yale University Press, 2014), 9, 18, 24–25, 45–46. See now, most recently, Stephen L. Young, *Paul among the Mythmakers: Sins, Gods, and Scriptures* (Edinburgh University Press, forthcoming).

41. See Heidi Wendt, *At the Temple Gates: The Religion of Freelance Experts in the Roman Empire* (Oxford University Press, 2016), and her contribution to this volume.

and power among mortals.[42] In heuristic terms, Paul is understood not *apart from* or *over against* so-called paganism, but, as it were, *within* it.

This is by no means to deny that Paul, as an individual, was creative, innovative, or even idiosyncratic within his religious environment.[43] Quite to the contrary. As a Jewish religious expert promoting the Jewish god to nonnatives, Paul's letters exhibit a highly original concoction of social, ethical, and cultic features distinct to his own group-making project,[44] clustering together to form a social *novum*.[45] Rather, it is more simply to affirm what Jennifer Eyl has argued should "go without saying," namely, that Paul was intelligible and recognizable among his "pagan" peers as one peculiar case relative to wider classes of social practice:

> [Paul] was not wildly unlike his contemporaries and he did not "make up" what he was doing from whole cloth. Even when he engaged in practices and made statements that may have been perceived as exotic and mysterious, he did so in a cultural arena where exoticism and secrecy held discernible functions and values. Even when he innovated, he innovated upon the cultural practices familiar to him and to his peers. To be clear—Paul was not a stranger "borrowing" practices

42. For a masterful overview of the issues involved, see Emma Wasserman, "Paul and Religion," in *The Oxford Handbook of Pauline Studies*, ed. Matthew V. Novenson and R. Barry Matlock (Oxford University Press, 2022), 217–35.

43. On "individuality" as a taxonomic and reciprocal kind of "uniqueness," which affirms individual difference while nevertheless maintaining affiliation to a larger class, see Smith, *Drudgery Divine*, 37–38, 40.

44. On "group-making projects" (or "groupism"), see Rogers Brubaker, *Ethnicity without Groups* (Harvard University Press, 2004), 13–14. On group formation as a central practice and guiding concern of Paul's religious project, see Richard Last, "What Purpose Did Paul Understand His Mission to Serve?," *HTR* 104, no. 3 (2011): 299–324.

45. On innovation and novelty in Paul, see Stephen L. Young, "Paul the Mythmaker" (PhD diss., Brown University, 2016), 57–60. On the category of "religious distinctiveness" as a "clusters of features" or a "cocktails of features" (informing my use of "concoction" above), see Matthew V. Novenson, "Beyond Compare, or: Some Recent Strategies for How Not to Compare Early Christianity with Other Things," in *The New Testament in Comparison: Validity, Method, and Purpose in Comparing Traditions*, ed. John M. G. Barclay and Benjamin G. White (T&T Clark, 2020), 79–94, at 84.

> from the world around him; rather, his choices were constituted by and intelligible in that world.[46]

Such an approach is not, then, by and large concerned with the questions that so preoccupied the "history-of-religions school" (known in German as *religionsgeschichtliche Schule*) in both its "older" and "newer" varieties—that is, questions fixated on origins, borrowings, backgrounds, and influences (whether Greek, Roman, Jewish, or otherwise).[47] Rather, it takes for granted that Paul lived and died a Jew "within Judaism," but it further insists that he, like other early Jews, participated in and contributed to religious practices traditionally attributed to Greeks, Romans, or other non-Jews, such as mythmaking,[48] divination,[49] magic,[50] deification,[51] spirit possession,[52] polytheism,[53]

46. Jennifer Eyl, *Signs, Wonders, and Gifts: Divination in the Letters of Paul* (Oxford University Press, 2019), 2. On intelligibility and recognition, see Young, "Paul the Mythmaker," 37–66.

47. For a programmatic critique of the fixation on "origins," see Willi Braun, *Jesus and Addiction to Origins: Toward an Anthropocentric Study of Religion*, ed. Russell T. McCutcheon (Sheffield: Equinox, 2020).

48. Stowers, *Christian Beginnings*, 101–41; Young, "Paul the Mythmaker"; Heidi Wendt, "Mythmaking and Exegesis," in *T&T Clark Handbook to the Historical Paul*, ed. Ryan S. Schellenberg and Heidi Wendt (T&T Clark, 2022), 199–214.

49. Eyl, *Signs, Wonders, and Gifts*; Matthew Sharp, *Divination and Philosophy in the Letters of Paul* (Edinburgh University Press, 2022).

50. Morton Smith, "Pauline Worship as Seen by Pagans," *HTR* 73, nos. 1/2 (1980): 241–49; Laura Salah Nasrallah, *Ancient Christians and the Power of Curses: Magic, Aesthetics, and Justice* (Cambridge University Press, 2024). Further on "magic" among religious experts, including early Christian traditions about Paul, see Wendt, *Temple Gates*, 114–45; Shaily Shashikant Patel, "Magical Practices and Discourses of Magic in Early Christian Traditions: Jesus, Peter, and Paul" (PhD diss., University of North Carolina at Chapel Hill, 2017); Patel, "Rehabilitating 'Magic' in the Study of Early Christian Literature," *Religion Compass* 15, no. 10 (2021): 1–12.

51. M. David Litwa, *We Are Being Transformed: Deification in Paul's Soteriology* (De Gruyter, 2012); M. David Litwa, *Iesus Deus: The Early Christian Depiction of Jesus as a Mediterranean God* (Fortress, 2014); Matthew Thiessen, *Paul and the Gentile Problem* (Oxford University Press, 2016), 129–60.

52. Giovanni B. Bazzana, *Having the Spirit of Christ: Spirit Possession and Exorcism in the Early Christ Groups* (Yale University Press, 2020); cf. Christopher Mount, "1 Corinthians 11:3–16: Spirit Possession and Authority in a Non-Pauline Interpolation," *JBL* 124 (2005): 313–40.

53. Emma Wasserman, *Apocalypse as Holy War: Divine Politics and Polemics in the Letters of Paul* (Yale University Press, 2018); Matthew V. Novenson, "The Universal Polytheism and the

ethnic reasoning,[54] iconicity,[55] and the like. In this way, Paul is redescribed in terms derived from the study of ancient Mediterranean religion more broadly, which deliberately cut across disparate categorizations of Greek, Roman, or Jewish "religions" as self-contained entities or discrete rival systems. Paul, as a Jew, was not at variance with Mediterranean religion, but an ethnically coded variation on it.[56]

As a result, such studies firmly resist analyses perceived to privilege—or, more dubiously, to "protect"[57]—Paul as categorically unique within the religious context of Mediterranean antiquity, that is, set beyond the bounds of comparison with his "pagan" contemporaries and so set apart from the implication of "pagan contamination."[58] They seek instead, as the twin goal

---

Case of the Jews," in *Monotheism and Christology in Greco-Roman Antiquity,* ed. Matthew V. Novenson (Brill, 2020), 32–60; Paula Fredriksen, "Philo, Herod, Paul, and the Many Gods of Ancient Jewish 'Monotheism'," *HTR* 115, no. 1 (2022): 23–45.

54. Denise Kimber Buell and Caroline Johnson Hodge, "The Politics of Interpretation: The Rhetoric of Race and Ethnicity in Paul," *JBL* 123 (2004): 235–511; Caroline Johnson Hodge, *If Sons, Then Heirs: A Study of Kinship and Ethnicity in the Letters of Paul* (Oxford University Press, 2007); Concannon, *When You Were Gentiles*; Stephen L. Young, "Paul's Ethnic Discourse on 'Faith': Christ's Faithfulness and Gentile Access to the Judean God in Romans 3:21–5:1," *HTR* 108, no. 1 (2015): 30–51; Paula Fredriksen, "How Jewish Is God? Divine Ethnicity in Paul's Theology," *JBL* 137, no. 1 (2018): 193–212; Fredriksen, "God Is Jewish, but Gentiles Don't Have to Be: Ethnicity and Eschatology in Paul's Gospel," in *Message of Paul*, 3–20; Patrick McMurray, *Sacrifice, Brotherhood, and the Body: Abraham and the Nations in Romans* (Fortress Academic, 2021); Stephen L. Young, "Ethnic Ethics: Paul's Eschatological Myth of Jewish Sin," *NTS* 70 (2024): 235–48.

55. Alexander Chantziantoniou, "Paul and the Politics of Idolatry: Ancient Mediterranean Cult Images and Iconic Ritual in the Letters of Paul" (PhD diss., University of Cambridge, 2023); Chantziantoniou, "Paul's Iconic Christ among Mediterranean Cult Statues: A Comparison of Divine Images," *JSNT* (forthcoming); Chantziantoniou, "The Politics of Paul's Image Parodies: Material Epiphany, Human-Divine Reciprocity, and Social Power," *NTS* (forthcoming).

56. So Wendt, *Temple Gates*, 30–31. Eyl ("Putting the End Back into the Beginning") suggests "a kind of integrated Greco-Roman-Judeanness."

57. For a metacritical account of "protectionism" in the study of Paul, see Young, "Let's Take the Text Seriously."

58. For an eloquent analysis of the issues, see Novenson, "Beyond Compare." On scholarly attempts to keep Judaism or Christianity "pure" or "protected" from "pagan contamination," see Smith, *Drudgery Divine*, 1–35, 54–84; followed by Litwa, *We Are Being Transformed*, 6–10; Eyl, *Signs, Wonders, and Gifts*, 21–30; Young, "Let's Take the Text Seriously," 345–43;

of comparison between Paul and his peers, the historical contextualization of Paul within his own time and place, and the subsequent correction of academic categories used to understand Paul and his Judaism in relation to those already at large in Mediterranean religion. In the words of J. Z. Smith, what is sought is *redescription* and *rectification*, pursued in order to equip scholars and laypeople alike to pose historical boundaries for a disciplined imagination of what was intelligible and recognizable in Paul's own religious environment.[59]

Such a project normalizes Paul's social formations and others like them in the early Jesus movement "as phenomena that belong to the spectrum of social practices of the ancient Mediterranean instead of exoticizing them as something unparalleled, incomparable, and sui generis."[60] This is a practice-oriented approach. It traces various types of social practice involving gods, and the various enactments of those practices throughout the Mediterranean basin, which "shared a basic intelligibility tinted with regional distinctiveness."[61] As a result, it offers a large-scale hypothesis by which "it may be possible to tilt the scales towards an assumption that the Jews were similar to their non-Jewish contemporaries until proved otherwise."[62] Paul, as one such Jew himself, may well have been odd in some ways. But his oddities were no greater than those of the many other religious actors and experts in the ancient Mediterranean, whether Greek, Roman, Jewish, or otherwise, who between them created the varied tapestry of religion in this region and period.[63]

Robyn Faith Walsh, *Origins of Early Christian Literature: Contextualizing the New Testament within Greco-Roman Literary Culture* (Cambridge University Press, 2021), 4–15.

59. Jonathan Z. Smith, "The 'End' of Comparison: Redescription and Rectification," in *A Magic Still Dwells: Comparative Religion in the Postmodern Age*, ed. Kimberley C. Patton and Benjamin C. Ray (University of California Press, 2000), 237–41.

60. John S. Kloppenborg, *Christ's Associations: Connecting and Belonging in the Ancient City* (Yale University Press, 2020), x.

61. Wendt, *At the Temple Gates*, 79.

62. Martin Goodman, "Jews, Greeks, and Romans," in *Jews in a Graeco-Roman World*, ed. Martin Goodman (Oxford University Press, 1998), 3–14, at 4.

63. This is a play on Goodman, "Jews, Greeks, and Romans," 4–5: "The hypothesis I propose is that the oddities of the Jews in the Graeco-Roman world were no greater than that of the many other distinctive ethnic groups, such as Idumaeans, Celts, or Numidians, who between them created the varied tapestry of society in this region and period."

Paul "within Paganism"

This is the ancient Mediterranean religion within which Paul stands. And he is no less Jewish for it. But this brings us back to the heuristic, catchall category of "paganism." The earliest known use of the Latin *paganus* refers to a "villager," a "country-dweller," or a "peasant," while the most common known use of the word referred more specifically to a "civilian" or a "private citizen," including nonmilitary personnel or those without official positions.[64] It is this latter usage that appears to inform its transliteration into Greek as *paganos* around the first century CE. While the Greek *paganos* remained relatively stable over time, continuing to refer to private citizens, in the latter half of the fourth century the Latin *paganus* quickly became the standard designation for non-Christian peoples as religious others. By the fifth century, *paganus* had effectively replaced "gentile" (Greek, *ethnē*; Latin, *gentes*, *gentiles*, or *nationes*) as the standard nomenclature for non-Christians.[65]

As it happens, the earliest extant use of *paganus* along these lines is from 360 CE, in Marius Victorinus's commentary on Paul's letter to the Galatians. When Paul calls Titus a Greek, Marius explains that "he was a Greek, that is, a pagan" (2.3). Elsewhere he repeats the equivocation ("among Greeks, which is to say, among pagans," 4.3) and explicitly refers to "Greeks" as those "whom they call *Hellenes* or pagans" (1.7). The nearest equivalent to *paganus* in postclassical Greek, then, is not its own transliteration as *paganos* but its conceptual counterpart in *Hellenes*, hence the Latin coinage of *paganismus* ("paganism") on the model of the Greek *Hellenismos* ("Hellenism," 4.9).[66] The word "paganism" thus came to define and police the boundaries of Christianity, lumping together "a wide variety of Greek, Roman, and other

---

64. See Maijastina Kahlos, *Debate and Dialogue: Christian and Pagan Cultures, c. 380–430* (Taylor & Francis, 2007), 22–26; Alan Cameron, *The Last Pagans of Rome* (Oxford University Press, 2011), 14–25.

65. Maijastina Kahlos, "The Shadow of the Shadow: Examining Christian Fourth and Fifth Century Depictions of Pagans," in *The Faces of the Other: Religious Rivalry and Ethnic Encounters in the Later Roman World*, ed. Maijastina Kahlos (Turnhout: Brepols, 2011), 165–95; Kahlos, *Religious Dissent in Late Antiquity, 350–450* (Oxford University Press, 2020), 92–104.

66. So, in no uncertain terms, when Evagrius of Antioch translated Athanasius's *Life of Anthony* 78 from Greek into Latin, he rendered *Hellenismos* ("hellenism") as *paganismus* ("paganism").

cults, beliefs, and practices" as a negative foil that represents "the Christian keenness to be defined as separate and different from other, non-Christian people."[67] And it still functions this way today: "in current historical discourse, by long-established convention, it is regularly employed as a shorthand for various facets of the non- or pre-Christian society of the Graeco-Roman world and its neighbors, excluding (for historical reasons) Judaism."[68]

This being the case, what business do we have applying the category to Paul or to early Judaism? What could we possibly mean by "paganism" in the phrase "Paul within paganism," when that troublesome word itself refers to social practices traditionally attributed to Greeks, Romans, and other non-Jews but emphatically denied of Jews or Christians? In fact, we mean precisely that. While many Pauline scholars are rightly reticent to come anywhere near the category due to its clear limitations as a form of Christian exceptionalism, I use the term not despite these limitations, but, to some extent, because of them. In other words, I use "Paul within paganism" as a *strategic anachronism* that deliberately applies to Paul an "othering" category invented by late antique Christians, which, by its very definition, refers to religious practices long thought *not* to apply to Jews or Christians.

What is more, in late antiquity the charge of "paganism" was often bound up with the use of magic and divination,[69] while in early modernity it was (and still is) much more commonly associated with polytheism and idolatry.[70] This makes "paganism" a surprisingly precise shorthand for just the sorts of religious practices that scholars of comparative religion are increasingly finding in the

---

67. Kahlos, *Religious Dissent*, 94.

68. Cameron, *Last Pagans*, 28; cf. Kathryn Gin Lum, *Heathen: Religion and Race in American History* (Harvard University Press, 2022), 29–33.

69. Kahlos, *Religious Dissent*, 195–213. See further Kahlos, "*Artis heu magicis*: The Label of Magic in the Fourth-Century Disputes and Conflicts," in *Pagans and Christians in Late Antique Rome: Conflict, Competition, and Coexistence in the Fourth Century*, ed. Michele Salzman, Marianne Sághy, and Rita Lizzi Testa (Cambridge University Press, 2015), 162–77; Kahlos, "'A Christian Cannot Employ Magic': Rhetorical Self-Fashioning of the Magicless Christianity of Late Antiquity," in *Rhetoric and Religious Identity in Late Antiquity*, ed. Richard Flower and Morwenna Ludlow (Oxford University Press, 2020), 128–42.

70. Jonathan Z. Smith, "Religion, Religions, Religious," in *Critical Terms for Religious Studies*, ed. Mark C. Taylor (University of Chicago Press, 1998), 269–84; Tomoko Masuzawa, *The Invention of World Religions: Or, How European Universalism Was Preserved in the Language of Pluralism* (University of Chicago Press, 2005), 37–71.

study of Paul and early Judaism, namely—magic and divination, polytheism and iconicity, among others. The self-consciously self-contradictory category of "Paul within paganism," then, is pitched with tongue planted firmly in cheek, heeding the transgressive advice of J. Z. Smith to "reflect on and play with the necessary incongruity of our maps."[71] Applying the category to Paul is deliberately intended to show that the category itself does not work. That is to say, it is not intended to defend or to reclaim the concept of paganism, much less to redeem it from its troubling history of colonialism. Rather, it playfully manipulates traditional categories and historical dichotomies in the attempt to disrupt the uncritical transmission of Pauline uniqueness and to dismantle the divide between Paul's Judaism and other ancient Mediterranean religion. By placing Paul "within paganism," the colonialist capstone of Christian exceptionalism is shown to be just that. The very category weaponized against ostensibly "non-Jewish" and "non-Christian" practices long dismissed as "foreign," "odd," "strange," or "unfamiliar" can be seen to include Paul within it.

71. Jonathan Z. Smith, *Map Is Not Territory* (University of Chicago Press, 1978), 309.

CHAPTER TWO

Jews in a Pagan World

Erich S. Gruen
University of California

The Question

What place did Jews have in a pagan world? Did they hunker down in closed communities, making themselves as inconspicuous as possible, hoping not to be noticed by hostile authorities, clinging to isolated enclaves in order to minimize public awareness, keeping their heads down to avoid repression or persecution? Or did they strive to become a part of the majority culture, to accommodate, assimilate, or integrate, thereby to play as full a part as possible in the larger society, even at the cost of compromising with principles and traditions? The dichotomy, framed in that fashion, is, of course, stark and simplistic. One might expect Jews to fall somewhere within that spectrum rather than at one of its ends. But even to pose the alternatives in that fashion may be misguided and unproductive. It presumes a need to choose between a maintenance of Jewish precepts and practices and a blending of them in syncretistic mode with the mores and expectations of an embracing paganism. Those postulated alternatives may miss the point.

The idea of such a choice constitutes a fundamental misconception. What would it mean to assimilate to paganism? There would surely not be an act of conversion. What would Jews convert to? There was no such animal as "paganism." The word *pagan* simply served as a label applied by Christians to non-Christians, a pejorative designation signifying "rustic" or "country bumpkin." There was no pagan entity, no pagan religion that converts would be expected to join, no uniform set of beliefs to which they would be expected to conform. And if there was nothing to convert to, what was there to assimilate to? The idea is a nonstarter.

As for Jewish isolation and separatism as a lifestyle to which Jews could retreat for self-preservation or disappearance from notice, that possibility runs afoul of the evidence. To be sure, some classical writers characterized Jews as keeping rigorously to themselves, shunning the company of non-Jews, and maintaining a single-minded attachment to their own clan.[1] Such comments, erroneous or exaggerated as they may be, do attest that Jews were indeed noticed and commented upon, hardly an inconspicuous minority hidden away in secretive enclaves. Remarks by pagan authors abound, mostly to point out peculiarities and idiosyncrasies in Jewish diet, circumcision, and keeping of the Sabbath. Whether hostile, mocking, or simply puzzled, they disclose a Jewish presence familiar to gentiles, no underground dwellers sheltered from view.

Indeed, one can raise the question of what Jews had to fear in a pagan world that would induce them to keep their heads down. Through much of their history, they had lived under the suzerainty of one foreign power or another: Assyrians, Babylonians, Persians, Greeks, and Romans. In the Greco-Roman era, the hand of the suzerain was relatively light. The notion that this was a period of regular or frequent oppression and persecution needs to be seriously questioned. Reconstruction of Jewish experience is all too often colored by the most spectacular and memorable events: The ferocious depredations by Antiochus IV Epiphanes in Jerusalem in the 160s BCE leading to the Maccabean rebellion, the "pogrom" in Alexandria in 38 CE, and the numerous Jewish uprisings in the first century CE culminating in the calamitous Great Revolt that brought about the destruction of Jerusalem and its Temple. But how representative were these dramatic episodes and how characteristic of Jewish history under Greek rulers and Roman emperors?

The Hellenistic Context

The larger picture of Judaea under the rule of Hellenistic kings needs to be stressed. Antiochus IV's actions, in fact, constituted a striking aberration. Jewish life in Palestine under the Ptolemies of Egypt in the third century BCE has left little on the record. But what remains is far from alarming. The

1. See, for example, Diodorus Siculus, *Library of History* 34/35.1–2; Tacitus, *Histories* 5.5.1–2; Juvenal, *Satires* 14.104–5. Discussion of these and other passages by Peter Schäfer, *Judeophobia* (Cambridge, MA: Harvard University Press, 1997), 170–95; Louis Feldman, *Jew and Gentile in the Ancient World* (Princeton University Press, 1993), 123–76; Benjamin Isaac, *The Invention of Racism in Classical Antiquity* (Princeton University Press, 2004), 450–61.

Ptolemaic administration leased out tax collection to contractors, some of whom at least were local or regional figures, like the Jewish family of the Tobiads. And the Jewish high priest retained a position, with extensive religious and political authority. The Ptolemies had little need for suppressing local governance so long as the area remained stable and continued to supply revenue. Jewish institutions evidently remained intact, and there is little sign of oppressive measures imposed by the regime in Egypt.[2]

A major shift in power in the Levant occurred at the beginning of the second century BCE. The Seleucid dynasty, centered in Antioch, under its most dynamic monarch, Antiochus III, wrested control of Palestine from the Ptolemies and, among other things, brought Judaea under its hegemony. But the Jews proved to be beneficiaries rather than victims. Their leadership had been wise enough to transfer allegiance in time to present themselves as allies of the Syrian monarchy, and they assisted the Seleucid cause by expelling Ptolemaic forces from the citadel in Jerusalem. Antiochus III brought significant rewards. The king paid for the reconstruction of Jerusalem and the temple after the ravages of war, offered substantial tax and tribute relief, and declared that Jews would henceforth be permitted to govern themselves under their own ancestral laws.[3] The collaboration bore fruit. Appointment of the Jewish high priest was subject to ratification by the king, but that office remained in the hands of the Oniads, a Jewish family that had long enjoyed its prerogatives. Relations between the Syrian throne and the subordinate state proceeded without notable friction or upheaval under Antiochus's successor, Seleucus IV, who, we are told, even paid out of his own revenues the expenses incurred by the temple cult for its official sacrifices.[4]

In a word, the bizarre actions of Antiochus IV in polluting the temple, installing a garrison in Jerusalem, and conducting ruthless persecution against

2. See, in general, Aryeh Kasher, *The Jews in Hellenistic and Roman Egypt: The Struggle for Equal Rights* (Mohr Siebeck, 1985) 29–74, 106–7; Joseph Mélèze Modrzejewski, *The Jews of Egypt: From Ramses II to Emperor* Hadrian, trans. Robert Cornman (Princeton University Press, 1995), 73–98; John M. G. Barclay, *Jews in the Mediterranean Diaspora from Alexander to Trajan (323 BCE—117 CE)* (T&T Clark, 1996), 19–47.

3. Josephus, *Jewish Antiquities* 12.138–46. On the reign of Antiochus III, see John D. Grainger, *The Seleukid Empire of Antiochus III (323-287 BC)* (South Yorkshire: Pen and Sword Books Limited, 2015).

4. 2 Macc 3:3.

defiant Jews, far from reflecting standard Seleucid practice, constituted a gross exception, unanticipated and unrepeated. The victorious resistance of Judah Maccabee, celebrated annually by the festival of Hanukkah, ought not to be seen as a defining victory by champions of Judaism over Hellenic domination. Engagement with a Greek presence had long since been part of the life of Palestinian Jews. Nor did Judah Maccabee represent himself as an undeviating enemy of Greeks and the Seleucid regime. He directed his military campaigns in large part against enemies who had dwelled in the land surrounding Judaea long before the advent of the Greeks, as for the most part did his successors in the Hasmonean dynasty. The notorious outburst of Antiochus IV proved to be brief and temporary. The Seleucids, both before and after him, required no abandonment of Jewish faith or conformity with Hellenic practices. Indeed, each of the Hasmoneans received official recognition by a Seleucid ruler, in effect restoring the situation that held prior to Antiochus IV: The Jewish high priest exercised authority in Jerusalem under the patronage of the Seleucid king (or pretender). Nor did the Hasmoneans shun the emblems of Hellenistic authority. They adopted Greek names. The high priest wore the purple vestments that echoed Seleucid court practice. Simon the brother of Judah constructed a massive family tomb that imitated Hellenic archetypes; his son John Hyrcanus inaugurated the practice of minting coinage in Judaea and hired foreign mercenaries, as did Seleucid kings. Simon's successor Aristobulus adopted the diadem and royal title to place himself on a footing with Hellenistic monarchs, even styling himself a "philhellene." Jewish leadership readily borrowed institutions from the wider world of Hellenistic reality.[5]

The Roman Context

Nor did the coming of Rome sharply reverse that reality. A Roman army under Pompey the Great entered the scene at a time when the Hasmoneans were riven with rivalries and civil strife. The Roman general proceeded in 63 BCE to seize control of Jerusalem, entered the temple, and set a Roman official over territories now seized from Hasmonean dominion. The Romans, however,

5. For this interpretation, see Erich S. Gruen, *Heritage and Hellenism: The Reinvention of Jewish Tradition* (University of California Press, 1998), 1–40. Recent works on the Hasmoneans include Eyal Regev, *The Hasmoneans: Ideology, Archaeology, History* (Göttingen: Vandenhoeck & Ruprecht, 2013); Kenneth Atkinson, *A History of the Hasmonean State* (Bloomsbury, 2016).

were no more interested in oppressing the Jews than the Ptolemies or Seleucids had been. Only internal friction brought about the demise of the Hasmoneans. Herod the Great gained supreme power in Judaea, even obtaining the title of king in 40 BCE, endorsed by the Romans under Antony and Octavian. Herod's lengthy reign, well over three decades, earned immense wealth and international prestige for his nation, backed ultimately by the power of Rome. But while Rome bestowed its favor, it did not dictate Herod's actions. He had largely free rein in domestic and foreign policy. Among other things, he authorized the building of a theater, an amphitheater, and a hippodrome in Jerusalem itself, striking emblems of classical culture in the very heart of the nation. None of this meant diminution of piety toward the ancestral faith. Herod's most dazzling legacy, in fact, was his rebuilding of the temple in Jerusalem in the most elaborate and splendiferous style. His embrace of classical culture went hand in hand with the maintenance of a Jewish heritage. The people of Judaea, for good or for ill, were in the hands of Herod the Great, not victims of foreign oppression.[6]

Family intrigue and struggles followed the death of Herod in 4 BCE, and the emperor Augustus finally took the step hitherto avoided. He converted Judaea into a province of the Roman empire in 6 CE. Did this new status entail that Jews would now be crushed under the weight of a repressive regime, a state of distressful subjugation culminated by the desperate rebellion of 66 to 70 CE, whose failure snuffed out a last hope for the nation? It is tempting and indeed common to read Jewish history in light of that calamity and to reconstruct the hostilities leading inescapably to the final conflagration and disaster. Better to resist the temptation of hindsight. In the six decades between the inception of the Roman province in 6 CE and the onset of the revolt in 66 only a relatively few episodes of insurgency can be identified, and most of those involved local disturbances not directed against Roman rule, hardly a harbinger of disaster. The great rebellion arose out of a combination

6. Works on Herod abound. The classic study remains Abraham Schalit, *König Herodes: der Mann und sein* Werk [English: *King Herod: The Man and His Work*] (De Gruyter, first published 1960, new edition in 2001). Among the more recent works, see Samuele Rocca, *Herod's Judaea* (Mohr Siebeck, 2008); Adam Kolman Marshak, *The Many Faces of Herod the Great* (Eerdmans, 2015); Mertin Goodman, *Herod the Great: Jewish King in a Roman World* (Yale University Press, 2024). And see Erich S. Gruen, "Herod, Rome, and the. Diaspora," in *Herod and Augustus*, ed. David M. Jacobson and Nikos Kokkinos (Brill, 2009), 13–27.

of contingent factors, personalities, errors, and miscalculations, not a long-standing sense of grievance and suffering that led inexorably to disaster.[7]

A single episode has often been reckoned as emblematic of the shaky, indeed fearful, character of Jewish life in pagan society: The horrendous "pogrom"" in Alexandria in 38 CE. This is not the place to explore the intricate and baffling features of that notorious event.[8] It needs to be stressed, however, that the complicated and highly unusual circumstances of Alexandria and its inhabitants make its use as a representative example of Jewish experience in Greco-Roman society quite dubious. The histrionic narrative of Philo on which we rely lacks plausibility. The idea that this expressed a general Hellenic hostility to Jews is well off the mark. The crowds who conducted pillage, murder, and destruction in the Jewish community of Alexandria were not Greeks at all but native Egyptians. Their jealousies and resentments over Jewish privileges in the city triggered events that were exploited by unscrupulous leaders, and the whole situation was badly mishandled by the recently appointed and inept Roman governor of Egypt. In short, a combination of exceptional circumstances provoked an urban uprising that proved, at least for a short time, to grow beyond control. What requires emphasis, in any case, is that this upheaval stands out as nearly unique in the previous history of Alexandrian Jewry. No outburst of this sort had raised its ugly head before. To reckon it as in any way typical ignores the wealth of testimony for flourishing Jewish life in Hellenistic and Roman Egypt, including service by Jews in the Ptolemaic armies; their participation in a wide range of occupations, both public and private, and in the social and economic life of Alexandria; their untroubled worship in the synagogues of Egypt; and their contributions at a high level to the literary and intellectual activity in Alexandria as a cultural capital.[9]

---

7. The case is argued by Erich S. Gruen, "Contingency and Context: The Origins of the Jewish War against Rome," in *Empire and Religion in the Roman World*, ed. Harriet Flower (Cambridge University Press, 2021), 94–114. For thorough treatments, see especially Steve Mason, *A History of the Jewish War, A.D. 66-74* (Cambridge University Press, 2016); Guy Maclean Rogers, *For the Freedom of Zion: The Great Revolt of Jews Against Romans, 66-74 CE* (Yale University Press, 2021).

8. The tangled issues are discussed by Erich S. Gruen, *Diaspora: Jews Amidst Greeks and Romans* (Harvard University Press, 2002), 54–83. See the detailed studies of Sandra Gambetti, *The Alexandrian Riots of 38 CE and the Persecution of the Jews: A Historical Reconstruction* (Brill, 2009); Bradley Ritter, *Judeans in the Greek Cities of the Roman Empire* (Brill, 2015), 77–112, with further bibliography.

9. See above, n2.

The image of Jews crowded in ghettoes, subject to harassment, and maintaining a largely secluded existence out of self-preservation can be confidently discarded.

Dwelling in Diaspora

The vast majority of Jews in the Second Temple period dwelled outside Judaea itself, a fact well worth accentuating. Although some Jews had made their homes abroad earlier, the conquests of Alexander the Great marked a major milestone. The capitulation of Persia, with its vast empire, to the forces of the Macedonian king in the later fourth century BCE cleared a path for extensive migration and settlements by Greek-speaking peoples to various parts of the Near East, from Anatolia to Afghanistan. The movement of peoples brought Jews also in its wake. Jews found themselves drawn to Hellenistic cities like Alexandria, Antioch, Ephesus, and Seleucia. Over the next three or four centuries synagogues sprang up in communities in Anatolia, both Middle and Lower Egypt, North Africa, Cyrenaica, the Black Sea, the Aegean, and Italy.[10] The freedom of movement is noteworthy. Nothing suggests that Jews spread abroad because they were expelled or exiled, forced out of their homes, and compelled to seek refuge in alien lands. Our sources record no mass exodus. Specific reasons for migration rarely appear in the evidence, but motives no doubt varied from place to place and time to time. Some must have moved to acquire land, others to gain employment, still others to serve as mercenary soldiers, to profit from commercial or business opportunities, or generally to improve their life-styles.

Did life in scattered communities dominated by Greek culture and Roman power prove to be a burden that had to be shaken off or escaped? The idea that diaspora Jews in any numbers had a hankering for the homeland lacks testimony. They were expected to pay an annual donation to the temple in Jerusalem. Many also engaged in occasional pilgrimages, sometimes in large numbers, to the holy city. Those practices signaled the profound link between diaspora and homeland but did not compromise the attachment to the lands in which they now dwelled.

---

10. On the synagogues, see the excellent survey by Lee I. Levine, *The Ancient Synagogue* (Yale University Press, 2000). On the diaspora generally, Barclay, *Jews*; Gruen, *Diaspora*; and the essays in John R. Bartlett, *Jews in the Hellenistic and Roman Cities* (Routledge, 2002).

The existence of synagogues in a wide variety of places from Egypt and Syria to Rome speaks eloquently to the comfort level of Jews who, in many cases, may have made their homes in pagan cities for several generations, without abandoning their sense of distinctive identity. We have records of synagogues from literary texts, inscriptions, and archaeology that have revealed remains of some of the actual structures. The earliest references go back to sixth century BCE Egypt, where a large dossier of papyri discloses the existence of a Jewish military colony at Elephantine in Upper Egypt that, among other things, included a temple of Yahweh and provided for celebration of the Passover.[11] Jewish communities had established themselves in Middle Egypt too by the third century, as we know from inscriptions recording dedications of synagogues made by Jews honoring the ruling family of the Ptolemies, and others have turned up in Lower Egypt in the second century. We also know that numerous synagogues arose in Alexandria, home to a very large community of Jews.[12]

The phenomenon was not confined to Egypt. We know of synagogues in Antioch and Damascus in Syria, in Cyrene in north Africa, in various cities of Asia Minor. Epigraphic evidence further reveals Jewish communities with synagogues in cities on the shores of the Black Sea. Jews indeed had synagogues in Rome, sanctioned by the Emperor Augustus. Funerary epitaphs from the Jewish catacombs in Rome show that at least eleven synagogues existed in the city by the third century CE.[13] Most strikingly, a structure on the island of Delos, a hallowed site for the Greeks, birthplace of Apollo, has been reasonably identified as a synagogue, thus setting Jews in a key center of pagan ritual and worship.[14]

Synagogues served more purposes than just houses of worship. Evidence from scattered sources indicates that they could provide means for a range of

---

11. Bezalel Porten, *The Elephantine Papyri in English: Three Millennia of Cross-Cultural Continuity and Change*, 2nd ed. (Brill, 2011).

12. Levine, *Ancient Synagogue*, 75–84.

13. Harry J. Leon, *The Jews of Ancient Rome* (Hendrickson, 1960), 135–66; Leonard V. Rutgers, *The Hidden Heritage of Diaspora Judaism* (Peeters, 1998), 45–71.

14. See Levine, *Ancient Synagogue*, 100–5; Donald D. Binder, *Into the Temple Courts: The Place of the Synagogues in the Second Temple Period* (Society of Biblical Literature, 1999), 297–317.

social and educational activities, including study of the Scriptures, instruction of the young, celebration of festivals, communal dining, neighborhood meetings, adjudication of disputes, and maintenance of the community's archives.[15] Not that all synagogues performed all these functions. Given the diversity of locations, we can infer that local practices and needs determined decisions as to what would take place at any individual site. But the ubiquity of these institutions stands out. And we even have evidence of patronage and financial support supplied to one such structure by a wealthy non-Jewish donor.[16] The extensive spread of the synagogue and the evidently laissez-faire attitude by Greek and Roman authorities toward their operation indicate the security of Jews in their own institutions in the pagan world.

Jewish activities in their communities extended well beyond the synagogue. In some places at least Jews set up governing bodies of their own. The Greek geographer Strabo, who had no axe to grind for Jews, reports that the Jewish community of Alexandria had an official with the title of ethnarch who governed them, oversaw contracts and decrees, and decided disputes.[17] At Sardis in Asia Minor, Jews had a governing body, a *synodos*, that exercised oversight and adjudication within their ranks.[18] Documentary evidence comes from the city of Berenike in Cyrene recording decisions made by the *politeuma*, evidently the corporate political entity of the Jewish community.[19] A recent and quite remarkable find turned up an invaluable cache of papyri from Herakleopolis in Middle Egypt. The documents record a Jewish officialdom headed by a politarch, together with other archons (chief officials), who adjudicated disputes within the community and occasionally between Jews and gentiles, a striking bit of evidence for the stature of Jews in that city.[20] Self-governing Jewish institutions did exist and were evidently sanctioned by the

15. See, briefly, Gruen, *Diaspora*, 115–19.

16. *IJO*, II, no. 168.

17. Strabo, as quoted by Josephus, *Jewish Antiquities* 14.117.

18. Josephus, *Jewish Antiquities* 14.235, 260–61.

19. *CJCZ.* no. 70, line 12; no. 71, lines 21–22.

20. James M. S. Cowey and Klaus Maresch, *Urkunden des Politeuma der Juden von Harrakleopolis (144/3—133/2 b. Chr)* [English: *Documents of the Politeuma of the Jews of Heracleopolis (144.3–133/2 BCE)*] (Westdeutscher, 2001), 10–18.

powers that be in the cities of the Greco-Roman world. The thin evidence that we have is too scanty to show that such institutions existed in every city or even in many cities. Circumstances differed widely in these multifarious communities. But even our fragmentary testimony suggests significant self-governance within Jewish society. Jews could, at least up to a point, run their own show.

Jews and Pagan Civic Society

Can one go beyond this? Did Jews play a part in the larger civic world of Greco-Roman society? The testimony here is even scantier than the scraps that we possess on Jewish self-governance. We have a small window on the Jews of Alexandria. Extant literary texts speak of a Jewish *politeia* or to Jewish political rights. Jews freely referred to themselves as "Alexandrians." [21] Greeks in the city did not have a monopoly on that term. Jewish inhabitants of Greek cities generally could be described as *Ioudaioi politai*.[22] The language is nontechnical, and it need not signify that Jews were "citizens" of these cities in a full sense. But it does show, and quite revealingly so, that Jews enjoyed civic privileges of some sort, recognized by the authorities. And not in Alexandria alone. We have evidence of Jews as part of the citizenry, at least to some degree, in Antioch and Sardis, and this doubtless held elsewhere where we lack explicit testimony.[23] The scanty evidence is evocative rather than definitive. But it does give a sense that Jews could, and in some places certainly did have a part to play in civic society beyond any isolated or segregated commune.

A picture begins to take shape. The imperial authorities, in our evidence, whether Hellenistic kings or Roman emperors, do not appear to have found Jewish communities troublesome or in need of repression. One might be tempted to see this as an exercise of tolerance on the part of pluralistic societies. Yet tolerance or intolerance may not be the best designation of alternatives. The terms are modern rather than ancient. There is no Greek or Latin word for tolerance. Nor did any Greek or Roman writer articulate a policy of toleration, let alone formulate a philosophy advocating freedom

---

21. Philo, *On the Embassy to Gaius* 150, 183, 194; Josephus, *Jewish Antiquities* 19.281; *Against Apion* 2.23–39.

22. Philo, *Flaccus* 53; *On the Embassy to Gaius* 150, 193–94, 349, 363, 371.

23. Antioch: Josephus, *Jewish Antiquities* 12.119; *Against Apion* 2.39. Sardis: Josephus, *Jewish Antiquities* 24.235, 14.259.

of religion. The practice has a different meaning: In the Greco-Roman world alien cults were often added to traditional religious institutions, without strain on any established system. This was not a matter of benevolence or generosity. Pagans lacked a religious establishment or a centralized apparatus to demand uniformity. Hence the very idea of extending or withdrawing tolerance is simply irrelevant. Addition or embrace of foreign cults was simply a long-standing ingredient of pagan societies. Jewish beliefs or rituals did not disturb that pattern.

Another point, often overlooked, deserves to be highlighted. Jews were eligible for *Roman* citizenship. Paul is only the most familiar example. We know that Roman officials who were responsible for recruiting soldiers for the army in Asia Minor during the civil war between Caesar and Pompey explicitly exempted Jews who were Roman citizens from conscription.[24] Plainly there were Jews in Asia Minor (and doubtless elsewhere) of sufficient number to make the granting of exemptions from military service a meaningful act. The privileges accorded by Roman citizenship are well illustrated by an episode in the reign of Augustus. When monthly distributions of grain in Rome took place on the Sabbath, many Jews could not take advantage of the bounty. Augustus intervened and directed that when allocations were scheduled on the Sabbath the officials in charge should reserve a portion of the grain for the following day so that Jews could have access to it.[25] As we know from other sources, recipients of the grain distribution had to be citizens. An important inference follows. Many Jews in Rome, even those of slender means, thereby eligible for allocation of grain, were Roman citizens.

Jews and Pagan Religious Life

The lives of "ordinary" Jews around the Mediterranean are largely closed to us. We lack official documentation of them, and the literary sources pay them little heed. We possess, however, some intriguing and revealing data, although fragmentary, from inscriptions, whether funerary epitaphs, private dedications, or lists of contributors to institutions, that provide valuable insights into the experience of the humbler members of society.

---

24. Josephus, *Jewish Antiquities* 14.223–28, 234, 240.

25. Philo, *On the Embassy to Gaius* 158.

A particularly evocative example deserves mention. In the third century BCE a certain Moschos (otherwise unknown) from Oropus in central Greece commemorated his emancipation from slavery by making a dedication to divine powers. He identifies himself explicitly and unabashedly as Moschos the Jew (Moschos Ioudaios). Yet he gives thanks to the Greek gods Amphiarios and Hygieia for sending him a dream that promised him manumission under their auspices.[26] This votive dedication by a Jew to pagan divinities, without qualification or embarrassment, indeed quite unselfconscious, is an arresting statement. Moschos appealed to the protective authority of the pagan shrine to guarantee the endurance of his new status as a freedman. At the same time he openly declared himself a Jew. Homage paid to the pagan gods did not entail abandoning his identification with the broader Jewish community. The inscription is powerful testimony that an assertion of Jewishness was perfectly compatible with acknowledging the authority and the agency of pagan divinities.

Further attestation of this surprising but evidently comfortable combination is readily found. Two inscriptions set up at the temple of Pan at El-Kanais near Edfu in Egypt, probably from the Ptolemaic period, serve as illustration. Each delivers praise to "god" (*theos*) for his benefaction. The first dedicator describes himself as "Theodotus the Jew," the second as "Ptolemy the Jew."[27] They show no hesitation about those labels. Expressing gratitude to divinity, a common practice among pagans, evidently did not dilute these dedications. And they represent more than just civic conventions; these are religious offerings. The "god" in question is evidently Pan, half-man, half-goat. But the Jewish dedicators did not shrink from associating themselves with this hybrid divinity.

Another epigraphic text from a different part of the Mediterranean reveals still a different instance of Jewish engagement with gentile observances in the Hellenistic period. From the city of Iasos in Asia Minor we possess a list of donors who contributed to a Dionysiac festival in that city. Among the benefactors of that pagan celebration was a certain Niketas, son of Jason, from Jerusalem.[28] Although he is not explicitly designated as a Jew, the name

26. *IJO*, I, Ach. 45.

27. William Horbury and David Noy, *Jewish Inscriptions of Graco-Roman Egypt* (Cambridge University Press, 1992), nos. 121–22.

28. *IJO*, II, no. 21.

Jason is a common one among Jews in this era, and the fact that he is from Jerusalem should clinch the matter. Jewish contributors to a pagan ceremony in a Greek city evidently did not raise eyebrows. None of this behavior should be understood as "conversion" or "apostasy." Jews simply shared in some of the rituals and practices of the pagan society in which they dwelled.

The intertwining of Jewish identity with gentile religious institutions and practices can be further exemplified in a notable conjunction. Two funerary epitaphs from different parts of the Roman Empire offer insight into the subject. One stems from the province of Pannonia, the other from Cirta in North Africa, both probably from the second or third century CE. In each case, the deceased woman carries the ethnic marker "Judea." But the gravestone is headed by initials *DM*, that is, *dis manibus*, a standard formula in pagan epitaphs, alluding to the divine spirits of the dead.[29] Not that allusion to *dis manibus* occurs all that often in Jewish inscriptions. But plainly no prohibition prevented Jews from adopting a gentile formula referring to the shades of the dead, indicating communication with them, and interpreting them in their own fashion.

A unique but evocative example of Jewish engagement with the pagan world comes from the Greek market city of Apamea in central Anatolia. The impact of the Jewish community in that city surfaces in a series of coins minted under the authority of Roman emperors, but sporting the biblical scene of Noah and the ark. The Jews found a place for that tale amid a welter of Anatolian legends.[30]

One can go further and into yet another realm of social and religious life. A number of relevant inscriptions attest to the manumission of slaves, a frequent feature of pagan society. And Jews were among the participants in that institution, both as liberators of slaves and as slave beneficiaries. At Delphi, seat of the Delphic oracle, a certain Ioudaios emancipated his slave in standard Hellenic fashion through fictitious sale to the god Apollo in the late second

29. Pannonia: *IJO*, I, Pan. 4. Cirta: Yann Le Bohec, "Inscriptions juives et judaisantes de l'Afrique romaine" [English: "Jewish and Judaizing Inscriptions from Roman Africa"], *Antiquités Africaines* 17 (1981): #71.

30. For discussion, see Paul Trebilco, *Jewish Communities in Asia Minor* (Cambridge University Press, 1991), 86–95.

or early first century BCE.[31] Here again adaptation to Greek practices seems quite comfortable and smooth, and the recourse to Apollo perfectly natural. The Jewish manumitter chose to liberate his slave in a pagan shrine under the aegis of a pagan god. More tellingly, we have a manumission document from the Black Sea region, dated explicitly to the year 41 BCE, in which the emancipator invokes *theos hypsistos* (god the highest). That invocation frequently appears in Jewish inscriptions with reference to Yahweh. And the slave is freed in the synagogue. But the slave owner, plainly a Jew, accompanies his freeing of the slave with the assertion that the new freedman will come under the protection of "Zeus, Earth, and Sun."[32] Evidently the dedicator felt no strain or tension between appealing to the Jewish god and at the same time invoking divinities as conceived by gentiles. So, even in the sphere of religion Jews did not stand altogether as a caste apart, neither excluded by the majority culture nor segregating themselves to remain untainted by the majority culture.

Another pointed instance underscores this overlapping. A sarcophagus from the town of Hierapolis in Phrygia in Anatolia, dating to the mid-second century BCE, sports the inscription of a certain Hikesios "also called Judah." The name is unmistakably Jewish. The inscribed statement calls him "the most famous victor in sacred contests" and indeed adds "multiple victor."[33] Whether Hikesios-Judah's triumphs came in athletic or musical contexts is unspecified. But that a man who carried the name Judah could enter—and win—numerous "sacred contests," that is, contests consecrated to pagan deities, holds real significance. Not only could Jews take part in gymnasial games, a Greek institution, but they could advertise their participation proudly in these preeminently pagan competitions.

A much later funerary text, also from Hierapolis, probably from the early third century CE, deserves notice in this connection. Here P. Aelius Glykon announces two endowments that he will supply for decorating the gravesites on specified occasions annually. The first is a gift to the guild of purple dyers to administer the ceremony each year at Passover. The second is a gift to the association of carpet weavers to distribute the proceeds, half at the celebration of

31. *IJO*, I, Ach. no. 44.

32. *IJO*, I, BS, no. 20.

33. *IJO*, II, no. 189.

the Kalends and half at the festival of Pentecost (Shavuot).[34] It is quite remarkable that Glykon, doubtless a Jew, specified two Jewish holidays, Passover and Pentecost, as occasions for commemoration, but also designated the festival of Kalends, a pagan event that celebrated the Roman new year. It is altogether unnecessary to propose, as some have, that Glykon was a partial convert to Judaism, a sympathizer, or a "god-fearer" who sought to balance his allegiance in this fashion. Such speculations, of course, depend on the presumption that Glykon's links to both Jewish and pagan festivals create a problem that needs to be resolved. But no such problem may have existed. That one of of the guilds would honor the gravesite both on a Jewish holiday and on a civic holiday was perfectly acceptable and requires no special explanation.

Two last examples help to confirm the picture. First, a Phoenician epitaph from the fourth century BCE gives the Hebrew name of a father and the Phoenician name of his son.[35] Both of them possess names that allude to divinity. The notable fact is that one of the names alludes to Yahweh and the other to the Canaanite deity Astarte. That is a remarkable form of shared religious and ethnic identity. The second document exhibits the reverse face of the adaptation that has been discussed here. Pagans could appropriate from Jews, just as Jews appropriated from pagans. In a text from Aspendos in Pamphylia in Asia Minor, dating from the first or second century CE, we can witness Jewish influence upon a pagan dedication. The text directs itself to a god who is infallible and not made by hand.[36] The document is pagan but the unusual expressions sound decidedly more Jewish than gentile. The resonance could echo from either side.

Reciprocity is worth stressing. Not only did Jews have access to and have association with gentile religious practices, but gentiles also sought and obtained a relationship with Jewish religious practices. An inestimable number of non-Jews found Judaism enticing. We can no longer recover the reasons, and they doubtless varied from place to place and person to person. But the fact of gentiles entering into Jewish society is incontrovertible. This did not require anything like conversion, let alone an abandonment of previous identity and associations. It might take the form of imitating the Jewish way of life,

---

34. *IJO*, II, no.196.

35. *IJO*, III, Cyp 7.

36. *IJO*, II, no. 218.

observing the Sabbath, or adopting certain codes of behavior, or taking part in synagogue activities, or providing material support for the Jewish community.[37] The Jews did not turn such people away.

Jews and Pagan Culture

Social and practical interaction is thus clearly attested, even if the available testimony is much thinner than we would like. But what about the realm of high culture? Did Jews play a part in the echelons of higher learning and literary productivity of the pagan world?

A development of critical importance took place sometime in the third century BCE: The Hebrew Bible, or at least the Pentateuch, was translated into Greek. As the famous story has it, Jewish sages from Jerusalem visited Alexandria at the behest of King Ptolemy II, who wanted a Greek version of the Bible for the great library in Alexandria. According to the narrative, the scholars collaborated carefully, compared translations, discussed and refined the wording, and eventually reached a consensus on a version acceptable to all.[38] The story is doubtless a fiction, concocted well after the fact. A process of this scale must have occupied an extensive period of time, with a good deal of revising and rephrasing and probably multiple versions, before one of them gained authority. But, whatever the truth of the celebrated tale, a Greek translation did emerge, a matter of tremendous import. It presumes the existence of Jewish intellectuals literate in both Hebrew and Greek. They were not reaching out to an alien world, absorbing and appropriating the learning of an otherwise alien civilization. Familiarity with Hellenic mythology, literature, and traditions had become part of the cultural life of many Jews themselves.

The best evidence for this phenomenon exists in a quintessential Greek institution: The gymnasium. That establishment represented the capstone of higher education in Greek cities everywhere around the Mediterranean and persisted for the Greek elite well into the period of the Roman Empire. Participants in the gymnasium came from the best families and entered as youths (boys only, of course) into the corps of ephebes, the blue bloods who would be trained for leadership in the city. One would not expect to find many

37. See Feldman, *Jew and Gentile*, 340–52.

38. *Letter of Aristeas* 9–11, 295–321.

Jews in those select circles, and indeed the record is sparse. But the gymnasium was not an altogether closed shop. We possess numerous inscriptions that disclose the names of those enrolled as ephebes in various gymnasia. And Jews do occasionally turn up. Two ephebic lists from Cyrene, for example, one from the late first century BCE and one from the early first century CE contain the names of some participants who are unmistakably Jewish and several others who could be as well.[39] Jews may not have entered the ranks of the ephebate in notable numbers, but they were certainly not excluded from a gymnasium education, the prerequisite to acceptance in the tiers of the intelligentsia. A gymnasium even surfaced in Jerusalem in the 170s BCE. Its installation proved to be quite controversial in some circles. But it is vital to note that the Judaean high priest himself inaugurated it, and that other members of the Jewish priesthood engaged enthusiastically in the competitions held therein.[40] They evidently did not see it as compromising their role as custodians of the nation's heritage.

The gymnasium and the ephebate were springboards of pagan literary and political elites. Jews were no strangers to it. Jewish intellectuals, for example, were quite familiar with Greek mythology. Is that surprising? One might think that Jews would shun stories of divine and heroic figures engaged in deception and lies, slaves to their passions, driven by avarice, jealousy, and lust. And, indeed, various Jewish writers, like Philo and Josephus, blasted the myths of Greek poets and denounced their fabrications and fantasies. Yet they were clearly and closely familiar with them. Tales of mythical Hellenic figures turn up in many Jewish texts, and only rarely are they rejected or dismissed. Indeed, they are exploited. That was the case with the tale by a certain Cleodemus Malchus who combined the Abraham saga with one of the labors of Heracles, having the Greek hero marry one of Abraham's granddaughters, and making the biblical patriarch responsible for the lineage of one of Greece's most iconic figures. The audacious fabrication linked Hellenic myth to patriarchal progeny.[41] The idiosyncratic Jewish writer Artapanus made Moses the teacher of Orpheus, thus portraying the iconic Hebrew figure as the cultural

39. Lüderitz #6–7.

40. 2 Macc 4.7–15.

41. Josephus, *Jewish Antiquities* 1.239–41; Eusebius, *Church History* 9.20.2–4.

progenitor of Hellenic literature and song.[42] Some of these concoctions may be more playful than serious. But the acquaintance with Greek traditions that such authors could count on for their audiences provides a revealing window on Jewish literary consciousness in the Hellenistic era.

Perhaps the most striking instance of this sort of Jewish outreach to the legendary world of Greek gods and heroes was the incorporation of the Sibylline oracles. Although Greek in origin, their subsequent complilation was largely due to Jewish and Christian revisers. The earliest of them, from the second century BCE, summarizes the biblical account of the Tower of Babel and blends it with the myth of the origin of the Olympian gods derived from Hesiod's *Theogony*.[43]

Knowledge of Hellenic legends and fanciful figures, even without embracing them, can be found widely scattered in the treatises of Philo and the works of Josephus. Jewish intellectuals did not resist the lure of Greek mythology. They resorted to it with some frequency to deliver a lesson or simply to enrich a story for a knowledgeable readership, they refashioned it freely, and they incorporated it into their own tradition.

The availability of the Scriptures in a Greek translation proved to be a spur for an explosion of literary activity in which Jewish authors reimagined and refashioned biblical tales in new forms and genres. Those composed in Greek obviously directed themselves for the most part to a Greek-speaking Jewish readership. The compositions took shape in nearly all the literary categories that Greeks had made their own: Epic, tragedy, philosophy, historiography, didactic poetry, and the novel. Educated Jews evidently commanded the whole range of Hellenic intellectual tradition and had engaged deeply with that broader cultural environment. It is noteworthy, however, that, although they looked to Hellenic models, they conveyed reformulated tales from their own heritage. So, for example, the Jewish playwright Ezekiel produced a wholesale drama on the model of Aeschylus, but its topic was the Hebrew exodus from Egypt.[44] A Jewish poet named Theodotus wrote in Homeric hexameters and produced an entire epic dealing at least with the life of Jacob, although we

42. Eusebius, *Church History* 9.27.3–4.

43. *Sibylline Oracles* 3.110–58, 199–201.

44. Carl R. Holladay, *Fragments from Hellenistic Jewish Authors*, vol. 2, *Poets* (Scholars Press, 1989), 301–529.

possess only a fragment of it.[45] And the very creative historian Artapanus composed a treatise that has Moses as a military hero who defeated Ethiopians and brought culture to the Egyptians, including even the introduction of animal worship and the invention of hieroglyphics.[46] The adaptation of Hellenic prototypes is clear enough. But the restriction of their works to traditions growing out of the Bible itself and to the celebrated figures from their own ancestral past reinforced the Jews' sense of self-esteem and stressed the ongoing history of their nation in the wider world of classical culture.

The intellectual discourse can be illustrated elsewhere in Jewish writings. The philosopher Aristobulus reached back to the teachings of Pythagoras, Socrates, and Plato but saw them through the prism of a (somewhat strained) Jewish perspective. In Aristobulus's conception these celebrated Hellenic thinkers borrowed heavily from the books of Moses and incorporated them in the formulation of their own doctrines.[47] The fact that the early Greek philosophers did not have access to the books of Moses in Greek presented a problem. So Aristobulus postulated that prior parts of the Pentateuch had already circulated in translation, making Moses's words accessible to Hellenic intellectuals.[48] The inventiveness of Aristobulus here exhibits the challenges that Jewish thinkers sometimes faced in framing the Jewish part in a pagan cultural realm and the creative way in which they responded to them.

Numerous Jewish authors (mostly obscure to us) provide instances of this pointed creativity. One concoction, whose origin is unknown, has the Jewish high priest discover evidence of a blood relationship between Jews and Spartans, both of them stemming from the house of Abraham.[49] The forging of fake lineages was a staple item of Hellenistic diplomacy; the blending of Jews and Spartans signaled a Jewish buy-in to a Greek convention but served the ends of the Jews' own self-reimagining. A further angle of vision on this overlap comes from the Third Sibylline Oracle, largely a Jewish composition

45. Holladay, *Poets*, 51–204.

46. Carl R. Holladay, *Fragments from Hellenistic Jewish Authors*, vol. 1, *Historians* (Scholars Press, 1983), 189–243.

47. Carl R. Holladay, *Fragments from Hellenistic Jewish Authors*, vol. 3, *Aristobulus* (Scholars Press, 1995), 152–55, 158–61, 162–71.

48. Holladay, *Aristobulus*, 152–55, 158–61.

49. 1 Macc 12.6–23, 14.16–23.

of the Hellenistic period expropriating the quintessentially Greek prophetess. The text shows a close familiarity with the Hellenic myth of the Titanomachy, dating back to Hesiod but refashioned by the Sibyl in a new Jewish version.[50] It also provides allusions to the tale of Troy, to Homer, and to several events in the Hellenistic era. The Sibyl presents herself as transcending Jew and gentile, for she claims to be daughter-in-law of Noah, thus preceding both the Hebrew and the classical worlds, her wisdom extended to all.[51]

Conclusion

These examples display the multiple means whereby Jewish intellectuals navigated the currents of Hellenic culture. But to see this feature as Jewish adjustment to or as reaction to Hellenism puts the matter the wrong way around. Jews who wrote in Greek were not so much confronting Hellenic culture as exhibiting their participation in it. The breadth and diversity of their works illustrate a wide familiarity with Greek literary traditions in which they themselves were steeped, often as consequence of gymnasium education. Educated Jews in Alexandria, Antioch, Corinth, and even Jerusalem reckoned these Hellenic traditions not as alien elements to which they must adjust, but as part of their own intellectual upbringing. This was no matter of strained adaptation but a natural mode of expression. Jews gave voice to their own Hellenism.

50. *Sibylline Oracles* 3.110–55.

51. *Sibylline Oracles* 3.809–29.

CHAPTER THREE

Paul and Roman Freelance Expertise

Heidi Wendt
McGill University

The last decades have witnessed a substantial repositioning of Paul's religious activities not only within Judaism but also within a wider landscape of Greco-Roman religion. While the latter is hardly a new development in Pauline studies, the analytical precision with which scholars present that landscape and redescribe Paul as an integrated participant has advanced considerably. Concurrent developments in Roman-period intellectual history likewise aid in reconciling Paul's command of contemporary philosophy and rhetoric with the intuition that he was at his core not just another popular philosopher, but a *religious* expert in some meaningful sense. Scholarship on the historical convergence of intellectual and religious practice, however, places Paul in the company of assorted *intellectualizing* religious experts operating within the same ancient Mediterranean nexus. In their company, he appears increasingly unexceptional, or rather *no less* exceptional than others who joined proprietary teachings with religious offerings—initiation, purification, healing, and so on—which they cast as exclusive and unique. What *is* exceptional about Paul is the survival of some of his letters. As relics of this broader phenomenon, they capture a rare insider perspective on how one such specialist operated, at a time when their influence was on the rise.

This essay traces the rise of self-authorized or "freelance" religious experts from the late Roman republic through the first century of empire.[1] Paul's floruit falls squarely within this broader trend. Evaluating him from this perspective furnishes vital context and fresh explanations for several perennial problems in Pauline studies: The punishments and opposition that Paul

1. See Heidi Wendt, *At the Temple Gates: The Religion of Freelance Experts in the Roman Empire* (Oxford University Press, 2016).

alleges to have suffered as an apostle of Christ; the tricky matter of whether he received material support; his dealings with the Jerusalem assembly; and his complex statements about and relationship to "Judaism" (the law, circumcision, *Ioudaioi*).

After locating Paul's general religious activities within this context, we will briefly explore two niches that help to pinpoint him more exactly: Freelance religious experts who leaned heavily on texts and intellectual practices (philosophical language or concepts, formal rhetoric, allegorical interpretation, etc.), and Judean experts who drew upon priestly or oracular texts. Consideration of the latter ventures a bit beyond Paul's lifetime, since Roman interest in these texts gathered considerable momentum just as our evidence for the apostle trails off. However, the prominence that Judean oracles and their expert interpreters would achieve in the final decades of the first century are integral to understanding the early reception of Paul's letters among the "Christian" experts who would later claim him.

The Rise of Freelance Experts

The last decades of the Roman republic heralded profound societal changes that would redefine the imperial age. General factors relevant to tracing the rise of "freelance" religious experts include the nascent empire's increasing cultural heterogeneity, its dynamic intellectual life, and its web of human networks connecting its vast territories. Beyond facilitating imperial bureaucracy, military movement, trade, travel, and other forms of migration, these networks were also conduits for would-be specialists in education, medicine, philosophy, and religion.[2] Assorted prophets, astrologers, and religious professionals played a significant role in the political competition that characterized the final years of the republic, which culminated with Augustus in autocratic rule.[3] Since the institutions of Roman civic religion guarded against

2. See in general Anna Collar, *Religious Networks in the Roman Empire: The Spread of New Ideas* (Cambridge University Press, 2013). For Paul in this context, see Timothy Luckritz Marquis, *Transient Apostle: Paul, Travel, and the Rhetoric of Empire*, Synkrisis (Yale University Press, 2013).

3. E.g., Andrew Wallace-Hadrill, "*Mutatas Formas:* The Augustan Transformation of Roman Knowledge," in *The Cambridge Companion to the Age of Augustus*, ed. Karl Galinsky (Cambridge University Press, 2005), 55–84; Andrew Wallace-Hadrill, *Rome's Cultural Revolution* (Cambridge University Press, 2008).

the concentration of religious authority in individual officients or families, the divine legitimacy emboldening such ambitions needed to derive from external sources. Julius Caesar, for example, placed foreign experts at the center of Roman religion by enlisting Alexandrian *mathematici*—a more technical term for astrologer—to intercalate the calendar after charging its pontifical custodians with neglect (Pliny, *Natural Histories* 18.211; Plutarch, *Life of Caesar* 59.5).[4] Julio-Claudian Rome also witnessed several trials for political intrigue wherein the accused allegedly consulted some foreign expert about imperial affairs, a poignant reminder of the power the latter wielded. And yet, the prominence of such experts was as much a source of attraction as of notoriety.

The centrality of the pact between heaven and earth, the *pax deorum* ("peace of the gods"), to Roman *imperium* also rendered religion a conceptual site for negotiating difference in ways that promoted the recognition of foreign experts.[5] Depictions of ethnic or provincial peoples often featured their peculiar cultic institutions and personnel, gods, theologies, and religious competencies. While such descriptions could tip over into caricature, reductive, exoticizing, and mere foils to Roman *religio*, they also rendered this religious diversity legible, even alluring. Inhabitants of the Roman world could scarcely avoid multimedia representations depicting exotic gods, temples, rites, and religious personnel. Libraries, bookstalls, and more personal literary networks teemed with ethnographic writings, natural histories, and other encyclopaedic efforts to catalogue and to rationalize the empire's territorial and cultural scope. The foregrounding of religious distinctiveness within the Roman imperial project created strong associations between competencies and the peoples or regions best known for them.

Freelance religious experts both contributed to and drafted off this mounting interest in foreign religion. Indeed, many seem to have exaggerated their own ethnic credentials in appearance, language, nomenclature, or by otherwise meeting audience expectations about whatever foreign idiom

4. See Jörg Rüpke, *The Roman Calendar from Numa to Constantine: Time, History, and the* Fasti, trans. David M. B. Richardson (John Wiley & Sons, 2011), 109–20.

5. E.g., Eric M. Orlin, *Foreign Cults in Rome: Creating a Roman Empire* (Oxford University Press, 2010); Jörg Rüpke, "Historicizing Religion: Varro's *Antiquitates* and History of Religion in the Late Roman Republic," *HR* 53 (2014): 246–68; Duncan MacRae, *Legible Religion: Books, Gods, and Rituals in Roman Culture* (Harvard University Press, 2016).

they alleged to represent.[6] Affectation and performativity were de rigueur for Rome's agnostic intellectual scene, wherein aspirants to all manner of specialty played the part in displays of skill and authenticity, the validation of which lay largely in the eye of beholders.[7]

Punitive Reactions to Freelance Experts

Although most ancient authors find the religion of freelance experts risible at best, none can deny its popularity among followers across the social spectrum, all over the empire. The inadequacies of our evidence hinders confident quantitative analysis, but circumstantial clues suggest an uptick in the number of would-be specialists, especially in the cosmopolitan cities to which many flocked (e.g., Rome, Athens, Alexandria, Ephesus, Corinth). One index is an escalation in the frequency and severity of legislative actions taken against varieties of specialists at the capital, which supplied in turn legal precedents for the provincial administration of justice (e.g., Pliny, *Letters* 10.96.1–2, 9; 10.97.1).[8] Many of these actions targeted certain kinds of specialists, astrologers for instance, although it is important to bear in mind that there existed no formal mechanisms for identifying those intended, let alone for broadly enforcing the penalty.[9]

That Roman magistrates issued such bans, confiscations, and expulsions more often, and with graver consequences, in the early imperial period indicates a regulatory frustration with a form of religiosity that was salient and prolific yet difficult to pin down. Since the culprits were typically foreign, scholars have tended to posit such underlying motivations as xenophobia or a perceived threat to Roman identity. And yet, many of the emperors or magistrates who acted in these ways against specialists and associated practices were

---

6. Wendt, *At the Temple Gates*, 74–113; Jennifer Eyl, "'I Myself Am an Israelite': Paul, Authenticity, and Authority," *JSNT* 40 (2017): 148–68.

7. Tim Whitmarsh, *The Second Sophistic*, Greece & Rome 35 (Oxford University Press, 2005).

8. Heidi Wendt, "*Ea Superstitione:* Christian Martyrdom and the Religion of Freelance Experts," *JRS* 105 (2015): 183–202; Heidi Wendt, *At the Temple Gates*, 42–54; Ryan S. Schellenberg, *Abject Joy: Paul, Prison, and the Art of Making Do* (Oxford University Press, 2021), 25–55.

9. Pauline Ripat, "Expelling Misconceptions: Astrologers at Rome," *CP* 106 (2011): 115–54.

also their consumers.[10] Roman law was a dull instrument for whittling these layers, although some experts were clearly more tolerable and tolerated than others. But as much of the problem lay in how specialists responded to such efforts. Lucian's Peregrinus is instructive. He lands in prison during his stint as a Christian, "which itself gave him no little reputation as an asset for his future career and the charlatanism and notoriety-seeking that he was enamored of" (*Passing of Peregrinus* 12.1–4). While incarcerated, Peregrinus is shown every attention: Visitors bring him elaborate meals, among other forms of care and devotion; he continues expounding the sacred books, earning him greater reverence; and he receives lavish gestures of material support from Christians across the eastern empire (12.5–13.7). "Much money came to him from them by reason of his imprisonment, and he procured not a little revenue from it" (13.6–7). Christians were especially vulnerable to the predations of charlatans and tricksters, as Lucian reflects in an aside, although they are hardly the only victims.

Paul as Freelance Expert

Paul shared much in common with other freelance religious experts. He was not only *like* them, but he also was an ordinary participant in this broader cultural phenomenon. His extant writings serve as a rare form of evidence for the insider perspective(s) they capture. Importantly, even very critical sources suggest that textuality was pervasive for experts of all varieties, although few texts comparable to the epistles survive. Even fewer experts enjoyed the historiographic rehabilitation that later Christian authors—keen to extract them from the fray of "magicians"—would perform for Paul and his apostolic contemporaries. It is a testament to their efforts that authorities on Christ have been so routinely excluded from this context despite every indication of belonging. Thus, a plausible case for reconceiving Paul's message as a variation of the religion of freelance experts may invite a more ambitious reimagining of early Christianity in similar terms.

One reason why Paul has seemed incomparable to his similar contemporaries stems from an elision of emic or insider perspective—in this case, how he

10. The most obvious example is the second Julio-Claudian emperor, Tiberius, who regularly consorted with astrologers—most famously Thrasyllus—and was allegedly himself a student of divination, although he was hardly the only member of the imperial family to do such things.

calls, explains, and justifies his own practices—with a more objective, analytical account of his activities. For example, most scholars take up the language of "apostle" uncritically, neglecting to reconcile it with the assorted titles that self-authorized experts adopted to lend an air of exceptionality or distinction to their roles.[11] That Paul and many of the figures mentioned in his epistles were *apostles*—not "magicians" or "false prophets"—then becomes the reason to exempt them from comparison with religious actors with whom they otherwise share many similarities. Apostles become a category unto themselves. However, labels such as "magician" were devised precisely to "other" those to whom they were applied. Only rarely were they embraced self-referentially, and such cases of claiming a once-derisive label are complex.[12]

Likewise, that vocabulary used for Paul—that he proclaimed a "gospel" and performed (or at least facilitated) "baptisms"—sets him apart from most other religious teachers or initiators. Yet employing unusual language—or common language with an unusual inflection—was par for the course among freelance experts, who insisted upon the novelty of their offerings to competitive advantage.[13] Paul defends the novelty of *his* gospel (e.g., Gal 2:2–5), objects to followers quibbling about who baptized them (1 Cor 1:11–17; 3:6), and characterizes as veiled or defective any interpretations of "God's oracles" (Rom 3:2) that do not arrive at his conclusions about Christ (2 Cor 3:12–18). Hence the need to transform his distinctive language into more generalizable terms and concepts: for example, religious expert ("apostle"); his transformative initiation rite ("baptism"); his revealed message ("gospel"); and his religious activities ("mission"). Redescription yields a version of Paul that is legible beyond Judaism and Christianity.

Rendered in such terms, Paul's practices accord well with those of other ancient Mediterranean religious experts. His frequent reference to imprisonments, beatings, and other hardships endured for the sake of his gospel

11. Matthew Novenson, "Messiahs and Their Messengers," *Svensk Teologisk Kvartalskrift* 95 (2019): 3–16.

12. The term *magos* is claimed on occasion in the Greek Magical Papyri, for example, although the choice to do so is not straightforward and may result from sensitivity to the term's primary connotations of Persian religious expertise.

13. For Paul's use of *to evangelion* to this effect, see Steve Mason, "Paul's Announcement (τὸ εὐαγγέλιον): 'Good News' and Its Detractors in Earliest Christianity," in *Josephus, Judea, and Christian Origins: Methods and Categories* (Hendrickson, 2009), 283–302.

are the other side of the coin to the parodied expert whose evidence of punishment breeds confidence in his skill. Paul complains to the Thessalonians of having suffered and been shamefully mistreated at Philippi, and also of having been driven out of Judea; to the Corinthians he speaks of experiencing affliction in Asia that was tantamount to a death sentence, and, in a previous letter, of fighting with beasts at Ephesus.[14] He recalls a nail-biting escape from Damascus as the ethnarch under King Aretas searched the city to apprehend him.[15]

Here and elsewhere, Paul invokes hardships to assert his authenticity and legitimacy. Punishments, especially, attest his disinterest—he is willing to forego freedom and personal safety for the urgency of his message. The authorities who enacted such measures appear to have been largely unconcerned with the *content* of expert offerings per se; rather, their impetus was regulatory and lay in such palpable factors as a potential for influence, economic liability, and sometimes sheer nuisance. Notwithstanding, in Philippians Paul exhibits how a recipient of punishment might capitalize on his circumstances by implying a causal connection: "I have been put here [in prison] for the defense of the gospel" (Phil 1:16b). The same verses speak to the paradoxical value of incarceration. It has become manifest to everyone that his chains are for Christ, resulting in the progress or success of the gospel (1:12–13). And most brothers in the lord, having become ever more confident in his chains, are emboldened to speak the *logos* without fear (1:14).

Paul belabors his suffering in greatest detail when on the back foot, amid other competing experts. In 2 Cor 11:23–25, he asks of would-be rivals: "Are they ministers of Christ? . . . I am a better one: With far greater labors, far more imprisonments, with countless floggings, and often near death. Five times I have received from the Judeans the forty lashes minus one. Three times I was beaten with rods. Once I received a stoning. . . ." The structure and function of his recollections are modeled on those of Greco-Roman philosophers, who saw in the endurance of adverse circumstances confirmation of one's philosophical virtue and exemplary character.[16] As Paul's contemporary, the Stoic

14. 1 Thess 2:2, 15; 2 Cor 1:8–9; 1 Cor 15:32.

15. 2 Cor 11:32–33.

16. John T. Fitzgerald, *Cracks in an Earthen Vessel: An Examination of the Catalogues of Hardships in the Corinthian Correspondence* (Society of Biblical Literature, 1988). See also

philosopher Epictetus, explains, "[The sage] suffers no harm even though he is soundly flogged, or imprisoned, or beheaded" (*Discourses* 4.1.127) but bears all of this with personal profit. Adversity occasioned the exhibition of virtue because it tested and revealed the person who is truly wise from charlatan pretenders.

The very fact that Paul is so enmeshed in rivalries itself corroborates his freelance status. So too do Paul's recourse to prophetic texts and collections taken on behalf of a foreign god have longstanding legislative precedents that might account for punishments received or that he expects to receive, especially at Rome or in Roman colonies (e.g., Philippi, Corinth) whose bureaucracies were patterned consciously after those of the capital. Again, none of this would result from Paul's eschatology or his teachings, but from how his practices or general modus operandi conformed to broader activities under suspicion or deemed illicit. As the matter of his collection anticipates, this context also makes good sense of Paul's uneasy relationship to the issue of receiving compensation for his "religious labor."[17] He variously draws himself into line with priests whose perquisites are easily misrecognized by dint of institutional setting (1 Cor 9:11–18), affirms his rights as an apostle, denies having exercised them (2 Cor 11:7–9), and thanks followers for material support they have provided (Phil 4:15–19; 2 Cor 11:8). Freelance experts were ever vulnerable to accusations of profit mongering, a charge the apostle both sustains and inflicts in turn (Phil 2:3; Rom 2:21–22).

Another indication that Paul participated in the religion of freelance experts is his sensitivity to and satisfaction of audience expectations about the kind of expertise he claims, even as he stakes out contrary positions on certain matters, for instance, whether (male) gentile adherents of the Judean god need undergo circumcision or observe the law. That is, Paul presents himself to his audiences and seems to be recognized by them as a credible authority on religious skills and on the benefits associated with Judeans, as well as certain intellectual abilities that were not mutually exclusive with Judean expertise but gestured beyond that frame of reference. At the same time, he differentiates

---

Ryan S. Schellenberg, *Rethinking Paul's Rhetorical Education: Comparative Rhetoric and 2 Corinthians 10–13*, ECL 10 (Society of Biblical Literature, 2013), 123–40.

17. Brigidda Bell, "The Cost of Baptism? The Case for Paul's Ritual Compensation," *JSNT* 42 (2020): 431–52.

his religious authority and program from those of a broad range of actors, even ones who were similarly self-authorized but not *religious* in the sense of enlisting divine beings (e.g., the gods, Christ, or agentive *pneuma*) directly in their activities.

Regarding the first prerogative, establishing his ethnic expertise, Paul adopts tactics consonant with what we see of other Judean experts. He speaks authoritatively about law observance, dietary restrictions, and circumcision; he alleges to have undergone dedicated training in ancestral teachings, even aligning himself with a specific interpretive group by claiming to be a Pharisee in matters of the law; he cites or alludes to prophecies from Judean writings that he interprets eschatologically and in reference to Christ; he offers allegorical exegesis of episodes from Judean myth; and he alleges the ability to perform any sign or wonder.[18] Whereas Pauline scholars long read his seemingly critical stance toward the law or circumcision as further evidence that he repudiated Judaism, the last few decades have restored the implicit caveat *for gentiles* to such statements.[19] At the same time, the pervasive and enduring ethnic dimension of Paul's religious program has been demonstrated for everything from his theology and the centripetal logic of the ethno-religious transformation he brokers—that gentiles in Christ can acquire Judean ancestry—to his self-positioning. In short, his ethnic credentials are foundational to his gaining recognition in the form of the expertise that he claims.[20]

Like other Judean experts, Paul seeks to harness the authority of illustrious figures from Judean tradition, foremost Moses.[21] He likens himself to a religious figure of unequalled stature within his ethnic idiom. This extension of authority is no one-way street: He also projects back onto Moses the essence of his own transformative rite when he informs the Corinthians "that *our*

18. See Heidi Wendt, "Mythmaking and Exegesis," in *T&T Clark Handbook to the Historical Paul*, ed. Ryan S. Schellenberg and Heidi Wendt (T&T Clark, 2022), 199–214; Jennifer Eyl, *Signs, Wonders, and Gifts: Divination in the Letters of Paul* (Oxford University Press, 2019).

19. John G. Gager, *Reinventing Paul* (Oxford University Press, 2002).

20. See, e.g., Caroline Johnson Hodge, *If Sons, Then Heirs: A Study of Kindship and Ethnicity in the Letters of Paul* (Oxford University Press, 2007); Paula Fredriksen, *Paul: The Pagans' Apostle* (Yale University Press, 2018).

21. For Paul's cultivated self-presentation as a figure akin to Moses, see Luckritz Marquis, *Transient Apostle*, 95–97, 103–111; Wendt, "Mythmaking and Exegesis," 208–13.

ancestors [the Israelites] were all under the cloud, and all passed through the sea, and all were baptized by Moses in the cloud and the sea, and all ate the *same* pneumatic food and drank the *same* pneumatic drink. For they drank from the pneumatic rock that followed them, and the rock was Christ" (1 Cor 10:1–4, modified). The isomorphism is telling. Presumably, Paul implies that the special food and drink consumed by the Israelites had the quality and effect of the ritual meal he will prescribe his listeners in 11:23–26. Like many of his "pagan" counterparts, then, he mobilizes the past in support of his own initiation rites. In so doing, he forges a mythic precedent that anticipates a mystery initiation and the receipt of Christ's divine *pneuma* in baptism, as well as the commemoration of this event by a ritual meal.

Even if they differ at the level of particulars, these elements of Paul's religious program trade on expectations about Judean religion that were widespread among non-Jews of the Roman period. As many Greek and Latin sources attest, the Judeans' inspired, oracular writings were a key element of that concept, although the interest they garnered was of a piece with the Romans' general enthusiasm for ostensibly ancient ethnic literatures, particularly prophetic books. Hence many a would-be Judean religious expert enlisted the former texts somehow in their practices, even if only indirectly, as is implied of Juvenal's priestess and interpreter of the laws of Jerusalem, but who is ultimately offering her services as a dream interpreter (*Satires* 6.542–47). Similarly, one Eleazar is said to derive his techniques and incantations from the books of Solomon, although the exorcism he performs presupposes that knowledge; the books are not consulted during the ritual (Josephus, *Jewish Antiquities* 8.44–49).

Where Paul is concerned, such textual engagement is front and center in most though not all of his letters. (Philemon lacks it entirely, while 1 Thessalonians and Philippians allude only obliquely to biblical writings.) Romans and Galatians especially display this textual expertise, although the Corinthians occasion some of his boldest biblical mythmaking in relation to Adam and to Moses. The apostle's performative displays of interpretive acumen likely catered to existing curiosity about the Judean literary heritage, which is not to say that his gentile audiences had studied these texts or necessarily knew them in any detail. Rather, it would suffice to be aware that this *ethnos* was in possession of so illustrious a corpus—which Roman-period authors variously characterize as priestly, holy, oracular, divinely issued, and riddled with secrets and mysteries—at a time when texts in general and religious texts in particular were symbols that communicated power, prestige, and social mobility. Indirect testament to the Romans' esteem for Judean writings occurs in narratives about the reconstitution of their own oracular corpus, the Sibylline Oracles, which had perished in 83 BCE when fire ravaged the Capitoline temple of Jupiter where they were stored A few years later, the Senate dispatched envoys to active sibyls in Ilium, Erythrae, Samos, Sicily, and Africa with a view to compiling anew the classical collection; later authors posit a Judean sibyl, too, as a contributor to its prophecies.[22]

A significant gain of redescribing Paul as a freelance expert in Judean religion is that his relationship to "Judaism" becomes a matter of position-takings vis-à-vis *other* Judean experts, ones with whom he was in competition and from whom he needed to distinguish himself.[23] This context both attenuates and localizes: Paul rejects the value of circumcision (for gentiles), or general law observance (again, for gentiles), for the simple reason that he has devised *an entirely different* mechanism for gentiles to establish a relationship with the Judean god. So too do other readers of Moses have hardened and veiled minds, a safeguard against disagreement with his interpretation of the prophetic writings, whence his "unveiled mind" has deduced a mystery kept secret for long ages, the gospel of Christ (2 Cor 3:15; Rom 16:25–26). Taking Judean rivals as the target of Paul's prescriptions or criticisms narrows their scope, transforming entirely how he intended them. The contrast is not between "Christianity" and a former religion he repudiated but between his religious program and the proprietary claims and practical arrangements of his closest competitors.

Paul as Intellectualizing Religious Expert

If some of Paul's interpretive insight stems from revelations and heavenly journeys, he locates its foundation in his prior time in *Ioudaismos* (Gal 1:13–14), which consisted in assiduous devotion to ancestral traditions, possibly texts. Josephus similarly tethers prophetic acumen to knowledge sourced from dreams, which only bolsters other bases: His priestly ancestry, extensive education, natural aptitude for memory and understanding, knowledge of the prophecies in

22. Aelian, *Historical Miscellany* 12.35; Pausanias, *Description of Greece*, 10.12.9; Origen, *Against Celsus*, 7.3.

23. Mark Nanos and Heidi Wendt, "Galatians," in Schellenberg and Wendt, *T&T Clark Handbook to the Historical Paul*, 329–48.

the sacred books, passage through the Judean philosophies, and skill in divination (*Life* 9–11; *Jewish War* 3.352). This background primes Josephus to recall the awesome visions of recent dreams in which God revealed to him the impending fate of the Judeans and the destinies of the Roman sovereigns.[24] He is then inspired to apply these visions to the holy books, but only after offering up a prayer to God (*Jewish War* 3.353–54). For Josephus and Paul alike, divine inspiration could cooperate with other human abilities and intellectual skills in complex configurations. Paul's description of *Ioudaismos* conveys precisely the sort of learned credentials that Josephus boasts. Although the apostle disavows in the same breath that such learning is the source of his revealed gospel (Gal 1:11–12), the literary unit showcases his possession of knowledge in both forms.

But Paul had more than other Judean experts in his sights. He is equally attentive to locating himself among (while likewise differentiating himself from) types of intellectuals, foremost philosophers. (Such categories hardly exclude Judean versions thereof, as his rough contemporary Philo serves as an apt reminder.) Whereas Pauline scholars have been content to catalogue parallels between Paul and other intellectuals only to conclude that he retained a unique status, a more grounded account of his philosophical habits invites fresh consideration of how he compares to other *intellectualizing* actors. Again, the critical difference lies in the joining of philosophical or intellectual discourses with *religious* practices, ones that involved or communicated with gods and other divine beings (e.g., *pneuma* ["spirit"] or Christ, in Paul's case).

There is ample evidence that some first-century Judeans were a salient type of Greco-Roman intellectual, who, like Philo and Josephus, interwove biblical and philosophical materials in ways both intuitive—primed by intellectual formation—and more self-conscious, as when Josephus maps the main "Judean *haireses*" ("schools") onto specific Greco-Roman philosophical schools. Interestingly, where Philo and Josephus are concerned, scholars never sever their status as intellectuals from their ethnicity. Philo might reorient his philosophical allegiances, adopt new literary genres, and exchange allegorical criticism for practical ethics, but that he was and remained a *Ioudaios* is always entailed in this intellectual versatility.[25]

24. Matthew T. Sharp, *Divination and Philosophy in the Letters of Paul* (Edinburgh University Press, 2022).

25. Maren R. Niehoff, *Philo of Alexandria: An Intellectual Biography* (Yale University Press, 2018).

The situation is more complicated with Paul, for whom ethnicity has sat uneasily with his intellectual abilities, to say nothing of his proclamation of Christ. And yet, he was also fluent in the rhetorical and philosophical dialects of his day, even if his representational horizons were shaped and limited by a particular ethnic idiom and collection of texts. Moreover, and *unlike* Philo and Josephus, he also mobilized these intellectual discourses to animate *religious* claims. In this respect, too, his self-positioning is a variation on a particular form of Greco-Roman religion, one attested in such contemporaneous sources as the Egyptian Hermetica or the Chaldean Oracles. Although these sources express different genres from Paul's letters, an improved account of his philosophical sampling permits fresh consideration of how he compares to other intellectualizing religious experts who drew upon that repertoire to similar effect, although articulated in another ethnic lexicon.

Earlier scholarship on Paul's resemblance to popular philosophers found affinities in their respective moral psychologies, ethics, educational and psychagogic approaches, or comportment. Work of the last two decades has explicated the physics and ontology that underpin his eschatology, revealing the apostle to be more philosophically adroit than in just his behavior and techniques. The results include recognition of a debt to Stoic materialism in his extensive use of *doxa* to describe God's visible splendor, in his concept of *pneuma* as an agent with extensible, transformative properties, and in the participatory force of being "in Christ" as a way of explaining that Jesus Christ, whose human body God refashioned from his own qualitatively superior *pneuma*, has now extended *his* pneumatic body to gentiles through the transformative rite of baptism. Their acquisition of Christ's *pneuma* not only activates assorted religious talents—the ability to prophesy, to utter and interpret divine speech, to heal, to discern spirits (1 Cor 12:4–11)—but is also foundational to the greater mystery at the core of his religious program: Upon Christ's return, those "in Christ" will not die but will be transformed themselves into immortal divine beings (15:50–57).[26] Other scholars have highlighted such Platonic elements as Paul's parts-based moral psychology, conception of a *nous* that can ascend to and be renewed in higher realms, and goal of divine assimilation through the contemplation of Christ.[27]

26. M. David Litwa, *We Are Being Transformed: Deification in Paul's Soteriology* (De Gruyter, 2012).

27. Emma Wasserman, *The Death of the Soul in Romans 7: Sin, Death, and the Law in Light of Hellenistic Moral Psychology*, WUNT 2/256 (Mohr Siebeck, 2008).

These "mixed" philosophical allegiances might be misdescribed as eclecticism. But Paul inhabited an emerging philosophical terrain in which Plato's writings and person were the source of a new philosophical ethos.[28] Three features of this first-century movement proved especially attractive to intellectual figures focused on the gods: First, the relative openness and flexibility of thought; second, the importance of religion; and third, the idea that primitive wisdom—whether oracular or philosophical—might be recovered from ancient books using the tools of textual criticism and allegorical interpretation.[29] For intellectualizing religious experts who employed them—as Paul does in Galatians when he explains that God's promise to Abraham and his *offspring*, one versus many, anticipates Christ (3:16), or reveals the story of Sarah and Hagar to be an allegory (4:24)—these interpretive methods constituted a skilled form of divination. It was precisely the *lack* of a standard Platonism that encouraged creative appropriations of Platonic thought for a variety of intellectual and practical projects. Roman-period figures put it to the task of explaining or justifying religious offerings. An expert such as Paul could pick and choose Stoic and Platonic elements that best suited his aims, integrating these with divine wisdom, secrets, or mysteries preserved in ancient, exotic texts.

Platonizing tendencies in Christian sources were long understood to be later "gnostic" developments that originated with "heretics" such as the second-century Alexandrian teacher Valentinus. Hence much scholarship on texts like the Hermetica and Chaldean Oracles insists that recurrent concepts such as faithfulness and love are not to be understood as "spiritual qualities," as in Paul's usage, but in a "theurgic sense," as virtues that facilitated assimilation to God.[30] The Paul whom these scholars have in mind, however, more closely resembles the apostle of later Christian heresiologists, who argued that the contamination of Scripture with philosophy was a secondary and erosive development in the transmission of Christian orthodoxy. But "spiritual virtue" is a

---

28. G. R. Boys-Stone, *Post-Hellenistic Philosophy: A Study of Its Development from the Stoics to Origen* (Oxford University Press, 2001).

29. Stanley Stowers, "The Dilemma of Paul's Physics: Features Stoic-Platonist or Platonist-Stoic?" in *From Stoicism to Platonism: The Development of Philosophy, 100 BCE–100 CE*, ed. Troels Engberg-Pedersen (Cambridge University Press, 2018), 231–53, here 250–51.

30. Ruth Dorothy Majercik, *The Chaldean Oracles: Text, Translation, and Commentary*, Studies in Greek and Roman Religion 5 (Brill, 1989), 11, quoting Hans Conzelmann.

poor characterization of the special force Paul assigns to faithfulness, by which he means unwavering confidence in God's ability to bring about whatever he promises, however improbable, above all, to create life from dead things. It is such trust or confidence, specifically, that establishes the line of faithfulness by which gentiles in Christ, through his divine *pneuma*, become coheirs to Abraham's inheritance, cast here in eschatological terms. The Stoic-Platonic Paul who has come increasingly into focus complicates such distinctions.

Paul advocates constant prayer (e.g., 1 Thess 3:10; 5:25), explaining in Romans that the indwelling divine *pneuma* itself prays through those "in Christ," sighing with unspeakable utterances since they do not know how to pray as they ought (Rom 8:26). Elsewhere, he reiterates this connection between *pneuma* and prayer, and also song, nevertheless encouraging active mindfulness when singing and praying (1 Cor 14:14–15). He also enjoins such contemplative techniques as self-examination and testing (1 Cor 11:28; 2 Cor 13:5), and discernment, with the ritual practices, as when he instructs those in Christ to discern the Lord's body when consuming his bread and cup "to call him to mind" (cf. 1 Cor 11:25, 26). The mastery of these techniques works to cultivate the portion of divine *pneuma* they received in baptism, but failure to adhere to his instructions may result in a reversal or physical decline. "For this reason," he admonishes the Corinthians, that is, eating and drinking without discerning the body, "many of you are weak and ill, and some have died" (1 Cor 11:30). Owing to their common Platonic heritage, Paul's letters also share with Hermetic and Chaldean texts a depiction of the mortal condition as one of inescapable death and decay, and the sole remedy, assimilation to God, as the acquisition of immortality.

All these authors proceed from an epistemological foundation with significant Platonic features, which each adapts to proprietary religious teachings, rites, and auxiliary practices (e.g., a ritual meal that renews or amplifies a rite's effects). The Chaldean Oracles are an especially intriguing comparandum for Paul—both the historical figure as well as the "remembered Paul" of later letter receptions—insofar as the texts, prophecies recorded in Greek hexameter, were attributed to a father-son pair of religious experts active in the Antonine period but who piqued fervent exegetical interest among Neoplatonic circles. According to early commentators, Julian the father, remembered as a Chaldaean and philosopher, made his son, Julian the "theurgist," act as a medium for the deified soul of Plato, uttering *logia* that his father then recorded and explicated in prose (*Suda* nos. 433–34). Scholars question this tradition of authorship for the pedigree and unity it supplies to the Chaldean corpus, the few extant fragments of which are preserved mainly in the pages of later Christian critics. Regardless of whether the Julians were merely co-opted as figureheads for a composite collection of texts, the claim itself had a plausible pretext in activities of freelance religious experts. The commentary culture that developed around the Chaldean Oracles—literary output that went together with disciplinary formation and institutionalization—is likewise suggestive of the afterlife of Paul's letters, which inspired everything from pseudepigrapha to commentary-style exposition, to "historical" narratives to maybe even gospels.

Conclusion

The study of Paul once proceeded from a premise of uniqueness—his own as well as that of Christianity writ large—within the religious landscape of the Roman Empire. More recent work not only restores him to that landscape, but also considers his letters rare evidence for broader religious transformations occurring within it. Although this essay examines Paul as a freelance religious expert, this type of religiosity was not mutually exclusive and, indeed, often overlapped with others, for example, certain "voluntary associations" with a religious dimension, whose members might provide a ready-made audience for someone like Paul, whatever their raison d'être (e.g., professional, ethnic, cultic, neighborhood) or connection to him.

Approaching Paul as one such expert, and one among other *Judean* experts, limits the scope of his varied positions on Judaism, casting these instead as poses struck to differentiate his authority and practices from those of proximate rivals. The same context addresses such perennial historical questions as whether he and other early Christ followers were "persecuted," or the reason for his ambivalence about receiving material support. This essay further highlights Paul's affinities with other intellectualizing experts, some of whose writings or legacies sparked considerable literary activity in the second and third centuries. Hence one of the most important questions remains his trajectory from "Judean" to "Christian" apostle, the answers to which may likewise be sought among later would-be specialists for whom proprietary receptions of the Pauline letters offered one means for distinction within a crowded field of expertise.

II

A World Full of Gods

CHAPTER FOUR

The Universal Polytheism and the Case of the Apostle Paul

Matthew V. Novenson
Princeton Theological Seminary

My twelve-year-old son recently learned in school—as I myself learned in school in the 1980s—that Jupiter is Zeus, Juno is Hera, Minerva is Athena, and so on. Only some years later did I learn the term of art *interpretatio Romana* (which we moderns borrow from Tacitus),[1] but the phenomenon signified by that term was clear enough for a child to grasp.[2] Because my school was an American public school, my teachers steered well clear of the question how the Jewish or the Christian god (let alone other gods worshiped in the Reagan-era United States) may or may not relate to Jupiter, Zeus, Juno, Hera, and others. Ancient writers, by contrast, did not avoid that question. Many of them were very interested, indeed, in proposing, denying, correcting, and otherwise litigating various *interpretationes Judaicae* and *Christianae*.

1. Tacitus, *Germania* 43.4: "Among the Nahanarvali is shown a grove, the seat of a prehistoric ritual. A priest presides in female dress; but according to the Roman interpretation [*interpretatione Romana*] the gods recorded in this fashion are Castor and Pollux. That at least is the spirit of the godhead here recognized, whose name is the Alci. No images are in use; there is no sign of foreign superstition. Nevertheless they worship these deities as brothers and as youths" (Tacitus, *Germania*, trans. M. Hutton and W. Peterson, rev. R. M. Ogilvie, E. H. Warmington, and Michael Winterbottom [Harvard University Press, 1914], modified). Throughout, translations of primary texts are my own unless otherwise noted.

2. Though, upon reflection, one quickly finds complex linguistic and theological questions lying just below the surface, as rightly noted by Clifford Ando, "*Interpretatio Romana*," *Classical Philology* 100 (2005): 41–51, here 46–47: "What might have appeared a simple problem of translation stands revealed as but one moment in a complex nebula of personal accommodation and cross-cultural dialogue whose implications reach far beyond the merely lexical. Or perhaps I should say, *translation* is here so revealed."

I have written elsewhere about the ample literary evidence for *interpretatio Judaica* in antiquity, arguing that ancient Jews and their god did not—contrary to ancient and modern stereotype—dwell in splendid isolation from the prevailing ancient Mediterranean cultural practice of *interpretatio*.[3] In our extant sources, gentile writers render the Jewish god intelligible in terms of their respective pantheons, and Jewish writers do likewise for gentile gods. To be sure, there is considerable anxiety on all sides about getting local ritual practice right: One does not worship Capitoline Jupiter *as* Zeus Hypsistos or *as* Iao, even if, deep down, x is y is z. Divine identity is one thing, ritual practice quite another.[4] But *interpretatio* is attested among ancient Jews no less than among ancient Greeks, Romans, and others, so that Robert Parker is well warranted in speaking of a universal polytheism:

> [It is] the shared assumption, grounded in *interpretatio*, that at bottom the gods you worship are also the gods I do or might worship. . . . Perhaps it is a mistake to speak of ancient polytheisms in the plural at all. From an actor's perspective the world was divided between different countries and tribes and political systems, but it was not divided between different gods: there was only one ancient polytheism, one set of gods ruling the entire world.[5]

---

3. Matthew V. Novenson, "The Universal Polytheism and the Case of the Jews," in *Monotheism and Christology in Greco-Roman Antiquity*, ed. Matthew V. Novenson, NovTSup 180 (Brill, 2020), 32–60. Further on this topic, see Collin Cornell, "*Interpretatio* among Levantines in Hellenistic Egypt," in *What's in a Divine Name? Religious Systems and Human Agency in the Ancient Mediterranean*, ed. Alaya Palamidis and Corinne Bonnet (De Gruyter, 2024), 713–33.

4. See Ando, "*Interpretatio Romana*," 49: "Cult practice diverges strongly from philosophical theology, for it was Plato who set the terms for virtually all traditions of Hellenistic theology, and they believed in gods whose identities were fixed and unchanging. The ontological presuppositions of cult were quite different. How should one then name a god? And how did one recognize another's god as identical to one's own, not least in light of their radical difference?" And Robert Parker, *Greek Gods Abroad: Names, Natures, and Transformations* (University of California Press, 2017), 172: "Even if the gods of every nation were in some sense the same, no one ever supposed that the local traditions for worshipping them, sanctified by time, should be neglected. In that sense, *interpretatio* is revealed as ineffective: your god may be my god, but their cults are not combined."

5. Parker, *Greek Gods Abroad*, 76.

In that previous essay of mine, I only briefly mentioned the case of the apostle Paul,[6] but it really is worth examining in more detail, which is the burden of this essay.[7] As a late Second Temple–period diaspora Jew, Paul properly belongs to the body of evidence for *interpretatio Judaica*, though because his letters rapidly became Christian Scripture, by dint of reception he is also part of the story of later *interpretatio Christiana*.[8] Like many other Jewish writers in the early Roman Empire, Paul frequently distinguishes between the god of the Jews on the one hand and the gods of the nations on the other. We shall therefore consider each of these in turn.

The God of the Jews

Marcion of Sinope (fl. mid-second century CE) famously proposed that the god whom Paul preached was an alien god, hitherto unknown to human beings until he sent his son Jesus into the world.[9] This is a misreading of Paul, but part of the reason Marcion thought this was that Paul does often designate his god simply as "god the father of Jesus Christ" (e.g., Rom 15:6) or "the god who raised Jesus from the dead" (e.g., Gal 1:1).[10] That is, Paul names this god with reference to his recently deceased and resurrected son, Jesus. With a bit of theological creativity, therefore, and a willingness to ignore a considerable mass of counterevidence (on which more in a moment), Marcion was able to read Paul as announcing an altogether new god to the world.[11]

6. Novenson, "The Universal Polytheism and the Case of the Jews," 52–53, on 1 Cor 8–10.

7. I take it that Paul's participation in *interpretatio* is—as per the theme of this volume—an aspect of his operating within ancient Mediterranean religion, or "paganism," more generally.

8. On Paul as a figure in the histories of both Judaism and Christianity, see the discussion in Matthew V. Novenson, *Paul, Then and Now* (Eerdmans, 2022).

9. For Marcion's works, we are unfortunately dependent on anti-Marcionite writers, above all Tertullian, as sources. Marcion apparently edited a gospel and a recension of Paul's letters, and also wrote the *Antitheses* explicating his gospel of the alien god.

10. This habit of naming is helpfully discussed by Francis Watson, "The Triune Divine Identity: Reflections on Pauline God-Language, in Disagreement with J. D. G. Dunn," *JSNT* 80 (2000): 99–124; and Wing Yi Au, *Paul's Designations of God in Romans*, WUNT 2/590 (Mohr Siebeck, 2023).

11. On Marcion's theology, see further Judith M. Lieu, *Marcion and the Making of a Heretic: God and Scripture in the Second Century* (Cambridge University Press, 2015).

But Paul also speaks—and this is how we know that Marcion's reading of Paul is wrong—of this same god making promises to father Abraham, giving the law to Moses, and leading the children of Israel through the wilderness (Gal 3; Rom 4–5; 1 Cor 10), among other biblical things. In other words, Paul's "god the father of Jesus Christ" is also the patron god of the Jews, the divine hero of the Jewish sacred law and prophets.[12] (In this respect, at least, the ancient catholic Christians with their two-testament Bible got Paul right where Marcion got him wrong.) Admittedly, Paul does not normally call him "the god of the Jews," but then, neither did most ancient Jewish writers. Just as how, in Scotland, Scotch whisky is usually just called "whisky," so also, among ancient Jewish writers, including Paul, the Jewish god is usually just called "god." It is not that the adjective is not apt, just that it does not need saying.[13]

Once, in his Letter to the Romans (3:29), Paul does expressly call this god *Ioudaiōn ho theos*, "the god of the Jews," confirming the point we have been making. Paul goes on, however, to argue that this patron god of the Jews is also the god of all the nations of the earth: "Is god of the Jews only? Is he not also of the nations? Yes, indeed, also of the nations" (Rom 3:29). This, too, is a well-attested ancient Jewish idea: That the god of the Jews is also the high god over all the nations and all their pantheons.[14] Probably this idea comes from the very ancient conflation of the regional god Yhwh with the high god El.[15] Already by the Hellenistic period, then, centuries before Paul, it was

12. A point decisively made by Richard B. Hays, *Echoes of Scripture in the Letters of Paul* (Yale University Press, 1989).

13. See further Paula Fredriksen, "How Jewish Is God? Divine Ethnicity in Paul's Theology," *JBL* 137 (2018): 193–212.

14. E.g., Ps 113:4: "Yhwh is high over all the nations"; Ps 95:3: "Yhwh is a great god, a great king over all the gods."

15. And also Elyon, if we read that as a separate theonym rather than just an epithet for El, which it sometimes is. In any case, compare, e.g., Deut 32:8–9: "When Elyon apportioned the nations, when he divided humankind, he fixed the boundaries of the peoples according to the number of the sons of god. Yhwh's portion was his people, Jacob his allotted share"; and Gen 14:22: "Abram said to the king of Sodom: I have raised my hand to Yhwh, El, Elyon, maker of heaven and earth." See further Mark S. Smith, *God in Translation: Deities in Cross-Cultural Discourse in the Biblical World*, FAT 57 (Mohr Siebeck, 2008); and Thomas Römer, *The Invention of God*, trans. Raymond Geuss (Harvard University Press, 2015).

commonplace for Greek writers to identify this Hebrew god Yhwh/El with Zeus Hypsistos.[16]

It is interesting, in this connection, that Paul himself in his extant letters never makes a particular theological move that his second-century biographer Luke makes for him. Luke writes his character Paul announcing to a crowd of philosophers at the Areopagus in Athens that the deity worshiped by the Athenians as *agnōstos theos*, "the unknown god," is in fact, unbeknownst to them (hence *agnōstos*), the god who long ago created the cosmos and who has just now raised Jesus from the dead.[17] What is more, he quotes a Greek poem in praise of Zeus—"We are his [Zeus's] offspring" (Aratus, *Phaenomena* 5 apud Acts 17:28)—as referring to this god. Luke's Paul does not expressly say to the Athenians that this god is also the patron god of the Jews, but from the rest of Luke's story it emerges that Luke thinks he is.

For Luke, then, the gentiles—or some gentiles, at least—do indeed worship the living and true god, albeit as one unknown. For Paul in his letters, by contrast, the gentiles neither know god nor worship him. "The gentiles do not know god," full stop (1 Thess 4:5). But—and here lies a tragic tale—it was not always so. Once upon a time, the gentiles' ancestors *did* know god via his handiwork in creation (Rom 1:19–20). But then, perversely, these prehistoric gentiles rejected this knowledge and resolved to worship images of human and nonhuman animals instead (Rom 1:21–23), so that the gentiles of Paul's own day, he reckons, are ignorant of god unless or until he, Paul, rectifies that

---

16. Most of the relevant literary evidence is collected in Menahem Stern, ed. and trans., *Greek and Latin Authors on Jews and Judaism*, 3 vols. (Israel Academy of Sciences and Humanities, 1974–1984). It is expertly discussed by George H. van Kooten, "Moses/Musaeus/Mochos and His God Yahweh, Iao, and Sabaoth, Seen from a Graeco-Roman Perspective," in *The Revelation of the Name YHWH to Moses*, ed. George H. van Kooten, TBN 9 (Brill, 2006), 107–38.

17. Acts 17:22–24, 30–31 RSV: "Men of Athens, I perceive that in every way you are very religious. For as I passed along, and observed the objects of your worship, I found also an altar with this inscription, 'To an unknown god.' What therefore you worship as unknown, this I proclaim to you. The God who made the world and everything in it . . . commands all men everywhere to repent, because he has fixed a day on which he will judge the world in righteousness by a man whom he has appointed, and of this he has given assurance to all men by raising him from the dead." See discussion in Clare K. Rothschild, *Paul in Athens: The Popular Religious Context of Acts 17*, WUNT 341 (Mohr Siebeck, 2014).

ignorance.[18] This is arguably why Paul never makes the move of identifying his god with Zeus or Jupiter or another familiar high god. It is not (contra Marcion) that Paul preached an altogether alien deity, just that he took a very dim view of gentiles' capacity for religious knowledge.

Stephen Ahearne-Kroll has recently made a compelling case that, although Paul does not identify his god with any particular gentile god, Paul's motif of a family of related deities who together receive divine honors—father, son, and holy pneuma—would have been familiar and indeed attractive to his audiences in Corinth and elsewhere.[19] Ahearne-Kroll cites Robert Parker, who in turn cites L. Preller and F. G. Welcker, to the effect that "Greeks typically prayed not to individual gods but to 'chords of gods.'"[20] In actual religious practice, that is, gods often came in bundles, or chords: Demeter and Kore; Poseidon and Palaimon; Asklepios and Hygieia; Jupiter, Juno, and Minerva; and so on. Paul's chord of father, son, and pneuma, then, is not a case of *interpretatio* strictly speaking, as if they were identical with, say, Jupiter, Juno, and Minerva. The point, rather, is that they came in a familiar-shaped package, as it were. Thus far the god of the Jews in Paul's letters. But what about his many divine neighbours?

The Gods of the Nations

As we shall see, Paul mostly paints the gods of the nations with a broad brush. Ancient Jewish writers could sometimes be much more specific. The book of Tobit, set partly in ancient Persia, features a local daemon named Asmodeus, probably a Greek gloss on Avestan (Persian) *aeshma daeva*, daemon of wrath. (This same character goes by the equivalent Hebrew name Ashmedai in later rabbinic demonology.)[21] The early medieval Jewish antichrist figure Armilus

18. See further Stephen L. Young, "Ethnic Ethics: Paul's Eschatological Myth of Jewish Sin," *NTS* 70 (2024): 235–48.

19. Stephen Ahearne-Kroll, *The Origins of the Corinthian Christ-Group: Paul's Chord of Gods*, ESRA (Edinburgh University Press, 2024).

20. Robert Parker, *On Greek Religion* (Cornell University Press, 2011), 66. L. Preller, "Das Zwölfgöttersystem der Griechen" [English: "The Twelve-God System of the Greeks"], *Verhandlungen der neunten Versammlung deutscher Philologen, Schulmänner und Orientalisten zu Jena* (Jena, 1846) credits F. G. Welcker with the phrase.

21. Kaufmann Kohler and Louis Ginzberg, "Asmodeus, or Ashmedai," in *Jewish Encyclopedia*, ed. Isidore Singer, vol. 2 (Funk & Wagnalls, 1906), 217–20.

may get his name either from Latin Romulus (mythical founder of Rome) or from Persian Ahriman (a Zoroastrian evil spirit), though, alternatively, it could come from Greek *eremolaos*, "destroyer of a people" (perhaps paralleling the Hebrew name Balaam in Num 22–24).[22] Other ancient Jewish writers identify particular gentile gods with particular biblical heroes. According to Pseudo-Eupolemus, the titan Atlas is actually Enoch (Eusebius, *Preparation for the Gospel* 9.17). According to Artapanus, Olympian Hermes is actually Moses (9.27). And in Bavli Avodah Zarah, the Egyptian goddess Isis is said to be Eve, and the Greco-Egyptian god Serapis the patriarch Joseph (b. Avodah Zarah 43a).[23] In short, some ancient Jewish writers know particular gentile gods by name and assign them Jewish equivalencies.[24]

Paul generally does not do this. In fact, Paul rarely speaks of any particular divine beings other than god the father and his son Jesus. There are a few exceptions, but none of them is clearly a gentile god. Some seven times in the undisputed letters, Paul speaks of a divine troublemaker called the satan, or the opponent,[25] a character Paul knows from the Jewish holy books.[26] But this satan is a member of the Jewish pantheon, not any gentile pantheon. Likewise another hostile being called Beliar, who appears once in Paul's letters (2 Cor 6:15), though the passage is subject to some text-critical dispute.[27] This Beliar (or variant spellings Belial, Beliab, Belian) is an evil spirit

22. David Berger, "Three Typological Themes in Early Jewish Messianism: Messiah Son of Joseph, Rabbinic Calculations, and the Figure of Armilus," *AJS Review* 10 (1985): 141–64.

23. Gerard Mussies, "The *Interpretatio Judaica* of Sarapis," in *Studies in Hellenistic Religions*, ed. M. J. Vermaseren, EPRO 78 (Brill, 1979), 189–214; Gerard Mussies, "The *Interpretatio Judaica* of Thot-Hermes," in *Studies in Egyptian Religion*, ed. M. Heerma Van Voss, E. J. Sharpe, and R. J. Z. Werblowsky, *Numen*Sup 43 (Brill, 1982), 89–120.

24. On all this, see further Novenson, "The Universal Polytheism and the Case of the Jews."

25. Rom 16:20; 1 Cor 5:5; 7:5; 2 Cor 2:11; 11:14; 12:7; 1 Thess 2:18; cf. also 2 Thess 2:9; 1 Tim 1:20; 5:15.

26. In Greek: 3 Kgdms 11:14; Sir 21:27. The famous satan of the Hebrew Book of Job (1:6–9, 12; 2:1–7) comes over into Greek Job as *diabolos*, "slanderer," a word unknown to the undisputed letters of Paul (though cf. Eph 4:27; 6:11; 1 Tim 3:6, 11; 2 Tim 2:26; 3:3; Titus 2:3).

27. On the text-critical question, which has in part to do with the mention of Beliar, see Joseph A. Fitzmyer, "Qumran and the Interpolated Paragraph in 2 Cor 6:14–7:1," *CBQ* 23 (1961): 271–80; and Hans Dieter Betz, "2 Cor 6:14–7:1: An Anti-Pauline Fragment?" *JBL* 92 (1973): 88–108.

in 1QM, 1QH, Jubilees, Testaments of the Twelve Patriarchs, Ascension of Isaiah, and other contemporary Jewish texts.[28] It is possible that the name derives from the ancient Mesopotamian goddess Belili, but this is far from certain, and even if true this *interpretatio* would have been a distant memory by Paul's time.[29] There is one cryptic passage where Paul speaks of an anonymous "god of this age" who has blinded the thoughts of religious outsiders lest they perceive the truth about the divine Christ (2 Cor 4:4).[30] Is "the god of this age" the satan? Beliar? God the father of Jesus? Capitoline Jupiter? Paul does not say. He makes no clear identification with a god from any pantheon, Jewish or gentile. The same is true of Philippians 3:19, where Paul says about certain people—disapprovingly, in the context of a dispute over proselyte circumcision—that "Their god is the loins, and their glory is in their shame." This "god of the loins" could conceivably refer to a god of male fertility: Greek Priapus, Roman Liber Pater, or some such.[31] But here, again, Paul offers no specific *interpretatio*.

Paul does, however, make relatively frequent reference to the gods of the nations *as a class*, which is the most common kind of *interpretatio Judaica* in ancient sources generally.[32] While he takes for granted the Deuteronomic axiom *heis ho theos*, "God is one" (Deut 6:4; Rom 3:30; 1 Cor 8:6; Gal 3:20), Paul also—like Deuteronomy—speaks of the plural gods of the nations. One locus classicus is 1 Corinthians 8:4–6, where Paul considers the question whether people-in-Christ may eat food offered to cult statues of gentile gods:

28. In the Hebrew Bible, however, *belial* is generally just a common noun meaning "worthlessness" (see BDB, ad loc.).

29. T. K. Cheyne, "The Origin and Meaning of Belial," *ExpTim* 8 (1897): 423–24; Morris Jastrow, *The Religion of Babylonia and Assyria* (Athenaeum, 1898), 589.

30. This text is a classic theological puzzle, since if it refers to god the father then it might seem to impugn his character, but if it refers to some hostile deity (e.g., the satan) then it might seem to suggest a dualism of a kind intolerable to the orthodox (e.g., Marcionism, Manichaeism). As far back as the second century, therefore, some Christian interpreters have tried—against the syntax of the clause—to read the genitive phrase "of this age" as modifying "unbelievers" rather than "god." But this is implausible. The text almost certainly speaks of "the god of this age"; the question is who that god is.

31. On this theme in Phil 3, see Ryan D. Collman, "Beware the Dogs! The Phallic Epithet in Phil 3.2," *NTS* 67 (2021): 105–20.

32. On the latter point, see Novenson, "The Universal Polytheism and the Case of the Jews."

> Concerning the eating of sacrifices to images: we know that an image is nothing in the cosmos, and that no one is god except the one. For if indeed there are so-called gods either in heaven or on earth, just as there are many gods and many lords, nevertheless for us there is one god the father—out of whom everything proceeds, and we into him—and one lord Jesus Christ—through whom everything proceeds, and we through him.[33]

There are, Paul says, accurately, many gods and many lords out there (which is, of course, why the problem of food sacrificed to images arises in the first place). "For us," however—that is, for Paul and other people baptized into Christ—there are only two who properly command allegiance: One god, namely the father, and one lord, namely, Jesus. The cult images ("idols") of gentile gods are nothing at all, Paul says, as if trying to speak them onto the rubbish heap.[34]

But the gods themselves *are* things in the cosmos, though Paul—like some other ancient Jewish writers—is a bit conflicted about how exactly to classify them.[35] In 1 Corinthians 8 he allows them the name "gods," but insists that they are not "for us." A bit later on in the same discourse, however, Paul withholds the name "gods" and classifies them as follows: "What am I saying? That sacrifices to images are anything? Or that an image is anything? Rather: that what they sacrifice, they sacrifice to divinities, not to god. I do not want you to be participants with divinities. You cannot drink the cup of the lord and the cup of divinities. You cannot partake of the table of the lord and the table of divinities" (1 Cor 10:19–21).[36] Here Paul says that when gentiles sacrifice,

---

33. Paul's claim here that all things proceed out of god and resolve back into him dovetails with some Stoic cosmogonies, which, in turn, could help make sense of another well-attested *interpretatio Graeca* of the Jewish god: that he is Ouranos or Kosmos or Physis (see Strabo, *Geography* 16.2.35).

34. Alexander Chantziantoniou ("Paul and the Politics of Idolatry" [PhD diss., University of Cambridge, 2023]) argues convincingly that Paul's language here is a rhetorical, as opposed to physical, means of defacing or absencing the images of rival gods.

35. For obvious reasons: If you insist that god is one, and you want to be strictly consistent, then you have to find another word for all the other beings that you might otherwise—and most everyone else does—call gods.

36. On the logic of Paul's prohibition here, see Matthew T. Sharp, "Courting Daimons in Corinth: Daimonic Partnerships, Cosmic Hierarchies, and Divine Jealousy in 1 Corinthians

they sacrifice not to god (*theos*), but rather to *daimons* or divinities.[37] English Bibles often render this word "demons," which to modern ears might suggest something essentially evil. Greek *daimonia*, however, is a commonplace and usually morally neutral word for divine powers (thus my gloss "divinities"). James Rives summarizes, "It generally denoted a superhuman force or being that was less well defined than a god or hero."[38] What is more, at least as far back as Plato, *daimons* were said to play a role in cult, mediating prayers and offerings between mortals and the gods.[39] So it is by no means unreasonable for Paul to mention *daimons* in the context of gentile sacrifices. But whereas Plato says that the *daimons* courier sacrifices onward to the gods, Paul says that gentile sacrifices go to the *daimons* and no further.[40]

Some other ancient Jewish texts that share Paul's anxiety about calling gods "gods" resort to the very useful category of angels. Recall the story in Deuteronomy 32, noted above, where the high god Elyon parcels out all the

8–10," in *Demons in Early Judaism and Christianity*, ed. H. M. Patmore and J. Lössl (Brill, 2022), 112–29.

37. Here Paul quotes a line from the Greek version of Deut 32:17, where god complains about Israel, "They provoked me with foreign things; they embittered me with their abominations; they sacrificed to *daimons* and not to god, to gods which they did not know." Here the *daimons* are none other than the gods of foreign nations.

38. J. B. Rives, *Animal Sacrifice in the Roman Empire (31 BCE–395 CE)* (Oxford University Press, 2024), 185.

39. In Plato, *Symposium* 202e–203a, Diotima says to Socrates that Eros is not a god but a *daimon*, by which she means a class of being "between divine and mortal . . . interpreting and transporting human things to the gods and divine things to humans; entreaties and sacrifices from below, and ordinances and requitals from above; being midway between, it makes each to supplement the other, so that the whole is combined in one. Through it are conveyed all divination and priestcraft concerning sacrifice and ritual and incantations, and all soothsaying and sorcery" (Plato, *Symposium*, trans. Harold N. Fowler [Harvard University Press, 1925], modified).

40. For Justin Martyr (mid-second century CE), *daimons* are evil through and through, much closer to the sense of English "demon": "Since, in ancient times, wicked *daimons*, in apparitions, committed adultery with women and seduced boys and made people see horrifying things, so those who did not rationally evaluate what the *daimons* were doing were stunned with terror. Carried away with fear, they named them gods, not knowing that they were wicked *daimons*" (*1 Apology* 5.1–2; in Justin, *Apologies*, ed. and trans. Denis Minns and Paul Parvis [Oxford University Press, 2009], modified). But Paul does not yet use the word in this loaded way.

nations of the earth among the sons of god: Every deity gets a nation, and Yhwh gets Israel. In the Greek translation of Deuteronomy, these "sons of god" become *angeloi theou*, "angels of god." This is the seed of the influential Jewish myth of the angels of the nations: The idea that god gave to each of the nations of the world—seventy of them, according to Genesis 10—its own patron angel. In the biblical book of Daniel (10:10–21), the patron angels of Persia, Greece, and Israel tussle with one another for geopolitical supremacy. In the Book of Dreams in 1 Enoch, the seer has a vision of seventy shepherds (i.e., angels) overseeing seventy flocks (i.e., nations; 1 En 89:59). In Targum Pseudo-Jonathan to Genesis 11 (the story of the tower of Babel), god first deliberates with the seventy angels of the nations before deciding to go down to confuse the human languages. And this is just a tiny sampling; the myth recurs in myriad other forms through late antiquity and the middle ages.[41]

For his part, Paul does not have an express theory of the angels of the nations à la Deuteronomy 32:8–9, but one passage suggests that he probably assumes some such schema. At the end of Romans 8, Paul imagines a rogues' gallery of divine beings trying and failing to hinder himself and his coreligionists, over against the force of god's love which ensures the cosmic victory of all the baptized. Paul writes, "I am certain that neither death nor life nor angels nor rulers nor present things nor future things nor powers nor height nor depth nor any other creature will be able to part us from the love of god in Christ Jesus our lord" (Rom 8:38–39). Here "angels" are coordinated with several other, related taxons, in particular "rulers" (*archai*) and "powers" (*dynameis*). This is no accident. As Emma Wasserman has shown, these and related terms are widely used in Hellenistic-period Jewish texts (including the Book of the Watchers, Animal Apocalypse, book of Daniel, and more) for lower ranks of divinities deputized by the high god to oversee their respective jurisdictions, whether in the sky or on the earth.[42] When speaking of Jewish texts, we often politely call

41. See the survey in Ludwig Blau and Kaufmann Kohler, "Angelology," in *Jewish Encyclopedia*, 1:583–597; and further detail in Novenson, "The Universal Polytheism and the Case of the Jews."

42. Emma Wasserman, *Apocalypse as Holy War: Divine Politics and Polemics in the Letters of Paul*, AYBRL (Yale University Press, 2018). See also Robert Ewusie Moses, *Practices of Power: Revisiting the Principalities and Powers in the Pauline Letters* (Fortress, 2014), who fascinatingly reads Paul's talk of "rulers" and "powers" in theological relation to West African indigenous gods, which is to say, a particular set of gentile gods.

lower ranks of divinities "angels" (rather than "gods"), as Paul himself does here in Romans 8. Why, though, would these angelic middle managers want to cause Paul trouble? Paula Fredriksen has plausibly argued that, because Paul took it to be his vocation to turn gentiles away from cultic images of their gods and to the god of the Jews, he might well have feared harassment ("persecution") at the hands of disgruntled gentile gods. Given his meddling in the *pax deorum*, Paul would have good reason to worry that these "rulers" might want to separate him from the protection of his patron deity.[43] In short, this text from Romans 8 makes the most sense if we assume that Paul has in mind a set of angels of the nations along the lines of what Deuteronomy 32 imagines.

Another text from a different letter of Paul confirms this impression and supplies further detail on Paul's vision of the divine populus. Near the end of the First Letter to the Corinthians, Paul sketches how he thinks the final resurrection of the dead must happen. (The occasion for this discussion seems to be that some of his auditors conceded the resurrection of Jesus but did not believe in the resurrection of all the righteous, so Paul undertakes to persuade them of the latter.) The resurrection of the righteous, Paul says, immediately precedes the end of all things. At the end, Christ must subject all the lower-ranking divine beings in the cosmos to himself. Then, once this hierarchy is all tidied up, he, Christ, hands over the sole rule to god, his father. The last of the lower-ranking divine beings to be wrangled is death,[44] which is why the resurrection happens last of all. The key thing for our purposes is that here Paul again speaks of "rulers," "authorities," and "powers"—the same terms that we saw in Romans 8, above. "Then the end comes, when he [Christ] hands over the kingship to his god and father, when he undoes every ruler and authority and power" (1 Cor 15:24). As per Wasserman's account, noted above, these divine rulers are best understood as the angels of the nations. For now they harass Paul as he goes about his work (Rom 8:38–39), but Christ will put them in their place once and for all (1 Cor 15:24).[45]

43. Paula Fredriksen, *Paul: The Pagans' Apostle* (Yale University Press, 2017).

44. Literally *thanatos*, Thanatos, "death," which in Greek is an abstract noun but can also be a theonym: the god of death, death personified, like Hebrew Mot. Compare Rev 1:18; 6:8; 20:13, where Thanatos and Hades appear as gods who threaten humanity but are conquered by Christ.

45. See discussion in Emma Wasserman, "Gentile Gods at the Eschaton: A Reconsideration of Paul's 'Principalities and Powers' in 1 Corinthians 15," *JBL* 136 (2017): 727–46.

One suspects that these undone "rulers and authorities and powers" are precisely the "many gods and many lords" of 1 Corinthians 8, though here in 1 Corinthians 15 Paul prefers not to dignify them with the name "gods." We might compare another Pauline account of the final victory of the divine Christ, this one from Paul's Letter to the Philippians: "God supremely exalted him [Jesus] and granted him the name that is above every name, so that at the name of Jesus every knee might bow—of heavenly beings and earthly beings and chthonic beings—and every tongue confess that Jesus Christ is lord, to the glory of god the father" (Phil 2:9–11). Like 1 Corinthians 15, this passage in Philippians 2 paints the final victory of Christ as the subjection of all other divine beings (except the father, of course) to him. Here, however, we also catch a further glimpse of Paul's cosmology: The layers of the cosmos in which different species of divine beings dwell. They come in three types: Heavenly, earthly, and chthonic (or underworld). It is likely that what Paul calls "rulers and authorities and powers" and also "gods" are the most powerful and therefore uppermost in the heavens. Meanwhile, "earthly beings" perhaps include the *daimons* that eat the gentile sacrifices at cult statues, and "chthonic beings" the *daimons* that drink the gentile libations poured into the ground. But all of them, no matter their relative ranks, must and shall be brought into submission to Christ.[46]

There is one more category that calls for discussion in this connection. In his Letter to the Galatians (4:1–11), Paul several times mentions what he calls the *stoicheia tou kosmou*, "elements of the cosmos," to which he says that baptized gentiles-in-Christ were previously enslaved. This might seem a strange thing to say, except that Paul also suggests that these elements are, or are thought to be, gods.[47] He writes, "Formerly, when you did not know god, you were enslaved to things that by nature are not gods. But now that you know god, or rather are known by god, how can you return again to the weak and poor elements to which you again want to be enslaved? You are observing days and months and seasons and years" (Gal 4:8–9). The elements, Paul insists, are nongods, but nongods to which his auditors were previously

46. On this text, see further Wasserman, *Apocalypse as Holy War*, 132–39.

47. See discussion in Emma Wasserman, "Gods and Non-Gods in Galatians: Reconsidering Paul's *Stoicheia*," in *The Social Worlds of Ancient Jews and Christians*, ed. Jaimie Gunderson, Tony Keddie, and Douglas Boin, NovTSup 189 (Brill, 2023), 19–41.

enslaved. What is more, these auditors' present observation of sacred festivals ("days and months and seasons and years") is—in Paul's biased view—a voluntary re-enslavement to the elements.[48] All of this strongly suggests that Paul is referring here to natural phenomena, either the classical elements themselves (earth, water, air, fire, and aether) or the heavenly bodies (sun, moon, stars, planets) that regulate sacred time and are superintended by—or, depending on one's physics, just *are*—the gods.[49] By calling them nongods, Paul is rhetorically robbing them of status but also simultaneously conceding that they are in fact recognized as gods.[50] This is one rhetorically loaded kind of *interpretatio Judaica*: The reclassification of gentile gods as mere elements.[51] Here in Galatians Paul denies them the name "gods," whereas in 1 Corinthians he allows it. This ambivalence is typical of much ancient Jewish—and, for that matter, subsequent Christian—discourse on gentile gods. On the one hand, those gods are a prominent part of the social world and so warrant recognition; on the other hand, though, Paul wants to avoid dignifying them with the same name (*theos*) that he normally uses for the high god over all.

Conclusion

As is well known, Paul preached an exclusivist religious message: Gentiles must abandon their cultic images of other gods, serve the one god over all (i.e., the god of the Jews), and wait patiently for the appearing of his son Jesus (thus, e.g., 1 Thess 1:9–10). But this exclusivist message did not by any means exempt Paul from the prevailing cultural practice of *interpretatio*, of assimilating other people's gods into one's own pantheon. The god whom Paul calls "god" without qualification created all things, adopted Israel as his people, and sent his son Jesus in the fulness of time. Paul does not identify this god with the highest

48. On these sacred festivals and their relation to indigenous deities of Asia Minor, see the discussion in Christina Harker, *The Colonizers' Idols: Paul, Galatia, and Empire in New Testament Studies*, WUNT 2/460 (Mohr Siebeck, 2018).

49. See discussion in Ernest P. Clark, *Weak Elements, Weak Flesh: Reading Galatians in Conversation with Philo and Greek Medical Discourse* (Lexington/Fortress, 2023).

50. Thus rightly Chantziantoniou, "Paul and the Politics of Idolatry."

51. There is a partial parallel here to ancient Euhemerism, the reclassification of gods as once-great but now-deceased mortals, on which see Nickolas P. Roubekas, *An Ancient Theory of Religion: Euhemerism from Antiquity to the Present*, RMCS (Routledge, 2016).

god of other pantheons—as Luke, for instance, does—but neither does Paul expressly deny such an equivalence.

The gods of the nations are, for Paul (as for Isaiah, Daniel, Jubilees, and other Jewish writers before him), so many subordinate divine "rulers," "authorities," and "powers" deputized by the one god over all to superintend their respective jurisdictions. They are not evil, but they are insubordinate, which is obvious from the political facts on the ground: Babylon, Persia, Greece, and Rome, in turn, have run roughshod over Israel. But the one god over all has now sent his son to subject all these powers to himself, to bring them to heel, and thereby to effect the rightly ordered kingship of god (*basileia tou theou*).

Gentile religious *practice* is a different kettle of fish. The chief problem there, by Paul's lights, is "idolatry" proper, that is, the cultic use of figural art representing the divine in human or animal form. These figural images are, Paul insists, nothing at all. But the beings who eat the sacrifices offered to these images are very real *daimonia*, "divinities." In light of all this, we may say that for Paul, as for Robert Parker in his theory of the universal polytheism, there is one set of gods ruling the entire world. The really interesting question is where all those gods fit in one's own—in the present case, Paul's own—pantheon. At a number of places in Paul's letters, we can see him hazarding partial answers to this question, sketching an *interpretatio Paulina*. Like Strabo, Tacitus, and other near contemporaries, Paul renders other people's gods intelligible to himself.

CHAPTER FIVE

Pauline Polytheism and the Triumph of the Davidic Messiah[1]

Paula Fredriksen
Boston University and The Hebrew University

God, Gods, and Jews

"Pagans were polytheists, believing in the existence of many different gods. Jews were monotheists, believing that there was only one god."

This statement is only half true. Pagans did indeed believe in the existence of many and various gods. But so did Jews.

Jews encountered these gods, first of all, in their own sacred texts. Jewish scriptures teem with other deities. In situations of war, they contest with YHWH. In Exodus 12:12, YHWH proclaims, "On all the gods of Egypt I will execute judgments." Jeremiah speaks of God capturing the gods of Egypt (Jer 43:12); at 46:25, God brings punishments upon these gods; at 49:3, he sends the Ammonite god into exile. "Who is like you . . . among the gods?" enthuse Moses and the Israelites after the defeat of the Egyptians (Exod 15:11). God champions Israel against the gods of the nations, while Israel battles their people.

But relations between these deities and Israel's god were not always hostile. These other gods attend God in his heavenly court. They bow down to him: "Worship him, all you gods," the Psalmist exhorts (Deut 32:34). "In the midst of the gods he holds judgment" (Ps 82:1). "All the peoples walk, each in the name of its god; but we will walk in the name of the Lord *our* god forever and

1. The following essay is excerpted from my article, "Philo, Herod, Paul, and the Many Gods of Ancient Jewish 'Monotheism,'" *Harvard Theological Review* 115, no. 1 (2022): 23–45. I thank the *Harvard Theological Review* and Cambridge University Press for their permission to reproduce elements of that article here.

ever" (Mic 4:5). In Deuteronomy, God even appoints these other, lower divine beings over the nations (32:8 NRSVue), and he permits the nations, though not Israel, to worship celestial beings (Deut 4:19). Whether as enemies or as courtiers or as divine powers over the nations, then, these other gods are just *there*. Israel's god was never the only god, not even in his own book.

Beginning in the fourth century BCE, once Jews began to move into the Hellenistic city (Greek, *polis*)—itself a pagan religious institution—foreign gods took on a higher cultural tone. In ways different from their earlier Canaanite and Philistine colleagues, Greek gods were deeply integrated into the life of the polis. Through the literary canon that shaped Hellenistic culture, these gods dominated education itself. And much of the life of the polis pulsed around public displays of respect to these gods. This was simple prudence: Gods superintended the well-being of their cities.

Jews in the western diaspora acknowledged the existence of these other gods. Moses himself, in Greek, had advised as much when he taught, "Do not revile the gods" (Exod 22:28 LXX). These gods might be *daimonia*, "godlings," gods lesser and lower than Israel's god (Ps 95:5 OG), but gods they were. They manifested in a dream to Moschos Ioudaios son of Moschion, who erected a votive inscription in their temple. Jewish ephebes, like Jesus son of Antiphilos and Eleazar son of Eleazar, were involved with Heracles and Hermes, the gods of their gymnasium; as mature citizens, they would have improvised demonstrations of respect to the gods of their cities of residence as well. Pothos son of Strabo called upon Zeus, Gaia, and Helios to witness a synagogue manumission. Jews both watched and funded athletic events dedicated to these gods and, if contestants, also participated in them. Jews, like Glykon in Phrygia, measured time by the holy days of both the Jewish and the Roman calendar.[2] Jewish town councilors, actors,

2. For Moschos, see *Inscriptiones Judaicae Orientis* 1, Ach 45; for Pothos, *IJO* 1, BS20; for Glykon, *IJO* 2, No. 196. The gymnasium stele naming Jesus and Eleazar is discussed in John M. G. Barclay, *Jews in the Mediterranean Diaspora: From Alexander to Trajan (323 BCE–117 CE)* (T&T Clark, 1996), 234; further on Jews, gymnasium educations, and civic life, pp. 235–41. On Jews as ephebes, town councilors, and officers in pagan armies, Margaret H. Williams, *Jews among Greeks and Romans: A Diasporan Sourcebook* (Johns Hopkins University Press, 1998), 107–31; specifically on Jews in foreign armies, Raúl González Salinero, *Military Service and the Integration of Jews into the Roman Empire* (Brill, 2022). On Jews both as spectators and as actors in (pagan) theatres, René Bloch, "Part of the Scene: Jewish Theatre in Antiquity," *JAJ* 8 (2017): 150–69.

and athletes, soldiers and gladiators, though in principle not active participants in public cult,[3] would at least have been respectfully present when such cult was enacted.[4]

Even for Jews, then, God was not the only god. Like their pagan and, later, Christian contemporaries, ancient Mediterranean Jews organized their cosmos hierarchically. "One god"—for Jews, the god of Israel; for pagan "monotheists" and hypsistarians (pagan worshipers of "the highest god"), their own particular "highest" god—reigned "on top," with as many others lower gods and divine powers as cosmologies, local culture, and personal experience required ranging beneath. Antiquity's universe was a god-congested place. Jews knew this as well as did the next ancient person.[5]

God, Jews, and Pagans

Jews mixed not only with pagan gods. They mixed as well with pagan humans. Jewish diaspora communities ("synagogues" or "prayer houses" or "assemblies") were open to outsiders. This is remarked on by pagan authors such as Juvenal, and by the author of the Acts of the Apostles as well. These pagan sympathizers and synagogue patrons were sometimes labeled "pious ones," that is,

3. An imperial law from the early third century CE eventually exempted Jewish town councilors from performing the rites attendant upon that position that would "transgress their religion," *Digest* 50:2:3:3.

4. For discussion of many of these sources, see Williams, *Jews among Greeks and Romans*; P. van der Horst, *Saxa iudaica loquuntur* (Brill, 2014), esp. ch. 2 ("Early Jewish Epigraphy: What Can We Learn?"). Further on the ethnicity and the religious Jewishness of these inscriptions, Tessa Rajak, *The Jewish Dialogue with Greece and Rome* (Brill, 2002), 366–70.

5. Charms and amulets to avert harm show that Jews, whether as clients or as adepts, attributed much power to Mediterranean gods, angels, and spirits (*pneumata*), especially in local, multireligious contexts: e.g., the Sicilian amulet that calls on angels to help Judah escape the negative attentions of a Greek goddess: "Artemis, flee from Judah!" #33, lines 13–14, in Roy Kotansky, *Greek Magical Amulets* (Springer Fachmedien, 1994); cf. Mika Ahuvia's analysis of an incantation bowl, "An Ancient Jewess Invoking Goddesses," *AJS* 2019 (https://www.associationforjewishstudies.org/docs/default-source/ajs-perspectives/ajs-perspectives-transgression.pdf). Further on the local variations and quotidian practicalities of Jewish "reciprocal exchanges" (offerings made to secure divine favors) with lower divinities, Stanley K. Stowers, "Why 'Common Judaism' Does Not Look Like Mediterranean Religion," in *From Strength to Strength: Essays in Appreciation of Shaye J.D. Cohen*, ed. Michael L. Satlow (Brown Judaica Series, 2018), 235–55, esp. 247–51.

"God-fearers."[6] The centurion Cornelius of Acts 10, fictive or not, provides a ready example: Though a Roman army officer, he "fears God" (Acts 10:22). Juvenal pokes (exasperated) fun at the *metuens Sabbata*, the "Sabbath-fearing" pagan whose sons, in light of their father's Jewish sympathies, themselves receive circumcision and thus "become" Jews (*Satires* 14.96–105).

Inscriptions support the literary data. Julia Severa, a Roman contemporary of Paul's, was a patron of the Jewish community in Acmonia in Asia Minor: A priestess in the imperial cult, she also built the Jewish community's "house." The theater of Miletus had an area reserved for "the Jews" and "the God-fearers." A fourth-fifth century Jewish inscription in Aphrodisias lists the names of fifty-four God-fearers among those of native Jews and of *proselytoi* (our "converts"). Later Christian authors like Commodian complain of pagans who "rush" between traditional altars and synagogues, calling them "half-Jews." (Some later Gentile Christians will frequent synagogues too, much to the disapproval of these ecclesiastical writers.) And of course, for as long as the temple stood, Jerusalem welcomed pagans into the temple's largest courtyard.[7]

Jews and pagans, divine and human, thus mixed in pagan cities, within civic, cultural, educational, and political institutions. And pagans mixed with Jews in Jewish communal and sacred spaces. This interpenetration of populations stabilized the religious ecology of the Greco-Roman city. The gods were honored, the city safeguarded. And the synagogue found its place in the urban landscape.

---

6. For a review of the epigraphical and literary evidence for God-fearers, see Irina Levinskaya, *The Book of Acts in Its Diaspora Setting* (Eerdmans, 1996), 51–126. On the continuing paganism of synagogue God-fearers, Paula Fredriksen, "If It *Looks* Like a Duck, and It *Quacks* Like a Duck . . . : On *Not* Giving Up the Godfearers," in *A Most Reliable Witness: Essays in Honor of Ross Shepard Kraemer*, ed. Susan Ashbrook Harvey et al., BJS 358 (Brown Judaic Studies, 2016), 25–34.

7. On Julia Severa, *IJO* 2, No.168; the inscription at Miletus (the translation is contested), *IJO* 2, No. 37; Aphrodisias, *IJO* 2, No. 14. For a discussion of this evidence for Jews in pagan places and pagans in Jewish ones, Paula Fredriksen, *Paul. The Pagans' Apostle* (Yale University Press, 2017), 54–60, 73–77. On the pagan presence in the precincts of Jerusalem's temple, Emil Schürer, G. Vermes et al., *History of the Jewish People in the Age of Jesus Christ* (T&T Clark, 1973; 1979; 1986), 1:176, 378; 2:222, 284–85; on God-fearers, 3.1:150–76. For Commodian's complaint, *Instructions* 37.1.

Paul, Gods, and Gentiles

Relations between Jews and foreign gods were not always so untroubled. Jewish tradition was not universally tolerant of pagan deities. The "liberal" position and *modus vivendi* ("way of life") charted above were more than matched by a teaching of contempt, one that condemned the gods of the nations and their material representations as "nothings"; one that attributed flamboyant social and sexual malfeasance to those who worshiped "idols" (*eidola*, "images"). "How miserable, their hopes set on dead things, are those who give the name 'gods' to the works of human hands!" (Wis 13:10). Some apocalyptic traditions anticipated the destruction of these false gods—sometimes, together with their worshipers—at the end of days, when the dead would rise and God would establish his kingdom. Other apocalyptic traditions, more inclusive, foretold the turning of the nations to the universal worship of Israel's god.

Paul himself speaks emphatically of the social agency, the presence, the power, and the cosmic (thus, religious) significance of pagan gods. They played a defining part in Paul's vision of his own role as Christ's emissary to the nations. And these gods also served in crucial ways to shape the apostle's Christology.[8]

Prophetic traditions hostile to the gods underlie Paul's letters. As he traveled the eastern Mediterranean spreading his *evangelion* ("good news"), Paul perforce dealt with pagan gods at close quarters: After all, he roamed in their territories. For example, corresponding with his gentile community in Corinth, he complained that "the god of this age" (*theos tou aiōnos toutou*) had blinded the minds of unbelievers (2 Cor 4:4). Modern commentators will insist that by "god" in this sentence, Paul must intend "the devil," that is, Satan. But that is not what Paul says. He is perfectly capable of naming Satan when he wants to: 1 Thessalonians 2:18 (cf: 3:5); 1 Corinthians 5:5, 7:7; 2 Corinthians 2:11, 11:14, 12:7; Romans 16:20. His frequent recourse to "Satan" in fact makes Paul's use of *theos*, "god," in 2 Corinthians 4:4 that much more striking, because deliberate. Which particular god did Paul have in mind? He does not say.

Elsewhere, Paul simultaneously sounds the biblical tropes of denial and defiance when speaking of these gods. Thus, at 1 Corinthians 8:4–6,

8. I will consider here material drawn from only six of the seven undisputed epistles. Philemon—basically a memo about the return of a runaway slave—is irrelevant to our topic. See J. Albert Harrill, *Paul the Apostle* (Cambridge University Press, 2012), 18.

instructing his ex-pagan gentile assembly, he states: "We know that 'an idol has no being in the world' and that 'there is no god but one.' [5]For even if there are so-called gods either in heaven or on earth—*as indeed there are many gods and many lords*—[6]yet *for us* there is one God, the Father, . . . and one lord, Jesus Christ" (au. trans.). Verse 6 does not deny the truth of verse 5, which plainly acknowledges the theological congestion of the first-century cosmos. Rather, it situates Paul's hearers within their newly *Judaized* cosmos: The existence of these many gods and other deities (*kyrioi,* "lords") notwithstanding, Paul's people are to adhere solely to Paul's god, enabled to do so through the spirit of that god's son, the messiah (*christos*).[9]

Who are these many "gods" and "lords"? We might look, first, again, to the stars and planets, divine intelligences for all ancient peoples. Paul's elder contemporary and coreligionist Philo of Alexandria, in his commentary on Genesis, had referred to these beings quite simply as *theoi*, "gods" (*On the Creation of the Universe* 7.27). In his letter to Rome, Paul names hostile heavenly intermediaries (*angeloi*), principalities (*archai*), and powers (*dynameis*), cosmic agents encircling the earth (Rom 8:38). Communicating with his expagan assembly in Philippi, Paul invokes the divine plenum of celestial, terrestrial, and subterranean superhuman beings, those above the earth and upon the earth and below the earth: They will kneel in acknowledgment of the returning, triumphant Christ "to the glory of God the father" (Phil 2:10–11). Eating sacrificial meat in temple settings can effect a real fellowship with these beings (1 Cor 10:20–21). The nations are wrong to sacrifice to such "godlings" (*daimonia*; 10:20). Among other baneful acts, they had arrayed themselves against Christ: The celestial "rulers of this age" (*archontes*) had crucified the divine son of Paul's god (1 Cor 2:8).[10] Cosmic elements (*stoicheia*), themselves

9. On gods as "lords," Nicole Belayche, "*Kyrios* and *Despotes*: Addresses to Deities and Religious Experiences," in *Lived Religion in the Ancient Mediterranean World: Approaching Religious Transformations from Archaeology, History and Classics*, ed. Valentino Gasparini, Maik Patzelt, Rubina Raja, Anna-Katharina Rieger, Jörg Rüpke and Emiliano Urciuoli (De Gruyter, 2020), 87–113; though, as Harrill points out, "kyrios" also functioned regularly as a term of respectful address to any social superior, human or divine; *Paul the Apostle*, 88.

10. Those entities currently combatting Paul, soon to be overwhelmed by the victorious Christ, are clearly super- or nonhuman powers, interpreted as such by an early deutero-Pauline pseudepigraph, Eph 6.12: "For our conflict is not against blood and flesh [i.e., human opponents], but against the principalities (*archas*), against the powers (*exousias*), against the cosmic rulers (*kosmokratoras*) of the present darkness, against evil pneumatic beings (*pneumatika tēs*

"not gods by nature (*physei*)"—though once considered and worshiped as gods by those in Galatia—had previously "enslaved" Paul's *ethnē,* "gentiles," before he had brought them to the exclusive worship of his own god (Gal 4:3–9). And, as we have seen, "the god of this age" got in Paul's way (2 Cor 4:4).

How had Paul and his gentile communities ended up on the wrong side of these gods? Why, given the extremely uneven distribution of power, did he and his people think that they could possibly prevail against superhuman opponents? And in what ways did pagan gods actually *confirm* Paul's conviction that Jesus was indeed God's warrior champion, the final, Davidic christ (Rom 1:3; 15:12)?

To answer these questions, we need to glance backward, briefly, to Jesus of Nazareth, and to events in and around Jerusalem some two-plus decades prior to Paul's letters. An itinerant prophet, exorcist, and healer, Jesus had gathered around himself a core group of followers. And he deputized them to work the same acts of power as he himself did, and through which he established his own authority to pronounce his message. For, like his mentor John the Immerser before him and like Paul his apostle after him, Jesus too proclaimed the imminent approach of God's kingdom. "The kingdom of God is at hand!" (Mark 1:15 RSV).

Whatever other end time hopes Jesus may have attached to this message, the coming resurrection of the dead must have figured prominently. The intensity of his followers' expectation of this event alone accounts for their behavior in the wake of Jesus's crucifixion as "King of the Jews."[11] They were convinced, despite his death, that Jesus lived on. Their community relocated permanently to Jerusalem, terrestrial epicenter of the coming kingdom (cf. Rom 11:26). From the largest court of the temple mount, they continued to proclaim Jesus's message, linked now to their belief that Jesus would himself

---

ponērias) in the heavens." Planetary "rulers" cohere with this cosmos. For definitions of *archē*, *exousia*, and *dynamis* as independent cosmic forces (that is, "gods"), see BDAG; for discussion, M. David Litwa, *We Are Being Transformed* (De Gruyter, 2012), 177–79.

11. "Easter faith may have been born after the crucifixion, but it was conceived before. Schweitzer saw the truth: the 'resurrection experiences' are 'intelligible' only if they were 'based upon the expectation of the resurrection, and this again as based on references of Jesus to the resurrection.' Without antecedent expectation of the imminent resurrection of the dead in general, there would have been no proclamation of the resurrection of Jesus in particular," Dale Allison, *Constructing Jesus* (Baker Academic, 2010), 59, citing n129 to Albert Schweitzer, *The Quest of the Historical Jesus* (1906; repr., Fortress, 2001), 343.

play a defining role in its establishment. Within a few years, some began to fan out, continuing to promulgate their messiah's message to Israel via the networks of synagogue communities ringing the Mediterranean—Joppa and Caesarea in Roman Judea; Damascus and Antioch further abroad.

It was there, within the Jewish communities of ethnically mixed, pagan-majority cities, that sojourning apostles encountered a social reality that their earlier itineraries through Jewish villages in the Galilee and Judea had not prepared them for: The presence of interested pagans, "God-fearers." Some of these synagogue-going pagans, too, responded positively to the apostles, who in turn welcomed them into the assemblies of Christ-followers forming within the synagogues' penumbra. But joining the Christ-assembly (*ekklēsia*) came with a radically Judaizing demand, one that urban synagogues themselves had never made of local pagan sympathizers. Christ-following non-Jews, insisted the apostles, had to break, completely, with their native gods.

This drastic requirement—universally demanded, so far as we know, by all factions of the Christ-movement—gives us another measure of its intense anticipation of God's kingdom. The nations' repudiation of the images of their "false" gods and their turning to the "living and true god" (1 Thess 1:9) was an apocalyptic trope featured prominently in Jewish end time prophecies.[12] At the end, the nations would stream to Jerusalem and worship together with Israel (Isa 2:2–4). Both peoples will together eat on the temple mount the feast that God will prepare for them (Isa 25:6). Gentiles will accompany Jews at the ingathering (Pss Sol 17:31; Zech 8:23). Gentiles will direct their sight to uprightness (1 En 91.14). Many nations will come from afar to the name of the Lord God, bearing gifts (Tob 13:11) and all the nations will turn in fear to the Lord, and bury their cultic images (14:5–6). Once God restores Jerusalem, "all who are on the earth" will know that he is the Lord God (Sir 36:17). At the coming of the Great King, the nations will bend knee to God (Sibylline Oracles 3.616). They will send to the temple and renounce their images (3.715–24), and from every land they will bring incense and gifts to the temple of the great god (3.772).

This turning of the nations was an event anticipated only at time's end. But for the members of the early Christ movements, Jesus's resurrection had

12. For a review of these traditions—and an appropriate refusal to attempt to systematize them—see Terence L. Donaldson, *Judaism and the Gentiles: Jewish Patterns of Universalism (to 135 CE)* (Baylor University Press, 2007).

tipped time into a new phase: The kingdom was being realized, the nations turning to God, through their own work in spreading the good news. Expagan gentiles joined the Christ assemblies in anticipation of Christ's glorious return. By midcentury—the point by which, with Paul's letters, we begin to have written evidence—various apostles of Christ disagreed heatedly over *how* to integrate (male) expagan gentiles into their movement. (Circumcision? Immersion alone? Immersion plus circumcision?) But no one seems to have disputed the principle of gentile inclusion as such. Indeed, the phenomenon itself was another confirmation of the movement's core message: If gentiles voluntarily repudiated gentile gods, then the kingdom must indeed be at hand.

How did their gods feel about this? Temperamental at the best of times, gods were quick to take offense. And offended gods acted out. Earthquake or flood, fire or famine, disease or violent death: Ancient people were all too familiar with these expressions of divine displeasure. Greco-Roman cities represented intricate religious ecosystems whose dynamic equilibrium was maintained by human solicitude: Attention to traditional repertoires of showing respect to the gods. The phenomenon of gentile "God-fearing"—a typical Mediterranean both/and model of dealing with divine diversity—enabled Jewish diaspora communities to settle comfortably within these ecosystems. And why not? Absent apocalyptic aspirations, the paganism of majority culture was entirely normal. The nations of course had their own gods. Israel had theirs (cf. Deut 32:8; Mic 4:5).

The gospel message—spreading from itinerant apostles to resident gentiles via diaspora synagogues; turning the local synagogue's pagans into expagans—disrupted the careful balance of relations between heaven and earth. Little wonder, then, that Paul experienced so much pushback: From anxious synagogue authorities, from angry urban mobs, from Roman magistrates attempting to keep the peace (e.g., 2 Cor 11:24–29; 12:10), and, as we have seen, from the gods themselves.[13] Yet he and his gentile *ekklēsiai*

13. On fear of heaven as the fundamental reason for pagan hostility both toward Jewish apostles and toward Christ-following gentiles, Martin Goodman, "Galatians 6.12 on Circumcision and Persecution," in Satlow, *From Strength to Strength*, 275–80. "Neglect of the traditional observances" offending "against the gods and therefore against the state" accounted for this hostility, G. E. M. de Ste Croix, "Why Were the Early Christians Persecuted?—a Rejoinder," *Past and Present* 27 (1964) 28–33, at 32–33. This diaspora urban context of angry and anxious pagans (human and divine) and vulnerable resident Jewish communities accounts for Paul's experience with "persecution," both giving and getting: Fredriksen, *Paul*, 61–93.

continued to defy their opposition, whether human or divine. Paul and his people were bound together—literally and materially—by a stronger power: The holy *pneuma* ("spirit") of Christ, and of Israel's god.

Paul assigns godlike attributes to Christ, despite his notable reticence about calling him a god *tout court*. Rather, he insists, Christ is a "human being" (*anthrōpos*), albeit "from heaven" (1 Cor 15:47). In his supramundane state, Christ had been in "god form" before his descent into "slave form" (*morphē theou/morphē doulou*; Phil 2:6–7), that is, into a body of flesh and blood. Presumably, in his postmortem manifestations—the only way that Paul would have experienced him—Jesus appeared in or as his pre-descent god form, a spiritual body (*sōma pneumatikon*), which was the sort of body that characterized ancient divinity more generally. Transformation into pneumatic body, Paul taught, was guaranteed to believers whether living or dead: Human flesh and blood ("which cannot inherit the kingdom of God") would transition into bodies of spirit (1 Cor 15:50, cf. v. 44; Rom 8:29).[14]

Paul's phrasing sometimes implies that the risen Christ presented as a visual object ("Have I not seen Christ our lord?" 1 Cor 9:1; "Christ . . . was seen," 15:5–8). More often, though, he uses locative language: Christ or Christ's spirit is "in" Paul, "in" the body of the believer, "in" the assembly at large (e.g., Gal 1:16, Paul's god revealed his son "in me"; spirit is "in" the body both of the individual and of the group, 1 Cor 6:15–17). Christ's indwelling spirit manifests by enabling charismatic acts: Works of power, divinatory expertise, prophecy, angelic speech, exorcisms, and healing. In effect, this sharing of spirit binds the assembly into "one body," or specifically into Christ's body (e.g., 1 Cor 12:12–14, 27).[15]

The key indices of *pneuma* for Paul the Pharisee, however, were ritual and ethical. Christ's *pneuma* had enabled his pagan *ethnē* to become those

14. For Paul's views on bodily (though not fleshly) redemption, see esp. Matthew Thiessen, *Paul and the Gentile Problem* (Oxford University Press, 2016), 129–60. On Christ's god form preceding his slave form, Fredriksen, *Paul*, 133–41.

15. For two recent and generative redescriptions of "spirit" in Paul's letters, see esp. Giovanni Bazzana, *Having the Spirit of Christ: Spirit Possession and Exorcism in the Early Christ Groups* (Yale University Press, 2020), 103–205, interpreting Paul's language and these performative phenomena by appeal to crosscultural studies of spirit possession; and Jennifer Eyl, *Signs, Wonders, and Gifts* (Oxford University Press, 2019), situating such types of empowerment within their broader Mediterranean context of divine/human reciprocity and allegiance (*pistis*).

long-prophesied "eschatological gentiles" who (finally!) repudiated the images of their gods and worshiped the right god in the right ways. Paul's expagans were thus nothing less than a "new creation," reformatted through pneumatic infusion to live according to (idealized) Jewish standards (2 Cor 5:7; Gal 6:16). Their newly Judaized conduct in fact gave the empirical measure of *pneuma*'s efficacy. Worship only Israel's god; no other gods; no idols; chaste marriages; settle disputes within the assembly; contribute funds for the group back in Jerusalem; and a lot of other idealized Jewish community behaviors, summarized by Paul as "fulfilling the law" (Gal 5:14; 1 Cor 7:19; Rom 13:8–10). Spirit had separated Paul's gentiles from those *ethnē* who did not know God, connecting them to Abraham via Abraham's *sperma* ("seed"), the "eldest of many brothers," Christ (Gal 3:16, 29; Rom 8:29). Spirit effected gentile *huiothesia*, "son-adoption," into God's family, making these gentiles "sons" and thus heirs, together with Israel, of God's kingdom. How long could these expagan *hagioi* ("holy ones") keep on keeping on? Until Christ manifested to the cosmos as God's Davidic son. The happy elect few, chosen both from Israel and from the nations, already knew that "the ends of the ages have come" (1 Cor 10:11). Soon everybody would know. It was all happening *en taxei* ("soon"), *nun* ("now"; Rom 16:20, 26).[16]

Scholarly analyses of Paul's letters often view the first generation of the Jesus movement as a series of accomplished or anticipated punctiliar events. "The" baptism of Jesus. "The" mission of Jesus. "The" resurrection. "The" apostolic community in Jerusalem. "The" gentile mission. "The" Parousia ("second coming"). But as Paul's letters imply, as the depictions in the later Gospels and Acts suggest, and as the physics of ancient material *pneuma* would support, all of these events—Jesus's activities and exorcisms; his various and continuing postmortem manifestations; the movement's settling in Jerusalem and then spreading abroad; its acceptance of expagan gentiles; the commitments and behaviors of Paul, of his apostolic rivals and colleagues, and of his expagan assemblies—do not describe a series of discrete moments. They *define a zone, a single kinetic arc of eschatological*

16. *Pneuma* enables expagan gentiles to "fulfill the law" (Gal 5:14, cf. Rom 13:8–10). On pneumatic adoption, as opposed to fleshly circumcision, Thiessen, *Gentile Problem*, 129–60; also Paula Fredriksen, "How Jewish Is God? Divine Ethnicity in Paul's Theology," *JBL* 138, no. 1 (2018): 193–212, at 205–9. On the ethnic specificity of Paul's ethics, Paula Fredriksen, "Judaizing the Nations: The Ritual Demands of Paul's Gospel," *NTS* 56 (2010): 232–52; also Stephen L. Young, "Ethnic Ethics: Paul's Eschatological Myth of Jewish Sin," *NTS* 70 (2024): 235–48.

divine empowerment and redemption, soon to transform the cosmos at and as the kingdom. The medium of that empowerment—continuous from Jesus's immersion by John (Mark 1:10–12 and parr; cf. John 1:32–33)—was divine *pneuma*. Its eschatological means of conveyance was Christ.

The Return of Christ and the Gods of the Nations

"Messiah" (*christos*) was a term that could admit of many meanings.[17] Its application to the figure of Jesus testifies to that semantic versatility. But for Paul, Christ's function as *Davidic* messiah is surprisingly, recognizably traditional.[18] Manifesting through *pneuma* in the quotidian to and in an elect few, those called from Israel and from the nations who are already being transformed (2 Cor 3:18), Jesus's status as God's son—thus, as the royal Davidic warrior—will be manifest *in power*, globally, when he raises, thus transforms, the dead (Rom 1:3–4; cf. 1 Cor 15:51–52).[19] But to do that, Christ first needs to get past the nations' gods.

Paul, like many other Jewish apocalyptic visionaries, foresees a final battle between the forces of good (Israel's god, his son the Davidic messiah, good angels and archangels; 1 Thess 4:16) and evil (cosmic gods, "every *archē* and every *exousia* and every *dynamis*," and even death itself; 1 Cor 15:24–26; cf. Phil 2:10, where these errant powers are subdued but not destroyed). Paul's language

17. On the varieties of Jewish messianism, two recent fine studies by Matthew V. Novenson: *Christ among the Messiahs* (Oxford University Press, 2012), and *The Grammar of Messianism* (Oxford University Press, 2017).

18. Though, as Matthew Novenson points out, "manifest diversity" describes even the specific subcategory of "Davidic messiah:" "Paul has a Davidic messiah who dies and rises from the dead (Rom 1.3–4). 4 Ezra has a Davidic messiah who dies but does not rise from the dead (4 Ezra 7.28–29). The Qumran *Community Rule* has a Davidic messiah who is an accessory to a priestly messiah (1 QS IX, 11). The epistle to the Hebrews has a Davidic messiah who is himself a priestly messiah (Heb 7.11–17). Bavli Sanhedrin even has a Davidic messiah who judges cases by a divinely inspired sense of smell (b. Sanh. 93b). All of these texts represent defensible ancient interpretations of certain biblical house of David texts, but they do not remotely constitute a single model of the Davidic messiah," "The Messiah ben Abraham in Galatians: A Response to Joel Willitts," *Journal for the Study of Paul and His Letters* 2 (2012): 163–69, at 165.

19. On reading Rom 1:4 not as Christ's *own* resurrection *from* the dead but as "*the* resurrection *of* the dead"—which is what the Greek happens to say (cf. 1 Cor 15:12–21), see Fredriksen, *Paul*, 141–45; cf. Bazzana, *Spirit*, 121–24.

in this passage of 1 Corinthians 15 resonates with the Davidic enthronement psalms: The messiah will reign "until he [God] has put all his [the Davidic king's] enemies under his feet" (15:25; cf. Ps 110:1).[20] In 1 Corinthians, Christ "destroys" or "abolishes" these cosmic forces.[21] In 1 Thessalonians, he descends from heaven "with a cry of command, with the archangel's call and the sound of the trumpet of God" (1 Thess 4:16 NRSVue modified)—more martial imagery. In Philippians 2, Paul's exalted Christ returns—presumably in his *morphē theou*—to subjugate these gods: Nonhuman knees, celestial, terrestrial, and subterranean, all "bend" to their messianic conqueror, ultimately acknowledging his father, the god of Israel (cf. Ps 97:7, "all gods bow down to him").[22]

In short: Redemption, for Paul, is preceded by a cosmic theomachy, a battle of the gods. Both his definition of Jesus qua Davidic messiah and his vision of the establishment of God's kingdom presuppose—indeed, require—the active agency of pagan gods: The son of David is a warrior. The pacification of the pagan cosmos will occur once the Redeemer manifests from Zion, to gather humanity—"the fulness of the nations and all Israel" (Rom 11:25–26). Transformed into bodies of *pneuma*, Paul proclaims, the redeemed will enter their celestial commonwealth, ascending above the moon to God's eternal kingdom (Phil 3:20–21).[23] It was through his defeat of these other deities that biblically sanctioned royal lineage and Davidic valor came together for Paul to define Jesus as the eschatological Christ.

Conclusion

As we have seen from our brief review of biblical texts and our consideration of some Jewish inscriptions, incantations, and amulets, ancient Jews were well

20. Even though "messiah" does not appear in these lines, it occurs four times in the lines immediately preceding. As Novenson concludes, "The Davidic messiahship of Jesus is not the point of 1 Cor 15:20–28, but it is axiomatic for the argument," *Christ among the Messiahs*, 146.

21. "At the End," Christ descends and "delivers the Kingdom to God the Father, "having destroyed every rule and every authority and every power" (1 Cor 15:24).

22. See too Rom 8, another collage of bodily transformation, pneumatic adoption, and cosmic conquest; cf. Eph 3:10; 6:12–13. On Phil 2:10 as presuming Christ's final, cosmic manifestation, Fredriksen, *Paul*, 133–41.

23. For Paul's ideas on *pneuma*, star bodies, and sidereal redemption, esp. Thiessen, *Gentile Problem*, 133–60; Troels Engberg-Pedersen, *Paul on Identity* (Fortress, 2021), 35–42.

aware of "the gods of the nations." The stars in Philo's firmament are divinities, created as gods by his god. Gods appear in a dream to Moschos, who places a votive in their temple. Pothos son of Strabo invokes witnessing gods within a synagogue ceremony of manumission. And besides skirmishing with offended lower deities in the course of his own mission, Paul narratively deploys them in essential ways to shape his Christology. Pagan gods define Jesus's role as God's end time champion: Were there none such opponents to fight, Christ would not be a Davidic messiah. Paul's messianism is of course Jewish. But that Jewish messianism sits within its defining, broader, and native first-century context, Mediterranean Greco-Roman culture.

What set (most? many? some?) Jews apart from their pagan contemporaries was their behavior, not their "beliefs."[24] Jews generally seemed to decline (or were thought to decline) to sacrifice to foreign gods, even if that god were the emperor. And this Jewish disinclination was respected (save by Caligula[25]) because it was grounded in ancestral custom, the hallmark of respectable religion.

Voluntary expagan pagans who joined the Christ movement were another matter altogether. These Pauline Judaizers were the particular objects of pagan disapproval, a source of anxiety and a precipitating factor of Paul's many "persecutions." But lines could be blurred. Native Jews were themselves clearly present at pagan cult. They filled the theaters, the council chambers, the gymnasia and stadia and schools of their Mediterranean cities. They availed themselves of the public baths and of mixed professional guilds, where foreign gods could be found. They served as soldiers and as gladiators, as actors and as athletes. They managed, doubtless variously, to do what they thought they could do or should do to attenuate cultic participation—though, as our inscriptions, papyri, and amulets attest, they also directed devotions to various

24. So too Larry W. Hurtado, "'Ancient Jewish Monotheism' in the Hellenistic and Roman Periods," *JAJ* 4, no. 3 (2013): 379–400. Note the scare quotes around "ancient Jewish monotheism." Hurtado acknowledges the difficulties with deploying this term in the ancient context (380–82), but defends its continued use by redefining it, emphasizing behavior rather than "belief." "Monolatry" in fact defines what his scare quotes signal.

25. The emperor Gaius (Caligula) sought to introduce the imperial cult of his own divinity into the temple in Jerusalem. His assassination ended the effort: his successor Claudius rescinded Caligula's order. See Philo, *Embassy to Gaius* 162, 188; Josephus, *Antiquities of the Jews* 18.261–309.

divine intermediaries as circumstance required. It was their ascribed behavior regarding pagan civic and imperial cult—not their "beliefs," and certainly not a more generalized Jewish cultural self-segregation—that stimulated classical authors' rhetorical criticisms (perhaps better: "stereotypes"?) of Jewish *amixia* ("antisociability"), *misoxenia* ("hatred of strangers") and *asebeia* ("atheism"). But Jews did "mix" (variously) with pagans, both human and, as we have just seen, divine.[26]

Our scholarly reliance on "monotheism" as a term of historical description occludes this vibrant and vital aspect of ancient Mediterranean religiousness.[27] It distorts much more than it putatively clarifies. It invites anachronism, allowing austerely monotheistic theologies to be imputed to Jews and, later, to Christians, theologies that our Jewish and (retrospectively) Christian texts themselves belie. It masks the degree to which Jews were comfortably settled within their pagan cities of residence, within their natal Mediterranean cultural context and, thus, within contemporary paganism(s). And it leaves us as historians unprepared, even unable, to see what stands before us in our evidence: The many gods who look back at us from the stones of the eastern Empire, from the songs of the ancient Psalmist, from Philo's learned commentaries, and from the urgent epistles of the apostle Paul.

---

26. Accusations of antisocial behaviors were common coin for interethnic insult: see esp. Benjamin Isaac, *The Invention of Racism in Classical Antiquity* (Princeton University Press, 2002). But mixing was the rule, not the exception. No less a personage than Rabban Gamaliel—unclothed, one assumes, and in the immediate company of unclothed pagans—frequented the baths at Akko, m. Avodah Zara 3:4; and, as the canons of the Council of Elvira (c. 300) reveal, Christians, pagans, and Jews of all sorts shared food, sex, public entertainments, and assorted liturgical acts involving various divinities. See further Paula Fredriksen and Oded Irshai, "'Include Me Out': Tertullian, the Rabbis, and the Graeco-Roman City," in *L'identité à travers l'éthique: nouvelles perspectives sur la formation des identités collectives dans le monde gréco-romain*, ed. K. Berthelot et al. (Brepols, 2015), 117–32.

27. The gods are eventually reformatted in Christian mythology as malevolent demons. Speaking of post-Late Antique/pre-Carolingian theological developments, David Brakke observes that "entire classes of lower gods and goddesses had either disappeared or suffered demotion" while "new faces"—human saints—"joined the celestial regions. . . . The once bustling community of diverse . . . *daimones* settled into a stable two-party system of angels and demons," "Valentinians and Their Demons: Fate, Seduction, and Deception in the Quest for Virtue," in *From Gnostics to Monastics*, ed. David Brakke, Stephen J. Davis, and Stephen Emmel (Peeters, 2017), 13–28, at 13.

III

Deification and Spirit Possession

CHAPTER SIX

Paul among the Sons of God

Matthew Thiessen
McMaster University

> If you say that angels stand before God who are not subject to feeling and death, and immortal in their nature, whom we ourselves speak of as gods, because they are close to the Godhead, why do we dispute about a name? . . . The difference therefore is not great, whether a man calls them gods or angels, since their divine nature bears witness to them.
>
> Macarius Magnes, *Apocritus* 4.21[1]

> If the Platonists prefer to call these angels gods rather than demons, and to number them among the gods who their founder and teacher Plato writes were created by the supreme God, let them say this if they like, for there is no need to trouble ourselves over a merely semantic issue. For if they say that these beings are immortal but created by the supreme God, and that they are blessed not in their own right but only by adhering to the one whom made them, then they say what we say, no matter what they call them.
>
> Augustine, *City of God* 9.23[2]

1. Translation taken from Thomas Wilfrid Crafer, trans., *The Apocriticus of Macarius Magnes* (SPCK, 1919).

2. Translation of William Babcock, *The City of God (de Civitate dei) (Books 1–10)*, The Works of Saint Augustine: A Translation for the 21st Century (New City Press, 2012), 301. For the Platonic text to which Augustine alludes, see Plato, *Timaeus* 40a.

Paul did not just believe in multiple gods, he believed the gods were multiplying. And not only did Paul believe the gods were multiplying, but he also believed they were doing so through his own mission as the divinely appointed herald of the Messiah to non-Jews.

Such statements fly in the face of the persistent belief that ancient Jews and early Christians were monotheists, that is, believing that one and only one God exists.[3] But there has been a growing consensus that this modern definition of monotheism fits poorly with the evidence of both early Judaism and of Christianity.[4] Consequently, scholars have applied different terms such as *monolatry*, *henotheism*, *megatheism*, and *polytheism* to both early Judaism and Christianity in an effort to describe various forms of belief in multiple gods combined with different sensibilities about which God or how many gods are to be worshiped.[5] This development in the study of Judaism and Christianity in antiquity parallels developments in Classics, which has pushed back against simplistic understandings of "pagan" polytheism, arguing that ancient "pagan" polytheism had tendencies that have often been described as monotheistic.[6] This polytheistic monotheism (or monotheistic polytheism) is captured concisely in the words of Maximus of Tyre, a second-century CE Greek philosopher, who asserts that all humanity, both Greeks and barbarians, agrees:

---

3. See, for instance, the first definition of monotheism in the *OED*: "The doctrine or belief that there is only one God (as opposed to many, as in polytheism)." The *OED* traces the first usage of the term *monotheism* back to the 1660 work of the English theologian Henry More, *An Explanation of the Grand Mystery of Godliness* (Flesher, 1660), who contrasts monotheism to both atheism and polytheism.

4. One can see arguments against monotheistic accounts of early Judaism already in the work of Peter Hayman, "Monotheism—a Misused Word in Jewish Studies?" *JJS* 42 (1991): 1–13, and Michael Mach, *Entwicklungsstadien des jüdischen Engelglaubens in vorrabinischer Zeit* [English: *Developmental Stages of the Jewish Thinking about Angels in the Pre-rabbinic Period*], TSAJ 34 (Mohr, 1992).

5. For instance, Michael S. Heiser, "Monotheism, Polytheism, Monolatry, or Henotheism? Toward an Assessment of Divine Plurality in the Hebrew Bible," *BBR* 18 (2008): 1–30.

6. Cf. Javier Teixidor, *The Pagan God: Popular Religion in the Graeco-Roman Near East* (Princeton University, 1977), Polymnia Athanassiadi and Michael Frede, eds., *Pagan Monotheism in Late Antiquity* (Oxford University Press, 1999), and Stephen Mitchell and Peter van Nuffelen, eds., *One God: Pagan Monotheism in the Roman Empire* (Cambridge University Press, 2010).

> In the midst of so much conflict, discord, and disagreement, you can discern one law and one account agreed upon all over the earth, that there is one god (*theos heis*), the king and father of all, and that there are many other gods (*theos polloi*) who are his offspring and who share in his rule. (*Philosophical Orations* 11.5)[7]

Here, in a few short clauses, we see a "pagan" expression of polytheistic monotheism: There are many gods, but all but one play a subordinate role. Only one is supreme, the father and king over all others. The subordinate divinities rule and have power, but it is a power and authority they participate in at the behest of this supreme God.

That Paul and other Jews and then later Christians were polytheists, that is, that they believed in the existence of more than one god even as they almost universally rejected the worship of gods other than the God of Israel, remains a controversial claim in some circles. It should not be. Such was the shared theology of the ancient Mediterranean world. After all, the central Jewish Scriptures that we call the Pentateuch frequently refer to other gods. In his contest with Pharaoh, Yhwh strikes down the firstborn animals and humans of Egypt in a sobering execution of his judgment on the Egyptian gods (Exod 12:12). As God leads Israel out of Egypt, Moses and the Israelites hymn this question: "Yhwh, who is like you among the gods [Hebrew, *elim*; Greek, *theoi*]?" (Exod 15:11). In the wilderness, Jethro declares that Yhwh is greater than all the gods (Exod 18:11: *Elohim/theoi*) and Moses claims that Israel's god is the "God of gods and Lord of lords" (Deut 10:17), asserting that this God divides the nations according to the numbers of the gods (Deut 32:8).[8]

7. Translation comes from LCL. It is worth noting that the phrase rendered as "his offspring" could be translated either as "children/sons of God," stressing their familial relationship, or as "servants/slaves of God," stressing their inferiority and subservience to the supreme God.

8. Following the Hebrew of 4QDeut[j] with support from the LXX, which, in many manuscripts, reads "sons of God" (*huioi theou*). Cf. the *gods* of the MT in v. 43 and the *angels* of God of the LXX. For a discussion of the latter verse, see Arie van der Kooij, "The Ending of the Song of Moses: On the Pre-Masoretic Version of Deut 32:43," in *Studies in Deuteronomy in Honor of C. J. Labuschagne on the Occasion of his 65th Birthday*, ed. F. García Martínez, A. Hilhorst, J. T. A. G. M. van Ruiten, and A. S. van der Woude, VTSup 53 (Brill, 1994), 93–100. Unless otherwise indicated, all Bible translations are the author's.

Israel's god is the Supreme God, reigning over all other gods who necessarily must exist if Israel's god is to reign over them (cf. Ps 82:1; 95:3; 96:4; 97:7).

The Pentateuch and other sacred Jewish texts also refer to a group of lower deities as the *sons of God* (*bene ha-elohim/hoi huioi tou theou*: Gen 6:2–4; Job 1:6; 2:1; 38:7;[9] and *bene elim/huioi theou*: Ps 29:1 [LXX 28:1]; 89:7 [LXX 88:7]).[10] Like their neighbors, ancient Israelites were polytheistic even as many of them devoted themselves to the worship of one God. Believing in the existence of multiple divine beings was not the same as devotion to or worship of them. I will not rehash all the evidence in later periods of Judaism, which is incontrovertible to all but the most obstinate modern monotheists.[11] But I briefly point to this small amount of important data to serve as a launching pad for thinking about Paul's mission to gentiles. The terminology differs—gods, sons of God, angels, even *daimonia*[12]—but the genus remains the same: Divine beings.

The Son of God and Many Sons of God

Paul believed himself to be an ambassador to the gentiles, appointed by God (e.g., 1 Cor 1:1). As such, he believed that there was only one supreme divinity, the God of Israel. He makes this clear throughout his writings, but especially in the Corinthian letters where he addresses the practice of eating foods related

9. Here the LXX translator of Job renders the Hebrew as "angels." Some Greek manuscripts of Genesis also render *bene ha-elohim* in Gen 6:2–4 as angels. Cf. 1 En 6, Jub. 5; T. Sol. 5:3.

10. Mark S. Smith, *The Origins of Biblical Monotheism: Israel's Polytheistic Background and the Ugaritic Texts* (Oxford University Press, 2003); Nathan MacDonald, *Deuteronomy and the Meaning of "Monotheism"*, FAT 2/1 (Mohr Siebeck, 2003).

11. E.g., Peter Schäfer, *Two Gods in Heaven: Jewish Concepts of God in Antiquity*, trans. Allison Brown (Princeton University Press, 2020), Silviu Bunta, *The Lord God of Gods: Divinity and Deification in Early Judaism*, Perspectives on Hebrew Scriptures and Its Contexts 35 (Gorgias Press, 2021), and Paula Fredriksen, "Philo, Herod, Paul, and the Many Gods of Ancient Jewish 'Monotheism,'" *HTR* 115 (2022): 23–45.

12. E.g., the translator of LXX Psalms renders pagan gods as *daimonia* (Ps 96:5) and the LXX translator of Deut 32:17 renders foreign/unknown gods as *daimonia*. On the question of when *daimonia* became demons, that is, categorically evil creatures, see Annette Yoshiko Reed, "When Did *Daimones* Become Demons? Revisiting Septuagintal Data for Ancient Jewish Demonology," *HTR* 116 (2023): 340–75. Even as late as Acts 17:18, Luke depicts Greek philosophers using the term *daimonia* to refer to seemingly benevolent gods.

to the cults of other gods. There he alludes to the Shema, claiming that "there is no god but one" (1 Cor 8:4; cf. Deut 6:4). And even as he acknowledges the existence of other gods (8:5), he qualifies this acknowledgement, saying, "*but* for us, there is one God, the Father" (1 Cor 8:6).[13] These statements are remarkably similar to the pagan claims of Maximus of Tyre, who as noted above could claim, "There is one god, the king and father of all, and . . . there are many other gods who are his offspring and who share in his rule" (*Philosophical Orations* 11.5). While Maximus does not conclude from this hierarchical structure to the realm of the divine that only the one supreme God should be worshiped, Paul does. Similarly, to the Romans Paul exclaims that "God is one" (Rom 3:30).[14] For both Jews and non-Jews, then, Paul believes that one supreme God exists. Only this God is worthy of worship. Consequently, participation in the cults of other gods should be avoided (1 Cor 10:20–22).[15]

Nonetheless, and reminiscent of the language of ancient Jewish Scriptures, Paul calls Jesus God's son on numerous occasions and in numerous letters.[16] Paul's message focuses on Jesus, descended from David, himself God's son according to various psalms (e.g., Ps 2:7), who was declared God's son with power through resurrection (Rom 1:3–4).[17] And this son seems to have

13. On the tensions in this passage, see Emma Wasserman, "'An Idol Is Nothing in the World' (1 Cor 8.4): The Metaphysical Contradictions of 1 Corinthians 8.1–11.1 in the Context of Jewish Idolatry Polemics," in *Portraits of Jesus: Studies in Christology*, ed. Susan E. Myers, WUNT 2/321 (Mohr Siebeck, 2012), 201–27.

14. See here, Wolfgang Schrage, *Unterwegs zur Einzigkeit und Einheit Gottes: Zum "Monotheismus" des Paulus und seiner alttestamentlich-frühjudischen Tradition* [English: *Toward the Uniqueness and Unity of God: On the "Monotheism" of Paul and His Old Testament-Early Jewish Tradition*] (Neukirchener Verlag, 2002).

15. For a coherent account of what appears, at first glance, to be Paul's contradictory teachings on food offered to idols, see Martin Sanfridson, *Paul and Sacrifice in Corinth: Rethinking Paul's View on Gentile Cults in 1 Corinthians 8 and 10*, WUNT 2/623 (Mohr Siebeck, 2025).

16. Rom 1:3, 4, 9; 5:10; 8:3, 29, 32; 1 Cor 1:9; 2 Cor 1:19; Gal 1:16; 2:20; 4:4; 1 Thess 1:10. Cf. Eph 4:13; Col 1:13. There are 41 occurrences of *huios* in the thirteen letters attributed to Paul. And *huiothesia* ("adoption as sons") occurs in Rom 8:15, 23; 9:4; Gal 4:5; cf. Eph 1:5. For whatever reason, (divine) *sonship* language is missing entirely from Philippians and Philemon, as well as the deutero-Pauline 2 Thessalonians and Pastorals.

17. See the valuable article of Joshua W. Jipp, "Ancient, Modern, and Future Interpretations of Romans 1:3–4: Reception History and Biblical Interpretation," *JTI* 3 (2009): 241–59.

pre-existed his incarnation, since God sent him to be born of a woman and under the law (Gal 4:4; cf. Phil 2). Scholars continue to debate what, in Paul's mind, this makes Jesus in relation to Israel's God, throwing around impressively weighty terms like "early high Christology," "adoptionism," "trinitarianism," and so on.[18] Obviously, that is an important question, but it will not occupy me here.[19] Rather, I am interested in focusing on Paul's belief that in the coming, death, and resurrection of this particular and peculiar *son* of God, a whole new generation of *sons* of God *has* come and *is continuing* to come into existence.

Paul himself serves as a prime example of new gods coming into existence, claiming that the Messiah now lives *inside* him (Gal 2:20). If the son of God lives inside Paul, it follows that Paul participates in the divine sonship of the Messiah and is thus also a son of God. Those whom God's *pneuma* ("spirit") leads are sons of God and they will one day be revealed to the *kosmos* ("universe") as such (Rom 8:14, 19).[20] Even non-Jews will be called sons of the living God, something Paul believes the prophet Hosea had predicted long ago (Rom 9:26; LXX Hos 2:1).[21] How? Like Paul himself, those who are both clothed in and inhabited by the Messiah are sons of God (Gal 3:26). Being in the Messiah means having the Messiah, who is God's son (Gal 4:6).[22] People infected or

---

18. For classic treatments see David Capes, *Old Testament Yahweh Texts in Paul's Christology*, WUNT 2/47 (Mohr [Siebeck], 1992), Larry Hurtado, *Lord Jesus Christ: Devotion to Jesus in Earliest Christianity* (Eerdmans, 2003), Richard Bauckham, *Jesus and the God of Israel: God Crucified and Other Studies on the New Testament's Christology of Divine Identity* (Eerdmans, 2008), and Chris Tilling, *Paul's Divine Christology*, WUNT 2/323 (Mohr Siebeck, 2012).

19. For a recent treatment of the question, see Paula Fredriksen, "How High Can Early High Christology Be?" in *Monotheism and Christology in Greco-Roman Antiquity*, ed. Matthew V. Novenson, NovTSup 180 (Brill, 2020), 293–319.

20. On divine sonship in this passage, see more fully Brendan Byrne, *Sons of God, Seed of Abraham: A Study of the Idea of the Sonship of All Christians in Paul against the Jewish Background*, Analecta biblica 83 (Biblical Institute, 1979).

21. See Jill Hicks-Keeton, *Arguing with Aseneth: Gentile Access to Israel's Living God in Jewish Antiquity* (Oxford University Press, 2018).

22. Caroline Johnson Hodge, *If Sons, Then Heirs: A Study of Kinship and Ethnicity in the Letters of Paul* (Oxford University Press, 2007), and Stanley K. Stowers, "What Is 'Pauline Participation in Christ'?," in *Redefining First-Century Jewish and Christian Identities: Essays in Honor of Ed Parish Sanders*, ed. Fabian E. Udoh et al., Christianity and Judaism in Antiquity 16 (University of Notre Dame Press, 2008), 352–71.

invaded or possessed by the Messiah's *pneuma* are now God's sons, and they call out to God naming him *abba, father.*[23] The presence of the Messiah's *pneuma* and the experience of it eliciting a cry of "Abba, father" from gentiles in Galatia serves as evidence of this change in their identity: Those who formerly neither knew God nor were known by God have now become God's very sons (Gal 4:8–9).[24]

In fact, Paul claims in Romans that God conforms believers to the image (*eikōn*) of his son. The Messiah, Paul tells his readers, is the firstborn among many brothers (8:29). While the NRSV's efforts to render the Greek in an inclusive way may be admirable in relation to modern concerns about gender, its translation of *pollois adelphois* as "a large family" is unhelpful in that it obscures the fact that Paul's readers, as sons of God, are also brothers. The identity of Paul's readers is derived entirely from their relationship to the Messiah. This is because Paul's gospel centers around union with or participation in the Messiah.[25] Since Jesus is the son of God, all who are in him have become sons of God as well, thus making them each brothers.

The creation of new divinities also explains Paul's pervasive use of familial language throughout his letters: Paul begins his letters to Rome, Corinth (not 2 Corinthians), and Thessalonica (cf. Colossians) by calling his readers *adelphoi* ("brothers") and addressing them throughout these and other letters in fraternal terms.[26] Why? Because they truly are brothers, a new genus of humans

---

23. Giovanni B. Bazzana, *Having the Spirit of Christ: Spirit Possession and Exorcism in the Early Christ Groups*, Synkrisis (Yale University Press, 2019).

24. Here see Michael Peppard, "Adopted and Begotten Sons of God: Paul and John on Divine Sonship," *CBQ* 73 (2011): 92–110.

25. Scholars continue to debate the exact nature of this union or participation, but few dispute its centrality to Paul's theology. Cf., for instance, the classic treatments of Albert Schweitzer, *The Mysticism of Paul the Apostle*, trans. William Montgomery (Johns Hopkins University Press, 1953) and Morna D. Hooker, "Interchange in Christ," *JTS* 21 (1971): 349–61, as well as the most recent treatment of Barbara Beyer, *Determined by Christ: The Pauline Metaphor "Being in Christ"*, NovTSup 191 (Brill, 2024).

26. The thirteen letters attributed to Paul use *adelph-* language 139 times. Rarely, Paul uses *teknon* or *teknion* ("children"): Rom 8:16–17, 21; 9:8; Phil 2:15. And only once does Paul refer to both sons and daughters (2 Cor 6:18). This might be under the influence of Deut 32:19, where God rejects his idolatrous sons and daughters, as John W. Olley argues, "A Precursor of the NRSV? 'Sons and Daughters' in 2 Cor 6.18," *NTS* 44 (1998): 204–12, or under the influence of Isa 43:6, which envisions God restoring his wayward sons and daughters, as James

who are sons of God, related to one another through their pneumatic connection to God's son. As James Tabor put it some years ago: "The equation of Jesus the Son of God, with the *many* glorified sons of God to follow is God's means of bringing into existence a *family* (i.e., 'many brothers') of cosmic beings, the *Sons of God*, who share his heavenly *doxa* ['glory']."[27]

Paul and the Holy Ones

Finally, Paul's belief that those in the Messiah are in the process of being divinized makes sense of one of his favorite names for them: *Hoi hagioi*, "the holy ones." Of the forty-five uses of the plural form of *hagios* ("holy" or "sacred") in the thirteen letters attributed to Paul, thirty-nine of them refer to believers. Over half (24) occur in the undisputed letters.[28] Modern translators unhelpfully render the term as "the saints," evoking images of haloed humans such as Francis or Patrick, Joan or Teresa.[29] But how would first-century readers have understood this term? Jewish writers, especially in poetic works, frequently used the phrase "the holy ones" to speak of lower divinities. The Song of Moses depicts God as glorious "among the holy ones" (Exod 15:11). And Deuteronomy 33 refers to God coming from Sinai with

M. Scott argues, "The Use of Scripture in 2 Corinthians 6.16c–18 and Paul's Restoration Theology," *JSNT* 56 (1994): 73–99.

27. James D. Tabor, *Things Unutterable: Paul's Ascent to Paradise in its Greco-Roman, Judaic, and Early Christian Contexts*, Studies in Judaism (University Press of America, 1986), 12. Cf. James Tabor, "Paul's Notion of Many 'Sons of God' in its Hellenistic Contexts," *Helios* 13 (1986): 87–97; Michael Gorman, "Romans: The First Christian Treatise on Theosis," *JTI* 5 (2011): 13–34; Stephen Finlan, "Can We Speak of Theosis in Paul?" in *Partakers of the Divine Nature: The History and Development of Deification in the Christian Traditions*, ed. Michael J. Christensen and Jeffery A. Wittung (Baker Academic, 2007), 68–80; Ben C. Blackwell, *Christosis: Pauline Soteriology in Light of Deification in Irenaeus and Cyril of Alexandria*, WUNT 2/314 (Mohr Siebeck, 2011); and M. David Litwa, *We Are Being Transformed: Deification in Paul's Soteriology*, BZNW 187 (De Gruyter, 2012).

28. Rom 1:7; 8:27; 12:13; 15:25, 26, 31; 16:2, 15; 1 Cor 1:2; 6:1, 2; 7:14; 14:33; 16:1, 15; 2 Cor 1:1; 8:4; 9:1, 12; 13:12; Phil 1:1; 4:22; Philem 5, 7. Deutero-Pauline: Eph 1:1, 15, 18; 2:19; 3:8, 18; 4:12; 5:3; 6:18; Col 1:2, 4, 12, 26; 2 Thess 1:10; 1 Tim 5:10.

29. It is telling that the NRSV translators use *saint(s)* sixty-five times, but only *once* in the "Old Testament" (Ps 31:23) and twice in the Deuterocanon (Wis 5:5; 18:9). Such translation decisions (intentionally or otherwise) communicate that saints are Christian, not Jewish or Israelite.

myriads of holy ones (33:2–3).[30] The book of Job also refers to the holy ones, something the LXX translator renders as "holy angels" (5:1). Zechariah depicts God coming with all his holy ones (14:5). And the Psalter calls both God's people (15:3; 33:10) and lower deities "the holy ones" (88:6, 8). In referring to divinities as *the holy ones*, ancient Israel was, yet again, participating in the common polytheistic language of the ancient Near East as one can see from both Ugaritic and Phoenician texts, which use the language of holy ones in relation to divinities.[31]

Early Jewish writers continue in this usage. According to Ben Sira, God made Moses equal in glory to the holy ones (*doxē hagiōn*, 45:2). The underlying Hebrew is only partially preserved, but likely reads *elohim* ("gods"), confirming that some Jews referred to divinities as the "holy ones."[32] The high priest Simon, according to the author of 3 Maccabees, claims that God is holy "among the holy ones" (3:2, 21). The author of Jude, quoting 1 Enoch 1:9,

---

30. Here the LXX translator of Deuteronomy transliterates קדש (*qodesh*) as Καδής (*Kades*) in v. 2 but renders קדשיו (*qedoshav*) as οἱ ἡγιασμένοι (*hoi hēgiasmenoi*: the holy ones) in v. 3.

31. Ugaritic: *CTA* 2 i 21, 38; 17 i 4 and the *Epic of Aqhat* (*Context of Scripture*, 1:343–44), which states:
Girded, he gave the gods food,
  [girded, he gave] the Holy Ones [drink].
He cast down [his cloak, went up], and lay down,
  cast down [his girded garment[3]] so as to pass the night (there).[b]
A day, [even two,
  girded,] Dānî'ilu (gave) the gods (food),
  [girded,] he gave [the gods] food,
  girded, [he gave] the Holy Ones [drink].
A third, even a fourth day,
  [girded,] Dānî'ilu (gave) the gods (food),
  girded, he gave [the gods] food,
  girded, he gave the [Holy] Ones drink.
A fifth, even a sixth day,
  girded, Dānî'ilu (gave) [the gods] (food),
  girded, he gave the gods food,
  [girded,] he gave the Holy Ones drink.
Phoenician: *CIS* 16000.5: the first Arslan Tash inscription. For this and other evidence, see John A. Davies, "The Heavenly Access of the Holy Ones," *Reformed Theological Review* 68 (2009): 3–11.

32. See Pancratius C. Beentjes, *The Book of Ben Sira in Hebrew: A Text Edition of All Extant Hebrew Manuscripts and a Synopsis of all Parallel Hebrew Ben Sira Texts*, VTSup 68 (Brill, 1997), 79.

says, "See, the Lord is coming with ten thousand of his holy ones" (14). Most helpfully for this essay, the Wisdom of Solomon clearly equates the holy ones with the sons of God, asking about the fate of the righteous:

> Why have they been numbered among the sons of God (*en huios theou*)?
>
> And why is their lot among the holy ones (*en hagiois*)? (Wis 5:5)

But the most concentrated usage of "holy ones" language is attested in the various scrolls discovered at Qumran, where we see the phrase used almost one hundred times in numerous different works. The evidence suggests that the phrase can apply both to Israel and to God's divine council or his angels.[33] At the very least, then, when Paul calls believers "holy ones" he signals that they are a people set apart for God. But there are reasons to believe that Paul also thinks that these holy ones are *humans* who are in the process of becoming *angelic*.

A telling exegetical sleight of hand supports this claim. In 1 Thessalonians, Paul quotes Zechariah 14:5, which states: "Then Yhwh my God will come, and all the holy ones (*qedoshim/hoi hagioi*) with him." In the context of Zechariah, these holy ones are angelic beings, who accompany God into battle to deliver Israel.[34] Paul uses this prophetic passage in a reference to the imminent return of the Messiah, who will come with all his holy ones. Here Paul riffs on Zechariah 14:5, swapping out Yhwh for the Messiah. Further, if Paul's use of *hagioi* throughout his letters is indicative, his reference to holy ones in 1 Thessalonians 3:13 must refer to those in the Messiah.[35] Why has Paul swapped out God's divine beings for humans? Because Paul thinks that

33. The Gospels of Mark and Luke and John, as well as Acts of the Apostles (3:14; 13:35 [*hosios*]), also apply the singular *ho hagios* to Jesus, calling him *the holy one of God* (Mark 1:24; Luke 4:34; John 6:69).

34. Carol L. Meyers and Eric M. Meyers, *Zechariah 9–14: A New Translation with Introduction and Commentary*, AB 25C (Doubleday, 1993), 429–30.

35. E.g., Gordon Fee, *The First and Second Letters to the Thessalonians*, NICNT (Eerdmans, 2009), 129. For the argument that it is humans, see Justin D. King, "Paul, Zechariah, and the Identity of the 'Holy Ones' in 1 Thessalonians 3:13: Correcting an Un'Fee'sible Approach," *PRS* 39 (2012): 25–38.

believers in Jesus already participate in his divinity even as they await the resurrection where they become fully divine. In fact, Paul has good precedent for this erasure of the line between angel and human since Zechariah already attests the collapse of these categories, predicting that the house of David will be like gods, as the angel of Yhwh himself (Zech 12:8).[36] At God's coming, then, God's people would be made divine or angelic. For Paul, this is actually happening in his ministry and in the wake of the Messiah's initial appearance. Those in the Messiah have taken on a divine identity already, but it is one that is, for the most part, hidden. Hidden in jars of clay and all that. It will, nonetheless, be fully manifested in the future when the Messiah returns. This hidden identity should both dictate and enable how those in the Messiah behave morally here and now.

The Angelic Rule of Both the Messiah and His People

On a number of occasions Paul makes it clear that the glorious future of those in the Messiah includes reigning over the *kosmos* (Rom 4:13), lower divinities included: Even now neither *angeloi* ("angels") nor *archai* ("rulers") nor *dynameis* ("powers") can separate believers from God's love (Rom 8:38).[37] And Paul was convinced that God would soon crush the malevolent deity, the *satan*, under the feet of *believers* (Rom 16:20), a potential allusion to Genesis 3:15 and Psalm 8:6 (Ps 109:1 LXX). If Paul has the latter passage in mind, the *satan* is

36. LXX Zechariah states that they will be like the "house of God," which still suggests an angelic identity. One can see the permeable boundary between humans and angels at Qumran as well: Devorah Dimant, "Men as Angels: The Self-Image of the Qumran Community," in *Religion and Politics in the Ancient Near East*, ed. Adele Berlin (University Press of America, 1996), 93–103; Matthew L. Walsh, *Angels Associated with Israel in the Dead Sea Scrolls: Angelology and Sectarian Identity at Qumran*, WUNT 2/509 (Mohr Siebeck, 2019). Cf. Loren T. Stuckenbruck, "'Angels' and 'God': Exploring the Limits of Early Jewish Monotheism," in *Early Jewish and Christian Monotheism*, ed. Loren T. Stuckenbruck and Wendy E. S. North, JSNTSup 263 (T&T Clark, 2005), 45–70. A similar eschatological collapse of the sharp boundary between angels and humanity can be seen in the book of Daniel.

37. See here Nicola Frances Denzey, "Under a Pitiless Sky: Conversion, Cosmology and the Rhetoric of 'Enslavement to Fate' in Second-Century Christian Sources" (PhD diss., Princeton University, 1998). Of Rom 8:38–39, Denzey (98) notes: "Paul appears to draw the terms ὕψωμα [*hypsōma*] and βάθος [*bathos*], not directly from Jewish sources, but from technical astronomical vocabulary of the first century CE. These terms refer specifically to the range of influence of the stars," pointing to Vettius Valens, *Anth.* 241.26 for *bathos* and Plutarch, *Moralia* 149a and 782e for *hypsōma*.

identified as one of the angels who will be under the feet of humanity. At the end, believers will be elevated even above the angels, judging both the *kosmos* and the old order of angels (1 Cor 6:2–3). As David Litwa notes, Paul "tells his converts—as if it were common knowledge—that they will someday judge higher, superhuman beings ('angels,' 1 Cor 6:3). In promising this, he seems to assume that he and his community will one day have an existence—or at least a status—above those angelic beings."[38] The *new* sons of God that Paul's mission has given birth to will one day rule over even older sons of God.

Paul's belief that humans could become divine fits within ancient Mediterranean thinking, which frequently attests to the idea that the line between humans and divinities was at least semipermeable. For instance, Dominic J. O'Meara has argued that "divinization describes the goal of the major philosophical schools of the Classical and Hellenistic periods."[39] Such a goal arose out of Plato's admonition that humans "ought to try to escape from earth to the dwelling of the gods as quickly as we can; and to escape to become like God, so far as this is possible; and to become like God is to become righteous and holy and wise" (*Theaetetus* 176B).

While Paul was indebted to these philosophical traditions, he located the divinizing power not in one particular philosophical school or in one form of human activity, but in the arrival of Israel's Messiah.[40] With the Messiah, those who are in the Messiah will reign over the *kosmos*. According to Paul's gospel, multiple new and superior gods are coming into existence, and even formerly godless and immoral non-Jews can ascend to the stars. This doesn't threaten Paul's belief in one supreme God, it rather confirms it. The supreme God is God by *nature* (or *physis*), whereas these new gods are gods through

38. Litwa, *We Are Being Transformed*, 11.

39. Dominic J. O'Meara, *Platonopolis: Platonic Political Philosophy in Late Antiquity* (Clarendon, 2003). Cf. Spencer Cole, *Cicero and the Rise of Deification at Rome* (Cambridge University Press, 2013). With regard to early Judaism, see M. David Litwa, "The Deification of Moses in Philo of Alexandria," *SPhilo* 26 (2014) 1–27, and Daniel B. Glover, *Patterns of Deification in the Acts of the Apostles*, WUNT 2/576 (Mohr Siebeck, 2022).

40. See George H. van Kooten, *Paul's Anthropology in Context: The Image of God, Assimilation to God, and Tripartite Man in Ancient Judaism, Ancient Philosophy and Early Christianity*, WUNT 232 (Mohr Siebeck, 2008), and Max J. Lee, *Moral Transformation in Greco-Roman Philosophy of Mind: Mapping the Moral Milieu of the Apostle Paul and his Diaspora Jewish Contemporaries*, WUNT 2/515 (Mohr Siebeck, 2020).

participation and grace (*charis*). Only the supreme God has the power to make other gods. Paul's mission brings into existence divine beings, sons of God, only by participating in God's son through the gift (*charis*) available to Jew and non-Jew alike in and through the Messiah and the Messiah's *pneuma*.[41] As Paul puts it so succinctly to the Galatians, "God has sent the *pneuma* of his son into our hearts, crying, "Abba! Father!" (Gal 4:6).

41. Earlier I mentioned obstinate modern monotheists, who resist claims that Paul was a polytheist. To whatever degree such obstinacy results from modern theological commitments, it might help to point to some theological literature that is consonant with a polytheistic Paul: On distinguishing God by *physis* and gods by *charis*, see Kathryn Tanner, *Christ the Key*, Current Issues in Theology (Cambridge University Press, 2010). This distinction can already be seen in Origen, *Homilies on Exodus* 6.5 on Exodus 15:11: "The words 'Who is like you among the gods?' do not compare God to the images of the Gentiles nor to the demons, who falsely appropriate the name of gods to themselves, but means those gods who by grace and participation in God are called Gods." Cf. Origen, *Commentary on John* 2.3: "We are called Gods because of our participation in him." Similarly, Athanasius, *Letter to Serapion* 2.4.4: "But if some have been called gods, they are not gods by nature but by participation in the Son."

CHAPTER SEVEN

Paul on Becoming (a) God

M. David Litwa

If a god in Mediterranean antiquity is a being with superhuman power, deathlessness, and freedom from decay, then Paul's gospel is the good news of becoming a god.[1] Paul promises believers a cosmic and universal rule along with the inheritance of a deathless and undecaying body. This is not "Humanity 2.0." It is not even "Humanity 10.0." It is, rather, a transition to a divine state.

The attainment of this state was not some pie-in-the-sky promise that Paul made to his followers. The promise was considered prevalidated. The great experiment had already worked once. Jesus the Anointed, born of woman (Gal 4:4), had been "appointed son of god in power, according to a spirit of sanctification" (Rom 1:4 my trans.). Jesus attained full deification after death (Phil 2:6–9). If Paul did not call Christ "god over all" (Rom 9:5), he certainly treated him as a god, and bid believers to worship him. But believers were not only to worship the anointed god. They were to assimilate to him as well.[2]

Pauline salvation means assimilation to a divine being; and assimilation to a divine being is a form of deification (becoming god). Pauline deification involves three factors, all intertwined: (1) Ruling over "all things" (including superhuman beings); (2) the inheritance of a superhuman, deathless, and incorruptible body; and (3) moral assimilation to Christ through spirit.

Before exploring these factors, let's deal with objections.

---

1. In this essay, "god" is not capitalized so as to avoid introducing later theological assumptions about the existence (or nonexistence) of intermediate deities in contrast to a non-communicable "God."

2. This essay adapts and develops elements of my previous work on Paul including *We Are Being Transformed: Deification in Paul's Soteriology*, BZNT 187 (De Gruyter, 2012); *Becoming Divine: An Introduction to Deification in Western Culture* (Cascade, 2013), 58–68.

Wasn't Paul a Monotheist?

The philosopher Thales reportedly said, "All things are full of gods!"[3] The saying applies to Paul's letters. Not only do we have reference to "the" god in these letters (namely the Father), but we also find "the god of this world" (2 Cor 4:4) "many gods and many lords" (1 Cor 8:5) "elementals" (Gal 4:9) "angels" (Gal 3:19; 1 Cor 6:3) "daimonia" (1 Cor 10:20), a "spirit" (Gal 4:6) "rulers of this aeon" (1 Cor 2:6), not to mention "authorities, powers, thrones," and so on. If a polytheist is a believer in multiple divine powers, then Paul was a polytheist. To put it in more "kosher" terms, Paul assumed—like virtually everyone else in Mediterranean antiquity—that there were multiple superhuman entities flitting around the cosmos.[4] As a Jew, he believed that these superhuman powers and authorities were subordinate to a single creative power called "the" god (*ho theos*). In this respect, Paul was no different than many Stoic and Platonic philosophers who imagined a divine hierarchy with a chief power on top (the Good, or Zeus), who governed a whole bureaucracy of middle-management powers who performed the daily grunt work of running the cosmos. These born gods are often thought to be generated (directly or indirectly) from the primal god, just as the "son" is generated from the Father.

Isn't God "Transcendent"?

Christian notions of a fully transcendent God—an unmoved mover beyond the limits of thought and being—developed centuries after Paul. Paul believed that the Father was immensely powerful, but that he still resided in this cosmos, not outside of it. Similarly, the Roman emperor ruled the civilized world, but he could still be found on the Palatine hill in Rome. Paul did not limit creative power to the primal God, since this God created by and through Christ (1 Cor 8:6; cf. Col 1:16). "The" God is the center and source of divinity. But divinity is not a zero-sum substance. It can be shared like sunlight.

There are shareable and unshareable aspects of divinity. Not all beings can be the divine Father, eternal and unborn. But they can become immortal, just, and wise. Deification is not "idolatry"—the worship of false or foreign

3. Plato, *Laws* 899b; Aristotle, *Soul* 1.411a8.

4. Litwa, *We Are Being Transformed*, 229–57; Paula Fredriksen, "Philo, Herod, Paul, and the Many Gods of Ancient Jewish 'Monotheism,'" *HTR* 115, no. 1 (2022): 23–45.

gods (aka "daimonia") or of their images. Humans who share divine power and identity are not worshiped, nor are they foreign. Humans can legitimately become true gods. The first human to do so was Jesus of Nazareth. Paul did not care much about Nazareth, or about the particularities of Jesus's Galilean life. He understood Jesus to be the prototype of human destiny. Christ is the first fruits of the resurrection (1 Cor 15:20). If Christ attained godhood, so could everyone else.

Christification

As Orphic initiates identified with the god Dionysus, so Paul morphed with the divine Christ. "I have been crucified with Christ," he once claimed, "I no longer live—Christ lives in me" (Gal 2:19–20). In a letter to the Corinthians, he writes, "The one who cleaves to the Lord [Christ] is one spirit with him" (1 Cor 6:17). Paul talks about his converts sharing a single body with their divine Lord (1 Cor 6:15; 12:25). Paul wanted Christ to develop in Christians like a fetus (a single organism with its mother; Gal 4:19). He wrote that the metamorphosed (i.e., deified) Christ follower becomes "the same image" as Christ (2 Cor 3:18). We can call this "Christ mysticism," but we can be more precise. It is Christification—becoming Christ—and insofar as Christ is a god, it amounts to deification as well.

This union of Christ and believers is well demonstrated by Paul's striking use of "co-" compounds, *syn-* in Greek. Paul's converts are said to be "co-heirs" (*sugklēronomoi*) with Christ (Rom 8:17; cf. Eph 3.6) if they "co-suffer" with him (*sumpaschomen*; Rom 8:17; cf. 2 Cor 1:5; Col 1:24). Paul calls himself "co-crucified" (*sunestaurōmai*) with Christ (Gal 2:19; cf. Rom 6:6). He apparently expects a similar destiny for his followers, insofar as they are "co-grown" (*sumphutoi*) into the likeness of Christ's death (Rom 6:5; cf. 6:8; 2 Cor 4:10; Phil 3:10; Col 2:20), and "co-buried" with Christ (*sunetaphēmen*; Rom 6:4; Col 2:12). Subsequently they "co-live" (*suzēsomen*) with Christ (Rom 6:8; 2 Tim 2:11) by being "co-glorified" with him (*sundoxasthōmen*; Rom 8:17; cf. 2 Thess 2:14).[5] Perhaps the strongest statement of union between Christ and

5. According to Deutero-Pauline literature, Christians are "co-raised" (*sunegeirō*) with Christ (Eph 2:6; Col 2:12; 3:1), and are "co-enlivened" (*suzōopoieō*) with him (Col 2:13; Eph 2:5). Subsequently, they "co-reign" with Christ (*sumbasileuō*; 2 Tim 2:12), sitting "co-enthroned" with him in the heavenly realms (*sugkathizō*; Eph 2:6).

the believer is in 2 Cor 3:18, where believers become the "same image" (*tēn autēn eikona*) of (or as) Christ—who is also identified as the image of god (4:4).

This union with Christ assumes a kind of kinship. Pauline Christians become children of god (Rom 8:14; 9:26; Gal 3:26; 4:6) just as Christ was declared "son of god" (Rom 1:4). Christ and Christians are thus siblings (*adelphoi*; Rom 8:29), images of the same divine Father (cf. Gen 5:1–3). This kinship language expresses a kind of relatedness that is rightly called "genetic," that is, having to do with the *genos*—the group or class in which two entities belong. Christ and believers as kin belong to the same class of beings, namely divine "children of god." Christians as divine children of the Father are pictured as subordinate to Christ their elder brother. The fact, however, that believers are pictured as Christ's siblings, made in the same image, and heirs of the same world, indicates that Jesus and Jesus devotees can share the same destiny.

In short, Pauline deification means assimilation to a divine being, Christ. That assimilation is moral, physical, and political.

Moral Assimilation: Rule over the Body

Plato said that "one should make all haste to take flight from earth to heaven, and flight means assimilation to God as much as possible; and assimilation to God is to become just and holy with wisdom."[6] Plato created a program in which justice was achieved by self-subordination. The human mind (*nous*) is charged with control of two other human parts: Drive (*thumos*) and desire (*enkrateia*). In Plato's vivid imagery, the inner human (the rational mind) reins in the lion of drive (located in the chest) and the beast of desire (focused on the belly and the genitals). The resulting internal order is called justice: The state in which the true self (mind) conquers the lower or false manifestations of self (will and desire).

Paul adopts a similarly dualistic view of self with a like technology of self-subordination.[7] The self is essentially split into "inner human" versus "outer

6. Plato, *Theaetetus* 176a–b.

7. For treatments of Pauline anthropology, see Udo Schnelle, *The Human Condition: Anthropology in the Teachings of Jesus, Paul, and John*, trans. O. C. Dean Jr. (T&T Clark, 1996); George H. van Kooten, *Paul's Anthropology in Context: The Image of God, Assimilation to God, and Tripartite Man in Ancient Judaism*, WUNT 232 (Mohr Siebeck, 2008), 269–312. A tripartite anthropology in Paul does not (as in Plato) undermine a more deep-structure dualism in Paul's anthropological thought. See also George H. van Kooten, "St. Paul on

human" (2 Cor 4:16), the "law of the mind" versus one's "limbs" (Rom 7:23), and "pneuma" trying to dominate "flesh" (Gal 5:16–26).[8] Whatever the "flesh" is exactly, it is the source of the disobedient urges of the false self. It leads to acts and expresses itself in violent emotions which Greek moralists would identify with the "passions" (*pathē*).

In his famous vice lists, Paul names some of these passions: Injustice (conspicuously heading the list), evil, greed, vice, jealousy, murder, strife, deceit, malignity, and so on (Rom 1:29). The moral goal of life is to "crucify the flesh with its passions and desires" (Gal 5:24), and in turn to manifest virtues characteristic of the divine Christ: "love, joy, peace, patience, kindness, generosity, faithfulness, gentleness, and self-control" (Gal 5:22–23). "Self-control" (*enkrateia*) is duly emphasized at the end, and reveals Paul's basic point. The higher self has to control—and to transcend—the lower self (or passions) to live virtuously.[9]

This basic dualism is reiterated and developed in Romans 7, where Paul attempts to demonstrate the human inability to follow god's law due to their enslavement to the passions.[10] He sees an inward split between mind (which yearns to do good), and "the law of sin" (or flesh) which leads well-meaning people into sin (7:23). Negative emotions and unruly desires are too powerful for the rational mind to control. Human conventions and laws are no help either. In fact, they awaken desire by setting limits on the will. The mind needs to be renewed by an injection of Christ's pneuma, his "spirit." Pneuma is that bit of Christ's self that enters the believer and catalyzes a cognitive

---

Soul, Spirit, and the Inner Man," in *The Afterlife of the Platonic Soul: Reflections of Platonic Psychology in Monotheistic Religions*, ed. Maha Elkaisy-Friemuth and John Dillon (Brill, 2009), 25–44.

8. For instructive comments on Gal 5:16–26, see Troels Engberg-Pedersen, "Paul, Virtues, and Vices," in *Paul in the Graeco-Roman World: A Handbook*, ed. J. Paul Sampley (Trinity Press, 2003), 608–33, at 617–24; Karl Olav Sandnes, *The Challenge of Homer: School, Pagan Poets and Early Christianity*, LNTS 400 (T&T Clark, 2009), 261–62.

9. For a fuller treatment of self-mastery and control of the passions in Paul, see Stanley K. Stowers, *A Rereading of Romans: Justice, Jews, and Gentiles* (Yale University Press, 1994), 42–82; Stanley K. Stowers, "Paul and Self Mastery," in *Paul in the Greco-Roman World: A Handbook*, vol. 2, ed. J. Paul Sampley (Bloomsbury, 2016), 270–300, at 280–97.

10. Stowers, *Rereading Romans*, 251–84.

transformation (Rom 12:2). Believers gain the "mind of Christ" (1 Cor 2:16), which enables self-rule.

This is a simplified version of Pauline salvation, but it is necessary to keep it simple to reveal its basic structure. What we have here is in substance a dualistic anthropology in which a higher, true self (the redeemed mind) tames and transcends a lower self (the passions or flesh). We can begin to see here a basic analogy between Paul's anthropology and the anthropology of popular Platonism. To be sure, the lower self is not identical with the chest and belly—but still the basic structure of the anthropology pits one part of the self against another.[11] Injustice and lack of inward harmony are expressions of the lower, false self, but these vices are controlled by the higher self, which is driven by the divine pneuma (the mind of Christ). Due to their passions, people cannot live according to god's justice, but the one driven by divine pneuma can attain virtue.

Even though Paul is not partial to the word "virtue" (*aretē*)—using it only in Philippians 4:8—he presents several virtue lists which could be described as qualities of the divine Christ.[12] For Paul, the virtues are "fruits of the pneuma" (Gal 5:22)—the pneuma that Christ is (1 Cor 15:45; 2 Cor 3:17). Being inhabited by the divine pneuma is analogous to being in the state of justice (or inward harmony). The divine pneuma of Christ develops virtue in the believer so that the believer's old self can be controlled and eventually transcended. The human being driven by the pneuma becomes a "child of god" (Rom 8:14, cf. vv. 15–16, 19, 23; cf. 1:4), a kinship fully realized when the believer is delivered from the present bodily platform (v. 23), when it is transformed and glorified (vv. 17–18, 21, 30).

Physical Assimilation: Rule over Death

The gods are deathless (*athanatoi*) and the deathless ones are gods.[13] The creation story of Genesis shows that humans, though made in (or as) the image of god (Gen 1:26–27), were kept from eternal life (Gen 3). Paul's gospel taught

---

11. For Plato and Paul, "injustice" and "being in the flesh" are both states that are connected to the body. Although Paul has no animus against the body per se, he can be critical of the unredeemed, corruptible body and its lusts. Redemption, in my reading of Rom 8:23b, requires transformation of this corruptible body.

12. For a discussion of virtue in Phil 4:8, see Sandnes, *The Challenge of Homer*, 264–69.

13. Litwa, *We Are Being Transformed*, 44–45.

that humans can attain deathlessness through assimilation to the divine Christ (1 Cor 15:35–53). The Pauline mode of assimilation is corporeal. That is, believers assimilate to the glorious *body* of Christ.

According to Paul, Christ has a "body of glory" (*sōma tēs doxēs*; Phil 3:21)—or, as it can be translated, a "body constituted by glory" (genitive of material). This is the body that Christ gained in his resurrection, when he was raised by the "glory" of the Father (Rom 6:4) and became a "life-making spirit" (1 Cor 15:45). Accordingly, Christ is the "Lord of glory" (1 Cor 2:8). When believers "behold the glory of the Lord" (2 Cor 3:18), they behold Christ himself, who is the image of god (2 Cor 4:4; cf. 4:6; Col 1:15).

Body and spirit are not opposed. In fact, Christ's body of glory is what makes him a "life-making spirit" (1 Cor 15:45; cf. 2 Cor 3:17). The word translated "spirit" is again *pneuma*. Scholars and exegetes are increasingly realizing that pneuma does not mean a Platonic, immaterial "spirit." It is more suitably translated by "breath" or "wind." Among ancient philosophers and medical professionals, it was thought of as a corporeal substance, though not a solid, earthly substance like soil and water.[14] It was more like air. Air, however, was thought to be naturally cold and misty, whereas pneuma was hot, fiery, refined, or subtle. Stoics described pneuma as a fine mixture of air and fire, and identified it with the substance of aether, or the fiery air thought to exist in the upper reaches of the universe.

That Christ's pneuma is also his body is indicated by the fact that those conformed to Christ (1 Cor 15:49) are said to inherit a "pneumatic *body*" (*sōma pneumatikon*; v. 44). Christians become like Christ by conforming to the image of Christ's pneumatic body (vv. 48–49). Elsewhere Paul speaks of assimilation to Christ's body of glory (Phil 3:21). Pneuma and glory are thus parallel expressions: Both describe the "stuff" of the resurrection body, and the substance of this body was a subject of intense discussion.

In 1 Corinthians 15:39–53, Paul discusses the nature of the resurrection body in answer to the question "With what sort of body do they [i.e., those resurrected] come?" (v. 35). He responds:

> Not all flesh is alike, but there is one flesh for human beings, another for animals, another for birds, and another for fish. There are both

14. Cf. Origen: "It is a custom of holy scripture, when it wishes to point to something of an opposite nature to this dense and solid body, to call it pneuma" (*First Principles* 1.1.2; cf. his preface §8).

> heavenly bodies and earthly bodies, but the glory of the heavenly is one thing, and that of the earthly is another. There is one glory of the sun, and another glory of the moon, and another glory of the stars; indeed, star differs from star in glory.
>
> So it is with the resurrection of the dead. What is sown is perishable, what is raised is imperishable. It is sown in dishonor, it is raised in glory. It is sown in weakness, it is raised in power. It is sown an animalic body, it is raised a pneumatic body. If there is an animalic body, there is also a pneumatic body. Thus it is written, "The first man, Adam, became animalic life (*psychē*)"; the last Adam [Christ] became a life-giving pneuma. . . . The first man was from the earth, a man of dust; the second man is from heaven. As was the one of dust, so are those who are of the dust; and as is the one of heaven, so are those who are of heaven. Just as we have borne the image of the one of dust, we will also bear the image of the celestial one [i.e., Christ].
>
> What I am saying, brothers and sisters, is this: flesh and blood cannot inherit the kingdom of god, nor does the perishable inherit the imperishable. Listen, I will tell you a mystery! We will not all die, but we will all be changed, in a moment, in the twinkling of an eye, at the last trumpet. For the trumpet will sound, and the dead will be raised imperishable, and we will be changed. (1 Cor 15:39–52, NRSV, modified)

Paul characterizes the pneumatic body by incorruptibility, glory, and power (vv. 42–43)—all divine qualities. It is also conformed to Christ's body, consisting of "life-making" pneuma (v. 45) associated with "heaven" (v. 47). The nature of the pneumatic body is thus celestial (v. 48).

The celestial body is not, Paul adds, made up of "flesh and blood"—the constituents of present bodily life (v. 50). Most ancient peoples admitted that bodily life on earth is constituted by flesh—by which is meant not only skin, but bones, arteries, muscle, nerves and all the various tissues and organs that make life possible on this planet. Flesh is the stuff of terrestrial life. Mortals have blood in their veins. To exist in a body without flesh and blood is not to be human in the way the ancients normally conceived of it. It is to be celestial, not terrestrial. It is to exist in a corporeality transcending the conditions of earthly life, without disease or decomposition. It is to be "bloodless" (*anaimones*), an epithet of the gods.[15]

When Paul talked about the bodies of earthly beings, he used the term "flesh" (*sarx*, v. 39). When he turned to heavenly bodies, he used the term "glory" (*doxa*, vv. 40–41). Although glory may simply mean "brightness" or "illumination," there is strong indication that in the latter half of 1 Cor 15 glory is meant to contrast directly with flesh (v. 39). If flesh is the substance of earthly bodies, then *doxa* is the stuff of pneumatic bodies. In short, a pneumatic body is a glory body. Pneuma, like the aether in ancient cosmology, shines like the stars. Since Christ is pneuma (v. 45), he has a body of glory (Phil 3:21).

These glory bodies can be in heaven or on earth (1 Cor 15:40), but their proper location is in the heavens where the glory bodies—sun, moon, stars—shine according to their purity or weight of glory (15:41; cf. 2 Cor 4:17). An animalic body (made up of flesh, blood, sinew) belongs on earth, but a pneumatic body is a dweller in heaven, like the stars. A pneumatic body actually is a heavenly body like sun, moon, and stars.[16] There is an implicit contrast between heavenly and earthly bodies underlying 1 Corinthians 15:39–49, and Paul associates the future pneumatic body of believers with the heavenly bodies. The mention of the heavenly nature of Christ's body in 1 Corinthians 15:47 recalls the contrast between earthly and heavenly bodies in 15:40.[17] Paul seems, then, to be alluding to the fact that the pneumatic bodies of Christ and believers show the same brilliance (*doxa*) as the heavenly bodies.

In a word, divine bodies are "glorified." In a later letter, Paul promises believers a "glorification" (*doxazō*) of their bodies in conformity to the resurrected body of Christ (Rom 8:29–30).[18] This passage from Romans is structurally similar to 1

15. Homer, *Iliad* 5.342.

16. Troels Engberg-Pedersen, *Cosmology and Self in the Apostle Paul: The Material Spirit* (Oxford University Press, 2010), 28.

17. Engberg-Pedersen, *Cosmology and Self*, 30.

18. On Pauline glorification, see Preston Sprinkle, "The Afterlife in Romans: Understanding Paul's Glory Motif in Light of the Apocalypse of Moses and 2 Baruch," in *Lebendige Hoffnung—ewiger Tod?! Jenseitsvorstellungen im Hellenismus, Judentum und Christentum*, ed. Michael Labahn and Manfred Lang (Evangelische Verlagsanstalt, 2007), 201–234. Cf. Carey C. Newman, *Paul's Glory Christology: Tradition and Rhetoric* (Brill, 1992).

Corinthians 15:49: "Just as we have borne the image of the one of dust (Adam), we will also bear the image of the celestial one (Christ)." In Paul's Letter to the Romans, to be conformed to Christ's image means to be glorified; in 1 Corinthians, to bear Christ's image is to become celestial, like the pneumatic Christ himself. Paul's language of "glorification" is thus a way of talking about becoming pneuma and living a life among the stars.[19] Believers will "shine like stars in the cosmos" (Phil 2:15). While believers are on earth, this image is metaphorical; but when they inhabit their celestial domain (Phil 3:20), it will cease to be a metaphor.

Paul's language of meeting the Lord "in the air" (*eis aera*; 1 Thess 4:17), of having a heavenly city (or citizenship; Phil 3:20), and of bearing the image of the "Celestial Being" (*ho epouranios*; 1 Cor 15:48–49) indicates that he envisioned an ascent to heaven or celestial sojourn after death (or when Christ comes to earth). Paul himself had a preliminary sojourn to heaven (2 Cor 12:1–4). When believers make their ascent, their pneumatic element will wholly envelop and replace their mortal flesh.

In Phil 3:21, Paul proposes that Christians will share in the "glory body," or the brilliant corporeality of a divine being. The analogous passage in 2 Cor 3:18 ("We all, beholding the glory of the Lord as in a mirror, are being metamorphosed into the same image from glory to glory") indicates just how closely believers are conformed to the glory of the Christ: They are to become the *same* image, that is the *identical (corporeal) form* as their divine Lord. Insofar as the faithful participate in Christ's pneumatic corporeality, they participate in Christ's divine identity. The result is the human attainment of the clearest of all divine attributes: Deathlessness (1 Cor 15:50–52).

Political Assimilation: Rule over the Cosmos

When arguing against factionalism in Corinth, Paul told his converts that "all things (*panta*) are yours" (1 Cor 3:21). This is not just rhetorical hyperbole. In

19. Why does Paul not speak directly of glorification in 1 Cor 15? Although glorification and the "glory body" was a concept intelligible to a Jewish audience (or those familiar with the Jewish heritage), it would seem to be less intelligible to a Greek one. Paul's "pneumatic body" may then be an attempt to redescribe the concept of "glory" in terms intelligible to Greek physics. The closest physical concept to corporeal "glory" was the Stoic pneuma: an ethereal, fiery, fine, subtle substance, not subject to decay. Since it existed in the heavens, pneuma was envisioned as a bright or luminous body. Such was the substance of the Stoic soul—and, as it turns out, also the substance of the stars.

Paul's apocalyptic mindset, "all things" includes real superhuman entities: The powers of death and life, all present and future things, and even the world itself (*kosmos*; v. 22; cf. Rom 8:38).[20] To have possession of these cosmic realities—and of the cosmos itself—is at the very least to have some degree of power over them. But to have power over death is the prerogative of the divine Anointed one who will defeat death when the "end" comes (1 Cor 15:25–27, cf. 10:11). Christ as creator is the one who truly owns "all things."

Christ is the prototype and believers "in Christ" assimilate to his divine powers and prerogatives. They are "coheirs" with Christ (Rom 8:17) to whom the whole tri-tiered cosmos bows the knee (Phil 2:10–11). As participants in Christ, believers gain "shares" in the Father's cosmic government. Thus, believers should not be worried about mere human things (1 Cor 3:21). They are called to be something more than human (3:4).[21]

A backstory of future rule is also implied in 1 Corinthians 4:8. Here Paul chides the Corinthians: "Already you have all you want! Already you have become rich! Quite apart from us you have become kings!" That Paul was not merely mocking his converts but affirming his own doctrine appears from his next (not entirely sarcastic) remark: "Indeed, I wish that you had become kings, so that we might be kings with you!" Reigning as cosmic kings was evidently not the private fantasy of the Corinthians, or the doctrine of Paul's enemies. It is, it appears, what Paul had told them of their final destiny.[22] As owners of

20. The *kosmos* is variously understood in 1 Cor 3:22. Johannes Weiss understood it as "the unlimited fullness of all living beings, human and angel (cf. 4:9)" (*Der erste Korintherbrief* [English: *The First Letter to the Corinthians*], 2nd ed. [Vandenhoeck & Ruprecht, 1977], 89). Archibald Robertson and Alfred Plummer opted for "the physical universe" (*A Critical and Exegetical Commentary on the First Epistle of St. Paul to the Corinthians*, 2nd ed., ICC 33 [T&T Clark, 1914], 73). Commentators who want to limit "the world" to something smaller have trouble explaining why death, life, as well as all present and future things are included in it.

21. "For when one says, 'I belong to Paul,' and another, 'I belong to Apollos,' are you not merely human (*ouk anthrōpoi este*)?" Origen comments: "The pneumatic is greater than 'human,' who is characterized either by soul or by body or by both, and not by the pneuma which is more divine than these. By very strong participation in the pneuma the pneumatic gains this name" (*Commentary on John* 2.21.138, my trans.).

22. The problem of the Corinthians is not that they speed up the time of their rule (*pace* David H. Hay, *Glory at the Right Hand: Psalm 110 in Early Christianity*, SBLMS 18 [Abingdon Press, 1973], 62) but that they rule without Paul (*chōris hēmōn*, in an emphatic position; 1 Cor 4:8).

all things and heirs with Christ, they will rule as kings or emperors (*basileusousin*; Rom 5:17), and come into possession of all there is (*ta panta*; 8:32).[23]

Ownership of "everything" is a form of sovereignty—a universal sovereignty to which only Christ can lay claim. To Christ, god makes "all things" (*panta*) subject (1 Cor 15:27; Phil 3:21). Strictly speaking, sovereignty over "all things" is the sovereignty that only Christ the creator has. This is the sovereignty that makes up the divine identity of Christ, the Anointed, who is master and heir of the world. Paul envisions believers as sharing this universal sovereignty through their assimilation to Christ, the divine son (Rom 8:29).

If believers will rule over the cosmos as coheirs with Christ, they also will have the authority to judge it. In 1 Corinthians 6:2, Paul asks, "Do you not know that the holy ones will judge the cosmos [*ton kosmon*]?" Included in the cosmos are both humans and angels (4:9). Naturally, Paul asks: "Do you not know that we are to judge angels?" (6:2–3). Paul's "Do you not know . . . ?" indicates that the future world dominance of believers was a well-known teaching—and evidently his own. The *kosmos* may refer to those judged on judgment day. More broadly, however, it designates the creation in general. If this is correct, then the "judging" may not be viewed as a one-time event, but as a continuous action of believers ruling the cosmos.[24]

The authority to judge the world (both human and superhuman) is a widely recognized divine function.[25] According to Paul, it is the god who judges the world (Rom 3:6; cf. Ps 96:13), along with the divine Christ (2 Cor 5:10).

---

23. "All things" here probably refers to creation as a whole, the most common meaning in Paul (Rom 11:36; 1 Cor 8:6; 11:12; 15:27–28; Phil 3:21). In the words of James D. G. Dunn, "what seems to be envisaged is a sharing in Christ's lordship . . . over 'the all'" (*Romans 1–8*, WBC 38A [Thomas Nelson, 1988], 502).

24. A good case for the "ruling" sense of the verb *krinō* ("judge") can be made from LXX usage, where this is often the meaning of the term (e.g., Judg 4:4; 10:2–3; Ps 66:5 [MT 67:5]; Hos 13:10; cf. Luke 22:30). Cf. also Judg 3:10, 30; 12:7–9, 11, 13–14; 15:20; 16:31. It also seems to be the sense in Ruth 1:1, 1 Kgdms 4:18; 2 Chron 26:21; Ps 2:10; 9:9; 71:2, 4; 95:10, 13; 97:9; 134:14; Prov 29:14; Mic 4:3; Isa 19:20; 51:22; Wis 1:1; 3:8; 12:13, 18; Tob 3:2; 1 Macc 9:73; Pss. Sol. 17:29; Odes 3:10; Sir 4:15; 45:26. This sense of *krinō* does not seem to appear at all in the Pentateuch, although see Deut 32:36.

25. According to Paul M. Hoskins, "In Jewish thought the judge of angels is also a position that is held solely by God" ("The Use of Biblical and Extrabiblical Parallels in the Interpretation of First Corinthians 6:2–3," *CBQ* 63 [2001]: 287–97, at 292, citing 1 En 9–10; 90:20–27).

Christ who functions as god in judging shares in god's divine identity. The same applies to believers. For god (through Christ) to give humans ownership of "everything" (*ta panta*) and judgment over the "world" (*ton kosmon*) is to give them a share of divine sovereignty which constitutes Christ's divine identity.

The sovereignty that believers gain in Christ is greater than the sovereignty Adam had over beasts and birds in Genesis 1:26 and 28. It is a sovereignty of the image of god, who is a divine being, the Christ (2 Cor 4:4). It is a universal sovereignty insofar as it includes ownership of all things and the judgment of the cosmos. In sum, it is a divine sovereignty, appropriate to a divine being.

Believers will not judge animals, or even other people. They will judge "angels," beings—whether good or evil—that are normally held to be superior to humanity. Human superiority over angels is only natural for those who have been made into "the same image" as Christ, the image of god (3:18; 4:4). Properly speaking, only Christ has power over the angelic or superhuman world (1 Cor 15:24; Phil 2:10–11). His power to judge is what gives him the honor of the Father. Humanity granted the power to judge angels is humanity sharing in Christ's divine prerogatives and honor.

In 1 Corinthians 15, Christ's role as the divine Messiah is "to destroy every rule and authority and power" (v. 24). Cosmic conquering belongs not only to the Anointed son, but also to the many children of god. Christ is the precursor, the prototype of an entire class of transformed beings granted imperial rule over superhuman powers.[26] Some of those powers are evil, and there is a master of evil, Satan. But Paul is undaunted. He promises believers that Satan will soon be crushed beneath their feet (Rom 16:20). Christ himself tramples "Death," the "last" enemy (1 Cor 15:26). Even as a man living in a "body of death" (Rom 7:24), Paul sung a victory hymn against Death (1 Cor 15:53–56). Death has been gulped down and Satan is dust beneath the believer's feet. Properly speaking, only the divine Messiah uses his enemies as a footstool (Ps 110:1; 1 Cor 15:27). By stomping on Satan, Christians secure Christ's sovereignty.

But more: believers inherit, with Christ, the universal sovereignty of god. The supreme god made Christ an heir of the world (1 Cor 15:27). He will own it and rule over it. Christ does not horde divine power; he lavishly shares it with his siblings and coheirs. Christ's rule is a cosmic rule, and thus a divine one. It

26. James Tabor, "Paul's Notion of Many 'Sons of God' and Its Hellenistic Contexts," *Helios* 13 (1986): 87–97, at 94.

is this divine rule which he shares with believers. Christ as the prototype for believers is not just a human being. He is a *divine* agent. According to Paul's gospel, believers are made "heirs of god and co-heirs with Christ" (Rom 8:17).[27] As coheirs, they will have an equal share of Christ's divine ownership of the world and dominion over it. Christ has first priority to it as the elder brother, but he willingly shares it with all those called his "siblings" and "children of god" (Gal 3:26; Rom 8:17, 19, 29). They fulfill, or help Christ fulfill, a divine function. In short, the children of god are gods.

Conclusion

Paul's gospel was (and is) a gospel of deification. In the ancient world, typically only emperors and pharaohs claimed divine prerogatives. Only they were immortal, and boasted of world rule. Paul preached a gospel wherein those privileges were granted to all—including commoners, slaves, women, and children. The only conditions were belief in Christ and moral rectitude.

One might accuse Paul of preaching a gospel of compensation since he projected divine life and rule into the future. One must die to become a god; or Christ must come again—whichever comes sooner. On the other hand, Paul's version of deification avoids the dangers of self-promotion exhibited in the various ruler cults. For the apostle, one is deified not by heroic victories and acts of war, but by following the divine Christ who lived and died to benefit human beings.

Pauline deification means assimilation to—and ultimately identification with—the divine Christ. It is thus appropriate to call it Christification, or "Christosis," provided that one does not downplay Christ's divinity.[28] Like the true god(s) imagined by Plato, Christ is a moral god able to lead his devotees into a virtuous life. All who follow him with dedication will share the same divine destiny because they come to share his divine materiality and functions: A deathless and undecaying body, a plethora of divine virtues, and nothing less than cosmic kingship.

27. "The term 'heirs of God,'" notes C. E. B. Cranfield, "is not to be explained as meaning simply 'heirs of Abraham,' who are to receive in due course the blessings which God promised to him and his seed." Christians will share "not just in various blessings God is able to bestow but in that which is peculiarly His own, the perfect and imperishable glory of His own life" (*A Critical and Exegetical Commentary on the Epistle to the Romans*, 6th ed. [Clark, 1975], 1.927).

28. Ben Blackwell, *Pauline Soteriology in Light of Deification in Irenaeus and Cyril of Alexandria*, WUNT 2/314 (Mohr Siebeck, 2011).

CHAPTER EIGHT

Paul among the Other Possessed

Giovanni B. Bazzana
Harvard Divinity School

The present essay deals with an apparently very simple question: If possession as a religious phenomenon was present in the Pauline groups (and in Paul himself, as I will argue below), should this be considered an exceptional feature with respect to the rest of the Mediterranean religious and cultural context? The question, however, is only deceptively simple. For starters, it demands that one deals with a number of preliminary issues before it can be tackled appropriately. In the first part of this treatment, I will address a few of such preliminary matters in a way that will be necessarily simplified. The remainder of the paper will be devoted to the main question enunciated above.

"Paganism" and the Ancient Mediterranean

First of all, one may wonder about the historiographical opportunity of speaking about Paul in the context of "paganism."[1] Currently, at least in the English-speaking world, there is little doubt that the vast majority of publications are designed to contextualize Paul as fully Jewish. Thus, their focus is placed on understanding the apostle's theology and religious experience as part of the diverse Judaism of the first century CE. This is a completely legitimate course of action. And it is easy to understand this important trajectory

1. In itself, the very label *paganism* is an anachronistic misnomer and should probably be abandoned, as it inappropriately conflates a mass of diverse and often at odds religious practices and beliefs. In addition, the very term *pagan* emerged in Latin-speaking Christianity (*paganus*) only much later than the period examined here, and it was employed almost exclusively in a derogatory sense. Adopting "ancient Mediterranean" instead allows for a more appropriate comparative exercise that has also has the advantage of sidestepping and redescribing the outdated opposition of Judaism and Paganism.

within New Testament studies as a productive reaction to centuries in which the figure of Paul had been conceptualized by Christian authors in opposition to Judaism (often, naturally, the Judaism of their own time) and then used as a springboard for theological supersessionism. But, as in almost all scholarly trends, such a welcome and overdue change of perspective carries potential downsides.[2]

An analogous problem has emerged also in the scholarship devoted to the historical Jesus. It rightly became a more mainstream approach in New Testament studies to emphasize Jesus's Jewishness in the latter part of the twentieth century. Such an emphasis, however, is often used simply to co-opt Judaism as a tool to reaffirm the exceptionalism of Jesus (now relabeled as the "Jewish Jesus") with respect to his broader Mediterranean context.[3] The result has also been a thinly veiled intent of advancing once more a Christian (now conveniently relabeled "Judeo-Christian") agenda of exceptionalism via rehabilitating the old Judaism versus Hellenism dichotomy. It goes without saying that the only valid response is to reaffirm the need to study topics like Jesus, Paul, and the ancient Judaism that encompassed both of them within their broader context of ancient Mediterranean culture and society. The goal is to understand the apostle historically both as wholly part of the Judaism of his time and as fully part of the ancient Mediterranean sociocultural space. I ask the question, "How did Pauline possession fit within the Mediterranean religious space of his time?" Nevertheless, it should remain understood that this move does not deny the fundamental importance of the Jewish background for an adequate comprehension of Pauline possession.

Defining "Possession"

The second necessary premise has to do with the very phenomenon designated here as "possession." Possession is a very fraught and contested concept in the study of religion in general, and especially in New Testament studies. One can

2. Some have been already and convincingly illustrated by other scholars, including, for example, Jennifer Eyl, *Signs, Wonders, and Gifts: Divination in the Letters of Paul* (Oxford University Press, 2019), and Paula Fredriksen, *Paul: The Pagans' Apostle* (Yale University Press, 2017).

3. An early diagnosis of this problem in William E. Arnal, *The Symbolic Jesus: Historical Scholarship, Judaism, and the Construction of Contemporary Identity* (Equinox 2005).

state that "possession" is a locale in which the anxiety surrounding Christian exceptionalism becomes glaringly evident. A good example is provided by the endless discussions about the potential "ecstatic" nature of the experiences described by Paul himself in 1 Corinthians 12–14.[4] The hand-wringing concerning "ecstasy" is often accompanied and motivated by the desire to prove that the members of the Pauline group in Corinth (or at the very least Paul himself) were absolutely not subject to any phenomenon that entailed loss or alteration of consciousness. Indeed, scholarly efforts are also often directed to demonstrate that the Corinthians (or at least Paul) were the only ancient Mediterranean people impervious to the loss of control and rationality that is traditionally associated with ecstatic experiences.

In addition, the task of defining possession is further complicated by the fact that the term entered the study of religion toolkit inextricably implicated within a set of conceptual oppositions that have their roots in early European modernity. In turn, it must be noted that such oppositions have also profoundly shaped the epistemological and methodological arsenal of modern biblical criticism. For the sake of brevity, I will mention here only two among these binaries. The first one of course is linked to the very term *possession*. While this is originally a Latin word, its use to designate the phenomenon under discussion here is not for the most part ancient. *Possession* began to appear systematically only in early modernity when European colonizers and ethnographers met non-European peoples for the first time, among whom the phenomenon occurred as an ordinary practice. As pointed out both by anthropologists like Paul Christopher Johnson, the choice of *possession* to designate the phenomenon is quite telling and deeply imbricated with the enterprise of subjugation and colonization that took place at the very same time (and often also under the direction of the very same people).[5] The designation of non-Europeans as possessed immediately opposes them to Europeans whose selves (as attested in the thought philosophers like

4. For a perceptive and updated historiographical discussion (even though the new conclusions are not always convincing), see now Ekaputra Tupamahu, *Contesting Languages: Heteroglossia and the Politics of Languages in the Early Church* (Oxford University Press, 2023), 1–48.

5. Paul Christopher Johnson, "Toward an Atlantic Genealogy of 'Spirit Possession,'" in *Spirited Things: The Work of "Spirit Possession" in Afro-Atlantic Religions*, ed. Paul Christopher Johnson (University of Chicago Press, 2014), 23–45.

Locke or Leibniz) are conceived as completely self-possessed, impervious to external intrusions that may compromise the full control of their free will. In this perspective, it is easy to see how such binary could be invoked to justify colonial subjugation all the way to the point of enslavement for those human beings whose selves were already conceived as "porous" and open to possession to begin with.

The second binary that is worth mentioning here works in a manner that is similar to the first one, but in turn it focuses on rationality as the defining trait of an autonomous and "buffered" self.[6] Those selves that are open to external infringement and control are then by definition also incapable of the objective rationality that characterizes European selves. Such irrationality is ostensibly evident in phenomena like the above-mentioned "ecstasy" and the openness to enter altered state of consciousness like trance.

There is no need to recount here the long and tragic history of the intertwining of European colonization and European Christianity, nor the equally long and problematic history of how this combination produced almost all the categories later employed in the study of religion. But keeping these trajectories in mind is crucial to understand many of the difficulties that one encounters in analyzing possession in any biblical setting, and specifically here in relation to Paul and his groups. Both Christian theology and biblical scholarship were deeply influenced by the binaries that I have described above. Such an outcome is completely expected if one considers when and under which cultural conditions biblical criticism as an academic discipline first emerged in northern Europe. Such an influence had two consequences for the study of possession in biblical materials, and especially in the New Testament. These consequences remain very powerfully installed to this day not only in the way scholarship approaches the issue at hand, but also in how biblical stories are commonly understood beyond academic discussions.

The first and most important consequence has been the strategy of cordoning off the "good characters" within these stories (Jesus, Paul, and other disciples who are seen as the predecessors of contemporary Christianity) from "possession." This is exactly what happens with the issue of ecstatic

6. The identification of a type of self as "buffered" over against "porous" is indebted to Charles Taylor's theorization of Western modernity, on which see Denise Kimber Buell, "The Microbes and Pneuma That Therefore I Am," in *Divinanimality: Animal Theory, Creaturely Theology*, ed. Stephen D. Moore (Fordham University Press 2014), 63–87.

experiences, which, being irrational, must be kept as far away as possible from the likes of Jesus or Paul, lest these figures become too foreign for modern European tastes. Yet features of biblical narratives about Jesus and Paul are often dangerously similar to those occurring in cases of possession. One could mention here basically all the New Testament situations in which a divine spirit is active in and with humans.[7] Interpreters had to work hard to keep these episodes on the "good" side of the binaries sketched above, where one should encounter only autonomous and rational selves. The strategy most often adopted in these cases consists simply in denying the application of the term *possession*. For example, think about the habit of speaking of Paul's "mysticism" in contexts that for all intents and purposes are almost indistinguishable from those slotted under the label *possession*. Most famously, this happens in Albert Schweitzer's seminal book, which is a treasure of interesting observations once its argument is disentangled from the vagueness of "mysticism."[8] The early Christian archive is likewise rich with stories that are just as easily slotted on the "bad" side of the binary: Most prominent among these are the episodes of exorcism, performed by Jesus or his disciples, that we are habituated to understand as actual possession. In these cases, interpreters face no problem in bringing out the entire panoply of features that locate the possessed individuals on the negative side of modern binaries. Irrationality, self-harm, and external control are all fortunately healed by Jesus.

But what is possession, really? Are the exorcisms narrated in the Gospels or in Acts the only evidence we have of this phenomenon in the early Christian world? To answer such questions requires, in my opinion, some help from outside the discipline of New Testament studies. Since early modernity, interest in possession among anthropologists has coordinated with a number of theoretical developments. Especially over the course of the last three decades (in conjunction with a systematic rethinking of the colonial past of the discipline itself), ethnographies of possession have become more sophisticated and have contributed to highlight a seemingly new culturally

7. One can refer to the entering of the holy spirit in Jesus at baptism in Mark 1:10 or the episode of speaking in tongues in Act 2.

8. *Die Mystik des Apostels Paulus* (Mohr 1930); translated into English as *The Mysticism of the Apostle Paul*, trans. William Montgomery, intro. by Jaroslav Pelikan (Johns Hopkins University Press, 1998).

integrated aspect of this phenomenon. While possession remains a painful experience, often beginning with states of malaise and sickness, newer studies have pointed out that it does not only need to be exorcized. Just as often possession is integrated into cultural and religious scripts for individuals and groups. So, the impersonation of foreign spirits in possession rituals frequently becomes an opportunity for a group to reflect on its relationship with otherness and, even more importantly, to reexamine, sometimes under a mordantly ironic and parodic light, cultural assumptions and habits that are otherwise left unexplored. Likewise, possessed individuals—once they have started the protracted process of exorcism—become sources of beneficial interventions for their groups, providing them with support via divination or healing.[9]

In sum, far from being the epitome of irrationality (as it had been previously characterized), possession urges us to expand the boundaries of what one designates as "rational." Possessed individuals, far from being bereft of their autonomy and moral agency, appear more often than not to find a state that sustains their ethical growth and nourishes their psychological well-being. It turns out that "porous" selves may provide humans with a better support for individual as well as communal life than the "buffered" selves that were the conceptualized hallmark of Western modernity.

It can be argued that such an understanding of possession provides also a more appropriate and more useful opportunity to rethink our comprehension of the phenomenon in the early Christian world. To think differently about possession enables scholars to overcome the modern binaries reviewed above. Thus, possession is not only just the harmful condition that must only be healed through exorcism, but also a phenomenon whose outcome is more ambiguous, sometimes even potentially beneficial. One can then also look for possession in other places in early Christianity that just the narratives of Jesus's and the disciples' exorcisms. Shifting perspective like that can have an immediate impact on how one looks at the experiences of Paul and of his groups. At the same time, by taking advantage of the insights produced by recent ethnographic research, one can also appreciate other aspects of this phenomenon, going beyond the mere treatment of possession as illness.

9. Classic anthropological treatments of possession moving in this direction are Janice P. Boddy, *Wombs and Alien Spirits: Women, Men, and the Zar Cults in Northern Sudan* (Wisconsin University Press 1989); Michael Lambek, *Human Spirits: A Cultural Account of Trance in Mayotte* (Cambridge University Press, 1981).

Paul's and Pauline Possession

The third and final preliminary observation concerns Paul. I will assume that Paul experienced possession himself, and that this phenomenon became one of the cornerstones for the religious experience that he shared with his groups. What follows is a brief explanation of this assumption.[10]

Paul himself is possessed by a spirit that he designates using the Greek word *pneuma*. It is important to note that this *pneuma* that possesses Paul is identical with Christ. (How this transformation of Christ from human being to *pneuma* happened is hinted at by Paul at the very beginning of Romans.)[11] The puzzling phrase "to be in Christ (*en Christo*)"—which is almost a hallmark of Paul's style, and which has given so much stimulus for thought and for debate to scholars—should be understood within this context. A similar phrase is used repeatedly in the Gospels to indicate that humans are possessed by negative spirits, even though translations usually hide this fact. For instance, in Mark 3:22 scribes from Jerusalem accuse Jesus of casting out demons by "the ruler of demons," and in 5:2 we are told that Jesus encounters a man who is "in an unclean spirit." Despite its oddity—or perhaps exactly because of it—this Greek phrase is systematically used to indicate possession, and there is no reason to think that Paul differs, except for the identity of the *pneuma* that possesses him. This is also the reason why Paul can make statements like the one preserved in Romans 8:9, "You are in the spirit [*en pneumati*], since the spirit of God dwells in you [*en humin*]. Anyone who does not have the spirit of Christ does not belong to him."

As in many instances of possession attested in ethnographic literature, in the case of Paul as well the *pneuma* (who is Christ) controls completely his agency, and Paul is quite straightforward in making this clear in his surviving letters. To prove this point it suffices to read Galatians 2:20, "It is no longer I who live, but it is Christ who lives in me." The fact that passages like this one are universally interpreted in a metaphorical way in modern exegesis is further confirmation of the situation described above. The loss of autonomy

10. Two key works that pushed Pauline studies in this direction are John Ashton, *The Religion of Paul the Apostle* (Yale University Press, 2000) and Christopher Mount, "1 Corinthians 11:3–16: Spirit Possession and Authority in a Non-Pauline Interpolation," *JBL* 124 (2005): 313–40.

11. A more detailed discussion in Bazzana, *Having*, 102–33.

entailed in possession is too problematic to reconcile with notions of the self that are hegemonic within modern Western thought. Thus, it should be kept as far away as possible from figures that are heroized in the Christian tradition, such as Jesus and Paul. That being said, it is worth recalling that the experience of possession is often also an opportunity for self-development and ethical growth, even though of course in a form very different from the one presupposed in classic Western subjectivities. In this perspective, Romans 8:9 is quite telling. Being possessed by the Christ *pneuma* is equated there to "belonging to him" (in Greek, this literally reads "who does not have the spirit of Christ, is not his"). Ethnographic research on spirit possession indicates that the relationship between a medium or a host and their spirit is often described employing metaphors that are culturally coded as unequal. So, in many cases, anthropologists encounter descriptions of this relationship in which spirits are husbands or enslavers, while their hosts or mediums are wives (regardless of gender) or enslaved. In this perspective, it is far from surprising to see (already in Rom 8:9) that Paul speaks about the experience of being possessed by the *pneuma* Christ as "belonging" to him. In a society profoundly shaped by enslavement, this "belonging" must certainly be understood as precisely that: Enslavement. Indeed, Paul frequently describes himself as "enslaved" (*doulos*) to God: Such a terminological choice (which is naturally jarring and quite problematic for modern readers) is undergirded by the experience of possession.[12] Albeit understandably paradoxical to our eyes, it is exactly this state of affairs on which Paul's religious experience and subjectivity are grounded.

Finally, a prominent goal of Paul's mission is to extend the experience of possession to others, which translates in the spreading of a possession cult centered on the presence of the Christ *pneuma*. As illustrated in 1 Corinthians, other members of the Pauline group share the same experiences. That should not be taken as an aberration fueled by the influence of pagan "ecstatic" cults. Far from being an irrational derangement, the possession Paul describes follows a rather complex ritual script that is the product of a sophisticated triangular negotiation involving the possessing *pneuma*, the mediums, and the

---

12. Paul is not the only early Christian author to make use of enslavement as a means to think about possession: Hermas's *Shepherd* provides another prominent example, for which one can see Giovanni B. Bazzana, "Negotiating the Experience of Possession in Hermas's *Shepherd*," in *Experiencing the Shepherd of Hermas*, ed. Angela Kim Harkins and Harry O. Meier (De Gruyter 2022), 9–29.

group that authorizes the entire phenomenon.[13] In this case too, one can clearly see the benefits that the experience of possession brings to participants. Most evident in 1 Corinthians is of course the divination that is produced through possession (1 Cor 12:4–11), but one can count here also the complicated issues of group identity and authority that are negotiated through and around the manifestation of the Christ *pneuma* (1 Cor 14:6–19).

Pauline Terminology

It is time to come to the central subject matter of the present intervention. As I noted at the very beginning, this could be formulated as a question: Is Pauline possession something that stood out over against the surrounding "pagan" Mediterranean religious and cultural context, and, if so, then in what ways did it stand out? It goes without saying that, when one tries to address such a problem in historical comparative terms, it is unlikely that the outcome can be an absolute yes or no. In any comparative exercise there will always be some measure of similarity and difference between the two *comparanda* that are brought together. That is all the more true if one of the two, as in the present case, is a huge and largely undetermined construct like the entirety of the "pagan" world at the time of Paul. In this perspective, a conclusion that Pauline possession could be considered completely unique with respect to its religious and cultural environment must be judged fundamentally ahistorical in principle. Further proof of this is that, as I observed above, such a conclusion is often reached with the support of an ideological agenda that strives to keep early Christianity (and its heroes) away from the contaminating influences of ecstasy or irrationality. In that respect, it is telling that the opposite kind of conclusion, that early Christian possession was a phenomenon entirely indistinguishable from its context (albeit no less ideological than the other one), is almost never advanced.

Thus, one should expect a situation in which some traits and aspects of the phenomenon will probably be similar, while others will be radically different. A difference that comes immediately to the fore (but should not be overemphasized) is terminological. Paul is clearly making a point of avoiding the use of terms that he evidently considered too close to non-Jewish religious practices and beliefs. This happens most clearly with the use of the relatively obscure or confusing (for

13. For a more detailed discussion, see Bazzana, *Having*, 167–205.

a non-Jewish reader or hearer) term *propheteia* ("prophecy") that Paul employs extensively in 1 Corinthians 12–14 for "divination." In this case, the apostle avoids the more common term *mantikē*. Nevertheless, it is evident that he is describing a divinatory practice that an external observer would have easily classified as another instance of *mantikē*. Something similar happens for the kind of possession that Paul and his fellow Christ followers experience. In this case, to indicate the entities that come to possess humans, Paul prefers terms like *pneumata* ("spirits," which is also employed more generally in Greek for this kind of phenomena) or *angeloi* ("angels," which is instead very specific to the Jewish tradition, like *propheteia*).[14] The most common Greek terms that were available are of course *daimon* and *daimonion*, but Paul employs them only in a negative sense, to designate entities whose possession is harmful and should be avoided (1 Cor 10:20–21).

As in the case of *propheteia*, though, this terminological difference, while not inconsequential, should not be overemphasized to pit Paul as unique over against his environment. Sound scholarship should resist Paul's own rhetoric on this point and take a more phenomenological approach.

More-Than-Human Beings

Paul is consistent with his Mediterranean environment in seeing the world as full of more-than-human beings who have the ability to control humans. The nomenclature Paul uses already indicates the beginning of the shift that will lead to Christian theological taxonomies of angelology and demonology, respectively.[15] Nevertheless, *daimonia* are certainly real and active for Paul—so much so that he must warn the Corinthians in no uncertain terms that partaking of "pagan" sacrificial offerings will put them at risk of being possessed by hostile forces. In these verses to be *koinonoi*, often translated as being "partners" of demons, is in all likelihood a reference to possession.[16]

14. On *angelos* as interchangeable with *pneuma* in the Second Temple period, see Bogdan Bucur, *Angelomorphic Pneumatology: Clement of Alexandria and Other Early Christian Witnesses* (Brill, 2009), xxv–xxvii.

15. On this Late Antique development, see Heidi Marx-Wolf, *Spiritual Taxonomies and Ritual Authority: Platonists, Priests, and Gnostics in the Third Century C.E.* (University of Pennsylvania Press 2016).

16. "No, I imply that what [they] sacrifice, they sacrifice to demons and not to God. I do not want you to be partners with demons. You cannot drink the cup of the Lord and the cup

Apart from *daimonia*, though, Paul employs the term *pneumata* frequently and with a nuance that is consistent with the way in which such more-than-human entities were generally understood in the ancient Mediterranean world. These beings were normally conceived as occupying an intermediate position in the cosmos, straddling the divine and the human worlds. From such crucial location, their activities were decidedly ambiguous, capable of bringing to humans either great benefits or dire misfortunes. This is also true as far as possession is concerned: The manifestation of any more-than-human being needs a good deal of expert analysis to understand which effects and consequences its presence will have both on the individual medium and on their social group.

The situation with Paul is no different. On the one hand, *daimonia* are presented as being very bad, definitely to be avoided in any way possible. On the other hand, the *pneuma* of Christ is clearly very good, so much so that Paul is happy to invite everyone to be possessed by him. More importantly though, in between these two extremes, it is clear that Paul acknowledges also the existence of other *pneumata*, whose identity and intentions are much more ambiguous and difficult to ascertain. In 1 Corinthians 12, this is the very subject matter of debate: Who has the authority and the expertise to distinguish between *pneumata,* discerning between those worth cultivating through possession and those that should be avoided? The way in which Paul addresses such a question is rather inconsistent throughout the chapter, and the fact that we have only his side in a conversation that was in all likelihood much more articulated does not help at all. In the very first verses, the apostle seems to imply that good or bad *pneumata* should be identified on the basis of what they make their hosts say (cursing or proclaiming the lordship of Christ).[17] But later Paul also says that the ability to "discriminate among *pneumata*" (*diakrisis pneumaton*) is one of the gifts that are conferred on members of his possession cult (12:10). As I noted above, to reconstruct Paul's argument here in all its details is probably impossible, given the fragmentary nature of our evidence, but in all likelihood such discriminating ability is crucial for a

of demons. You cannot partake of the table of the Lord and the table of demons" (1 Cor 10:20–21).

17. "Therefore I want you to understand that no one speaking by the Spirit of God ever says, 'Let Jesus be cursed!' and no one can say 'Jesus is Lord' except by the Holy Spirit" (1 Cor 12:3).

master of possession and a religious expert, as Paul presents himself to be in his writings.

Exorcisms

Exorcism is notably absent from Paul's letters, even though this practice figures so prominently in other documents belonging to the early Christian archive. Especially if one sets aside the information that canonical Acts of the Apostles give us on Paul, it seems that the apostle is more interested in describing the "good" side of possession with its inherent benefits. In any event, exorcism appears to be quite a popular practice throughout the Mediterranean in the first and second centuries CE.[18] For instance, Philostratus in narrating (at the beginning of the third century) the *Life of Apollonius of Tyana* attributes to this renown Greek religious expert at least one exorcism and several other interactions with *daimones*. These episodes (as well as the fact that Apollonius himself is described as a *daimon* by some admirers of his wisdom in 1.19) are well known because they are often discussed in New Testament scholarship since they look so similar to the exorcisms attributed to Jesus.[19] Such narratives indicate that religious experts in the specific field of possession were very successful in attracting attention both at a popular and a literary level.

Some advocates of the uniqueness of Judeo-Christian religious experience within the ancient Mediterranean have seized on this evidence to advance the hypothesis that exorcism (and also possession, if the latter is reduced to its "bad" side, as traditionally done) was a relatively new import in the Greco-Roman world from the Levant, if not specifically from Judaism. Such a hypothesis finds some support, for instance, in another well-known account

18. See Roy Kotansky, "Greek Exorcistic Amulets," in *Ancient Magic and Ritual Power*, ed. Paul Mirecki and Marvin Meyer (Brill, 1995), 243–77.

19. "Apollonius was explaining how to pour libations.... The youth greeted his remark with a loud, licentious laugh, at which Apollonius looked up at him and said, 'It is not you that are committing this outrage, but the demon who controls you without your knowledge.' In fact without knowing it the youth was possessed by a demon. He laughed at things that nobody else did and went over to weeping without any reason, and he talked and sang to himself.... When Apollonius looked at the spirit, it uttered sounds of fear and fury, such as people being burned alive or tortured do, and it swore to keep away from the youth and not enter into any human. But Apollonius spoke to it as an angry householder does to a slave who is wily, crafty, shameless, and so on, and told it to give a proof of its departure" (Philostratus, *Life of Apollonius of Tyana* 4.20).

of exorcism, a satirical one included by Lucian in his *Philopseudes*, which is datable to the mid-second century. Lucian relates a generic episode of exorcism (where the possession is again attributed to a *daimon*) performed by a Syrian from Palestine, supporting the conclusion that such a practice might have been associated with people hailing from that region.[20] The hypothesis has some merit and it would require a much longer discussion. At the very least, one can observe that a certain type of exorcistic ritual became popular in this period and that its origin was attributed to religious experts coming from the eastern shore of the Mediterranean. Indeed, the exorcisms described by Philostratus, Lucian, and the New Testament sources share a few traits that are interestingly specific. One can mention in this context a couple of them: The rebuking of the possessing entity, and the detail that the more-than-human being communicates using foreign (non-Greek) languages (a phenomenon widespread in "magical" rituals, in which these incomprehensible sounds are technically designated as *voces barbarae*). The phenomenon occurs also in the Pauline groups in connection with manifestations of possession. This is how one should understand both the glossolalia of 1 Corinthians 12–14 and the Aramaic utterance "Abba" that the apostle attributes to the spirit in Romans 8:15 and Galatians 4:6.[21]

That being said, it would be incorrect to maintain that rituals to exorcize humans from harmful possession did not exist in the Greek or Western Mediterranean before the advent of the Christ movement. Features of ritual practices were certainly different from those described above, but several comparable cases can be gathered from a number of classical sources. For instance, a large portion of the plot of the only surviving example of a tragic trilogy

20. "Everyone knows about the Syrian from Palestine, how many he takes in hand who fall down in the light of the moon and roll their eyes and fill their mouths with foam; nevertheless, he restores them to health and sends them away normal in mind, delivering them from their straits for a large fee. When he stands beside them as they lie there and asks: 'Whence came you into his body?' the patient himself is silent, but the spirit answers in Greek or in the language of whatever foreign country he comes from, telling how and whence he entered into the man; whereupon, by adjuring the spirit and if he does not obey, threatening him, he drives him out" (Lucian, *The Lover of Lies*, 16).

21. "And because you are children, God has sent the Spirit of his Son into our hearts, crying, 'Abba! Father!'" (Gal 4:6); "For you did not receive a spirit of slavery to fall back into fear, but you received a spirit of adoption. When we cry, 'Abba! Father!,' it is that very Spirit bearing witness with our spirit that we are children of God" (Rom 8:15–16).

(Aeschylus's *Oresteia*) revolves around devising an effective means to exorcize Orestes from the Erinyes of which he had fallen prey after the murder of his mother. Interestingly, Aeschylus describes the behavior imposed on his hero by these demonic furies as very similar to the one suffered by the unnamed Gerasene demoniac in Mark 5 and parallels. In both cases, the possessed individuals are described as affected by madness and as forced to live at the very margins of human social interactions. In a less literary context, several Greek sources inform us about the techniques employed to exorcize the ghost of general Pausanias from the temple of Athena in Sparta where he had been forced to die of hunger (a highly contaminating event for a most sacred place in Greek religion). In this case as well, some sources report that the Spartan authorities were forced to ask for the help of foreign religious specialists, who are designated as *psychagogoi* ("leaders of souls").[22]

Subversive Spirits

The mention of these very negative entities (the Erinyes of Clytemnestra or the angry ghost of Pausanias) evokes another aspect that is remarkably similar between Pauline and other ancient Mediterranean forms of possession. Oftentimes, the more-than-human beings that possess humans were conceived as the surviving spirits of deceased humans. In several traditions, the most powerful among these revenants belong to categories of dead that have seen their life cycle cut short in sudden or violent ways: People who have died young, or without proper burial, or who have been killed by others.[23] That is the case for the *pneuma* of Christ that possesses Paul as well, inasmuch as this is the surviving spirit of a Judean who had been executed by the Romans at a relatively young age. Without entering the thorny question of how well acquainted Paul was with the historical Jesus, it suffices it to say that he knew that Jesus had been crucified by the Romans. That event certainly played a significant role in shaping Paul's experience of possession by the Christ *pneuma*. The Pauline possession cult might have been seen with suspicion by imperial authorities, as was the cult of Bacchus, which was banned in the second century BCE.

22. Fuller discussion and references in Bazzana, *Having*, 94.

23. A landmark treatment of this phenomenon in Sarah Iles Johnston, *Restless Dead: Encounters between the Living and the Dead in Ancient Greece* (University of California Press 1999).

Pauline possession is recast to be more acceptable to Roman eyes in Acts of the Apostles. The *pneuma* that possesses the members of the Christ groups may have acquired a seditious aspect.

That being said, it is also worth pointing out that a "bad" character (defined by marginality and foreignness) was not unusual for more-than-human beings involved in cases of possession in the ancient Mediterranean world. And, most importantly, these features were not necessarily an obstacle for the phenomenon of possession to prove beneficial for a group or a community. This is quite common for figures who are heroized in traditional Greek religion, for example. "Heroes" are often "wicked" characters who are honored after death to control their activities as *daimones*. The city of Temesa established a cult for an unnamed member of Odysseus's party who had been stoned after raping a girl from the town. Likewise, the city of Astypalea conferred similar honors on Cleomedes, a boxer who had killed an entire group of children in a school seeking revenge for a victory denied to him in the Olympic games.[24] Even though possession has sources that can be deemed "negative," its products can be beneficial and one could count possession by the Christ *pneuma* in this number as well. Besides Christianity, the most important example in the ancient world is certainly that of Bacchic possession. Dionysus starts out as a foreign and dangerous deity, while the people possessed by his power go into fits of frenzy and madness. Nevertheless, the cult of Dionysus was systematized into mainstream religious practice with the attached benefits of prophecy and healings. As attested also by ethnographic research on possession cults, spirits are often foreign and compel their hosts to behave in ways that are sometimes highly irregular or immoral. So, to establish whether an emergent case of possession should be considered "good" or "bad" is a complex task, carried out in a sophisticated triangulation between religious experts and the participating audiences. All the information at our disposal leads to the conclusion that ancient Mediterranean possession was evenly suspended between madness, subversion, and beneficial outputs. In this perspective, it is understandable that Paul may be concerned that the outward perception of the Corinthian group's meetings might be perceived as *mania* ("madness"), as he states in 1 Corinthians 14:23 ("If, therefore, the entire church comes together and all

24. Cases like these are treated in detail in Monica Visintin, *La vergine e l'eroe: Temesa e la leggenda di Euthymos di Locri* [English: *The Virgin and the Hero: Temesa and the Legend of Euthymos of Locri*] (Edipuglia, 1992).

speak in tongues, and outsiders or unbelievers entre, will they not say that you are out of your mind?").

Pneuma

In recent years, several prominent scholars have provided descriptions of the Pauline *pneuma* that look very different from the one presented here. For instance, John Ashton surmises that a good metaphor to describe the *pneuma* could be "electricity," while Stanley Stowers suggests that it could be considered akin to "cosmic stuff."[25] The latter proposal is especially important, because it is grounded in a much more fundamental redescription of Pauline thought. As such, it touches directly on the present issue of Paul's possession against its ancient Mediterranean context. Stowers's "cosmic stuff" is part of a more general thrust to revise our understanding of Paul in light of cosmological and ethical categories related to ancient philosophical tradition labeled as "Stoicism." Indeed, as pointed out also in a very convincing manner by Troels Engberg-Pedersen, the connections between Pauline thought and Stoic theories are undeniable and quite illuminating.[26] There is little doubt that ancient Stoicism assumed that the entire universe was pervaded by a constitutive and effective element that was designated as *pneuma*. In this perspective, it is quite useful to recognize that such a *pneuma* was not conceived as immaterial at all, which is very important in order to understand several complex Pauline passages, notably Paul's discussion of the resurrected body in 1 Corinthians 15. Moreover, the similarities between such conceptions and the language used by Paul in speaking about the body of Christ constituted through the pervasive presence of the Christ *pneuma* are also quite intriguing.

That being said, however, focusing too exclusively on Stoic concepts leads to a significant problem: The "spirit" conceived as something completely impersonal is certainly fitting for ancient Stoicism, but not so much for Paul in his very personal dealings with possession by the Christ *pneuma*. In principle, it is completely possible that Paul might have used the Stoic-looking categories

25. Stanley K. Stowers, "Kinds of Myth, Meals, and Power: Paul and the Corinthians," in *Redescribing Paul and the Corinthians*, ed. Ron Cameron and Merrill P. Miller (Society of Biblical Literature, 2011), 105–49.

26. Troels Engberg-Pedersen, *Cosmology and Self in the Apostle Paul: The Material Spirit* (Oxford University Press, 2010).

and language that were available to him to express and make sense of his new, emergent experience of possession. But the Pauline conception of *pneuma* also has other dimensions.

Interestingly, part of the issue here is the very understanding of Stoicism that is advanced as a crucial piece of supporting evidence for the hypothesis of Paul's use of Stoic ideas. It is by no means clear that ancient Stoics denied that demons existed alongside the impersonal *pneuma* that constituted the foundation of their cosmic providential order. As noted in a recent contribution on this subject by Keimpe Algra, to think that Stoics denied the existence of personal demons risks projecting modern Western cosmological and anthropological categories on these ancient philosophers.[27] On the contrary, even Stoics were fully part of the ancient Mediterranean world and so shared some fundamental religious ideas that would be difficult to expect in modern European philosophers like Spinoza or Locke. Despite the paucity of systematic evidence on ancient Stoicism at our disposal, it seems that belief on the existence of personal demons remained more or less present in the philosophical school, even though it may appear difficult to reconcile with other tenets. In particular, Stoic philosophers did write entire books about topics that are totally expected within such a cosmological scheme, for example on the participation of demons in divination. Indeed, some surviving fragments seem also to attest a Stoic understanding of demons as internal impulses of the human soul or of demons acting as supernatural guardian "angels" for humans. These are all traits that Paul could have easily reconciled with his experience of possession as we have seen above.

Conclusion

The brief observations assembled so far have shown that comparing Pauline possession with analogous ancient Mediterranean phenomena is an exercise that can yield a significant advance in our understanding both of Paul's groups and their context. Possession played a crucial role in shaping the religious imagination, group identity, and common practice of Pauline groups. As such, besides the foundational influence of Jewish traditions, Pauline possession

27. Algra emphasizes the analogy between Stoicism and Spinoza on this point; see "Stoics on Souls and Demons: Reconstructing Stoic Demonology," in *Demons and the Devil in Ancient and Medieval Christianity*, ed. Nienke Vos and Willemien Otten (Brill, 2011), 71–96.

shared important elements with similar phenomena attributed to other ancient Mediterranean groups, as, for example, the belief in the existence of more-than-human beings and in the influence that these could exert on the human world both in positive and negative terms. Naturally, ideas that are attested for Paul and his groups could also be different from those attested for others. For instance, the Pauline understanding of *pneuma*, while sharing more than a few traits with ancient Stoicism, was also different in emphasizing the personal and autonomous character of individual spirits.

IV

Divination, Magic, and Astrology

CHAPTER NINE

Paul among the Pagan Prophets

Matthew T. Sharp
University of St. Andrews

Most people living in the ancient Mediterranean would have assumed that gods existed and that they communicated with humans in various ways. Paul is no exception. Nevertheless, most biblical scholars isolate Paul's methods of divine communication from those of his ancient context. One common way of doing this is by dividing methods of divine communication into two discrete categories: Prophecy (Greek: *prophēteia*) and divination (Greek: *manteia, mantikē*).[1] Prophecy, it is held, is a means of divine communication in which a god intervenes on his or her own initiative to speak directly to or through a chosen individual. Divination, on the other hand, is often understood as the human endeavor to discover the will of a god through the rational interpretation of signs or omens. As one influential treatment put it, "The diviner seeks to obtain God's answer to man's questions; the prophet seeks man's answer to God's question."[2] More than just a heuristic distinction between divinatory practices, this distinction has often served as a dividing line to separate ancient Judaism and Christianity from all other ancient Mediterranean religious traditions. While Jews and Christians like Paul availed themselves of the direct revelation afforded by prophecy, divination is seen as a distinctly pagan practice.[3]

1. The English word "divination" is derived from the Latin word *divinatio,* which Cicero notes is a translational equivalent of *mantikē* (Cicero, *Divination* 1.1).

2. Abraham J. Heschel, *The Prophets* (Harper & Row, 1962), 459.

3. On the Hebrew prophets, see, e.g., Heschel, *Prophets,* 454–59. Such terminology and assumptions are embedded in most work on early Christianity, e.g., Craig S. Keener, *Acts: An Exegetical Commentary,* vol. 1 (Baker Academic, 2012), 886–902; Christopher Forbes,

This familiar division derives from a misreading and a conflation of two different streams of ancient evidence. It is true, on the one hand, that ancient Jewish literature polemicized against some of the ways in which foreign nations communicated with their gods, and they used the Greek terminology of "divination" in these polemics. Deuteronomy 18:9–14 in its Greek translation, for example, prohibits Israelites from practicing divination (*manteuomenos manteian*) alongside a number of related and overlapping practices prevalent in the foreign nations that they are about to dispossess (18:10). While the nations listen to "omens and divinations" (*klēdonōn kai manteiōn*), Israelites should heed only a prophet (*prophētēs*) like Moses (18:14–19). Here indeed is a distinction between divination and prophecy. But there is nothing in this passage to suggest that the distinction describes two fundamentally different types of communication divided along the lines of inspiration versus interpretation, or divine versus human.

This distinction derives instead from a different stream of ancient evidence in which certain (pagan) philosophical writers distinguished between natural or inspired divination on the one hand, such as oracles, dreams, and visions, and artificial or technical divination on the other, which involves the interpretation of signs (e.g., Plato, *Phaedrus* 244b–d; *Timaeus* 71e–72b; Cicero, *Divination* 1.12).[4] Like in the modern scholarly division, there is a clear value judgment built into this distinction, which favors those methods of divination that are more clearly seen as divine or inspired. Most recent scholars of ancient Greek divination now question how well these categories applied to the actual practice of divination in the ancient world, and they attribute this philosophical distinction rather to the particular rhetorical motives of Plato and Cicero.[5] Numerous examples do not fit neatly on either side of the line. Dreams, for instance, are inspired by a god but also often need interpretation. Interpretations themselves may also be inspired by a god. The figure of Calchas in Homer's *Iliad,* for example, is introduced as a "bird interpreter," but the

---

Prophecy and Inspired Speech in Early Christianity and Its Hellenistic Environment, WUNT 2/75 (Mohr Siebeck, 1995).

4. The Greek word for "inspired" is *entheos,* which literally means "to have a god inside."

5. See, e.g., Sarah Iles Johnston, *Ancient Greek Divination* (Wiley-Blackwell, 2008), 8–9, 28; Michael Attyah Flower, *The Seer in Ancient Greece* (University of California Press, 2008), 84–91; Peter T. Struck, *Divination and Human Nature: A Cognitive History of Intuition in Classical Antiquity* (Princeton University Press, 2016), 16–19.

text also says he was given this divinatory gift by Apollo (*Il.* 1.70).[6] Later Stoic thinkers would seek theories that explained the working of all types of divine communication within a single mechanism, so the distinction appears more rhetorical and heuristic than ontological. More importantly, though, none of the texts that make this distinction assign the label "divination" (*manteia, mantikē, divinatio*) to the purely technical methods. Divination is the broad category of divine communication under which further subdivisions can be made. If one were to restrict the term to one particular type of communication, the philosophical sources are clear that it should refer to the inspired type rather than the other way around (Plato, *Phaedrus* 244b–d; Cicero, *Divination* 1.5).

There is nothing in the ancient sources to support the distinction of Jewish or Christian inspired prophecy versus pagan technical divination. This distinction emerges from the conflation of Israelite polemic against foreign divinatory practices in texts such as Deuteronomy 18, with the pagan philosophical distinction between two different types of divine communication. If "divination" in ancient texts instead refers to a broad category encompassing a variety of types of divine communication, then it prompts us to reconsider what exactly the similarities and differences are between Paul and others in their ancient Mediterranean environment, who both claimed to relay the words and will of a god.

Pagan Divination in the Acts of the Apostles

A later text, Acts of the Apostles, which is closer to the apostle Paul, helps to focus the question. The Greek root for pagan divination occurs only once in the canonical New Testament (Acts 16:16). In this story, Paul encounters an enslaved girl whom the narrator says had a "python spirit" (*pneuma pythōna*) that enabled her to perform divination (*manteuomenē*).[7] She follows Paul and his companions, screaming, "these men are slaves of the Most High God, who

6. "Bird interpreter" = *oiōnopolos*. Plato uses the word *oiōnistikē* to refer to all types of technical, interpretive divination (*Phaedrus* 244c–d). The related word *oiōnizomenos* appears in the list of banned practices in Deut 18:10.

7. The NRSVue translates *pneuma pythōna* as "spirit of divination," which is a more interpretive gloss (on python spirits, see below). It translates *manteuomenē* as "fortune telling," which probably reflects the narrow and pejorative view modern scholars have of ancient divination.

proclaim to you a way of salvation" (16:17), until Paul becomes annoyed and casts the spirit out of the girl (16:18).[8]

The girl's divinatory actions and abilities in this passage fit none of the usual stereotypes about pagan divination. Divination here is not a merely human activity, since the girl is said to be inspired by a spirit. The extra detail about a "python" spirit links the girl's divination to the god Apollo and his famous oracular sanctuary at Delphi, where Apollo is said to have slain the giant serpent Python and established the Pythian games.[9] The prophetic priestess at Delphi, known as the "Pythia," was famous for giving oracles under Apollo's inspiration. Plutarch, a Platonist philosopher and priest at Delphi in the first to second centuries CE, knew of people called "Pythons" who claimed to have a god or daimon inside them, which enabled them to speak oracles (*On the Decline of Oracles* 414e).[10]

The inspired speech uttered by the girl shows that divination is also not limited to the interpretation of signs. The Greek verb *krazein*, which I have translated "screaming," is frequently used by Luke to describe the general shouting of a crowd, so it may mean nothing more here than that she is being loud and emotive. The same intensity of emotion, though, often characterizes the cries of spirits and possessed people (e.g., Luke 4:33, 41; 8:28; 9:39). Paul himself, in his letters, only uses this verb to introduce spirit-inspired speech, whether it be the Aramaic words that the spirit of Christ screams through believers (Gal 4:6; Rom 8:15) or the cry of the prophet Isaiah (Rom 9:27).

From the perspective of the narrator of Acts, the enslaved girl's spirit-inspired speech is also undeniably true. The description of Paul and his companions as "slaves of the Most High God, who proclaim to you a way of salvation" is perfectly consistent with the presentation of Paul in Acts and is also not a bad summary of Paul's own self-understanding in his letters (e.g., Rom 1:1–7; 16).[11] Paul still

8. All translations of ancient texts are my own unless, unless otherwise stated.

9. On the various versions of the Apollo and Python myth, see Daniel Ogden, *Drakōn: Dragon Myth and Serpent Cult in the Greek and Roman Worlds* (Oxford University Press, 2013), 40–48.

10. Plutarch also calls the same people "belly-talkers" (*engastrimythous*), another term that occurs on Deuteronomy's list of banned practices (Deut 18:11).

11. Paul prefers to call himself a slave of Jesus Christ rather than of the Most High God (Rom 1:1; Gal 1:10; Phil 1:1). He does, however, occasionally say that his audiences have been "enslaved to God" (Rom 6:22) and "serve the living and true God" (1 Thess 1:9).

exorcizes the spirit from the girl, which establishes his fundamental opposition to the spirit's activity. Scholars have long sought a rational reason for Paul's desire to silence the spirit's speech, but the only reason the text gives is that Paul was worn out or "annoyed" (Acts 16:18).[12] The text does draw attention to the exploitation of the girl's divinatory abilities by her masters for profit (16:16, 19), but this is not given as the reason for the exorcism. Even if this were a factor, it would be a comment on the use and exploitation of divinatory gifts rather than on divination itself.

Pagan divination, in Paul's only explicit encounter with it in the New Testament, is thus portrayed as both inspired and true. Its only major problem, as also appears to be the case in texts like Deuteronomy 18, is that it is inspired by the wrong god. The clash between Paul and paganism in this text is a clash between rival gods, and Paul's exorcism of the divinatory spirit shows his god to be more powerful. While the question of which god is speaking is undoubtedly an important theological distinction to make, we should not allow this distinction to occlude other more analytically oriented questions that aim to contextualize Paul within his broader pagan environment. If we temporarily suspend the theological polemics, we can engage in a more neutral comparison of how gods, daimons, or spirits were thought to communicate with humans in the ancient Mediterranean world. Divination is perhaps not the word Paul would have used to describe his activities, but it is the word used by most scholars of ancient Mediterranean religion (and probably much of Paul's pagan audience) to categorize similar practices.[13] In the rest of this essay, I will briefly survey some of the evidence in Paul's undisputed letters for the various ways that he engages in communication with divine beings, and how these fit into the broader context of ancient Mediterranean divination. I will then focus more detailed attention on a particular passage (1 Cor 1:18–3:4), which demonstrates that not only Paul's divinatory practices but also Paul's thought about divine communication can be profitably situated "within paganism."

---

12. Craig Keener discusses a number of scholarly rationales for Paul's opposition and offers his own solution: *Acts*, 3:2457–64.

13. For a complementary argument for "divination" as a useful category for analyzing Paul, see Jennifer Eyl, *Signs, Wonders, and Gifts: Divination in the Letters of Paul* (Oxford University Press, 2019).

Paul's Divinatory Practices in Context

Paul's means of divination can be heuristically divided into four categories: Inspired speech, visionary epiphanies, the interpretation of written oracles, and the interpretation of nonverbal signs. In practice, these four categories blur into one another as each type of divine communication can be understood as a "sign" of some sort, and each type of sign requires varied degrees of interpretation. Some of these divinatory practices also occur in conjunction with each other in various combinations. The fuzziness between these categories only demonstrates the utility of the category of divination as a whole since it brings together various related aspects of Paul's letters that scholars normally treat quite separately.[14]

We have already seen that the enslaved girl of Acts 16 produces spirit-inspired divinatory speech because she "has a python spirit," and this puts her in a class of other inspired figures who claimed to speak at the instigation of a god or spirit. Paul also claims to "have" a spirit (1 Cor 7:40; cf. 2 Cor 4:13; Rom 8:9), which enables him to speak with divine authority on a number of different issues.[15] The precise method varies. Sometimes the spirit directly cries out from within him (Gal 4:6; Rom 8:14–16; cf. 1 Cor 14:14). Sometimes he appears to be given particular words to say although these are notoriously hard to pinpoint with accuracy (e.g., 1 Thess 4:15–17; 1 Cor 7:12; 11:23). At other times, Paul's possession of this spirit provides him more generally with divine wisdom and knowledge on matters great and small that he can dispense to his assemblies (1 Cor 2:6–10; 7:40; 12:8; cf. Rom 11:25; 1 Cor 15:51).

As well as inspiring speech, gods were also widely known to appear to people, either in dreams or while awake, in order to dispense information.[16] Such divine epiphanies could be deliberately sought. Incubation shrines, particularly associated with the healing gods Sarapis, Isis, and Asclepius, offered inquirers a place to sleep in the hope that a god would encounter them in the night. Papyri from Egypt also preserve spells and initiations that a person

14. For a more detailed treatment of the categories and texts in this section, see Matthew T. Sharp, *Divination and Philosophy in the Letters of Paul*, ESRA (Edinburgh University Press, 2023).

15. On spirit possession, see Giovanni Bazzana's contribution to this volume.

16. On divine epiphanies, see Georgia Petridou, *Divine Epiphany in Greek Literature and Culture* (Oxford University Press, 2015) and Sarah Rollens's contribution to this volume.

could undergo in order to prepare for a visionary encounter. At other times a god might show up unannounced with information and instructions for a chosen individual.[17] Paul claims to have experienced multiple "visions and revelations of the Lord" (2 Cor 12:1), which provided him with privileged information, not least the contents of his gospel message (Gal 1:11–12). Like the visitors of incubation oracles, Paul may have also sought out an oracle for physical healing. He says in 2 Corinthians 12:8 that he invoked the Lord three times for deliverance from his "thorn in the flesh," using the same verb, *parekalesa*, as did suppliants at the shrines of Asclepius.[18] Paul reports that these invocations did eventually result in an oracle although not perhaps with the answer he was hoping for (2 Cor 12:9).

Oracles and epiphanies can still be generally seen to fall on the inspired side of the divinatory division. Opening up Paul's repertoire of divine communication to the whole range of divinatory methods helps us to further appreciate the ways in which Paul was not just a passive recipient of divine information but was actively involved in the interpretation of divinely sent messages.

Paul not only sought and spoke fresh oracles through the spirit, but he also devoted considerable space in his letters to interpreting past oracles that had been preserved in sacred texts. Paul calls these texts the "oracles [*logia*] of God" (Rom 3:2) and regularly claims that they predicted various facets of his gospel. With frequent recourse to the prefix *pro* ("before"), Paul says that his good news was "pre-promised" (*proepēngeilato*) by prophets in sacred texts (Rom 1:2). These texts foresaw (*proidousa*) that gentiles would be justified by faith and so pre-announced (*proeuēngelisato*) the good news to Abraham (Gal 3:8). Jesus's crucifixion was forewritten (*proegraphē*) in sacred texts as were many other things, which Paul says should give believers hope (Gal 3:1; Rom 15:4).[19] In these passages, Paul interprets scriptural texts like the oracles (*logia*)

---

17. On incubation shrines, see Gil H. Renberg, *Where Dreams May Come: Incubation Sanctuaries in the Greco-Roman World*, 2 vols. RGRW 184 (Brill, 2017). On the Magical Papyri, see Iles Johnston, *Ancient Greek Divination*, 155–58.

18. Adolf Deissmann, *Light From the Ancient East: The New Testament Illustrated by Recently Discovered Texts of the Graeco-Roman World*, trans. Lionel R. M. Strachan (Hodder & Stoughton, 1910), 310–11.

19. Heidi Wendt, "Galatians 3:1 as an Allusion to Textual Prophecy," *JBL* 135 (2016): 369–89.

that Thucydides reports were circulated during the Peloponnesian War, which predicted the outcome of various battles, or like the oracles collected in the Sibylline books at Rome, which were thought to predict various moments in Roman history.[20] All such oracles need interpretation and Paul demonstrates great exegetical prowess in deciphering and unveiling the true meaning of these divine messages and how they relate to his audiences' circumstances.

Just as Paul believed God was active in inspiring the words of ancient prophets, so too did he see God at work in sending signs and omens. A sign, sent by a god and needing interpretation, is the fundamental feature of all divination in the ancient Mediterranean. In one sense, oracles, epiphanies, and texts are all specific types of divine signs that need decoding. But the term more regularly applies to any number of nonverbal and nontextual signs. Some objects and occurrences developed conventional divinatory value and formalized systems of interpretation such as the flight of birds or the liver of an animal. At other times, one could discern a divine sign in any sort of remarkable or otherwise inexplicable occurrence ranging from extreme weather to a well-timed sneeze. Paul, on occasion, says that his activities were accompanied by "signs and omens" (*sēmeia kai terata*), which helped to validate his message and demonstrated that he came with divine approval (Rom 15:19; 2 Cor 12:12; cf. 1 Thess 1:5; 1 Cor 2:4; Gal 3:5). Paul is also adept at interpreting signs of divine displeasure, as when he tells the Corinthians that people have been getting sick due to ritual error at the Lord's Supper (1 Cor 11:27–32), or when he tells the Romans that God's wrath has been revealed from heaven against all impiety (Rom 1:18).

These examples are only a sample of all the passages in Paul's letters that show him to be actively engaged in seeking, interpreting, and communicating divine messages. But they are sufficient to demonstrate that Paul participated in a variety of divinatory practices that cohere with the broader ways that gods were thought to communicate with humans in the ancient Mediterranean world. These coherences are obscured by the usual categories we use, such as "revelation" or "Paul's use of Scripture," but the category of divination exposes

20. See Thucydides, *History of the Peloponnesian War* 2.8.3; 2.21.3; 2.54.2; 5.26.3–4; Dio Cassius, *Roman History* 57.18.4–5; 62.18.3–5.

the connections both between the practices themselves and Paul's broader religious environment.

The Physics of Divination

Redescribing Paul's access to divine knowledge in terms of divination opens up comparative angles on Paul's practices that show him to be a comprehensible figure within the broader Mediterranean world. The category of divination also helps shed light on Paul's theology. That is, the ways he publicly theorizes the nature and workings of the gods. A good example of this is 1 Corinthians 1:18–3:4, where Paul reflects on some of the mechanics of divine communication and justifies how his message can be classified as divine wisdom. Throughout, he wages a polemical war with alternative explanations while, at the same time, his own explanations depend and innovate upon established discourses in his wider context.

In 1 Corinthians 1:18, Paul speaks of the failure of mortal humans to comprehend the message of the cross: "For the message about the cross is foolishness to those who are perishing, but to us who are being saved it is the power of God" (1 Cor 1:18). In 1:22 Paul creates his own Judaism/ Hellenism divide when he says that "Jews ask for signs [*sēmeia*] and Greeks seek wisdom [*sophia*]." It is interesting, given the classic distinction between Jewish prophecy and Greek divination, that Paul characterizes his fellow Jews as those who seek after divinatory signs (*sēmeia*). The Greeks, on the other hand, Paul characterizes not for their pagan divinatory practices but their philosophy, their love of wisdom (*sophia*). In any case, the message of a crucified Messiah, he says, confounds them both.

Paul's dismissal does not mean, from his perspective, that Jesus's crucifixion does not demonstrate true wisdom, nor that it is not a genuine sign of God's disposition and activity in the world. He goes on to say a few verses later that "among the initiated we do speak wisdom, but not a wisdom of this age" (1 Cor 2:6). This true wisdom, however, can only be understood through divinatory means, namely through the possession of God's spirit:

> But God has revealed [these things] to us through the spirit. For the spirit searches everything, even the depths of God. For what person knows the things of a person except the person's spirit that is in him?

> In the same way, no one knows the things of God except God's spirit. And we did not receive the spirit of the cosmos but the spirit that is out of God, so that we might know the gifts given to us by God, things which we also speak in words not taught by human wisdom but taught by spirit, interpreting spiritual things to spiritual people. (1 Cor 2:10–13)

We have already seen spirit possession as one prominent means of conveying divinatory knowledge. In this passage, Paul begins to expand further on the nature of spirit, how it works, and what it can accomplish. While this discussion occurs in a critique of the adequacy of contemporary forms of divination and philosophy, Paul's own explanation draws from and innovates upon developing philosophical discussions about the role of spirits, souls, intellect, and daimons in the process of divination. His discussion of "spirit" (*pneuma*) in particular begins to take on a more philosophical nuance which is sometimes better translated as "breath." To appreciate these points, we need to take a step back and survey this conversation in a few different authors from Plato to Plutarch before returning to Paul's own engagement with this topic.

Plato: Images and Apparitions in the Liver

Plato's *Timaeus* was the most influential cosmological work in antiquity. Philo, for instance, a Jewish near-contemporary of Paul, used its philosophical framework as a lens through which to interpret the biblical creation account of Genesis 1.[21] In the *Timaeus*, the eponymous character gives an account of the creation of the world by a divine craftsman (or Demiurge) and the subsequent creation of humans by the newly created race of heavenly gods.

When recounting the creation of the human and the placing of the soul within the body, Timaeus specifies the soul as the part of the person that receives divinatory messages (*Timaeus* 70d–72b). He divides the human soul into three parts: The rational, the spirited, and the appetitive. The rational soul is closest to the divine and is elsewhere described as a *daimon* or divinity placed in the person's head (90a). Divination, however, is comprehended by the lowest, appetitive, part of the soul. This part of the soul does not understand reason but only responds to images (*eidōla*) and apparitions (*phantasmata*),

21. See David T. Runia, *Philo of Alexandria and the Timaeus of Plato*, PhA 44 (Brill, 1986).

and so it is encased in the belly of a person to prevent it from interfering with the rational soul in the head. Even though scholars are used to thinking of Plato as the architect of the immaterial soul, it is striking how physical the soul appears in this account. It occupies space in a physical body and physically interacts with the bodily organs.

The liver is placed in the same part of the body as the appetitive soul so that it can translate mental images from the rational, divine part to the appetitive part in order to keep it under control. One way this happens is when the rational soul breathes out gentle images, which use the liver's sweetness to put the appetitive soul into an ordered and measured state. In this state, this part of the soul can spend the night "experiencing divination in its sleep" (71d).[22] The term for "breath," *epipnoia*, is Plato's term for divine inspiration, used in other dialogues to speak of divination as a breath from Apollo (*Phaedrus* 265b). These impressions and this breath are not the divinatory images themselves, but they put the soul into the right condition to receive them.

It is not enough, however, for the more animal and disordered state of the soul to be tamed. In order to receive true divination, it must also be free of the influence of reason and intelligence. This can happen when in sleep, in times of sickness, or in moments of inspiration (*enthousiasmos*). Reason will be required again to interpret the significance of the things seen and heard in these states, but this should be done by someone other than the one who received the divinatory images and is an entirely rational and logical process (*Timaeus* 71e). Plato as we have seen, strictly separates inspiration from interpretation as two separate activities, although in this case they are both still necessary to be able to receive and understand divinatory information.

Thus, for Plato, divination takes place within the human body as information is breathed or inspired from the rational, divine part of the soul to the lower, appetitive part of the soul via the bodily organ of the liver. Divinatory knowledge is much lower on Plato's epistemological scale of value than rational, discursive reasoning. It does not provide wisdom, but it is still a divine gift given by God as compensation to the lower part of the soul so that it may attain some measure of truth (*Timaeus* 71e).

22. The use of the liver in this context reflects the traditional role of the liver in hepatoscopy. See further, Struck, *Divination and Human Nature*, 83–84.

Posidonius and the Stoics: Sympathetic Connections in the Pneuma

From Plato we move to Posidonius, a Stoic philosopher of the late second/early first century BCE. His views on divination are mainly available to us through Cicero's compendious work *On Divination*, which makes use of them. Cicero says that Posidonius enumerated three ways that the gods communicated with humans in dreams, although Cicero seems to expand this category to refer to broader moments of divine inspiration:

> In the first the soul foresees all by itself because of the relationship with the gods it possesses; in the second, the air is full of immortal souls on which the marks of truth are clear, as though hallmarked; in the third, the gods themselves speak with people as they sleep. (Cicero, *Divination* 1.64)[23]

Posidonius affirms direct visions of gods in dreams as well as the presence of multiple souls or spirits in the air that can communicate information. The first option is related to this idea: "The soul foresees by itself because of its kinship with the gods." For Posidonius and other Stoics, the human soul is a bodily substance composed of "hot breath" (*pneuma*), which is a partitioned piece of the breath that makes up the soul of the cosmos and can in some sense be identified with God.[24] The entire cosmos is a single living organism, connected and held together by divine spirit. It is these pneumatic connections between human and divine souls that make divination possible. According to Cicero, inspired types of divination can be explained physically with reference to the nature of the gods themselves:

> . . . From which, as the most learned philosophers agree, our own souls are drawn and gathered. Since the universe is filled and packed with

23. Translations of Cicero are all modified from *Cicero on Divination: Book 1*, ed. and trans. David Wardle (Oxford University Press, 2006).

24. "Hot breath": Diogenes Laertius, *Lives* 7.157. For a helpful overview and discussion of the God-cosmos-soul relation in Stoic physics, see Francesco Ademollo, "Cosmic and Individual Soul in Early Stoicism," in *Body and Soul in Hellenistic Philosophy*, ed. Brad Inwood and James Warren (Cambridge University Press, 2020), 113–144.

> eternal intelligence and the divine mind, human souls are necessarily affected by their sympathy with divine souls. (Cicero, *Divination* 1.110)

"Sympathy" is a technical Stoic term to talk about the interconnected nature of the cosmos by which human souls can communicate with divine souls in what Peter Struck calls a "*pneuma-pneuma* transfer of information."[25] In terms reminiscent of Plato, the soul is hindered from receiving this sort of communication in its normal waking state. Unlike Plato, though, it is not rationality from which the soul needs to be free, but rather the general necessities of waking bodily life:

> But when they are awake our souls are subject to the necessities of life, and hampered by the restraints of the body, are hindered from association with the divine. . . . In fact the human soul does not divine naturally, unless it is so unrestrained and free that it has absolutely nothing to do with the body, as happens only for prophets and dreamers. (Cicero, *Divination* 1.110–13)

While dreams obviously occur in the natural state of sleep, waking prophets often require an external divine impulse to remove the soul from bodily influence (1.66). This occurs, according to Cicero, through the gods diffusing their power throughout the cosmos, "sometimes enclosing it in caverns in the earth" (1.79). This power accounts for the inspiration of famous seers such as the Pythia at Delphi. The Pythia's inspiration comes from the "power of the earth," which was transmitted through subterranean vapours or exhalations (1.38, 80, 114). Greek writers described these exhalations with the same word used previously for breath or spirit (*pneuma*), calling it an "inspiring spirit" (*pneuma enthousiastikon*, Strabo, *Geography* 9.3.5) or a sacred spirit (*hieron pneuma*, Dio Cassius, *Roman History* 62.14.3). For Plato, this sort of inspired divination was distinct from the rational interpretation of signs. For Posidonius, however, the divine breath connecting the entire cosmos accounts for both inspired and

25. Struck, *Divination and Human Nature*, 210; see also the broader discussion in 208–11.

technical divination as the soul is able to discern the interlocking causes of events transmitted through *pneuma*.[26]

We can thus see in Posidonius a number of themes carried over from Plato, particularly the idea of an innate capacity of divination in the human soul, which is activated either when the body is asleep or inspired by some sort of divine breath. These themes are significantly transformed though so that rather than one part of the soul communicating with another, divination is projected onto the entire cosmos. Both natural and technical forms are enabled by the entire cosmos being connected through divine breath, which communicates information from divine souls to human souls.

Plutarch: The Divinatory Breath

One final author to discuss before returning to Paul is Plutarch. Chronologically, Plutarch comes slightly later than Paul, but he is a good example of the eclectic nature of post-Hellenistic philosophy that interprets Plato's dialogues in the light of Stoic and other later philosophical developments. Plutarch's Delphic dialogues are full of wide-ranging conversations about the nature and working of divination, particularly as it was practiced at Delphi, as well as a host of other philosophical matters. I will focus for now on how he builds on the common idea of the innate divinatory potential of the soul.

In discussing the manner of the Pythia's inspiration at Delphi, Plutarch, like both Plato and Posidonius, affirms that the soul possesses an innate power of divination that is activated in sleep, at the point of death, and in moments of inspiration. Like Plato, Plutarch links these moments with the relaxing and withdrawing of reason and thought, but like Posidonius he also ties it into a more general escape from the body's mortal nature (*On the Decline of Oracles* 432c). Again, like Posidonius, inspiration is kindled by "the earth [sending] forth many powers" that affect the disposition of the soul (432d). The most potent of these powers is a form of divine breath or spirit (*pneuma*). This spirit shares a similar nature to the soul, so that when it comes into contact with the soul it produces a special disposition in the soul that enables divinatory knowledge (432d–e).

26. Struck, *Divination and Human Nature*, 201–8.

Paul: Searching the Depths of God

Returning to Paul in this context, we can identify a number of ways that Paul's discussion of the reception of divine wisdom in 1 Corinthians 1–3 connects to and innovates upon the philosophical themes that I have just sketched. First, like the philosophical authors described above, Paul also discusses how divine communication can happen. In 1 Corinthians 2:9, he quotes an unknown oracle to the effect that God's plan cannot be known by the normal sensory perception of the eyes, the ears, or even the heart. In verse 10, he says that these things have been revealed to Paul and his associates by the means of spirit, which "searches everything, even the depths of God." This language, as Stanley Stowers has remarked, "indicates contiguity and extension" between God and people through shared possession of this same substance.[27] It is reminiscent of the descriptions of the soul in Posidonius and Plutarch that "sees everything in nature" (Cicero, *Divination* 1.115) when unencumbered by the body and "ranges amid the irrational and imaginative realms of the future" (Plutarch, *On the Decline of Oracles* 432c).[28] Spirit, or breath, by its very nature, can bridge the gap between the highest and lowest forms of matter in the universe, gaining knowledge of everything and connecting the divine and human spheres.

Paul goes on to distinguish different types of spirit: The spirit of a person, the spirit of the cosmos, and the spirit from God. The human spirit inside a person is best understood as something akin to the soul within the body. It is the breath that God breathed into Adam so that he became a "living soul" (Gen 2:7; quoted by Paul in 1 Cor 15:45). The Stoics gave the name *psychikos*, "soulish" or "animate," to the breath that made up the human soul and made people capable of movement and sensation (Galen, *Medical Introduction* 14).[29] Paul also calls people with human spirit inside them *psychikos* people (1 Cor

27. Stanley K. Stowers, "The Dilemma of Paul's Physics: Features Stoic-Platonist or Platonist-Stoic?" in *From Stoicism to Platonism: The Development of Philosophy, 100 BCE–100 CE*, ed. Troels Engberg-Pedersen (Cambridge University Press, 2017), 236.

28. Troels Engberg-Pedersen also cites the Stoic statement that "intellect (*nous*) permeates every part of [the universe]" (Diogenes Laertius, *Lives* 7.139). Troels Engberg-Pedersen, *Cosmology and Self in the Apostle Paul: The Material Spirit* (Oxford University Press, 2010), 228n42.

29. On this text, see Phillip Sidney Horky, "Cosmic Spiritualism among the Pythagoreans, Stoics, Jews and Early Christians," in *Cosmos in the Ancient World*, ed. Phillip Sidney Horky (Cambridge University Press, 2019), 279–80.

2:14) and later says that they have *psychikos* bodies (15:44–46). Being God's own breath, the soul shares some kinship with God, but Paul agrees with his philosophical contemporaries that in its current state it can only know human things (1 Cor 2:11). In order to understand the hidden plans of God, the human soul needs a fresh infusion of another breath directly from God (vv. 11–12).

Paul is careful to distinguish God's spirit from what he calls the spirit of the cosmos. In the philosophical context I have sketched, this most naturally refers to the breath that permeates the world and is particularly potent in caverns and subterranean vapours. Plutarch and Posidonius did not distinguish this breath from God but saw it as the diffusion of God's own power. Paul's denial of effective knowledge to the spirit of the cosmos would then appear to be an example of his polemic against the standard explanations for pagan divination. Similar to what we saw in Acts, though, Paul does not take issue with the actual mechanism of divination (they both involve varieties of spirit). Instead, the issue is which spirit is inspiring the Corinthians and where it comes from (cf. 1 Cor 12:3). Paul positions the spirit that he and his companions have received as the only one that comes directly from the true God and provides access to the depths of God's knowledge.

This spirit still acts in the ways a pagan would expect breath to act. Like Plutarch's description of the holy divinatory breath that enters the body and enables the soul to learn divinatory knowledge, Paul's divine breath also enters the body (in the heart, Gal 4:6; 2 Cor 1:22) and upgrades the person's cognitive capacity so that he can know the things of God.[30] On a broader scale, just as the Stoic spirit held the whole cosmos together as a single body providing it with both unity and differentiation, Paul's spirit also creates one body out of Christ's followers providing both unity and differentiation in roles (1 Cor 12:4–13).[31] When scholars notice these "pagan" elements in Paul's thought, they often explain them away as Paul's cynical appropriation of ideas in the

30. Plutarch's word for the temperament or mixture created in the soul is *krasis* (*On the Decline of Oracles* 432e). Matthew Thiessen argues that ancient discussions of *krasis* also provide the best analogy for understanding the reception of *pneuma* in Paul's letters. Matthew Thiessen, *Paul and the Gentile Problem* (Oxford University Press, 2016), 111–15.

31. See further, Michelle V. Lee, *Paul, the Stoics, and the Body of Christ*, SNTS Monograph Series 137 (Cambridge University Press, 2006); Horky, "Cosmic Spiritualism," 290–91; Engberg-Pedersen, *Cosmology and Self*, 169–71.

surrounding culture for the sake of promoting his gospel to a pagan audience. It is just as likely, though, that these ideas helped structure Paul's own theology and provided the formative categories that enabled him to articulate how he believed God had acted in the world.

As well as inspiration, God's breath also provides gifts of interpretation:

> Interpreting spiritual things to spiritual people. Now, the [merely] animate person does not accept the things of God's spirit, for it is folly to him and he is not able to know, because it is discerned spiritually. But the spiritual person discerns all things, but he is discerned by no one. (1 Cor 2:13–15)

Like the Stoic sage who can "discern with his soul the connection of every cause" (Cicero, *Divination* 1.127), the spiritual (or pneumatic) person can interpret and understand all things. This understanding puts Paul closer to Stoic ideas on divination than Platonic as interpretation is not a separate, purely rational process, but is included in the single operation of *pneuma*. This passage also suggests that receiving the spirit for Paul is more than just a temporary moment of ecstatic inspiration (although it can include that cf. 1 Cor 14). Rather it comes closer to what Michael Flower calls "intuitive divination," in which the gods grant particular people a special intuitive insight that enables them to correctly interpret divine signs.[32] Paul's contention that pneumatic things are "folly" to the merely animate person recalls his earlier assertion that a crucified Messiah is "folly" to the wisdom-loving gentiles. This whole discussion occurs in the context of how to correctly recognize and interpret the divine sign of a crucified Messiah and thus dissolves any rigid distinction between inspiration and interpretation in Paul's understanding of divine communication.

One final point of comparison with the philosophers before concluding. Once the human soul has been upgraded with divinatory gifts and connected to God's own spirit, Paul still identifies flesh as a factor that inhibits the proper use of the Corinthians' divinatory potential. In 1 Corinthians 3:1–4, he says he is not able to speak to the Corinthians as pneumatic people (even though they do have divine breath inside them), and they are not able to advance in

32. Flower, *Seer in Ancient Greece*, 87–88.

their use and understanding of these gifts because they are still fleshy (*sarkikos*). Paul points to their jealousy, strife and factionalism as evidence that they are still influenced by their flesh. We have seen that Plato saw rationality as the inhibiting factor in divination, and for Posidonius it was the bodily senses. Paul comes closest to Plutarch for whom it is the mortal, fleshly nature from which the soul needs to escape to receive divine revelation.

Conclusion

In the Myth of Timarchus, from Plutarch's work *On the Daimon of Socrates*, Timarchus visits the oracle of Trophonius for a divinatory consultation. At the oracle, his soul is transported from his body and given a tour of the cosmos by a daimonic guide. The guide explains to him:

> Every soul (*psyche*) partakes of mind (*nous*), and is not irrational or without understanding. But as much of it as is mixed with flesh and passions (*sarki . . . kai pathesin*), being altered in accordance with pleasures and pains, is turned toward the irrational. But not every soul is mixed the same way: rather some wholly sink into the body, and being thrown into disorder throughout, are altogether tossed about by passions during life. But others are mixed in part, and leave the purest part outside . . . Therefore, the part carried submerged in the body is called soul (*psyche*), but the part that is left free of corruption the many call mind (*nous*), thinking it is inside them . . . but those who surmise correctly name it *daimon*, as being external. (Plutarch, *Socrates' Sign* 591d–e)

Like Plato, with whom we began, Plutarch identifies the highest, rational part of the soul with a daimon, a divine being, which connects to the world soul that permeates the cosmos. Souls can submit in varying degrees to their outer daimons, but the responsive souls form the race of diviners (*to mantikon*) and inspired men among whom Plutarch counts Socrates (592c). Plutarch thus explains divine guidance in this instance as a mixture of the innate capacity of souls, freed from bodily, fleshly influence, and the external guidance of a divine soul identified as intellect or mind (*nous*) and divinity (*daimon*).

Paul can be read along similar lines. Even though believers now have Christ's own intellect (*nous*, 1 Cor 2:16), they are still being dominated by their flesh and passions. They instead need to let themselves be guided by their indwelling and possessing spirit, the intellect of Christ, which communicates divine things so that they do not sink back into the clouding influence of the flesh. Such an understanding connects with other Pauline passages such as Romans 8:5: "For those who are according to flesh set their minds on the things of the flesh, but those according to spirit set their minds on the things of the spirit," and Romans 12:2: "Do not be conformed to this age but be transformed by the renewing of the mind [*nous*] so that you may discover the will of God."

Discovering a god's will is one of the main aims of divination in the ancient world, and Paul's letters reveal the variety of methods he employs in this endeavor. By redescribing Paul's access to divine knowledge in terms of pagan divination we can cast fresh light on the many similarities that connect Paul's practices with his larger pagan environment. By reading Paul's arguments in the context of philosophical discussions about divination we can also see how his thought and theology sit comfortably within pagan philosophical discussions about spirit, souls, and daimons in the physics of divination.

CHAPTER TEN

Curses in the Pauline Letters

Laura Salah Nasrallah
Yale University

In Romans 9:3, Paul expresses a desire through the letter's writer, Tertius:[1] "I wish that I myself should be *anathema* (cursed) from the messiah for the sake of my siblings, my kinfolk according to the flesh."[2] In the letter we call 1 Corinthians (there was at least one earlier letter that we are missing), Paul and Sosthenes use vocabulary associated with cursing. First, a man is "handed over" to Satan (1 Cor 5:5). Second, the recipients of the letter hear that "no one is able to say, '*Anathema* Jesus,' in God's spirit, and no one is able to say, 'Master Jesus,' unless by a holy spirit" (1 Cor 12:3). Third, the letter ends with a curse: "Greetings by my own hand, that of Paul. If someone does not love the lord, let that one be *anathema*. *Marana tha* [Aramaic: Our Lord, come]" (1 Cor

---

Some materials for this essay were drawn from Laura Salah Nasrallah, "Judgment, Justice, and Destruction: *Defixiones* and 1 Corinthians," *JBL* 140 (2021): 347–67 and Laura Salah Nasrallah, *Ancient Christians and the Power of Curses: Magic, Aesthetics, and Justice* (Cambridge University Press, 2024). I express my gratitude to research assistant Austin Goodwin Andrews for help with the current essay.

1. Rom 16:22; see Candida Moss, *God's Ghostwriters: Enslaved Christians and the Making of the Bible* (Little, Brown, and Company, 2024), among others; Henrik Mouritsen, *The Freedman in the Roman World* (Cambridge University Press, 2011).

2. Translations of the New Testament are mine, sometimes modified with reference to the NRSVue and using Nestle-Aland 28. On curses and Rom 12:14–21, see Thomas Schumacher, "Feurige Kohlen und die Macht der Feindesliebe: Überlegungen zum Fluchmotiv in Röm 12, 14–21" [English: "Fiery Coals and the Power of Loving Your Enemy: Reflections on the Curse Motif in Rom 12:14–21"], in *Antike Fluchtafeln und das Neue Testament*, ed. Michael Hölscher, Markus Lau, and Susanne Luther, WUNT 474 (More Siebeck, 2021), 381–408.

16:21–22). The letter to the Galatians is stocked with curses and language of magic, from its very beginning:

> But even if we or a messenger from heaven should proclaim to you a gospel contrary to what we proclaimed to you, let that one be accursed (*anathema estō*)! As we have said before, so now I repeat, if anyone proclaims to you a gospel contrary to what you received, let that one be accursed (*anathema estō*)! (Gal 1:8–9)

Galatians also refers to the evil eye or magic (*ebaskanen*, 3:1) and refers to a curse (*kataran, epikataratos*) associated with "the one who is hung on a tree" (3:10–14; cf. LXX Deut 27:26).[3]

But surely *Paul* didn't use curses, and surely the first Christ followers wouldn't have tolerated such practices, you might think. This essay will argue that those who first received the letters of Paul and his cowriters would have understood these phrases and practices within their own social, cultural, and ritual contexts *as* curses.[4] Paul, among others, used curses and practices that scholars have associated with magic.

Magic and Curse

Religion and magic, miracle and medicine, curses and prayers are terms that often emerge in one ancient group's attempts to denigrate another, and in the attempts of one group (of modern scholars) to construct proper religiosity or primitive practices in the present.[5] These are categories often forged in polemical situations. Yet ancient Greek and Latin offer specific terms for

---

3. See Konrad Zawadzki, "Die Anfänge des ‚Anathema' in der Urkirche. Teil 1: Status quaestionis" [English: "The Beginnings of the 'Anathema' in the Early Church: Part 1: State of the Question"], *Vox Patrum* 28, no. 52 (2008): 1323–43; Konrad Zawadzki, "Teil 2: Anhaltspunkte für das Anathem im Neuen Testament" [English: "Part 2: Evidence for the Anathema in the New Testament"], *Vox Patrum* 29, nos. 53/54 (2009): 495–520.

4. Jennifer Eyl, *Signs, Wonders, and Gifts: Divination in the Letters of Paul* (Oxford University Press, 2019), 2.

5. See, e.g., Talal Asad, *Formations of the Secular: Christianity, Islam, Modernity* (Stanford University Press, 2003). On "religion" in antiquity, see, e.g., Brent Nongbri, *Before Religion: A History of a Modern Concept* (Yale University Press, 2013), 1–14, 132–53; on categories of miracle, religion, and magic, see, e.g., Attilio Mastrocinque, Joseph E. Sanzo, and Marianna Scapini, eds., *Ancient Magic: Then and Now* (Franz Steiner Verlag, 2020).

magic, and we find evidence of some legal restrictions regarding these ritual practices. Magic (*mageia*) was sometimes associated with political upheaval; indeed, magic is sometimes characterized as an engine for political resistance, and was placed under legal sanction even in the Roman Republican period.[6] The premature death of Germanicus, heir to the Roman throne, in early first-century Antioch, in mysterious circumstances amid a feud with the province's governor Gnaeus Calpurius Piso and his wife Plancina, is linked to curses and magical practices. According to Tacitus,

> explorations in the floor and walls brought to light the remains of human bodies, spells, curses, leaden tablets engraved with the name Germanicus (*carmina et devotiones et nomen Germanici plumbeis tabulis insculptum*), charred and blood-smeared ashes, and others of the implements of witchcraft (*malefica*) by which it is believed the living soul can be devoted to the powers of the grave. (*Annals* 2.69; trans. Moore and Jackson, LCL)[7]

Suetonius (a gossip writer, but still) notes that Augustus burned more than two thousand "prophetic writings (*fatidicorum*) of Greek or Latin origin [which] were in circulation anonymously or under the names of authors of little repute," sparing only some of the Sibylline oracles.[8] It is not clear if these were considered "magical" books, but tales of the destruction of magical materials, as well as the risk of holding them, continue to late antiquity. In the

6. The *Lex Cornelia de sicariis et veneficiis* of 81 BCE probably augmented preexisting laws against so-called magic. It was aimed particularly at homicides that were connected to those who "prepared, sold, bought, possessed, or administered a dangerous drug (*venenum malum*)" (James B. Rives, "Magic in Roman Law: The Reconstruction of a Crime," *Classical Antiquity* 22, no. 2 [2003]: 318); on the *Lex Cornelia*, see also Magali Bailliot, "Rome and the Roman Empire," in *Guide to the Study of Ancient Magic*, ed. David Frankfurter (Brill, 2019), 189–90. Yet, as Andrew Wilburn explains (*Materia Magica: The Archaeology of Magic in Roman Egypt, Cyprus, and Spain* [University of Michigan Press, 2012], 211): "Magic directed at the state, particularly aggressive magic aimed at harming members of the provincial administration, clearly would have been viewed as an illegal activity, endangering both parties, the practitioners and those who employed them. These proscriptions may suggest that the use of magical acts constituted resistance against Rome in the minds of the authorities."

7. Andrew T. Wilburn, "Building Ritual Agency: Foundations, Floors, Doors, and Walls," in *Guide to the Study of Ancient Magic*, ed. David Frankfurter (Brill, 2019), 555.

8. Suetonius, *Life of Augustus* 31.1; Lactantius, *Divine Institutes* 1.6.

fourth century, John Chrysostom tells of a book that lacked title or binding, thrown in the Orontes River in Antioch when soldiers scanned the city for magical texts. Chrysostom and a friend happened to grab it from the river and flipped it open to see its contents; they were terrified to find it was a book of magic (*Homilies on the Acts of the Apostles* 38).

So-called magical materials are sometimes part of a subversive ritual practice. The use of polemics against magic are sometimes entwined with gendered and classed invective launched to distinguish (right) self from (shifty or heretical) other, comparable to the formation of "orthodoxy" and "heresy" in early Christianity.[9] Among these so-called magical practices, curses can be understood as ritual objects and aesthetically complex judicial mechanisms that worked alongside the established court systems of the Roman Empire.[10]

More than two thousand *defixiones* or curse tablets have been found from the ancient Mediterranean world, dating over roughly a millennium, starting in the fifth century BCE.[11] Such tablets often appear to be a mere lump of encrusted dirt on an archaeological dig. We can therefore presume that many more existed and many are yet to be found.[12] Another example of

9. See Kimberly B. Stratton and Dayna S. Kalleres, eds., *Daughters of Hecate: Women and Magic in the Ancient World* (Oxford University Press, 2014); on gender and rhetoric, Jennifer Knust, *Abandoned to Lust: Sexual Slander and Ancient Christianity* (Columbia University Press, 2006), esp. 143–63; on magic as "alterity," David Frankfurter, "Preface," and "Ancient Magic in a New Key: Redefining an Exotic Discipline in the History of Religions," in *Guide to the Study of Ancient Magic* (Brill, 2019), esp. xi; on alterity, see 6 and 11; on it as "non-normative religious activity," Radcliffe G. Edmonds, III, *Drawing Down the Moon: Magic in the Ancient Greco-Roman* World (Princeton University Press, 2019), 5. Joseph E. Sanzo defends the category of magic in his "Deconstructing the Deconstructionists: A Response to Recent Criticisms of the Rubric 'Ancient Magic,'" in *Ancient Magic: Then and Now*, ed. Attilio Mastrocinque, Joseph Sanzo, Marianna Scapini (Franz Steiner, 2020), 27–48.

10. Henk S. Versnel, "Beyond Cursing: The Appeal to Justice in Judicial Prayers," in *Magika Hiera: Ancient Greek Magic and Religion*, ed. Christopher A. Faraone and Dirk Obbink (Oxford University Press, 1991), 60–106; Nasrallah, *Ancient Christians*, 43–89; Nasrallah, "Judgment, Justice, and Destruction."

11. Jessica L. Lamont, *In Blood and Ashes: Curse Tablets and Binding Spells in Ancient Greece* (Oxford University Press, 2023), 3; Daniela Urbanová, "Latin Curse Texts: Mediterranean Tradition and Local Diversity," *Acta Ant. Hung.* 57 (2017): 57.

12. For collections of curses available online, see University of Hamburg, "Thesaurus Defixionum (TheDefix)," https://www.thedefix.uni-hamburg.de/html/heurist/?db=The_dema&website&id=41774 (Greek) and Korshi Dosoo, Markéta Preininger, Julia Schwarzer

"activated" objects—that is, ritual objects meant to protect, to curse, to attain justice[13]—are amulets, whether in stone or papyrus or other materials.[14] In addition, fragments of "recipes" or spell books instructing a person how to *make* these curses and amulets also exist, giving further evidence of these ritual practices as widespread and iterative: To give only one example, you can insert the name(s) of those to be cursed.[15] Separate studies exist for ceramic incantation bowls, which combined words, images, and particular placement to enact their purpose.[16]

There is an astonishing range of objects often classed under magic that take quite different forms, and that often combine writing and the materiality of the object to empower its purposes, found from Britain to Babylonia. Once we recognize this, we can also read the letters of Paul and his coworkers within the multiple and varied local expressions of cursing, incantations, spells, and other practices often associated with magic. We can even recognize that

---

et al., eds., *Kyprianos* Database. Julius Maximilian University Würzburg, https://www.coptic-magic.phil.uni-wuerzburg.de/. See also Daniela Urbanová, *Latin Curse Tablets of the Roman Empire* (Innsbrucker Beiträger zur Kulturwissenschaft, 2018).

13. Richard Gordon, "Compiling P. Lond I 121 = PGM VII in a Transcultural Context," in *Cultural Plurality in Ancient Magical Texts and Practices: Graeco-Egyptian Handbooks and Related Traditions*, ed. Ljuba M. Bortolani, William Furley, Svenja Nagel, and Joachim F. Quack, Orientalische Religionen in der Antike 32 (Mohr Siebeck, 2019), 94.

14. The *Campbell Bonner Magical Gems Database* (*CBd*) emerged from Campbell Bonner's *Studies in Magical Amulets: Chiefly Greco-Egyptian* (University of Michigan Press, 1950); see also discussions of amulets in Christopher A. Faraone, *The Transformation of Greek Amulets in Roman Imperial Times* (University of Pennsylvania Press, 2018). On the importance of amulets to New Testament studies, see Theodore S. De Bruyn, *Making Amulets Christian: Artefacts, Scribes, and Contexts* (Oxford University Press, 2017); Theodore S. De Bruyn and Jitse H. F. Dijkstra, "Greek Amulets and Formularies from Egypt Containing Christian Elements: A Checklist of Papyri, Parchments, Ostraka, and Tablets," *Bulletin of the American Society of Papyrologists* 48 (2011): 163–216; Joseph E. Sanzo, *Scriptural Incipits on Amulets from Late Antique Egypt: Text, Typology, and Theory* (Mohr Siebeck, 2014); Brice C. Jones, *New Testament Texts on Greek Amulets from Late Antiquity* (Bloomsbury T&T Clark, 2016).

15. Christopher A. Faraone and Sofía Torallas Tovar, eds., *Greek and Egyptian Magical Formularies: Text and Translation* (California Classical Studies, 2022); Christopher A. Faraone and Sofía Torallas Tovar, eds., *The Greco-Egyptian Magical Formularies: Libraries, Books, and Individual Recipes* (University of Michigan Press, 2022).

16. Among others, see Simcha Gross and Avigail Manekin-Bamberger, "Babylonian Jewish Society: The Evidence of the Incantation Bowls," *Jewish Quarterly Review* 112, no. 1 (2022): 1–30.

in early Christian attempts to define orthodoxy and heresy, and their uses of the term *anathema*, we find a continued, acceptable practice of cursing between Christ followers. The Nicene Creed of 325, after all, not only asserts what a Christian should believe, but ends with a long list of anathemas: Condemnations or curses.

The Potential Problems of "Paul within Paganism"

Before we delve into curses, let me explain that interpreting Paul within "paganism," with a focus on magic and curses in particular, has four potential dangers. The first is that *pagan* itself is a scholarly term that does not do justice to the complexities of Greco-Roman religions. The second is that "Paul within paganism" could signal a return to a paradigm that understands Paul as a Hellenic thinker among non-Jewish communities of the Greek East. It could thus erode the positive work that has been done on the historical fact of Paul as a Jew whose own writing presents him within the paradigm of the prophets of Israel (Gal 1:15). A third danger is that the phrase "Paul within paganism" might imply a focus on Paul (alone). Yet it is better history, and a principle of feminist biblical scholarship, not to attend only to Paul's voice, but to reconstruct the communities—usually called *ekklēsiai* or assemblies, sometimes *koinōniai* or companies—to which he and his cowriters penned letters. Such an approach allows us to break with the great man model of history, which asks, What did Paul the hero, or Paul the philosophizer, or Paul the first Christian, think? Paul as hero, philosopher, and Christian are tropes of later scholarly characterization. A more rigorous history attends to the many to whom Paul and his cowriters addressed their letters, for, in their first instantiation, the letters of Paul and cowriters are timely letters sent to particular communities about particular issues—they were not universal, meant for everyone, or intended as scripture or univocal.

A fourth potential danger of the phrase "Paul within paganism" is that it might imply the model that this volume instead works against: It might imply that the lines of differentiation between Jew, Christian, and so-called pagan are clear in the first few centuries CE. This is what I call a "Tupperware model": It presumes that communities are sealed off from each other, or that there is a core or essence to a religion (an authentic Judaism, say) versus its syncretistic hinterlands. In fact, that study of the ancient ritual recipes, spells, and other data that has long gone under the label of magic teaches us the opposite: It teaches about the porosity of cult, the creativity and shared technologies of ritual experts, the utility of divinities of all kinds. Isis, Hekate, Iao, Sabaoth, angels, even Jesus: The names of gods from various cults can be invoked to do justice for one's cause.[17]

Paul still stands as a Jew within the diversity of Jewishness in the first century CE. The Christian author Origen, writing in the early third century CE, indicates that Jews *and* non-Jews used Jewish patriarchs, stories, and song for ritual purposes:

> It is clear that the Jews trace their genealogy back to the three fathers Abraham, Isaac, and Jacob. Their names are so powerful when linked with the name of God that the [formula] "the God of Abraham, the God of Isaac, and the God of Jacob" is used not only by members of the Jewish nation in their prayers to God and when they subdue *daimones* by song, but even by almost all those who do business in incantations and magic. Furthermore, "the God of Israel," and "the God of the Hebrews," and "the God who drowned the king of Egypt and the Egyptians in the Red Sea," are often named to overcome *daimones* or certain evil powers. (*Contra Celsum* 4.33–34).[18]

Paul, in the first century CE, writes at a time when the *ekklēsiai* or "assemblies" to which he writes are still largely non-Jewish (gentile). Yet they wish to affiliate with Judaism, and with the peculiar form of Judaism that Paul preaches: One that honors a crucified messiah. At the same time, these communities dwell in cities and regions in which so-called magical practices—including curses, spells, and incantations—were rife.

Words are powerful. Curses contain speech-acts, formulated in ritual ways—scratched on a lead tablet, incanted, or the like, made to *do* things. To put it another way: A curse is less the effluence of words after you stub your toe in the dark night; it is more like the "I do" of a wedding, an efficacious word spoken before human and nonhuman witnesses, in order to effect some

17. But Joseph E. Sanzo, *Ritual Boundaries: Magic and Differentiation in Late Antique Christianity* (University of California Press, 2024) argues that some magical objects seek to differentiate between religious affiliations.

18. Origen, *Contra Celsum*, trans. Henry Chadwick (Cambridge University Press, 1980), modified.

fundamental change.[19] A curse is a small ritual machine, made up of multiple components and constructed and performed within a broader world of ritual which included what has been labeled magic, what has been labeled liturgy, and what has been labeled religion.

Cursing near Corinth

The curses with which this essay began came from the letters of Paul and use terminology common to curses in the ancient Mediterranean world. We turn to Roman Corinth and environs for a local case study, which helps us to envision the gritty and compelling language, rituals, and ideas of the mid-first century CE.

Not far from Corinth, Megara lies on the isthmus; it is home to a first- or second-century CE curse tablet.[20] Written on both sides on a (now fragmentary) lead tablet (ca. 10 × 15 cm), the curse has two features of particular interest for the study of the letters of Paul. First, it uses the verb "to anathematize," *anathematizein*. The word "anathema" in antiquity usually refers merely to a dedication within a temple or to a god.[21] Yet it also comes to

19. David Frankfurter, "Spell and Speech Act: The Magic of the Spoken World," in *Guide to the Study of Ancient Magic*, ed. David Frankfurter (Brill, 2019): 608–25; see Nasrallah, *Ancient Christians*, 33, 108–9.

20. University of Hamburg, *TheDefix*, curse tablet ID no. 225; Auguste Audollent, *Defixionum Tabellae* (Fontemoing, 1904): 41; John Gager, *Curse Tablets and Binding Spells from the Ancient World* (Oxford University Press, 1992): no. 85; translation is Gager's. Also cited in relation to Paul in Susanne Luther, "Neutestamentliche 'Bindeformeln'? Eine Spurensuche in der paulinischen Korintherbriefkorrespondenz" [English: "New Testament 'Binding Formulae'? A Search for Clues in Paul's Corinthian Letter Correspondence"], in *Antike Fluchtafeln und das Neue Testament: Materialität—Ritualpraxis—Texte,* ed. Michael Hölscher, Markus Lau, Susanne Luther, WUNT 474 (Mohr Siebeck, 2021), 451–52. On Megara as site of mysteries of Demeter (and two cults to Demeter), see Jan N. Bremmer, *Initiation into the Mysteries of the Ancient World* (De Gruyter, 2014), appendix 1. Regarding the interaction of philosophical-theological thinkers like Plato, Philo, and Plutarch with so-called magical practices of their day, see Christopher Atkins, "Philosophical Piety and Lived Religion: Cosmos, Justice, and Ancestral Wisdom" (Ph.D. diss, Yale University, 2025).

21. Katell Berthelot, "The Notion of Anathema in Ancient Jewish Literature Written in Greek," in *The Reception of Septuagint Words in Jewish-Hellenistic and Christian Literature*, ed. Eberhard Bons, Ralph Brucker, and Jan Joosten, WUNT 2/367 (Mohr Siebeck, 2014), 50. Berthelot shows that "in Jewish literature written in Greek, one does not encounter the meaning of *anathema* as 'imprecation', 'curse', or 'excommunication' that will become

mean something accursed. Second, this curse refers to "Hekatean and Hebrew words" (*logois Hekatikiois horkismasite [H]abraikois*) as part of its ritual efficacy. That is, it refers both to the goddess Hekate of the crossroads, and it refers to "Hebrew words" of some sort, indicating a knowledge of Judaism, or at least of the idea of Jewishness as exotic and esoteric.

The spell from Megara calls upon multiple gods: On side A, Althaia, Kore, Hekate, and Selene; on side B, Hekate and Selene again.[22] While the names of those cursed are missing from this fragmentary inscription, side A makes clear how the curse operates:

> We curse those EPAIPĒN . . . them and we anathematize them. Althaia, Kore, OREGAZAGRA Hekate Moon who devours its tail . . . ITHIBI . . . we anathematize them—body, spirit, soul, mind, thought, feeling, life, heart—with Hekatean words and Hebrew oaths . . . Earth Hekate . . . commanded by the holy names and oaths of the Hebrews—hair, head, brain, face, ears, eyebrows, nostrils . . . jaws, teeth . . . so that their soul may sign, their health may. . ., their blood (and) flesh may burn and (let) him/her sign with what he/she suffers. . . .

"Anathematize" may be used again on side B, which also concludes, ". . . and enroll them for punishments, pain and retribution . . . the body. *Anathema*."

The Megaran curse is roughly contemporaneous and roughly proximate to the recipients of 1 Corinthians. With its interest in justice and in "Hebrew oaths,"[23] the Megaran curse helps us to understand the social world and ritual practices familiar to those siblings (*adelphoi*) in the assembly (*ekklēsia*) whom Paul and Sosthenes address. More than thirty-eight curses are known to have

frequent in Christian literature and inscriptions"; Berthelot points to Mark 14:71, where Peter swears and curses (*anathematizein*) that he does not know Jesus.

22. Gager, *Curse Tablets*, 183 for context and translation. See Gideon Bohak, *Ancient Jewish Magic: A History* (Cambridge University Press, 2008), 209 on the use of Hebrew or Aramaic script or transliteration in amulets or curses as a sign of Jewish authorship, but note that the Megara curse only has a vague reference to "Hebrew . . . oaths."

23. Versnel ("Beyond Cursing," 65) cites this Megarian curse as an example of a "prayer for justice" in which "several elements betray a Jewish influence."

been found in the environs of Corinth;[24] there are yet more to be published and studied.

First Corinthians, a letter of Paul and Sosthenes to the Corinthians, was written ca. 54 CE from Ephesos, and it contains a ritual text that is a curse. In a much-debated passage, a man who "has his father's wife" is consigned to "destruction of the flesh":

> It is actually reported that there is sexual immorality among you, and of a kind that is not found even among pagans; for a man is living with his father's wife. And you are arrogant! Should you not rather have mourned, so that he who has done this would have been removed from among you? For though absent in body, I am present in spirit; and as if present I have already pronounced judgment in the name of the Lord Jesus on the man who has done such a thing. When you are assembled, and my spirit is present with the power of our Lord Jesus, you are to hand this man over to Satan for the destruction of the flesh, so that his spirit may be saved in the day of the Lord. (1 Cor 5:1–5)

Scholars have been nervous about this passage. It is well known that curses in antiquity are often formulated in the name of an authoritative being, and we have evidence of so-called magical practices conducted "in the name of the Lord Jesus," even within the Christian Testament (e.g., Acts 4).[25] Yet some have argued that "in the name of the Lord Jesus" (1 Cor 5:4a) should be connected with "assembling together," not with consigning the man to Satan (5a).[26] Some have softened 1 Corinthians 5:1–5 into an "excommunication,"

---

24. John Fotopoulos, "Paul's Curse of Corinthians: Restraining Rivals with Fear and *Voces Mysticae* (1 Cor 16:22)," *Novum Testamentum* 56 (2014): 291–92n74.

25. Benedict H. M. Kent, "Curses in Acts: Hearing the Apostles' Words of Judgment alongside 'Magical' Spell Texts," *JSNT* 39, no. 4 (2017): 412–40.

26. Anthony C. Thiselton, *The First Epistle to the Corinthians: A Commentary on the Greek Text* (Eerdmans, 2000), 393–94, following Hans Conzelmann, *1 Corinthians: A Commentary on the First Epistle to the Corinthians* (Fortress, 1975), 97; see also P. E.-B. Allo, *Saint Paul Première Épitre aux Corinthiens* [English: *Saint Paul's First Epistle to the Corinthians*] (J. Balada, 1956), 121. Deut 27:20, Lev 18:8 and 20:11, and Cicero, *Pro Cluentio* 5.14–6.15 condemn a man "having" his father's wife.

reading later Christian practices into a first-century context.[27] As Susanne Luther puts it, scholars have wanted to set a boundary between Paul and curse tablets.[28]

Yet, the context of curses and so-called magic explains this passage. In 1908, Adolf Deissmann argued that 1 Corinthians 5 was similar to "execration" spells.[29] Many have since developed this insight.[30] Seon Yong Kim, for example, has detailed how the most curse-laden of epistles, Galatians, fits within this broader cultural context.[31] Christiane Zimmerman and I have read Paul's reference to *anathema* and his cursing of a man who is "with his father's wife" in 1 Corinthians as evidence of an act of justice in a world of god(s) who engage in judgment.[32] Susanne Luther has used the curse from

---

27. David R. Smith, *"Hand This Man Over to Satan": Curse, Exclusion and Salvation in 1 Corinthians 5* (T&T Clark, 2008), 3–56; Gordon D. Fee, *The First Epistle to the Corinthians*, NICNT (Eerdmans, 1987), 208; James South, "A Critique of the 'Curse/Death' Interpretation of 1 Corinthians 5.1–8," *NTS* 39, no. 4 (1993): 539–61.

28. Luther, "Neutestamentliche 'Bindeformeln,'" 464. Smith, *Hand This Man Over*, 181–82 mentions that some contemporary Christians do not want to face the idea that curses would be accepted among ancient or modern Christ followers.

29. Adolf Deissmann, *Light from the Ancient East*, trans. Lionel R. M. Strachan (1927; facsimile ed., Kessinger Publishing, 1997), 302–12. Tertullian calls it a curse (*On Modesty* 13–14; see Smith, *Hand This Man Over*, 27–31), as did Conzelmann, *1 Corinthians*, 97. Many would argue against this, e.g., Robert Ewuise Moses, *Practices of Power: Revisiting the Principalities and Powers in the Pauline Letters* (Augsburg Fortress, 2014), 99–102.

30. Adela Yarbro Collins ("The Function of 'Excommunication' in Paul," *Harvard Theological Review* 72, no. 1 [1980]: 255) has argued Paul's curse has similarities to the Greek magical papyri; citing Deissmann, she notes the technical use of the verb *paradidōmi* in both "magical" texts and 1 Corinthians 5. Papyrological evidence reveals *paradidōmi* as judicial language and as a term for handing over the enslaved; Peter Arzt-Grabner and Michael Ernst, *1 Korinther* [English: *1 Corinthians*], vol. 2 of *Papyrologische Kommentare zum Neuen Testament* (Vandenhoeck & Ruprecht, 2006), 207. Fotopoulos, "Paul's Curse," 275–309, discusses 1 Cor 16:22's use of Aramaic in light of curse practices

31. Seon Yong Kim, *Curse Motifs in Galatians: An Investigation into Paul's Rhetorical Strategies*, WUNT 2/531 (Mohr Siebeck, 2020); Konrad Huber, "Verhext—verflucht—am Leib gezeichnet. Aspekte von Magie im Galaterbrief?" [English: "Bewitched—Cursed—Marked on the Body: Aspects of Magic in Galatians?"], in Hölscher, Lau, and Luther, *Antike Fluchtafeln und das Neue Testament*, 465–88.

32. Christiane Zimmermann, "Anathema und Übergabe an den Satan als Aktualisierungen des göttlichen Gerichts in den paulinischen Gemeinden" [English: "Anathema and Surrender to Satan as Actualizations of Divine Judgment in the Pauline Churches"], *Novum*

Megara, among others, to set a context for the use of the term *anathema* in 1 Corinthians.[33] Jennifer Eyl has argued that Paul engages in divination practices as a ritual expert in antiquity.[34] Heidi Wendt characterizes Paul as one among many other ritual entrepreneurs.[35]

The curse states, "I have already pronounced judgment" (1 Cor 5:3).[36] We should picture 1 Corinthians 5:1–5 read not privately, but aloud in the assembly at Corinth; it would raise among its hearers a debate regarding justice and judgment. The passage would have been interpreted in the context of the city's legal processes, including local practices of cursing. The second-century travel writer Pausanias says that someone traveling the steep road from the Roman forum of Corinth to its high Acrocorinth passed several sacred sites, including a temple to the Mother of the Gods and a throne, and then a temple of the *Moirai*, the Fates.[37] These were located near, or perhaps to be identified with, the Sanctuary of Demeter and Kore, which Pausanias also mentions (*Description of Greece* 2.4.7). From the plain on which the city lay, one could raise one's eyes to the south to see this shining site about midway up the rugged mountain of stone

---

Testamentum 63, no. 3 (2021): 360–89; Nasrallah, "Judgment, Justice, and Destruction." John S. Kloppenborg ("Cursing in the Corinthian Christ Assembly," in Hölscher, Lau, and Luther, *Antike Fluchtageln und das Neue Testament,* 421) discusses the letter's concern about "the breaching of the boundaries of the physical body" and its effects on *pneuma* or spirit, seeking to understand how the curse would have been worked with Paul at a distance from Corinth

33. Luther, "Neutestamentliche 'Bindeformeln,'" 451–54.

34. Eyl, *Signs, Wonders, and Gifts.*

35. Heidi Wendt, *At the Temple Gates: The Religion of Freelance Experts in the Roman Empire* (Oxford University Press, 2016).

36. "Paul is resolved upon a judicial act of a sacral and pneumatic kind against the culprit." Conzelmann, *1 Corinthians,* 97. Christophe Senft (*La première épitre de saint Paul aux Corinthiens* [English: *The First Epistle of Saint Paul to the Corinthians*], 2nd ed. [Labor et Fides, 1990], 73) notes that the phrase is confusing, and that some give it a judicial meaning; Allo too emphasizes judicial elements, arguing that *sun tē dynamei tou kyriou* points to the tribunal (*Saint Paul,* 121–24). Thiselton discusses speech act, judgment, and guilt in *First Epistle to the Corinthians,* 394.

37. See Nancy Bookidis and Ronald S. Stroud, *The Sanctuary of Demeter and Kore: Topography and Architecture,* Corinth XVIII.3 (Princeton University Press, 1997), 437; Jorunn Økland, *Women in their Place: Paul and the Corinthian Discourse of Gender and Sanctuary Space,* JSNTSup 269 (T&T Clark, 2004), 90–91. New work on rereading the curse tablets associated with the sanctuary of Demeter and Kore, as well as work on unpublished curse tablets at Corinth, will enrich and likely change some of our extant data.

and brush. Eighteen curses have been found at this sanctuary, one in Latin and the rest in Greek, nine within what the archaeologists call the "Building of the Tablets" on the sanctuary's lower terrace.[38] The curses likely date to the second and third centuries CE. Some kind of ritual occurred, most likely with the help of religious experts and in an established ritual context.

The Corinthian curses invoke Kyria (Mistress) Demeter, and other gods, such as the *Moirai Praxidikai* (Fates who enact justice), *Anankē* (Necessity) and Hermes Chthonius (Hermes of the underworld).[39] A nailed-together double curse (Stroud nos. 125, 126) contains a complex literary structure. It is one of three aimed against a garland-weaver named Karpimē Babbia, likely a woman of low status who plaited together flower and leaves for religious ceremonies.[40]

> I entrust and consign Karpimē Babbia, weaver of garlands, to the Fates who exact justice, so that they may punish her acts of insolence, to Hermes of the Underworld, to Earth, and to the children of Earth, so that they may overcome and completely destroy her soul and heart and her mind and the wits of Karpimē Babbia, weaver of garlands. I adjure you and I implore you and I pray to you, Hermes of the Underworld, that the mighty names of Ananke, Nebezapadaieisen[.]geibebeohera, make me fertile; that the mighty name, the one carrying compulsion, which is not named recklessly unless in dire necessity, EUPHER, mighty name, make me fertile and destroy Karpimē Babbia, weaver of garlands, from her head to her footprints with monthly destruction.[41]

The double curse reveals a "poetics of magical formulas,"[42] beginning with two verbs commonly used "in lead tablets, especially prayers for justice,"

38. For archaeological context and thus ritual procedure, see Bookidis and Stroud, Corinth XVIII.3, 277, 279, 281; Stroud, *The Sanctuary of Demeter and Kore: The Inscriptions*, Corinth XVIII.6, 151; summary in Nasrallah, "Justice, Judgment, and Destruction," 356–57.

39. Stroud, Corinth XVIII.6, 84–85.

40. See Plutarch, *Moralia* 41F (= *On Listening to Lectures* 8), LCL 136 and discussion in Nasrallah, *Ancient Christians*, 196.

41. Stroud, Corinth XVIII.6, 105–7.

42. H. S. Versnel, "The Poetics of the Magical Charm: An Essay in the Power of Words," in *Magic and Ritual in the Ancient World*, ed. Paul Mirecki and Marvin Meyer (Brill, 2002),

parathitomai and *katathitomai* ("entrust" and "consign").[43] While the curse does not name the curser or *defigens*, the accursed's name and occupation of the accursed are clear: Karpimē Babbia, garland weaver. She is consigned to the Fates, who exact justice. The purpose or hoped-for result of this action is stated: That they might punish or perhaps prove, demonstrate, or display (her) "acts of insolence."[44] She is also consigned to chthonic Hermes,[45] Earth, and Earth's children. The curse's hoped-for result is that these figures should "overcome and completely destroy her soul and her heart and her mind and the wits of Karpimē Babbia, garland weaver." The curse twice uses the verb destroy (*ergazomai*) in a poetic move of repetition and uses polysyndeton—the repetition of "and" builds up the "rhythmic prose" and emphasizes the body of the accursed.[46]

The text then starts anew with a strong first-person voice, addressing Hermes Chthonius: "I make you swear and I adjure you and I pray to you." The verbs intimately decrescendo from near command to plea. Archaeologist Ron Stroud wondered if this phrasing "echo[ed] an oral chant as in a prayer or a hymn, perhaps one that was chanted in Room 7 of the Building of the Tablets with lamps burning and incense from the thymiateria filling the air in this very confined space."[47] The tablet then calls upon the great names of Anankē or Necessity, and *voces magicae*, "magical voices" or letter sequences that we cannot understand.

The petitioner gives another command (line 11): "Make me fruitful" (*karpisai me*), an imperative repeated at line 14 and conjoined with a balancing curse for Karpimē Babbia. The curse ends by twice using language of destruction: "Destroy Karpimē Babbia, garland weaver, from head until

---

140, 152; he also cites Patricia Cox Miller to suggest that so-called magical texts "transcend not only writing but speech itself" (145–56).

43. Stroud, Corinth XVIII.6, 108, cites multiple authorities, including Henk S. Versnel; by the latter see "Prayers for Justice, East and West: New Finds and Publications Since 1990," in *Magical Practice in the Latin West: Papers from the International Conference Held at the University of Zaragoza, 30 Sept.—1 Oct. 2005*, ed. R. L. Gordon and F. Marco Simón (Brill, 2010), 338.

44. Stroud, Corinth XVIII.6, 109, commentary on line 3.

45. See Jessica L. Lamont, "A New Commercial Curse Tablet from Classical Athens," *Zeitschrift für Papyrologie und Epigraphik* 196 (2015): 159–74: 164 on chthonic Hermes.

46. Stroud, Corinth XVIII.6, 110. For a more ancient example and helpful discussion of poetics, see Lamont, "A New Commercial Curse," esp. 165.

47. Stroud, Corinth XVIII.6, 111.

footprints by means of monthly destruction."[48] The spell's command may also be a pun: *Karpisai me*: Make *me* fruitful, destroy the fruitfulness of Karpimē Babbia. The Greek word for "fruit" is *karpos*; the use of the word "fruitful" alongside the phrase "monthly destruction" hints at some sort of reproductive envy or competition.[49] The curse is punctuated at beginning, middle, and end by the name of its recipient (lines 1–2, 7, 14). The Bab(b)ia family at Corinth was prominent, as we know from monumental inscriptions—they dedicated a fountain on the forum, for example. Given this, we can wonder whether Karpimē [50] is a personal name or instead a code to refer to a specific woman who is considered fruitful, from the *oikos*, or household, of Babbius. Karpimē engages in low-status work as garland weaver; perhaps it is the nickname of an enslaved woman: The fruitful one. The *defixio* postdates 1 Corinthians, but it reveals conceptualizations of the world that were long-lasting. The idea of the destruction of the soul, heart, mind, and wits of Karpimē Babbia finds an echo in 1 Corinthians 5:5's injunction to hand over someone to Satan.

Speaking in Tongues at Corinth

I have so far skipped over the curse's "Nebezapadaieisen[.]geibebeohera" and "eupher." Scholars name this phenomenon of Greek letter streams that make no sense as "magical voices" (*voces magicae*). Common within curses and amulets, their use may add to the esoteric authority of the ritual practitioner.[51] So-called magical texts, among other practices and literatures in antiquity, indicate the use of linguistically, sonically nonnormative elements such as aphasia, stuttering, and speaking in tongues. Such unusual forms of language sometimes also extend to the process of writing itself: They may include retrograde writing (writing a word backward), crafting a palindrome,

48. See also Stroud, Corinth XVIII.6, 123, "and (?) she will be destroyed from this day today—I beg (?)—sinews—underworld—herself—" and the two curses against Maxima Pontia, both of which use the word *katergasia* (nos. 130, 131).

49. Stroud, Corinth XVIII.6, 114.

50. Stroud, Corinth XVIII.6, 109, mentions that the name Karpime is attested for both free and enslaved women.

51. See Richard Gordon, "The Healing Event in Greco-Roman Folk Medicine," in *Ancient Medicine in Its Socio-Cultural Context, vol. 2: Papers Read at the Congress Held at Leiden University, 13–15 April 1992*, ed. H. F. J. Horstmanshoff et al., Clio Medica 28 (Brill, 1995), and Versnel's engagement with Gordon in "The Poetics of the Magical Charm," 142–43.

writing a Greek text in Latin letters, writing with the "wrong" (left) hand, or writing in a pattern, producing "an intentional and puzzling palimpsest,"[52] or writing letters that *look* like a known language (*charaktēres*) but are not.[53] These elements, largely incomprehensible to us, offer an alternative mode of thinking about language. Within 1 Corinthians, the Aramaic *Marana tha* used immediately after *anathema* in 16:22 may have the effect of esoteric ritual speech, the invocation of another language, unknown to some, to emphasize a curse.[54]

First Corinthians also mentions "kinds of tongues" (12:10) and indicates that the community heard angelic tongues ("If I speak in the tongues of humans and of angels but do not have love, I am a noisy gong or a clanging cymbal," 13:1). In 1 Corinthians we find sound, including tongues and song: "When you come together, each one has a hymn, a lesson, a revelation, a tongue, or an interpretation" (1 Cor 14:26). Yet the letter attempted to downgrade tongues as a form of sound, and attempted to limit women's speech in the assembly (1 Cor 14:33b–35). Numerous curse tablets and the recipes for spells include the term *epaoidē*, or incantation, which reminds us that such words were spoken or sung or chanted aloud.[55]

Voces magicae also engaged and demonstrated a range of theological and aesthetic strategies, which included either violence or play—the upending of normal communicative efforts, on the one hand, and some idea of transcendence, on the other.[56] They should be interpreted among other linguisti-

52. Ronald S. Stroud, *The Sanctuary of Demeter and Kore: The Inscriptions*, Corinth XVIII.6 (The American School of Classical Studies at Athens, 2013), 91 (catalog no. 118), a curse against Secunda Postumia, dated to pre-70 CE.

53. Richard Gordon, "Charaktêres between Antiquity and Renaissance: Transmission and Re-invention," in *Les savoirs magiques et leur transmission de l'Antiquité à la Renaissance*, ed. V. Dasen and J.-M. Spieser (SISMEL/Edizioni del Galluzzo, 2014), 253–300; Kirsten Dzwiza, *Schriftverwendung in antiker Ritualpraxis* [English: *The Use of Writing in Ritual Practice*] (Erfurt, 2013); Daniel James Waller, "Curious Characters, Invented Scripts, and . . . Charlatans? 'Pseudo-Scripts' in the Mesopotamian Magic Bowls," *Journal of Near Eastern Studies* 78, no. 1 (2019): 119–39.

54. Fotopoulos, "Paul's Curse," 291.

55. Nasrallah, *Ancient Christians*, 128–46, 203–60.

56. Versnel, "The Poetics of the Magical Charm," 145; he uses the important essay of Patricia Cox Miller, *In Praise of Nonsense: A Piety of the Alphabet in Ancient Magic* (Routledge, 2001).

cally effervescent or experimental modes: Glossolalia or speaking in tongues in 1 Corinthians, philosophical texts like the musings on language we find in Plato's *Cratylus*, and writings in the Nag Hammadi codices that discuss language or that break apart into vowels. The idea of "the bewitchment of language itself"[57] was sometimes framed as alternate language, sometimes as a transcending of language.[58] At other times, such practices were mocked as foreign-sounding.[59]

Voces magicae, such as the one found in Roman Corinth within a curse against Karpimē Babbia, are an important context for understanding *glōssai* in 1 Corinthians. This curse tablet or the larger phenomenon of *voces magicae* does not explain or fix the meaning of 1 Corinthian's discussion of tongues. I am not arguing that the phrase "kinds of tongues" for Paul and Sosthenes, writers, or for those who first heard this letter written aloud in assembly, evoked only one meaning.[60]

Yet the phenomenon of the letter streams of *voces magicae* is one piece of evidence within a larger context of ancient play with and theorizing about sound and language. In the case of ancient Corinth, transgressive linguistic practices occurred at different sites: At the Sanctuary of Demeter and Kore at Corinth and among Christ followers likely somewhere in the lower city,

57. Cox Miller, *In Praise of Nonsense*, 500–501.

58. Versnel, "The Poetics of the Magical Charm," 145.

59. See, e.g., Plutarch, *Moralia* 165F–166A (= *On Superstition*), Celsus (according to Origen, *Contra Celsum*, 7.9) polemically associates alternative sound or language with magic (Nasrallah, *Ancient Christians*, 189–90). See Birger A. Pearson, "Theurgic Tendencies in Gnosticism and Iamblichus's Conception of Theurgy," in *Neoplatonism and Gnosticism*, ed. Rich T. Wallis and Jay Bregman (State University of New York Press, 1992), 258. Maurice Olender, *The Languages of Paradise: Race, Religion, and Philology*, trans. Arthur Goldhammer (Harvard University Press, 2009) recounts the long debate regarding what language God spoke; see also Yuliya Minets, *The Slow Fall of Babel: Languages and Identities in Late Antique Christianity* (Cambridge University Press, 2021).

60. The first-century BCE Jewish worshippers at Qumran may have understood themselves as participating in angelic song and even worshipping in the presence of angels. See, e.g., 1QH[a] XI 19–23 (from the Thanksgiving Hymns or *Hodayot*), quoted in Peter Schäfer, "Communion with the Angels: Qumran and the Origins of Jewish Mysticism," in *Wege mystischer Gotteserfahrung: Judentum, Christentum und Islam: Mystical Approaches to God: Judaism, Christianity, and Islam*, ed. Peter Schäfer et al. (Oldenbourg Wissenschaftsverlag, 2009), 37–66; Janelle Peters, "Creation, Angels, and Gender in Paul, Philo, and the Dead Sea Scrolls," *Open Theology* 7, no. 1 (2021): 248–55.

folk who lacked a sanctuary or temenos for their practices. Despite their differences, both the curse tablet and 1 Corinthians remain as data for ritual practices that involved play with language.

Conclusions

So-called magical materials are improvisational and ecumenical,[61] crossing what we think of as cultic boundaries and transgressing our categories of curse, prayer, vow, and legal action.[62] *Defixiones* are sometimes legal instruments that ask Fate or other gods and beings to adjudicate a present situation or to redress a past wrong.[63] Sometimes, they hint at their own performance in incantation.

The letters of Paul and his cowriters, while they represent our earliest extant data regarding Christ followers, are not sui generis. Placing them within a broader context, including that of "magic," enhances our understanding of the letters themselves. One New Testament scholar has stated that *defixiones* are "far from the realm of ancient philosophy."[64] I would argue, instead, that objects such as *defixiones* and amulets are small, material distillations of larger ideas and debates about human futures, justice, and divine activity—the very ideas that the letters of Paul and his cowriters engage. Curses are an underutilized source to investigate philosophical-theological ideas about the agency, the will, and the efficacy of human and nonhuman subjects, whether gods or the materiality of the lead on which a *defixio* is incised.

61. Richard Gordon, "Queering Their Pitch: The Curse Tablets from Mainz, with Some Thoughts on Practising 'Magic,'" *Journal of Roman Archaeology* 27 (2014): 784; Pieter Willem van der Horst uses the term *ecumenical* in his "'The God Who Drowned the King of Egypt': A Short Note on an Exorcistic Formula," in *Wisdom of Egypt: Jewish, Early Christian, and Gnostic Essays in Honor of Gerard P. Luttikhuizen* (Brill, 2005), 135–39.

62. On legal language, see, e.g., Avigail Manekin-Bamberger, "The Vow-Curse in Ancient Jewish Texts," *Harvard Theological Review* 112, no. 3 (2019): 340–57, esp. 349, 356; Andrew T. Wilburn, *Magica Materia: The Archaeology of Magic in Roman Egypt, Cyprus, and Spain* (University of Michigan, 2012), 210, 174–5; Nasrallah, "Judgment, Justice, and Destruction" and "Making Justice: Justin Martyr and a Curse From Amathous, Cyprus," *Zeitschrift für Antikes Christentum* 28, no. 1 (2024): 76–99.

63. Nasrallah, *Ancient Christians*, 43–89 and "Judgment, Justice, and Destruction."

64. Smith, *Hand This Man Over*, 1.

CHAPTER ELEVEN

Paul, the Moon, and Cosmic Philosophy

Robyn Faith Walsh
University of Miami

In the competitive landscape of Greek and Roman intellectual life, taking a position on the nature of the moon and of the cosmos was essential to proving one's expertise. So common was this subject within physics, philosophy, literature, and among those seeking prestige for divine knowledge, one might even say that having an opinion on the moon was *expected* by ancient audiences. Paul the apostle was no exception to this rule.

Paul references cosmology and "the [starry] heavens" (*tois ouranois*)—often misleadingly translated as simply "heaven"—frequently, perhaps most famously in 2 Corinthians 12, where he reports on an elusive journey to the "third [starry] heaven" (*tritou ouranou*).[1] First Corinthians 15 is also noteworthy for its classifications of types of terrestrial and extraterrestrial bodies (including the moon, sun, and stars) and for its similarities to arguments made by Middle Platonists like Plutarch and Philo.[2] Throughout Paul's undisputed

---

*A more detailed version of this piece appears in Robyn Faith Walsh, "*Argumentum ad Lunam*: Pauline Discourse, 'Double Death,' and Competition on the Moon," *Harvard Theological Review* 117, no. 4 (Oct 2024): 720–43. My gratitude to *Harvard Theological Review* and Cambridge University Press for permission to reproduce elements of that argument here.

1. *Ouranos* possesses a general sense of "heaven" but also the far reaches of the concave ceiling of visible stars. Ocellus, for instance, divides the cosmos into three parts, including the "heavens" (*ouranos*) as the upper regions encompassing the moon, sun, and stars as distinct from both the earth and the "mid-air" region between the earth and moon (*On the Nature of the Universe* 9–10); also cited in Karen ní Mheallaigh, *The Moon in the Greek and Roman Imagination: Myth, Literature, Science and Philosophy* (Cambridge University Press, 2020), 104 and discussed below.

2. Cf. Phil 3:19–21 and 2 Cor 4:1–5:10. Colossians 2:16 also makes mention of a "new moon."

letters, his approach on matters from physics to moral psychology are often misread as "theology" without full attention to how similar his discussions are to thoughts expressed within Platonism, Pythagoreanism, and Stoicism. But recognizing the ways in which Paul was a very typical first-century popular philosopher helps us recalibrate our understanding not only of his ideas, but also why his message was compelling to gentiles in the first place.

Paul's use of technical terms like *pneuma* ("spirit"), *nous* ("mind"), and *logos* ("word") places him squarely in dialogue with the philosophy of his day. And this includes matters like the composition and purpose of the moon, planets, stars, and other celestial bodies. Couched within a larger trend of imperial "wonder culture" in the first century—and in competition with a variety of teachers, wonderworkers, superapostles, and the like—sufficient evidence remains to reconstruct portions of Paul's cosmological views.[3] Reading Paul in this way challenges our traditional understandings of the nature of Christ, the transformation of resurrected bodies, what the afterlife will look like, and even the sexual politics of extraterrestrial existence.

In what follows, I will sketch some of the predominant theories on the composition, purpose, and function of the moon relevant to Paul's thought. I will then demonstrate how the moon, sun, and "starry heavens" factor concretely into Paul's cosmology. In short, it is plausible that Paul, like other Middle Platonists, saw the moon as a clearinghouse for souls awaiting a cosmic judgment—similar to what Plutarch (and later Augustine) describes as a "double death."[4] In this construction, those who lived virtuous earthly lives enjoy eternal Elysium on the moon or find peace by merging their minds and souls with the cosmos, while those tethered to the passions either sink back toward the earth or perish. Paul is not unique by any means in these ideas, yet he distinguishes himself, in part, through his interpretation of Christ's role in this cosmic future. His utopian vision also participates in a kind of discourse about society and gender politics that may offer some insight into questions about astral existence in the afterlife—specifically, Paul likely envisioned a lunar afterlife as pneumatic or "spiritual," but also principally male. At

3. For more on the concept of wonder culture: Karen ní Mheallaigh, *Reading Fiction with Lucian: Fakes, Freaks and Hyperreality* (Cambridge University Press, 2014), passim, and Joseph A. Howley, *Aulus Gellius and Roman Reading Culture: Text, Presence and Imperial Knowledge in the "Noctes Atticae"* (Cambridge University Press, 2018), preface.

4. For Augustine on "double death" (*duplae morti*), *On the Trinity* 4.3.

minimum, Paul's rhetoric aligns with discourse about "wise men" as found in writers like Philo (e.g., *Special Laws* 2.42–45) who, on account of their virtue, give their souls wings and dance through outer space among the moon, sun, stars, and planets, spared from the ultimate death of the soul.[5]

By situating Paul's thought within this cosmological landscape, I also aim to add to our knowledge of what Stanley Stowers has called the "new terrain [of philosophy]" for thinkers of the imperial period like Paul, Philo, and Plutarch, which combines elements from Pythagoreanism with Platonism, "mixed with elements of Stoic thought."[6] Paul is not merely eclectic in his philosophical proofs for how one "participates in Christ" and achieves a promised pneumatic, lunar existence.[7] His descriptions of *pneuma*, his cosmology, and his astrobiology are completely ordinary given his social and cultural context. Thus, it may be that anachronistic translations and theologically driven prejudices against categories like "paganism," "astrology," and "magic" are responsible for setting Paul apart from his original meaning over time.

Fly Me to the Moon, Let Me Play among the Stars . . .[8]

From the pre-Socratics forward, there is near consensus that the visible cosmos was divine in nature. Plato, for instance, referred to the stars as "divine eternal animals ever abiding." Similarly, for Aristotle, the stars were "beings

5. Philo variously describes these wise men as wise scholars or associates, practitioners of wisdom, or "righteous" or "blameless" men. I have taken some liberties with "outer space" above for the sake of initial simplicity; a more literal translation is "ether," which I will discuss. Note that all translations in this piece are my own, unless otherwise noted. On the concept of soul death in Paul, see Emma Wasserman, particularly her *The Death of the Soul in Romans 7: Sin, Death, and the Law in Light of Hellenistic Moral Psychology*, WUNT 2/256 (Mohr Seibeck, 2008).

6. Stanley K. Stowers, "Paul and the Terrain of Philosophy," *Early Christianity* 6 (2015): 141–56, cit. 149.

7. On the concept of participation in Christ: Stanley K. Stowers, "Matter and Spirit, or What Is Pauline Participation in Christ?," in *The Holy Spirit: Classic and Contemporary Readings*, ed. Eugene Rogers (Wiley-Blackwell, 2009), 92–105.

8. Bart Howard, "Fly Me to the Moon" (1954), perhaps best remembered for Frank Sinatra's cover in 1964's *It Might as Well Be Swing* with Count Basie, released with Reprise records.

of superhuman intelligence, incorporate deities."[9] Both Plato and Aristotle also believed that human beings were integrally tied to the moon, sun, and planets. In the *Timaeus* and the *Republic*, Plato suggests that humans are "lower" beings in the cosmic hierarchy but ones that retain the potential to "return to the stars" should they lead virtuous lives. Plato agrees that "when once the human soul has entered upon this life, its destiny is henceforth subject to the courses of the stars," a position to which Aristotle adds the destiny of animals (incidentally leading to more than one debate as to whether a man and a donkey born at the same time are fated to lead the same life!).[10] Indeed, there is no shortage of discourse on the potential influence the cosmos may have on humanity's day-to-day existence. The popularity of astrology—including calculating the stars to predict the future, to predict one's death, or to invoke helper deities (like daemones)—also contributed to "outer space" becoming integral to this kind of discourse.[11]

Across philosophical schools and literature broadly, the moon often took "centre-stage" in such meditations.[12] Its relative proximity fostered discussion about its nature, its changeability (i.e., phases), and its prospective inhabitants, all while acting as a foil for claims about the earth itself and the mortal condition. Is the moon a giant celestial mirror reflecting earth? Is it a cosmic eye or

9. Lynn Thorndike, *A History of Magic and Experimental Science: During the First Thirteen Centuries of Our Era*, vol. 1 (Columbia University Press, 1923), 25–26. For an excellent overview on philosophical opinion on the nature of the stars as it relates to immortality: M. David Litwa, "Divine Corporeality and the Pneumatic Body," in *We Are Being Transformed: Deification in Paul's Soteriology* (De Gruyter, 2012) 119–51.

10. Thorndike, *A History of Magic*, 25–26.

11. Pliny the Elder laments about astrology, "There is no one who is not eager to learn the future about himself and who does not think that this is mostly truly revealed by the sky"; cited from Thorndike, *A History of Magic*, 60.

12. Here I am interfacing with Ní Mheallaigh's argument about the moon relative to the actions of Alexander of Abonouteichos, to be discussed: "Alexander proves himself to be a creative innovator of the ordinary bag of tricks. He also places the Moon centre-stage in a complex drama of religious belief and scepticism . . . between the gullible 'idiots' who belong 'over there' in far-flung cultural wastelands like . . . Pontus, and the sophisticated readers who are identified with the normative centre, the city of Rome" (*Moon*, 45). She ultimately nuances this claim, stating that to reduce reception to a binary of urban sophisticates and suburban boors is an oversimplification.

a pupil of the gods?[13] Could it be an ethereal cloud sitting "atop the Earth like a felted hat" buoyed by "terrestrial winds" or ocean vapors?[14] Or is it a galactic uterus "monthly swelling and shrinking [with] life-giving moisture and occasional reddening to the colour of blood"?[15] Certain Pythagoreans and, later, members of the Old Academy associated the moon with the afterlife: A stellar Isle of the Blessed. Theorizing that the soul (*psuchē*) was made of a similar ethereal-yet-material "light," it stood to reason that it would rise upward from the body (*soma*) after death.[16] There, the soul was likely to chance upon a host of other extraterrestrial beings in sublunar orbit. Beyond the variety of daemones (some oracles, some former mortals) described by Xenocrates or Herclides, Varro later adds the souls of immortals, made of "ether and air" (*aethere et aere*), as well as heroes, *lares*, and *genii* perceptible only by the mind and "not the eyes."[17] In a somewhat macabre scene, Macrobius suggests this same region is populated with the lifeless bodies of those waiting to be ensouled, a claim that matches some lines of Pythagorean though, which placed the moon in the uppermost starry heavens (*ouranos*)—that stratum between the moon and the earth teeming with daemones, immortals, and those "coming-to-be."[18] As philosophical schools honed their respective doctrines, prose and poetry invoked similar imagery,

13. There is a fair degree of overlap between theories of the moon as mirror and as eye in Greek literature and philosophy. This is due, in no small part, to its light and reflectivity and, thus, visibility. Parmenides, for instance, supported a theory of heliophotism, suggested that the moon is "ever-gazing at the rays of the sun," while also calling the moon "round-eyed"; for more examples and a detailed discussion of ancient theories on sight and reflectivity, including the moon as a dilating and contracting pupil, see Ní Mheallaigh, *Moon*, 68–82. Parmenides's fragments are cited from Ní Mheallaigh, *Moon*, 68.

14. Xenophanes and Heraclitus are representative examples in this case; Heraclitus suggests that the moon is a colossal concave bowl brimming with fire and aimed at the earth. Cf. Ní Mheallaigh, *Moon*, 58.

15. Ní Mheallaigh, *Moon*, 28–29. This uterine imagery also pertains to Plutarch's theory (also relevant to Paul) that the moon is a receptacle for souls and, therefore, has the potential to be penetrated with seed and/or ensouled and/or bring forth new life.

16. Herclides fr. 98a–99; Ní Mheallaigh, *Moon*, 107n209.

17. Cited from Augustine, *City of God*. 7.6 (fr. 226); Ní Mheallaigh, *Moon*, 108.

18. Macrobius, *Commentary on the Dream of Scipio*. I 11, 1–12, esp. 5–6; Ní Mheallaigh, *Moon*, 105, 107. cf. n7. Philo also describes this region as specifically "dusky" (*Abraham* 205–6),.which may convey a sense of "gloomy."

from Sappho's Selene gazing upon Endymion[19] to Cicero's *Dream of Scipio*, with its parade of virtuous souls dotting the Milky Way.[20]

The moon figured prominently in the discourses and actions outside of strict literate culture as well. Celestial objects or beings could direct or influence human lives; their power could be harnessed to one's benefit. Among seafarers and farmers, for instance, whether the moon, stars, and planets played a role in phenomena like weather or earthquakes had significant "real world" consequences.[21] A mastery of "the heavens" indicated privileged or divine knowledge; related displays of authority offered prestige and, in certain cases, encouraged or solidified social ties. Pliny the Elder was well within his rights, however, to express skepticism about tongue-shaped gems—*glossopetra*—raining down from the sky during lunar eclipses to give people divinatory powers.[22] Nonetheless, performative engagement with the moon to indicate specialized status was everywhere.

The so-called Thessalian Trick, or "drawing down the moon," was one such practice and a source of anxiety from the Greek period well into late antiquity. Associated with Thessalian "witches," it reputedly involved filling a bowl with water and creating an aperture in order to conjure the moon in front of eager spectators. Thought to be particularly convincing during an eclipse (as one might expect), the maneuver was so popular that the bishop Hippolytus was still condemning it in the third century CE.[23] That the infrastructure behind the trick itself was easily explained belied its purpose. The mere proposition that human beings could capture the moon—physically or conceptually—was tantalizing enough.

19. For example, Sappho fr. 96.

20. Cicero, *On the Republic* 6.16; Ní Mheallaigh, *Moon*, 107; Litwa, "Divine Corporeality and the Pneumatic Body," 139. There is a rich body of literature on what one might term journeys into heaven or space, including texts like the Testament of Abraham. For more on this genre, one useful source is Catherine Hezser, "Ancient 'Science Fiction': Journeys into Space and Visions of the World in Jewish, Christian, and Greco-Roman Literature of Antiquity," *Christian Origins and Hellenistic Judaism: Social and Literary Contexts for the New Testament*, ed. Stanley E. Porter et al. (Brill, 2013), 397–438.

21. Pliny, *Natural History* 2, 6 and 18. 5, 57, 69.

22. "[Pliny] is openly incredulous about the gem *glossopetra*, shaped like a human tongue and supposed to fall from the sky during an eclipse of the moon and to be invaluable in selenomancy"; Thorndike, *A History of Magic*, 98; *Natural History* 37, 59.

23. Hippolytus, *Refutation of All Heresies*. 4.37–38.

Indeed, interest in displays of lunar authority was pervasive across the social and economic spectrum. In the first century CE, for example, Plutarch describes certain elites in Rome—descendants of the "most ancient families"—wearing crescent-shaped trinkets on their shoes (*Roman Questions* 282A),[24] indicating "that after death their souls will again have the moon beneath their feet" (282A).[25] This kind of ostentation was in lockstep with a fondness among the imperial elite for "construct[ing] pseudo-genealogies which inserted [aristocrats] into the lineages of famous Greek heroes of history or myth."[26] Elsewhere, Plutarch describes such noble ancestors floating in the ether surrounding the moon or walking on its surface with "firm footing . . . like victors crowned with wreaths of feathers" (*On the Face of the Moon* 943D). And among them were "daimones and saviors" (*daimones . . . kai soteres*, 944D) who could elect to intercede in human events, from inspiring oracular speech to performing rescues at sea, and everything in between.[27]

Lucian's amusing caricature of Alexander of Abonouteichos (second century CE) also looms large. A self-styled "Neo-Pythagorean holy man" and reputed charlatan, Alexander claimed to be a prophet of Asclepius, founder of a cult to Glycon, son of Apollo, divination specialist, and consort to the moon

24. Concerning lunar-inspired amulets, of note are *lunulae*. Typically associated with young women, there are multiple styles of *lunulae* that have been found as grave goods and in funerary portraits throughout the Mediterranean. This raises the question of whether the crescent was always, as scholars tend to conclude, associated with fertility and menstruation. Supporting the idea that this kind of cosmic-themed jewelry was à la mode in the first century—and among the imperial family in particular—Domitia wears a *lunula* as she processes with the Augustan family on the Ara Pacis (my gratitude to John Bodel for bringing this to my attention). Beyond the elite and aristocracy, however, there is evidence that Flavian soldiers wore similar pendants on their belts and/or placed them on the bridles of their horses. There was also a general imperial-era penchant for placing crescents on pets like dogs and cats. For more on the *lunulae*, see Christopher A. Faraone, *The Transformation of Greek Amulets in Roman Imperial Times* (University of Pennsylvania Press, 2018).

25. Such associations with lineages may have additional significance for early Christianity insofar as Paul also argues for ties between *pneuma* and kinship.

26. *Lucian: Alexander or the False Prophet*, trans. Peter Thonemann (Oxford University Press, 2021), 34.

27. Iamblichus, for example, suggests that Pythagoras was from the moon (*Life of Pythagoras* 6.30); in the same passage cited above, Plutarch cites the Dioscuri.

goddess Selene, among other illustrious talents.[28] Perhaps remembered best for using a snake puppet to deliver his predictions and prognostications like a ventriloquist, he also leveraged his associations with the moon to enhance his paranormal résumé. Famously, he claimed his daughter had been conceived by the moon goddess and betrothed her to the Roman senator Rutilianus—who just happened to be one of his more generous sponsors.[29] Alexander himself performed their marriage ceremony, having his daughter descend like the moon from a rooftop into the arms of her groom. Alexander was also highly literate, composing hexameters and choreographing text-based prophecies, including slipping a self-serving proclamation about the resurrection of Asclepius into a snake egg that he preplanted and then recovered in yet another display of his divine abilities.[30] As an imperial-aged figure in competition with early Christians, among others, in Asia Minor, Alexander demonstrates that the moon remained a key touchstone for religious practitioners and writers seeking popular approval.[31] More directly, Alexander shows us what hitching your star to the moon, so to speak, can get you.

We All Shine on, Like the Moon and the Stars and the Sun. . . .[32]

That Paul is engaged in authorizing strategies involving the moon should not be a radical thesis. Scholarship has recognized for over a generation that Paul

28. For a thorough discussion of Lucian's approach and tone in *Alexander*, I recommend Thonemann, *Alexander*, 1–36.

29. Lucian, *Alexander the False Prophet* 26–40, esp. 35. John Kloppenborg's *Christ Associations: Connecting and Belonging in the Ancient City* (Yale University Press, 2019) presents a great deal of data on the senatorial sponsorship of both formal cultic associations and more entrepreneurial religious actors in the imperial period. On the question of conspicuous patronage among the curial classes, see his section "The Attraction of the Elite to Christ Assemblies," 332–39.

30. Lucian, *Alexander the False Prophet* 8–17; Ní Mheallaigh, *Moon*, 44–46.

31. Kloppenborg locates little evidence that Christ associations enjoyed sponsorship from the senatorial or equestrian strata until the late second century; Kloppenborg, *Christ Associations*, 327. Also consider Thonemann's analysis of "the widespread 'renaissance' of oracles in the Greek world under Trajan, Hadrian, and the Antonines" in *Alexander*, 30ff.

32. "Instant Karma! (We All Shine On)" by Lennon/Ono and the Plastic Ono Band, released in February 1970 as a single under the Apple Record label.

is utilizing the language of substances and forms common to the popular philosophy of his day.[33] He does so in the course of justifying his central claim that gentiles who share or participate in Christ's holy, god-given *pneuma* (again, often translated as "spirit") will be afforded a rarified status in the afterlife. Implicit in Paul's discourse is engagement with cosmology; yet few have drawn the direct connection between Paul and the moon.

One important exception is Stowers who, while arguing for a "new terrain" for Paul, briefly notes the following:

> Probably in Alcinous and clearly from Plotinus onward, Platonists insisted that the stars and planets had incorporeal minds or souls, but also bodies of pure fire. This solved the problem of their visibility among other things. The fire of which they were composed was like no gross element of the earth. As we have seen, later Platonists also gave bodies or vehicles composed of pneuma to daemons and other beings in the region below the moon. All of this shows that Paul's idea of a pneumatic body for Christ people who will be moving around the region below the moon could also make sense in the new thought inspired by Pythagoras and Plato that included significant elements from Stoicism.[34]

Building from Stowers's observation, there is substantial reason to understand that the cosmos—the moon, sun, and stars—is well within Paul's purview in a far more coherent and systematic sense than is traditionally acknowledged. A comprehensive survey of Paul's references to "the heavens" and to extraplanetary bodies reveals a clear concern for cosmology. For Paul, the natural and

---

33. Some representative examples include Abraham J. Malherbe, "'Gentle as a Nurse': The Lyric Background to I Thessalonians ii," *Novum Testamentum* 12 (1970): 203–17; Abraham J. Malherbe, *Paul and the Popular Philosophers* (Fortress Press, 1989); Troels Engberg-Pedersen, *Paul and the Stoics* (Westminster John Knox, 2000); Wasserman, *The Death of the Soul in Romans 7*; Troels Engberg-Pedersen, *Cosmology of the Self in the Apostle Paul: The Material Spirit* (Oxford University Press, 2010); Stanley K. Stowers, "Jesus as Teacher and Stoic Ethics in the Gospel of Matthew," in *Stoicism in Early Christianity*, ed. Tuomus Rasimus et al. (Hendrickson, 2010); Stowers, "Paul and the Terrain of Philosophy"; Jennifer Eyl, *Signs, Wonders, and Gifts: Divination in the Letters of Paul* (Oxford University Press, 2019).

34. Stowers, "Paul and the Terrain of Philosophy," 156.

divine worlds synthesize through Christ's God-given *pneuma*, allowing for a new covenant between God and his people that includes granting the same kind of pneumatic body to Christ followers that Jesus received at his resurrection. Perhaps obscured by later theological ideas about what constitutes "heaven" and the afterlife, Paul's astral logic adheres to established first-century philosophy and physics (e.g., the hierarchy of substances), placing him in far closer conversation with proximate contemporaries like Philo of Alexandria and Plutarch than with later thinkers like Augustine or Dante, who arguably still dominate our afterlife imaginary.

What I describe as Paul's "cosmic topography" is well represented by one of his earliest references to extraterrestrial life and afterlife in 1 Thessalonians 4:13–18. Advocating that his addressees not be "ignorant" or unknowledgeable (4:13) about "the ones sleeping" (4:13)—that is, "the dead in Christ" (4:16)—he describes an apocalyptic scenario in which the Lord "descends from [starry] heaven" and raises the dead "first" (4:16). For the living, however, he describes a far more jolting experience:

> Then, we—the living ones still remaining—together with [the dead] will be seized by force [up] into the clouds to a meeting with the Lord in the air: and so we will always exist with the Lord. (1 Thess 4:17)

This passage precedes Paul's well-known admonition that these events "will come like a thief in the night" (5:2) leaving behind destruction (5:3) for those not snatched up into the atmosphere. What Paul describes is an impending and tremendous event in which the pneumatic bodies of both the dead and the living will be supernaturally designated—a kind of assortment at altitude found in contemporaneous literature like Plutarch's *On the Face of the Moon* (hereafter, *Face*) in which the soul and *nous* ("mind") of a person are violently ripped away from their *soma* ("body") and propelled upward toward the moon either on the path to Elysium or into the interminable liminality of sublunar orbit. Cicero's *Tusculan Disputations* 1.43 similarly claims that after death, the soul "makes its escape . . . readily from our air. . . and breaks its way through, because there is nothing swifter than the soul." If the soul "survives" this blast-off intact and unchanged in substance, it will "pierce and divide" the stormy atmosphere like a missile until it "reaches . . . and recognizes a substance resembling its own," at which point it will hover motionless, nourishing itself with the same sustenance as the stars.[35] The soul will then continue to observe and gain knowledge—its true purpose—all the while observing the contours of its new "heavenly country" (*caelestium*, 1.44).[36]

Elsewhere, Paul indicates that living on "in the air" with the Lord is not merely a figurative idea. Rather, he repeatedly invokes extraterrestrial existence, citizenry, and cityscape. In Philippians 3:20, for instance, Paul characterizes those not in Christ as destined for "destruction" (Phil 3:19) and then locates the collective fate of those "in Christ" aloft:

> For those not in Christ their ending is destruction, their god is the belly and their glory is in shame, those whose minds are on earthly things. Whereas our citizenship/commonwealth is in the starry heavens, out of which we also expect/await a savior, the lord Jesus Christ, who will change the body of our submission, instead becoming conformed to the body of Christ's glory, according to the working of his power to make subject to himself all things. (Phil 3:19–21)

Those joining Christ in the "heavens" are described as part of a city state (*politeuma*). Thus, Paul and his followers eagerly await a heavenly Christ to gather his fellow citizens and transform their humble, susceptible, and corporeal bodies into something of a more ethereal stuff suitable for a heavenly city. Taking the entirety of Paul's correspondence into consideration, he means to indicate that they will be "conformed" into pneumatic bodies like Christ's; indeed, he explicitly states that those in Christ will be "raised in a pneumatic body" in 1 Corinthians 15:44.[37]

---

35. A portion of this passage is also referenced in Litwa, "Divine Corporeality and the Pneumatic Body," 139. Litwa additionally cites Josephus, who claims that the soul, once released from the body, settles "among the stars" (*Jewish War* 6.47).

36. I have borrowed the translation "heavenly country" from Cicero, *Tusculan Disputations*, trans. J. E. King, Loeb Classical Library 141 (Harvard University Press, 1927), 54–55. For additional examples of the "rising soul" motif—including in Plato and Plutarch—consider Alan Segal, "Heavenly Ascent in Hellenistic Judaism, Early Christianity and their Environment," *ANRW* 2: 23, no. 2 (1980): 1333–94, esp. 1346–51.

37. Stowers makes a similar, but more elaborate, point in his "Paul and the Terrain of Philosophy" (154) that I will discuss further below. For more on the composition—and

M. David Litwa argues for a similar reading in his "Divine Corporeality and the Pneumatic Body," citing numerous examples throughout popular and philosophical literature wherein ancient Mediterranean deities were understood to possess "'super bodies' built from superior substances" and were, by extension, of superior size, beauty, and luminosity, as well as superior moral and intellectual disposition.[38] For Litwa, this pneumatic body is in some sense corporeal, albeit "fitted for eternal life." Drawing examples from the Stoics, he demonstrates that the soul (*psuchē*) was understood "*to be a type of body* . . . pneuma . . . the highest 'part' of the human being" and thus the proper "eschatological 'stuff' " to survive in an astral or sublunar city.[39] To this, Litwa suggests Paul is influenced, in part, by the Platonic notion that the immortal soul is eternal.[40] Thus, like Cicero and others, Paul appears to have adopted a "Platonically modified Stoicism" characteristic of the first century in which the soul, made of *pneuma* and buoyant like ether, rockets toward the stars, retaining a certain sense of materiality, yet metamorphosing into a more refined starlike pneumatic form and, ultimately, finding an eternal home with God.

In 2 Corinthians 5:1–5, Paul once again hints at the ethereal "home" that God will make for his people "in the heavens," extending this imagery into a metaphor about shedding the earthly "tent" or tabernacle that houses the mortal body and eagerly "putting on" God's eternal heavenly dwelling (*tois ouranois*) in its place:

> For we know that if our earthly house of the tabernacle is destroyed, we have a building from God—a home not made by [mortal] hands

---

survival—of the soul in Greek and Roman philosophical thought: Christopher Gill, *The Structured Self in Hellenistic and Roman Thought* (Oxford University Press, 2006). I transliterate *soma* as body to indicate its distinction in Paul's thought from *sarx*, or "flesh," which has significance for my coming discussion of 1 Cor 15:35–58.

38. Litwa, "Divine Corporeality and the Pneumatic Body," 121. To Litwa's catalog of literary and philosophical examples we might add the resurrected hero described in some detail, and to similar effect, in Philostratus's *On Heroes*.

39. Litwa, "Divine Corporeality and the Pneumatic Body," 137, emphasis original.

40. The Stoics, rather, saw the corporate soul as immortal but not necessarily that of the individual; Diogenes Laertius, *Lives of Eminent Philosophers* 7.156; Litwa, "Divine Corporeality and the Pneumatic Body," 139.

> [and] eternal in the heavens.[41] For also in this we groan, greatly desiring to put on our home out of heaven [for in] being clothed, we shall not be found naked. For indeed the ones who are in the tabernacle groan, being burdened, since we do not wish to put off but to put on, in order that the mortal may be swallowed up by the life. Now the one having worked this very thing for us is God, the one having given to us the down payment of the *pneuma*.[42]

Paul simultaneously emphasizes the earthly and the heavenly, the corruptible and the incorruptible, and, crucially, the visible and the invisible in this passage. The implication of these comparisons is that true knowledge or the true nature of a material object—that is, correct judgment (*epistêmê*)—is not indicated by what is visible to the eye (its "glory") but by its innate or divine qualities. For example, in 2 Corinthians 4:18 he specifies that those in Christ "do not consider the things being seen, but . . . the things not being seen, for the things being seen are temporary, but the things not being seen are eternal."

The significance of this contrast is illustrated by means of the new covenant between God and his people "through Christ" in 2 Corinthians 3:1–18. Drawing an extended analogy with Moses at the center, Paul tells his addressees that they themselves are a letter (3:2) written not in ink, but by the "*pneuma* of a living God" (3:3); not chiseled into dead stones (3:7), but on tablets of the human heart (3:2). Reflecting on Exodus 34:29–35, he claims that the people of Israel, after establishing their covenant through Moses, were unable to fix their eyes upon Moses's face (3:7); he was forced to veil himself (3:13) in the aftermath of speaking directly with God, as "the glory of his face (3:7)" was too awesome to comprehend. Paul suggests that this same veil remains (3:14) now in the hearts (3:15) of those attempting to comprehend and follow the Law.[43] Rhetoric about the Law as an agent of death, sin, or misjudgment is rife within Paul's letters and linked to a larger discourse about the passions and

---

41. It is possible this passage is invoking the language of the LXX translation of 2 Chron 2.

42. When Paul speaks of "putting on" a heavenly body, he may have in mind the LXX translation of Isa 61:3 in which a "generation of righteousness" is given "a garment of *doxa* instead of a *pneuma* of neglect."

43. Oddly, several English translations replace "hearts" with "minds" in this passage.

moral weakness.[44] While the Law remains "spiritual" or pneumatic—as he plainly states in Romans 7:14—the new covenant through Christ offers greater permanence (3:11), "freedom" (3:17), and pneumatic connection to God. It is here that Paul once again uses the language of transformation, stating that with "unveiled faces" those in Christ will metamorphize into "the same image" as the Lord, as though reflected in a mirror (3:18).

If You Believe They Put a Man on the Moon. . . .[45]

Recognizing Paul's use of technical and philosophical language has done much over the years to help sharpen our understanding of his rhetorical strategies. Theological or anachronistic translations of words like *pistis* ("faith"), *pneuma* ("spirit"), *ekklēsia* ("community"/"church") assume a certain taken-for-granted quality. Translating *ekklēsia* as "church," for instance, signals a social cohesion and an institutional stability that is plainly ahistorical to Paul's moment.[46] Similarly, outside of contemporary Christianity, translating *pneuma* as "spirit" makes little sense as an argument for adherence to Christ without its materialist or Stoic context.

Scholars are frequently bedeviled by Paul's "systematic ambiguity" and the way he appears to "[combine] . . . Stoic materialism and Platonic mentalism."[47] He does not easily conform to an established school of Greco-Roman philosophical thought and therefore resists categorization. To refer to his specific brand of philosophy as "popular" accomplishes twin goals: First, it acknowledges his influences and intellectual debts including, and beyond, the Greek translation of Jewish scriptures; and, second, it helps us really to understand the social context in which Paul is functioning. To the best of our knowledge, Paul is attempting to render his claims acceptable to a first-century

44. For instance, Engberg-Pedersen, *Paul and the Stoics*; Wasserman, *The Death of the Soul in Romans 7*; Engberg-Pedersen, *Cosmology of the Self in the Apostle Paul*.

45. "Man on the Moon" by R.E.M. released on *Automatic for the People* in October 1992 under Warner Bros. Records.

46. Jennifer Eyl, "Semantic Voids, New Testament Translation, and Anachronism: The Case of Paul's Use of *Ekklēsia*," *Method and Theory in the Study of Religion* 26 (2014): 315–39.

47. John Dillon, *The Platonic Heritage: Further Studies in the History of Platonism and Early Christianity* (Routledge, 2012), passim.

pagan audience, not a gaggle of Stoic wonks. Likewise, his discourse on the heavens/cosmos is not random or metaphorical. Rather, it represents a remapping of the natural world with the promise of the transformation of the body through resurrection and continuing existence in a new realm—"the glory of the heavens/cosmos" (1 Cor 15:40).

The stakes for this kind of claim were incredibly high. Paul is not merely a letter writer but a divinatory and wonderworking specialist. His expertise as a philosopher cannot be meaningfully distinguished from his expertise as a purveyor of "pneumatic" knowledge and power. To this extent, Paul's focus on the moon and the cosmos represents a tangible afterlife strategy with material consequences. Karen ní Mheallaigh articulates a similar claim about Plutarch's focus and use of the moon as a "doxographical" symbol of the imperial period:

> If . . . Plutarch's goal . . . was to weld together the metaphysical and physical components of the Middle Platonic curriculum, then we may see the Moon as an icon of Plutarch's intellectual world. Especially Middle Platonism with its diet of physics and mysticism—and perhaps broadly still of the culture of what used to be called the "Second Sophistic," with its *enkyklios paideia* that included astronomy as well as linguistic, rhetorical, and literary expertise. This tendency of multiple theories and approaches to converge around the Moon converts it into a doxographical space, an archive of ideas. It is no accident that the selenographic impulse—the desire to collate all theories and write about the Moon—coincides precisely with the globalizing period of the Roman Empire.[48]

Paul adds to this "selenographic impulse" a connection via Christ to a rarefied genealogy and special status, a pneumatic body, and "victory" (1 Cor 15:57) over death and other enemies (1 Thess 4–5). More than a Thessalian Trick, Paul is not only willing to lasso the moon. He promises his audience a new world order as well.

48. Ní Mheallaigh, *Moon*, 188.

There's a Starman Waiting in the Sky. . . .[49]

Throughout 1 Corinthians 15:35–49, Paul invokes the language of *pneuma*, glory (*doxa*), power (*dunamis*), and the heavens as a prooftext for claims about the nature of a postresurrection reality in orbit. After delineating the glories of the cosmos, he proceeds to explain how those participating in Christ will receive pneumatic bodies in the afterlife, bearing the image or likeness of their new heavenly co-heir:

> The first man [Adam] was out of the ground and earthy, the second man [Christ] is out of [starry] heaven (*ouranou*). . . . Such [is] the earthy one, so too the earthy ones; and such [is] the heavenly one, so too the heavenly ones: and as we bear the likeness (*eikona*) of the earthy, we will also bear the likeness of the heavenly. (1 Cor 15:47–49)

Paul makes allied claims in 1 Corinthians 15:50–58 and in 1 Thessalonians 4:13–5:11 (discussed above) about the "mystery" (*musterion*) that awaits them when they will transform into heavenly, pneumatic beings, with Christ descending from the clouds at the sound of a trumpet to raise everyone, including the dead, into the air. But how this process is to take place seems as mysterious in Paul's extant letters as the so-called mystery itself.

As indicated above, Paul's cursory description of death and transformation shares much in common with more detailed treatises like Plutarch's *Face.* A dialogue set between a certain Sulla and Lamprias, *Face* establishes the moon as a celestial terrain at the "threshold of life and death" between the material earth and the ethereal sun (928B). There, refined substances like "light," "fiery bodies," and even mind and souls (*nous . . . psuchē*) experience a natural buoyancy and rocket into orbit (927C; 943A). Lamprias explains that mind and soul are intermixed with body (*somatos*) and, furthermore, that mind and soul are intermixed with each other; however, mind remains "superior and more divine than soul" (943A). Thus, when death occurs, the body remains with the earth that supplied it (the first death), returning to the soil as the soul and mind, intermingled, "swiftly and violently" (943B) extract themselves from the body and ascend toward the moon. In the "ether about the moon" (943D),

49. David Bowie, "Starman" released as a single from *The Rise and Fall of Ziggy Stardust and the Spiders from Mars* (1972) by RCA Records.

a transformation or second death occurs. The soul and mind are gently disentangled by Persephone—the moon drawing the soul, and the mind returning to its source of creative fire and light: The sun (943B–C). While all souls are "destined to wander [in this] region between earth and moon (*ges kai selenes*)" in order to experience their transformation, those who led less than virtuous mortal lives, or who are still attached to the corporeal world, find themselves in a rougher stream of air, forced to withstand an onslaught of purifying celestial winds that strip away miasma (μιασμούς) as if it were a foul odor (943C). Many of these unfortunate souls attempt to cling to the moon's craggy surface for refuge, but they are quickly swept away. The virtuous, by contrast, find "firm footing" on its surface and, wearing "crowns of feathers," move about freely (943D). Of these latter souls, some will venture to the side of the moon that faces the stars—Elysium—while others will elect to become daimons, oracles, or intercessors in human events (944D; 945B). In all cases, these souls retain the likeness or image of their mortal bodies, like a mold or the imprint of a wax seal (945A).

Paul's promise of pneumatic bodies for those in Christ corresponds in important ways with Plutarch's lunar afterlife predictions—from the rapid ascent of luminous souls to meeting other divine and intermediary beings in sublunar orbit. Compellingly Paul, like Lucian, also describes intergalactic military battles, with Paul's God neutralizing any competing authority or power (*dunamin*, 1 Cor 15:24), until all "enemies" are vanquished "under his feet" (15:25). Paul hints that God's cosmic warfare will conscript pneumatic Christ people into service, and they will meet Christ "in the aer, the region between the earth and the moon, and join him in defeating recalcitrant lower divine beings, and judge angels."[50] Ultimately, Christ and his pneumatic brothers (*adelphoi*) will bring God's new civilization (*basileian*) into fruition, and a new age will begin (15:30, 24).

As for the issue of the likeness of the heavenly pneumatic bodies of God's cosmic warriors, we only know that they will resemble that of "the starry man" (*Anthropos . . . ouranou*), but to what extent is not clear. Perhaps they will all take on the identical form of Christ (cf. 2 Cor 3:18). Perhaps they will be, as Plutarch describes, imprints of their former earthly bodies in all respects. Lucian compellingly suggests that such incorporeal forms will be

50. Stowers, "Paul and the Terrain of Philosophy," 154.

"intangible and fleshless, with only shape and figure," yet they will continue to "live and move and think and talk"—"naked souls . . . in the semblance of their bodies . . . like upright shadows," clothed in nothing but "delicate purple spider webs."

As a plain matter of textual and comparative analysis, the status of mortal women in Paul's afterlife remains murky. While there is ample evidence that women in Christ will be included in Paul's afterlife scenario, whether their physiological gender will remain the same or also be "transformed" is unclear.[51] With childbearing seemingly not a factor, what would be the need to preserve the lesser female body?[52] Plato, too, speaks compellingly about chaste love between men being far superior to procreation with women, as men produce offspring "more worthy and enduring than children, such as poetry, philosophy, and law codes." Given that Paul follows Plato's *Republic* in nearly all respects on how to run a utopian society—from endorsing communal property (462a9–e3), to envisioning a literal body politic (462b4–d3), to the destructive effects of marriage and procreation (462b8–c5; 1 Cor 7)—is he more likely to conform to Platonic thinking for God's interstellar army and civilization?[53]

With their undercurrents of warfare, destruction, death, and violence, whether it is Paul, Philo, Plutarch, Lucian, or even Alexander, discourses on the moon are ultimately about a promise of freedom. For some, it is the freedom of adventure; for others, it is freedom from the body, suffering, or oppression. In each case the moon represents currency, whether social, religious, or even economic. Philo, meditating on the ignorance and burdens of mortality, muses that "souls that are without flesh and body spend their days in the theater of the universe" (*On the Giants* 31.266–267).[54] And for a good number of imperial writers and wonderworkers, that theater's mezzanine is the moon.

---

51. For more on this topic, I recommend Taylor Petrey, *Resurrecting Parts: Early Christians on Desire, Reproduction, and Sexual Difference* (Routledge, 2015).

52. Aristotle, *The Generation of Animals* 737a 25–30.

53. Kathy L. Gaca, *The Making of Fornication: Eros, Ethics, and Political Reform in Greek Philosophy and Early Christianity* (University of California Press, 2017), 29–30.

54. I have taken some liberties with "the Theater of All," given the full context of this passage—i.e., contrasting those "without" flesh to those burdened by it, forced to stare at the ground instead of at the rotating stars and planets above them.

V

Authorizing Paul's Gospel

CHAPTER TWELVE

Paul, Epiphanies, and Social Formation

Sarah E. Rollens
Rhodes College

Introduction

The colloquial meaning of the English word *epiphany* denotes a sudden, dramatic realization about something. It also carries another, slightly less common meaning, which is the manifestation or appearance of something supernatural. Both meanings stem directly from a single word in ancient Greek: *Epiphaneia*, which means "appearance" or "manifestation." Epiphanies in the ancient Mediterranean world involved a deity or a communication from a deity and were usually characterized by some sort of spectacular or unexpected element. Perhaps the most well-known ancient example of this is when God "manifests" himself to the prophet Moses through a burning bush in Exodus 3. A close second known to most modern Christians might be the colorful version of the apostle Paul's vision of the risen Jesus on the road to Damascus in Acts 9. Even so, New Testament scholars have historically been reticent to use the term *epiphany* for Paul's encounter, because the appearance of the Christian God in Jesus's human form has traditionally been regarded as something unique and qualitatively different from the many stories in the "pagan" world.[1] Indeed, Christian modern readers may know the term *epiphany* more in reference

1. The terminology of *pagan* is challenging in the study of early Christianity for several reasons. Above all, its meaning has been dominated by its use as a polemical category that late antique Christians aimed at others who did not share their religious views. Even if we try to use it as a neutral descriptor for non-Christians (and usually it implies non-Jews as well), that, too, could be confusing, as many categories of identity could overlap in antiquity. For instance, one could be a "pagan," then become interested in the stories about Jesus and the practices associated with his worship, but have no plans of abandoning the worship of previous deities. Thus, any simplistic binary between the identity of pagans and Christians is always more complicated in reality, which this volume explores well.

to the Christian holiday of Epiphany, which commemorates appearance of the infant Jesus to his visitors from the east (*magoi*, Matt 2:1–12). The long-standing assumption of the uniqueness of the Christian epiphany in biblical scholarship stems from the fact that much of the history of biblical studies often had Christian theological or devotional aims, whether explicitly or implicitly.

This essay, which is a revised version of an earlier, more detailed article, has two very specific goals: First, to show that Paul's epiphanies closely resemble counterparts in the Greco-Roman ("pagan") world, and second, perhaps more importantly, to demonstrate that these Pauline epiphanies *functioned* just like their pagan counterparts in terms of group formation. Indeed, claims to have seen visions of Jesus after his death would not have been extraordinary at all to Paul's urban audiences. In fact, we can (and will!) look at evidence from a common Greek and Roman social form known as an "association" to see that his audiences would have had a very specific cultural framework into which to place his claims to have encountered the risen Jesus. In other words, far from being unique experiences that immediately stunned Paul's audiences into becoming followers of the Judean god and his son Jesus, Paul's epiphanies would have been exactly what they expected from *anyone* trying to found an association devoted to *any* sort of god or goddess.[2]

Greek and Roman Associations

Recent research has convincingly shown that many aspects of Paul's urban groups can be better understood by comparison with Greek and Roman associations. "Association" is a wide-ranging category for numerous social groups in the ancient Mediterranean world that could form for a number of reasons—something like "club" or "organization" might capture the meaning in English well. Associations could, for instance, be based on a shared commitment to a deity such as Zeus or Aphrodite, a mutual occupation (such as weaving, fishing, or sailing), or the regional or ethnic identity of its members (such as Egyptians, Judeans, or Phrygians). There are even associations made up of

2. This essay was published in a slightly different version in an academic journal: Sarah E. Rollens, "The God Came to Me in a Dream: Epiphanies in Voluntary Associations as a Context for Paul's Vision of Christ," *Harvard Theological Review* 111, no. 1 (2018): 41–65. That version contains more detailed bibliographical references, as well as more engagement with the ancient texts in their original languages. Readers wanting to go deeper into this topic are invited to read that article.

various people who lived in the same neighborhood and even some just for people who lived and worked within a particular household. No matter the reason for their forming or the basis for their membership, these associations were found all over the Roman Empire and attest to ancient people's desire to form communities with other people.

We know a great deal about these ancient associations based on the written records that they left. These records exist in papyri, in inscriptions on buildings and on public statues, and on ostraca (shards of broken clay vessels that have been repurposed as writing surfaces), among other forms. These recount such mundane affairs of associations as meeting frequency, membership lists, initiation requirements, fees and fines associated with the group, and regulations for meetings. By comparing Paul's letters with these records, it has been possible to generate new insights about the Christ groups he wrote to, namely, the likely size and frequency of their meetings,[3] their venues for socializing,[4] their financial dealings within the groups,[5] their group activities and leadership structures,[6] and their relationships to other Christ groups.[7] Whereas most comparative studies have focused on the structure and activities of Paul's groups, I argue that associations can help illuminate other aspects

---

3. For instance, Richard S. Ascough, "Reimagining the Size of Pauline Christ Groups in Light of Association Meeting Places," in *Scribal Practices and Social Structures among Jesus Adherents: Essays in Honour of John S. Kloppenborg*, ed. William E. Arnal et al, BETL 285 (Peeters, 2016), 547–65.

4. For instance, Inge Nielsen, *Housing the Chosen: The Architectural Context of Mystery Groups and Religious Associations in the Ancient World*, Contextualizing the Sacred (Brepols, 2014).

5. For instance, Richard Last and Sarah Rollens, "Accounting Practices in P.Tebt. III/2 894 and Pauline Groups," *Early Christianity* 5 (2014): 441–74.

6. For instance, Richard Last, *The Pauline Church and the Corinthian Ekklēsia: Greco-Roman Associations in Comparative Context*, SNTS Monograph Series 164 (Cambridge University Press, 2015); Philip A. Harland, "Familial Dimensions of Group Identity: 'Brothers' (ἀδελφοί) in Associations of the Greek East," *JBL* 124 (2005): 491–513; Philip A. Harland, "Familial Dimensions of Group Identity (II): 'Mothers' and 'Fathers' in Associations and Synagogues of the Greek World," *Journal for the Study of Judaism in the Persian, Hellenistic, and Roman Period* 38 (2007): 57–79; John S. Kloppenborg, "Greco-Roman *Thiasoi*, the *Ekklêsia* at Corinth, and Conflict Management" in *Redescribing Paul and the Corinthians*, ed. Ron Cameron and Merrill P. Miller, ECL 5 (Scholars, 2011), 186–218.

7. For instance, Richard S. Ascough, "Translocal Relationships among Voluntary Associations and Early Christianity," *JECS* 5 (1997): 223–41.

of his groups as well: In particular, the reason that they took Paul's authority seriously, and the persuasiveness of Paul's "backstory," which he conveyed in order to justify his undertaking his mission throughout the Mediterranean world.[8] This backstory, as we will see, easily served as a foundation for the groups' common identities.

Simply put: Many of Paul's audiences would have received his story about encountering the risen Jesus in a vision as rather commonplace, given the frequency of other similar claims among associations. That is, Paul's claim to have encountered a deity in a vision, which caused him to set out on a mission to set up Christ groups throughout the Mediterranean world, is an entirely ordinary way to narrate the origins of an ancient association, as we will shortly see. The people in his groups would thus not have assumed his vision of Christ was self-evidently exceptional or even unique in their world.

To be clear, this discussion is not about what actually happened to Paul to initiate his "conversion,"[9] nor is it about the genesis of his visions of Christ or their effect on him. Rather, my interest is in how Paul's (non-Jewish) audiences would have understood his claims within their wider cultural framework, especially if they considered his Christ group to be like the many other associations with which they were already familiar.

Epiphanies in Antiquity and in Greco-Roman Associations

At the outset, we should note that epiphanies are ubiquitous in Greek and Roman literature. For this reason, we can likely assume that Paul's audiences,

8. Backstory is in quotation marks here in my first usage, because it is a rather colloquial way of phrasing this idea. The most technical terminology for the very same idea (which I will be avoiding here) is "aetiology," that is, a story that explains how things got to their present state. The creation story in Genesis 1, for instance, is an aetiology for why Jewish people observe the Sabbath.

9. "Conversion" is in quotation marks as well, because it is a very tricky concept in religious studies—and even more so the study of *ancient* religions. In the polytheistic world of the Roman Empire, people could—and did—easily revere multiple gods. Thus, a person's interest in a new god (such as Jesus) would not necessarily mean that they had "converted" to an entirely new religion or that they even abandoned those gods they were previously interested in. See further Paula Fredriksen, "Mandatory Retirement: Ideas in the Study of Christian Origins Whose Time Has Come to Go," *Studies in Religion/Sciences Religieuses* 35, no. 2 (2006): 231–46, here 232–38.

whether they were highly literate or not, were generally familiar with stories of gods variously manifesting to people, whether it be through the form of an animal or of a traveler in disguise or of something altogether different. What's more, it was customary for authors to depict these visions of gods as taking place in dreams.[10] And given ancient people's desire to please as many gods as possible (or at least as many as they thought necessary and appropriate), one would want to be sure to do whatever the deity in one's dream told them to do.

Despite this cultural ubiquity, New Testament scholars have often treated Paul's vision of Jesus in the New Testament as unambiguously remarkable—an event that, when told to others, would immediately persuade them that something utterly unique had happened to Paul. Not only are such encounters *not* unique in the ancient world, they are not even unique cross-culturally.[11] Rather, in having encountered a god in a vision, Paul was simply doing what many others did in his cultural context.[12]

Before we look at evidence for epiphanies in ancient associations, it is helpful to consider examples in ancient literature, so that we can see how widespread they are as literary tropes. Our first example is the Roman historian Suetonius's description of prophetic dreams had by Emperor Nero and by (soon-to-be emperor) Vespasian in the first century CE:

> He [Vespasian] dreamed in Greece that the beginning of good fortune for himself and his family would come as soon as Nero had a tooth extracted; and on the next day it came to pass that a physician walked into the hall and showed him a tooth which he had just then taken out. . . . Omens were also reported from Rome: Nero in his latter days was admonished in a dream to take the sacred chariot of

10. J. S. Hanson, "Dreams and Visions in the Greco-Roman World and Early Christianity," in *ANRW* (1980) 23.2: 1395–1427, here 1397.

11. Pieter Craffert, "Altered States of Consciousness: Visions, Spirit Possession, Sky Journeys," in *Understanding the Social World of the New Testament*, ed. Richard DeMaris and Dietmar Neufeld (Routledge, 2009), 126–46.

12. As Heidi Wendt observes, Paul was "hardly unique among first-century Judeans in adducing literary mysteries, prophecies, and eschatological narratives from Judean writings, nor, for that matter, in receiving messages from God through revelations, dreams, or other methods of divination" (*At the Temple Gates: The Religion of Freelance Experts in the Roman Empire* [Oxford University Press, 2016], 154).

> Jupiter Optimus Maximus from its shrine to the house of Vespasian and from there to the Circus. (Suetonius, *The Lives of the Caesars* [Vespasian] 5.5–7)

A second example is the apostle Peter's dream about food in Acts 10:9–15, which is another well-known instance of receiving divine communication in a dream:

> Peter went up on the roof to pray . . . he fell into a trance. He saw the heaven opened and something like a large sheet coming down, being lowered to the ground by its four corners. In it were all kinds of four-footed creatures and reptiles and birds of the air. Then he heard a voice saying, "Get up, Peter; kill and eat." But Peter said, "By no means, Lord, for I have never eaten anything that is profane or unclean." The voice said to him again, a second time, "What God has made clean, you must not call profane." (NRSVue)

Many early Christian theologians treated this dream (or vision, since ancient people did not always distinguish between the two) as an authoritative pronouncement from God that Jewish Christ followers were allowed to eat nonkosher foods that other Jews typically avoided. The general idea, then, was that gods revealed themselves or important information through dreams and visions to select people who were thereby empowered to take some sort of action.

Turning now to the written evidence for ancient associations that we will be comparing with Paul's letters, we will quickly see how these dreams, visions, and other epiphanies were used to legitimate the founding of the associations and the authority of their most prominent leaders (whether they were founders, financial patrons, or others). These epiphanies take slightly different forms than the examples from Suetonius and Acts, because association records tend to be recorded in inscriptions and documentary papyri,[13] not in works of literature. But even when expressed in different forms, they nevertheless

13. Papyri from the ancient world are generally grouped into two categories: Literary papyri (novels, philosophical treatises, satirical works, plays and dialogues, etc.) and documentary papyri (records, archival materials, receipts, contracts, and other administrative documents).

contribute a great deal to the authority of the figure who received the epiphany and often explicitly approved the social formation in the association.

Our first example of an epiphany in the written records of associations is an inscription known as *SIG*[3] 985.[14] This documents the regulations of a household association and describes a man called Dionysios, who was singled out to receive instructions from a deity in a dream:

> To good fortune! For health . . . common salvation (?), and the best reputation, . . . the instructions (?) . . .which were given to Dionysios in his sleep were written down, . . . giving access (?) . . . into his house to men . . . and women (?), free people and household slaves. . . . For in this house altars (?) . . . have been set up for Zeus Eumenes and Hestia . . . his consort (?), for the other Saviour gods [a list of names of more than ten gods follows]. Zeus has given instructions to this man for the performance of the purifications, the cleansings, . . . and the mysteries (?) . . . in accordance with ancestral custom and in accordance with what has now . . . been written here (?).[15]

Admittedly, the text is fragmentary, but we can nevertheless make out the important claim that some sort of information was "given to Dionysios in his sleep . . . [and subsequently] written down." This information, the reader is told, came directly from a god, namely, Zeus himself. It is likely that Dionysios is the male head of the household already, and so to receive this epiphany straight from Zeus no doubt heightened his authority compared to the other

14. Textual evidence for associations is often referred to with a series of abbreviations and numbers that catalogue where the text was found and how it was archived by the primary scholars who worked on it. Many of the inscriptions are fragmentary or unreadable (hence, the ellipses to signal gaps in the text), and sometimes scholars propose wording that would have likely filled in a section that is otherwise unclear (those suggestions are followed by question marks to signal their conjectural nature).

15. The inscription continues and outlines the group's regulations, though it is not reproduced in full here. Greek text and translation taken from: Philip Harland, "[121] Divine Instructions for the Household Association of Dionysios (late II-early I BCE)," *Associations in the Greco-Roman World: An Expanding Collection of Inscriptions, Papyri, and Other Sources in Translation*, November 10, 2011, http://www.philipharland.com/greco-roman-associations/?p=141.

members of the association. The encounter, moreover, sanctioned him to pronounce the regulations of the household association. In other words, if anyone were to ask *why* the association carried out the rituals and practices that it did, this inscription gives a reason: Because Zeus specifically told Dionysios to do these things.

IG X/2.1 255 is another fascinating example of an epiphany rendered in an association inscription. This (again fragmentary) narrative reveals the complex history regarding how an association devoted to the Egyptian gods Sarapis and Isis came into being:

> . . . it seemed in his sleep that Sarapis stood beside him (Xenainetos) and told him that after having arrived in Opus, he should carry a message to Eurynomos, son of Timasitheos, to receive him (Sarapis) and his sister Isis, and that he should deliver to him (Eurynomos) the letter under the pillow. And waking up, he (Xenainetos) marveled at the dream and yet he was at a loss about what he should do, because he was a political rival to Eurynomos. But, falling asleep again and seeing the same things, when he awoke he found the letter under the pillow, just as it had been indicated to him. . . . [Later] he gave the letter to Eurynomos and reported the things that were decreed by the god. When Eurynomos received the letter and heard the things that Xenainetos said, he was at a loss because they were political rivals towards one other. . . . After having read the letter and having seen (that) the things that were written were in agreement with the things first having been said by him (Xenainetos), he (Eurynomos) received Sarapis and Isis. After he provided hospitality in the household of Sosinike, she received Sarapis and Isis among the household gods. . . .[16]

This is a truly complicated series of events, and, for that reason, it requires some unpacking. In short: A man named Xenainetos encounters the Egyptian god Sarapis in a dream, and Sarapis tells him to take a message to Eurynomos,

16. Greek text taken from the Packard Humanities Institute (PHI) database of inscriptions (Packard Humanities Institute, "PHI Greek Inscriptions," September 1, 2015, http://inscriptions.packhum.org/); translation from Richard Ascough, Philip Harland, and John S. Kloppenborg, *Associations in the Greco-Roman World: A Sourcebook* (Baylor University Press, 2012), 48–49.

who is unfortunately Xenainetos's political rival. Given that it is not wise to refuse the gods' instruction, Xenainetos does as he is instructed, which results in Eurynomos "receiv[ing]" Sarapis and Isis—which is another way of saying that he joined the association of Sarapis and Isis devotees. Eurynomos then also helped (probably with financial assistance) a woman named Soinike incorporate Sarapis and Isis into her household "cult."[17]

For the purposes of our analysis, we can notice that Xenainetos gains extensive authority from being visited by Sarapis in a dream. The inscription narrates that "in his sleep that Sarapis stood beside him and told him" a variety of messages and actions to take that allowed him to eventually convince his political rival to "receive Sarapis and Isis." In other words, it appears that Eurynomos was sufficiently persuaded by Xenainetos's claim: The former accepted his claim to have seen Sarapis in his dream to the extent that he acted on it.

In another inscription, *SEG* 15, 637, a householder named Poseidonios receives a message from the god Apollo who decrees that he and his family should honor Zeus Patroos (literally, "Zeus of the Fathers"), Apollo, and the Mother of the Gods (that is, they should found a household association to honor them). The inscription describes his epiphany thus: "When Poseidonios sent to inquire of Apollo for himself and for members of his family, past and present, both the men and the women, regarding what to do and what to accomplish, the god answered: 'It is more desirable and better for them to do as their ancestors did and to appease and honor [the following gods].'"[18] In

17. Using the words *cult* and *cultic* require some discussion, for this is a very difficult category in the academic study of religion. Jason N. Blum has explained clearly how the term *cult* has become a negatively marked label that people have historically applied to religions that they think are different or "weird" ("What Is the Difference between a Religion and a Cult?," in *Religion in 5 Minutes*, ed. Aaron W. Hughes and Russell T. McCutcheon [Equinox, 2017], 26–29, 27). However, scholars who study the ancient Roman and Greek worlds often use the word *cult* in an entirely different way than the one being critiqued by Blum. They use *cult* in a way that stems from the original Latin meaning of *cultus*, which describes the entire set of practices involved in worshipping and taking care of a deity. In many ways, this is similar to "religious practice," broadly conceived. So, for example, to talk about the "cult of Sarapis" is simply to talk about a particular expression of religiosity and practice that a person (or association) directed toward Sarapis.

18. Greek text taken from Packard Humanities Institute, "PHI Greek Inscriptions"; translation from Philip Harland, *Greco-Roman Associations: Texts, Translations and Commentary II North Coast of the Black Sea, Asia Minor*, BZNW 204 (De Gruyter, 2014), 187–88.

other words, this divine message authorized Poseidonios to guide his entire household in devotional practices aimed at pleasing these gods.

These examples show how ordinary people had epiphanies, dreams, and visions of gods that supported their status over their household and over the different groups of people who came together in associations. Whether members of an association *believed* the founder's claim of a divine encounter is not the point. Such claims are rhetorically functional, especially in a written medium.[19] In other words, ancient people would have been socialized to understand these claims not solely for their truth value, but also for what they indicated about the recipient's social status and prestige, which told them where they should place them on the social hierarchy. As we will see, when Paul arrived in cities throughout the Roman Empire, many people probably would have expected him to share similar stories.

Before turning to Paul, however, we should also explore a second important function of epiphanies: They provided a shared sense of identity for associations. This was especially crucial for groups that had diverse constituencies. As we saw, members of an association *might* share an occupation, ethnicity, or household, but in others, their group activities or their devotion to a particular deity may have been the main feature they had in common. This made it all the more critical to establish shared identity and origins story—what scholars in the academic study of religion call a "myth of origins"—that the group could hold in common.[20] Association inscriptions often contain these myths of origin that translate into a shared means of expressing belonging.

Let us look at some association inscriptions that generate this sense of belonging for a group. In fact, we have already seen two. Earlier we looked at the inscription known as *SIG*³ 985, which described Dionysios receiving instructions for how to establish the association in his household. Those in his

19. Harrisson, *Dreams and Dreaming*, 102.

20. In the study of religion, *myth* is not a derogatory word; nor does it indicate anything about the truth or falsehood of a story. Instead, a myth is simply an important story to a group. A myth of origins for a group is a story about where the people came from and how they came to be united as a group. Through the process of telling and retelling this story, members solidify their group identity and origins. Often, myths of origins cannot be verified with empirical evidence, but that is not really the point. The point is that, regardless of their truth value, they do important work in terms of identity creation and social formation for a group of people.

household (described in the inscription as including "men, women, free people, and household slaves") could have taken Dionysios's epiphany as a foundational moment for their association. They might explain it to their friends across the city in this way: "Zeus visited the head of our household and instructed him in how to carry out sacrificial, ritual, and social practices—that's why there is a Zeus association in our household." We can see, then, that by thinking creatively about how these stories might have worked for an association, we can understand how they provided a foundation for a group's identity.

Or recall another inscription, *IG* X/2.1 255, which told of the elaborate series of events that led to the founding of a Sarapis and Isis association. This time, the backstory for the association may have gone something like this: "The god Sarapis visited Xenainetos in a dream, spurring him to take a written message to his political rival Euronymos. Though he initially hesitated to accept it, Euronymos eventually conceded to receiving Sarapis and Isis and even helped establish an association for their devotion. That's why we have this particular association in Sosinike's house." For the members of this association, this foundational account is fairly exciting. It means that their association came into being against all odds, after a well-known political rivalry had been overcome with divine assistance. Everyone likes a good story of overcoming adversity!

When it comes to dramatic myths of origin, perhaps the most famous is found in an inscription known as *SIG*[2] 663, which describes how another association dedicated to Sarapis came into being on the island of Delos. The sequence of events is rather complex:

> The priest Apollonios [II] inscribed this according to the command of the god. For our grandfather, Apollonios, an Egyptian from the priestly class, having brought his god with him from Egypt, continued serving his god according to ancestral custom and, it seems, lived for ninety-seven years. My father, Demetrios, followed him in serving the gods and, because of his piety, he was honored by the god. . . . He lived for sixty-one years. . . . After receiving the sacred things and being appointed to perform the services in a diligent manner, the god instructed me through a dream that I should dedicate his own temple of Sarapis, and that he was not to be in rented rooms anymore. Furthermore, he would find the place where the temple should be

> located, indicating this by a sign. . . . Now since the god willed it, a contract of purchase was completed and the temple was quickly built in six months. Now certain people conspired against us and the god. They sought a judgment against the temple and myself in a public trial, seeking either punishment or a fine. But the god promised me in a dream that we would win the case. Now that the proceedings have ended and we have won as is worthy of the god, we praise the gods by demonstrating appropriate gratitude.[21]

To simplify this series of events somewhat: The dedicator (the priest Apollonios, who is the grandson of an Egyptian priest, also called Apollonios) describes being instructed in a dream that he must build a special temple for the god Sarapis on Delos (prior to this, Sarapis's devotees had rented space for meetings). He was even given a divine sign to indicate where it should be built. After the temple was built, there was a conspiracy against the group, perhaps involving a lawsuit, which culminated in a public trial. The speaker was *again* visited by the god in a dream during the trial and was promised that he would be victorious. The Sarapis devotees evidently won.

However, there is an even more elaborate backstory here. Before the dedicator describes his own divine vision, he recounts how Sarapis ended up on Delos in the first place: His grandfather Apollonios had brought Sarapis from Egypt and established his cult on Delos. Apollonios's son Demetrios continued to serve Sarapis, as does his son Apollonios, the dedicator. Thus, we see in this complex account the many exciting details of a legendary origin story, traversing several generations, that the entire group could share. This story tells the members of the Sarapis association *where they came from* and *how their god guided their success to the current moment*. This is not, we should note, unlike the many stories in the Hebrew Bible that similarly demonstrate the Israelite god's ongoing interest in the Hebrews and their successes.

Even if the legendary founding of an association is not present in an inscription, we sometimes find instead the backstory of a group's distinct practices. An example of this was already seen in *SIG*[3] 985, where Dionysios received instructions from Zeus himself regarding how to carry out their

21. Greek text taken from Packard Humanities Institute, "PHI Greek Inscriptions"; translation from Ascough, Harland, and Kloppenborg, *Associations in the Greco-Roman World*, 133.

association's practices. In other words, this inscription explains "why we do things the way we do." So also, in *SEG* 15, 637 above, we saw that, in addition to giving a backstory of the foundation of Poseidonios's household association, the inscription also explains why his family shows honor *specifically* to Zeus Patroos, Apollo, the Fates, the Mother goddess, and the other family gods. In all of these examples, members of the group would have an explanation for why their group met in a *particular* location and why they engaged in their *specific* practices—these can be traced all the way back to direct communication with divine sources narrated in these records. These brief narrative instances become the collective memory for the association's members.[22]

So far, we have explored the varieties of "work" that epiphanies accomplish within the context of ancient associations. Given that these epiphanies are common motifs within the surviving evidence for associations, it seems reasonable to conclude that members would have certain expectations when a founder approached them with such stories. If they bought into the claims, then they would typically assume that the epiphany attested to the founder's authority and prestige. For the members, the founder's story of encountering a god would then become part of "their" explanatory story for their association's origin. By attributing authority to the founder or leader, as well as to the collective identity to the group, such stories helped associations work. Paul's claims to encounter Jesus, I now suggest, would have fit neatly into this framework.

Pauline Epiphanies

We admittedly do not have the same sort of evidence for Pauline groups as we do for Greek and Roman associations. Instead of dedication plaques, public inscriptions, accounting documents on papyri, or records on ostraca, what we have are Paul's letters, which, to be sure, present some problems when trying to

22. Collective memory is a concept that has been variously defined over the years in different corners of scholarship. While the foundational work on this concept comes from Maurice Halbwachs (*On Collective Memory*, ed. and trans. Lewis Coser [1925; repr., University of Chicago Press, 1992]), an accessible definition of collective memory would be the following: "Collective memory refers to the memories that individuals have as members of the groups to which they belong, whether small (family, school) or large (political party, nation). Membership in some groups can form a strong part of a person's individual identity. Collective memory is history as people remember it; it is not formal history, because the 'memories' of a group are often contradicted by historical fact" (Henry L. Roediger, "Three Facets of Collective Memory," *The American Psychologist* 76, no. 9 [2021]: 1388–1400, here 1388).

access the social formation behind them. While we should not assume that the groups behind his letters looked precisely like his textual descriptions of them, or even that they saw themselves as a singular group, we can say, minimally, that there were real people in his audiences whom he was trying to persuade.[23] The remainder of this essay will take that simple point seriously and try to imagine the "narratives" that Paul likely told those audiences about his own epiphanies. These can be productively compared to the epiphanies in associations that we just explored. The guiding question will be this: *What would Paul's stories have sounded like to his audiences*, especially if they were familiar with the rhetoric of founder figures, their epiphanies, and the elaborate myths of origin that we explored above?

The most of famous of these epiphanies in Paul's letters is his claim to have seen the risen Christ. We can piece together details from several passing references to this encounter scattered through his letters. Along with this vision, Paul declares that he received a special communication directly from Christ (Gal 1:12), which initiated his mission to gentiles (1:15–16). The book of Acts has a more elaborate version of this event (Acts 9:3–19), which includes a heavenly light, a dialogue with Jesus, and an unfortunate blinding.[24] Though Paul's letters relate fewer details than Acts' version, there is no reason to think that Paul did not relay an equally vivid and exciting account to his audiences. What Paul says he "received" (1 Cor 15:3, Gal 1:12) at this moment was a body of knowledge about Christ and about a series of visions that his early followers had (1 Cor 15:3–7). This encounter spurs him on his mission to tell others about Christ. Surely, I suggest, Paul told the groups that he visited across the Mediterranean world about this fantastic epiphany.

But I suspect there was a more elaborate story that Paul shared with them. In 2 Corinthians 12:1–14, he describes a special visit to the "third heaven" or "paradise" wherein he was told amazing secrets, not all of which he could go on to share. It seems likely that when Paul relayed his miraculous accounts of seeing the risen Christ and of journeying to paradise to receive divine

23. On the social formation behind Paul's letters, see my wider discussion here: Sarah E. Rollens, "The Anachronism of 'Early Christian Communities,'" in *Theorizing "Religion" in Antiquity*, ed. Nickolas Roubekas, Studies in Ancient Religion and Culture (Equinox, 2018), 307–24.

24. Most scholars agree that Acts' version contains literary embellishments to make a more dramatic account.

secrets, his audiences would have received them as important, but nevertheless familiar, stories recounting the crucial moments in the emergence of their group, facilitated by Paul, their "founder."[25]

Like the accounts we saw in associations above, Paul's stories would have worked to establish his authority over those in his group. First, and perhaps obviously, his epiphanies would tell those in his groups that he was elected by a god to receive divine communication. Christ, he narrates in 1 Corinthians, "appeared also to me [or: Was seen by me]" (1 Cor 15:8). Elsewhere, he states that God "was pleased to reveal" his son in him (Gal 1:16; see also, 2 Cor 12:1). So, the very fact that Paul had this divine encounter at all (and that those in his groups did not) elevated his status within the group. In Paul's own telling, he was intentionally chosen over others for this encounter. In Galatians, he describes God as "the one who had *set me apart* before I was born and called me through his grace" (Gal 1:15, emphasis mine). This would, no doubt, underscore his importance and authority among those with whom he shared this epiphany.

In addition, Paul insists that the teachings about Christ that he shares came precisely from these divine encounters—that is, he did not just overhear them discussed by others who knew Jesus in his lifetime (Gal 1:17–22).[26] This claim of firsthand experience carries more authority than if he had only learned it secondhand from other authoritative. A final strategy Paul uses to prop up his authority is to emphasize the personal, sometimes difficult, effort that he exerted to spread these ideas that he received via the epiphanies. Indeed, as we noted above, overcoming adversity makes for a great story!

We can probably assume that he was, in fact, treated as an authority figure (at least initially) by the groups he visited, since many of his letters suggest that his recipients were writing to him to ask for clarification on

25. The term "founder" is in quotation marks because it seems too simplistic to me to simply say that a single person founds a social group. We often use that terminology, but, in my view, it occludes other social dynamics, as well as the cultural context, which all contribute to the ability of someone to "found" a successful group.

26. When Paul gives the series of events leading up to his vision of Christ and what he did afterward, he gives no indication that he knew Jesus before his crucifixion (Gal 1:13-17). He elsewhere refers to himself as "one untimely born" (1 Cor 15:8; the Greek term literally means something more akin to "abortion/miscarriage"), which some scholars have taken as an oblique way of admitting that he never knew Jesus in life. Without this firsthand knowledge, he probably faced regular resistance to his self-proclaimed expertise on Jesus.

theological matters or practical advice. In other words, like the founder figures in the associations above, these epiphanies reinforced a particular group hierarchy with the founder figure on top—in large measure because of his direct experience with a deity.

Paul's story of being "caught up into paradise" and seeing "visions and revelations of the Lord" in 2 Corinthians 12 shows us precisely how a founder figure like Paul might *deliberately* use an epiphany to undergird his authority to teach or to lead an association.[27] In fact, Paul brings this story up in the middle of discussing other Christ followers who are apparently trying to usurp his authority in Corinth (2 Cor 11:1–15; 12:11–21). The reference appears just after his discussion of his own struggles and sufferings (11:16–33), which is itself a common trope in Paul's letters that acts as a useful strategy to cultivate authority.[28] Thus, Paul's extraordinary heavenly visions and the special knowledge that he received from them function to remind his readers of his special role as their founder and of the exciting experience that compelled him to travel to share his ideas about Christ.

Of course, anyone can claim to have experienced any kind of incredible event, and not everyone will automatically believe it. However, there is reason to think that Paul was doing exactly what many others were doing in his day and that people took it seriously, because that is what they expected to hear from religious leaders. As Heidi Wendt has shown, claims to divine revelation are one of the many strategies that "freelance experts" used in the Roman Empire to establish their authority as religious leaders.[29] We can quickly see that Paul's rhetoric fits this pattern: His claim to have communicated *personally* and *directly* with a deity, as well as to have had a heavenly journey of some sort, became the authoritative bases by which he justified all of his work. And

---

27. Scholars largely agree that, although Paul narrates this story in the third person ("I know a person . . . ," 2 Cor 11:2), this is actually a story about himself. This is, indeed, how early Christian authors understood it as well.

28. According to James A. Kelhoffer, Paul's letters are among many texts in the New Testament that "construe the withstanding of persecution as a form of cultural capital convertible to power, authority, legitimacy, or standing within the Christian community" (*Persecution, Persuasion and Power: Readiness to Withstand Hardship as a Corroboration of Legitimacy in the New Testament*, WUNT 270 [Mohr Siebeck, 2010], 16; for specific remarks on Paul's rhetoric of suffering, see 30–65).

29. Wendt, *At the Temple Gates*, passim.

his groups appear to have initially endorsed his activity, instead of treating him as a charlatan.[30] Were he perceived as a charlatan, his teachings would not have been entertained by people in Corinth, Galatia, and elsewhere. Paul is thus akin to the founder figures assessed above, such as Dionysios, Xenaitenos, and Apollonios, who had special encounters with a deity and then share their story with a group.

Besides fortifying the authority of a founder figure or leader, the second major function of epiphanies discussed above was to provide a common identity for a group, which we also see happening in Paul's letters. His stories about his epiphanies craft a *common past* that diverse members of his groups could unite around—just like the associations in the inscriptions discussed above. The thinking might have gone something like this: Paul's legacy and authority are linked to the "pillars" in Jerusalem,[31] and the pillars had inherited their authority directly from Jesus during his lifetime. By being connected to Paul, his audiences are, in turn, brought into this identity and can claim the same origin story as the Jesus followers in Galilee and Judaea. What's more, *all* Christ groups across the empire participate in this identity, making them part of something much larger than their individual groups.

The construction of this shared identity is nowhere clearer than in 1 Corinthians 15. Here he describes a chain of recent history starting with Christ's death, his appearance first to Peter, then to five hundred other followers, then to James, and then to the rest of the apostles (15:3–7). Paul describes himself as the most recent link in this chain of tradition (15:8), which he then passes on to his audiences (15:3; see also 1 Thess 2:13). We already noted how this strategy of inserting himself into a list of important people who are ultimately connected to Christ encourages people to accept his authoritative status. Now we see that other Christ followers (here the Corinthians) can join this chain too: Whereas their group may have formed relatively recently, Paul wants to convince them that they are actually part of a wider identity that emerged during the lifetime of Jesus. Thus, through narrating his epiphanies, Paul answers questions that the group may have had,

30. Second Corinthians 11–12 demonstrates that the Corinthian Christ group may have later questioned his status as their singular authoritative leader.

31. Paul refers to the leaders of the Jerusalem Christ group (James, Peter, and John) as "pillars" (Gal 2:9).

such as, "Where did we (Christ followers) come from? Who came before us? Are Christ followers in Corinth the same as those in Jerusalem? How and why are we connected?"

The epiphanies also give an origin story for Paul's missionary activity. Think back to *IG* X/2.1 255 above, when Sarapis visited Xenainetos in a vision and convinced him to approach his political rival to establish a temple and an association; that event marked an important moment in the chronology of that association. Similarly, Christ's epiphany to Paul signals the moment when Paul set out to spread stories of Christ throughout the Mediterranean. Paul's claims to encounter Jesus thus provide his audiences with a reason why he had appeared in their cities in the first place.

In fact, his letters establish a much more distant legacy for his recipients than simply connecting them to other Christ followers in Judaea. Paul's frequent appeals to key figures in the Israelite tradition, namely Moses and Abraham, also extend the history of his contemporary Christ groups back through time (and space!) and connect them to those ancient, prestigious figures in Jewish Scriptures. To offer one example, in 1 Corinthians 10:2–4 Paul styles the ancient Israelites as "new ancestors" of the Corinthians.[32] This story represents a kind of "mythic precedent"[33] for the members of the group, who might have lacked a common identity before Paul convinced them of their new shared identity "in Christ." We could list numerous other examples, but the bottom line is this: Especially for non-Jewish audiences, Paul's incorporation of authoritative figures from the Hebrew Scriptures appended a common "history" onto a group that may have otherwise only come into existence rather recently. For Paul, it was their relationship to him and to Christ that established their "groupness"—and once they were in on that, they could also inherit the history of the Israelites, too.

Conclusions

Though written evidence for associations looks vastly different in style and form from Paul's letters, both engage in similar ways of using epiphanies to bolster a founder's or leader's authority and to craft a backstory for their respective

32. Wendt, *At the Temple Gates*, 151.

33. Wendt, *At the Temple Gates*, 152.

groups. Even more, I suggest that Paul's audiences were probably socially primed to accept—even to expect—these kinds of stories from someone who was trying to start a new cultic association.

The comparison of Christ groups and ancient associations is relatively recent, and many scholars remain uncomfortable with viewing Christ groups alongside this common Mediterranean social form. The concern is usually that Christ groups are somehow diminished through the comparison, that they are treated as "just" another association. It is important to underscore the methodological principle that guides us here: Our approach is *analogical*, that is, it compares Christ groups and ancient associations in order to raise questions about their similarities and differences. One is not simply a species of the other, nor vice versa. Instead, we have used associations to help us understand how claims about epiphanies worked in the social formations attested by association data, and then imagined how Paul's claims would have sounded to an audience familiar with such associations. We hypothesized that Paul's epiphanies would have fulfilled many of the same social functions as similar claims within associations: They bolstered his authority and prestige as a "founder"; they gave the group's members a sense of connection with each other; and they linked each group to a foundational period in Judaea—and then to an even deeper historical legacy in the time of the Israelites.

In short, by looking at the specific claims about epiphanies made in evidence for associations and by assuming that at least *some* of Paul's audiences must have regarded his Christ groups as similar to other associations, we can better envisage how they would have received his remarkable stories to have seen a vision of a deity who encouraged him to travel throughout the eastern Mediterranean to establish an urban network of Christ believers.

CHAPTER THIRTEEN

Paul, Martial Imagery, and Adjuring Gentile Loyalty

Jennifer Eyl
Tufts University

Pistis, most frequently translated as "faith," is the virtue that Paul promotes above all others. To the modern ear, that translation implies an interior psychological state: One "believes" sincerely or strongly. If we translate the word, more accurately, as "trust," or "loyalty," or "allegiance," we see how the term functions as part of Paul's strategy of group formation, emphasizing both internal disposition and outward behavior. And we see—especially in 1 Thessalonians—how *pistis* relates to Roman martial imagery, embedded in the ideas of struggle, opposition, war, fortification, and armor. By drawing extensively on martial imagery, Paul seeks to encourage and to conjure among his gentile followers the fidelity/*pistis* expected of Roman soldiers.

In 1 Thessalonians 5:8, Paul refers to the armament that will protect his followers at the eschaton: "But since we belong to the day, let us be sober and put on the breastplate of fidelity [*pistis*] and love [*agapē*] and for a helmet the hope of salvation."[1] In his so-called hardship list from 2 Corinthians 6:7, Paul refers to "the weapons of righteousness for the right hand and for the left." Later in the letter, he writes, "Indeed, we live as humans but do not wage war according to human standards, for the weapons of our warfare are not merely human, but they have divine power to destroy strongholds. We destroy arguments and every proud obstacle raised up against the knowledge of God, and we take every thought captive to obey Christ. We are ready to punish every disobedience when your obedience is complete" (2 Cor 10:3–6). These three examples are but a few of the many instances when Paul draws on martial

1. Unless otherwise noted, all New Testament translations are modified from NRSVue.

imagery—that of waging war, struggle, opposition, defeat, victory, weapons, standing firm, being strong, fortification, or armor—in all his letters from 1 Thessalonians to Romans.[2]

The recurrence of such imagery has received a healthy amount of scholarly interest, most of which explores precedence or influence. That is to say, where do such images come from? We certainly find metaphorical uses of martial imagery in a range of authors from antiquity. For example, some scholars have argued that Paul draws from Proverbs 21:22 (OG): "A wise man assaults fortified cities and demolishes the fortification in which the ungodly trusted." Perhaps Paul uses martial imagery simply because the Roman military was everywhere, and thus an obvious and familiar presence? This is the suggestion of Edgar Krentz and Jeremey Punt.[3] Or perhaps this imagery is drawn from philosophical traditions, as Nijay Gupta and Abraham Malherbe have suggested.[4] This essay sets aside questions of origins and focuses instead on some rhetorical (or, paraenetic) aspects of the martial imagery as found in the letters, primarily 1 Thessalonians. I do this, first, by showing that Paul tends to use martial imagery in conjunction with what I take to be Paul's premier virtue: *Pistis*, understood as faithfulness/loyalty/fidelity. And second, I argue that the conjunction of martial imagery and the virtue of faithfulness functions as a rhetorical strategy in support of social formation. In other words, Paul pairs fidelity with military imagery to foster the belonging and loyalty required for the configuration of tightly bounded social groups.

Pistis and *Fides*

To start, something must be said of *pistis*. The word appears over 162 times in Paul's undisputed letters, making it by far the virtue he most commonly

2. Nijay Gupta has observed that martial imagery appears in nearly all Pauline letters ("Fighting the Good Fight: The Good Life in Paul and the Giants of Philosophy," in *Paul and the Giants of Philosophy: Reading the Apostle in Greco-Roman Context*, ed. Joseph R. Dodson and David E. Briones [Intervarsity Press, 2019], 95).

3. Edgar Krentz,"Military Langauge and Metaphors in Philippians," in *Origins and Method—towards a New Understanding of Judaism and Christianity: Essays in Honour of John C. Hurd*, ed. Bradley McLean (Sheffield Academic Press, 1993), 105–27; Jeremey Punt, "Paul, Military Imagery, and Social Disadvantage," *Acta Theologica* 23 (2016): 201–24.

4. Gupta, "Fighting the Good Fight"; Abraham Malherbe, "Antisthenes and Odysseus, and Paul at War," *HTR* 76, no. 2 (1983): 143–73.

promotes.[5] When *pistis* appears in New Testament texts, it is nearly always translated as "faith."[6] In agreement with numerous recent scholars, however, I argue that *pistis* is better understood as the equivalent of the Latin *fides*: "Fidelity," "loyalty," "faithfulness," or "trust(worthiness)." Indeed, even ancient sources translate *pistis* as *fides* (the Latin Vulgate, for example).[7] Space here prohibits unpacking the long, complicated, and fascinating history of how *pistis* turns into "faith" and how faith becomes synonymous with "religion."[8] Suffice it to say that "faith," often equated with "belief," suggests the personal, the internal, and the private.[9] To understand *pistis* as "faith" or "belief" is to understand the word as reflecting a cognitive position regarding the veracity of a proposition—assenting to the notion that something either is or is not true, without empirical evidence to support it. Yet, among Greek speakers of the first century and the centuries prior, the word most often refers to relations of mutual trust, fidelity, trustworthiness, and loyalty. Indeed, it is a word of relationality more than of cognitive assent to a proposition. As Zeba Crook has observed, *pistis* is not a mental disposition but an allegiance or loyalty

---

5. For more on Paul and *pistis*, see Jennifer Eyl, *Signs, Wonders, and Gifts: Divination in the Letters of Paul* (Oxford University Press, 2019), 170–212.

6. RSV; NRSV; KJV; NIV; ESV. I have yet to come across a translation that eschews "faith" as a regular translation for *pistis*. One common exception is Gal 5:22, which is often translated as "faithfulness," "fidelity," or "trustfulness." My thanks to Michael Winger for this observation.

7. Theresa Morgan's *Roman Faith and Christian Faith:* Pistis *and* Fides *in the Early Roman Empire and Early Churches* (Oxford University Press, 2015) offers an indispensable analysis of *pistis* language in ancient Greek and its extensive overlap with Latin *fides*.

8. "Faith" and religion are often used synonymously in popular and scholarly accounts. See, for example, Nicholas Wade, *The Faith Instinct: How Religion Evolved and Why It Endures* (Penguin, 2009); Phil Zuckerman, *Faith No More: Why People Reject Religion* (Oxford University Press, 2012).

9. Indeed, faith is also frequently used interchangeably with belief, such as Adam Cohen, Joel Siegel, and Paul Rozin, "Faith versus Practice: Different Bases for Religiosity Judgments by Jews and Protestants," *European Journal of Social Psychology* 33, no. 2 (2003): 287–95. As per Paula Fredriksen, "To translate πιστεύω as 'believe' too easily conjures for us the sentiments and psychological states of post-Romanticism (e.g., authenticity, genuine affection, individual subjectivity, self-authenticating intensity, and so on). Especially when dealing with early Christian materials, such as the gospels or Paul's letters, πιστεύω as 'believe' runs head-on into the theological existentialism of Bultmannian hermeneutics, and more generally into the polemical jargon of the Reformation" ("Judaizing the Nations: The Ritual Demands of Paul's Gospel," *New Testament Studies* 56 [2010]: 225n7).

for which one demonstrates evidence through one's behavior.[10] This is not a sentiment or a thought unmoored from action. Furthermore, *pistis* often appears in conjunction with oaths and oath-taking and in descriptions of the behavioral demeanor expected of slaves, wives, children, and soldiers. I have lightheartedly argued elsewhere that if Paul could have imposed a Latin motto on his gentile followers, it would have been something akin to *Semper Fi*.[11]

Fidelity and Obedience

Paul's insistence on faithfulness/loyalty/fidelity is especially prominent when he pairs the virtue with obedience (*hupakoē*). As he greets and introduces himself to readers in Romans 1:5, for example, he thanks Christ through whom he has received the benefaction and commission to "bring about the obedience of fidelity [*hupakoēn pisteōs*] among all the gentiles." He reasserts the importance of "the obedience of fidelity" at 16:26. In some ways, *pistis* and *hupakoē* overlap in meaning. At Romans 1:8, for example, Paul expresses delight over the Christ followers in Rome because their *pistis*/loyalty has developed such a fine reputation "throughout the world." And he reiterates this notion at 16:19, swapping *pistis* for *hupakoē*: "Your obedience [*hupakoē*] is known to everyone, so that I rejoice over you." On thirteen occasions, Paul uses the explicit language of obedience (*hupakoē*),[12] often asserting that his job is to make gentiles obedient to the Judean god (and thus, to his understanding of that deity).[13]

Among ancient authors, Paul is hardly a rare bird in tying obedience (or disobedience) to loyalty or fidelity; the two are often associated. We will consider three examples. In his *Judean Antiquities*, Josephus recounts that story of Trypho, who intends to gain the trust of Jonathan Apphus in order to

10. Zeba Crook, *Reconceptualising Conversion: Patronage, Loyalty, and Conversion in the Religions of the Ancient Mediterranean* (De Gruyter, 2004), 200–208.

11. Jennifer Eyl, "A Reexamination of *Pistis* in the Letters of Paul," paper presented at the Boston Area Patristics Group, Harvard University, April 2019. Since 1883, *Semper Fi*, a shortened form of *Semper Fidelis* ("always faithful") has been the official motto of the US Marine Corps. The motto refers to the unwavering allegiance and loyalty Marines promise to their nation, their communities, and their fellow Marines.

12. Phlm 21; 2 Cor 7:15; 10:5, 6; Rom 1:5; 5:19; 6:12, 16a, 16b, 16c; 15:18; 16:19, 26.

13. For a deeper examination of Paul's emphasis on obedience, see Jason Myers, *Paul, the Apostle of Obedience* (T&T Clark, 2023).

kill him, during the Maccabean Revolt. Josephus tells us that Trypho tricked Jonathan by ordering his own generals to obey (*peitharchein*) the Maccabean, thereby building the sense of *pistis* between them (*toutois pistōsasthai boulomenos*). Once Trypho gained Jonathan's trust, the latter let down his guard and was captured and killed (13.189). In this story, the performance of obedience produces the appearance of *pistis* between parties. Even when enacted with an eye toward treachery, obedience and loyalty/fidelity are often coterminous.

Describing the conquest of Greece by Philip, the father of Alexander the Great, Polybius tells us that Apelles managed to thwart the king by drawing on his own reputation for trustworthiness. Apelles retires to Chalcis to disrupt Philip's plans by intentionally hobbling the supply line for the Macedonian army. When he gives orders that are strategically meant to sabotage, nobody questions him: "All yielding him obedience [*peitharchountōn*] due to his former trustworthiness [*pistin*] at court, that at length the king was in such need of money that he was forced to pawn some of the silverplate in use at his table and live on the proceeds" (*Histories* 5.2.10, my translation). Here, Apelles's reputation for loyalty engenders trust and obedience in others. It is simply assumed that his actions are loyal and obedient to the wishes of Philip, and therefore that compliance is necessary.

Finally, in Herodian, the obedient are contrasted with those who are *apistos* (disloyal or unfaithful). We learn that the prefect, Plautianus, has plotted the deaths of Septimius Severus and his son Caracalla, in order to usurp imperial power. He orders his most trusted tribune, Saturninus, to carry out the deed as he alone would have access to the emperor at night. Saturninus goes to Septimius's palace and reveals the assassination plot and himself as the would-be assassin. Thinking that the assassination has succeeded, Plautianus appears at the palace to assume his newfound power, but finds the Severan family alive and well. The guards are ordered to kill the disloyal prefect: "Obeying without delay the young emperor's orders, they killed Plautianus and threw his body into the street, so that the affair might be clear to all and he would be vilified by those who despised him. Such was the fate of Plautianus, who, maddened by his greed to have everything, was betrayed in the end by a faithless [*apistos*] subordinate" (Herodian, *Roman History* 3.12.12).[14] Here,

14. Herodian, *History of the Roman Empire*, trans. Edward C. Echols (University of California Press, 1961).

we behold the chess game of loyalty and obedience. Plautianus has been the lifelong friend of Septimius, and yet he plots the emperor's death in a move of abject disloyalty and treachery. Plautianus's most trusted tribune demonstrates disobedience and disloyalty to the prefect by revealing the plot, and, in doing so, shows unequivocal *pistis* toward the emperor. Throughout the account, Herodian draws on the language of *pistis*/loyalty, and (dis)obedience, consistently demonstrated by behavior.

As for Paul, Romans 1:5 is typically translated as, "through whom we have received the grace and apostleship to bring about the obedience of faith among all the gentiles." Given the widespread pairing of loyalty and obedience, "the obedience of faith" does not make much sense. Rather, Paul describes his job as bringing about the obedience of loyalty, or fidelity, of the gentiles. That is to say, "faith" is not an obvious companion of obedience, whereas loyalty/fidelity often are, especially insofar as being faithful or loyal demands a kind of discipline or firmness in the face of temptations to wander astray. The kind of *pistis* Paul calls for demands an unwavering conformity and dedication (i.e., obedience) to what followers are taught.

Martial Imagery and the Fidelity of Soldiers

If there were one arena in which calls to *pistis*/*fides* and obedience were most vociferous in the first century, it was in the military. Upon enlistment, and yearly thereafter, soldiers of the Roman army swore an oath of loyalty to the emperor, the *sacramentum militiae*. Such an oath became more instrumental in ensuring the discipline and obedience of soldiers as the republic moved away from a *gens*-based military that, by nature, functioned on clan loyalty.[15] By the early principate, enlisted soldiers, who were not connected by *gens*, professed not only loyalty to the emperor, but also an obligation to obey their commander and an obligation to not desert.[16] A military body comprising citizens, noncitizens, volunteers, and conscripts, many of whom were part of the auxiliary troops (*auxilia*) of *peregrinii*—that is, of noncitizens from far-flung places—were bound not by familial roots, language, or defense of

15. Tristan Taylor, "The Roman Military Oath: The *Sacramentum Militiae*," in *Religion and Classical Warfare: The Roman Empire*, ed. Matthew Dillon and Christopher Matthew (Penn & Sword, 2022), 19–42, at 20.

16. Taylor, "Roman Military Oath," 32, quoting fourth-century Servius.

homeland, but by oaths of loyalty and obedience. The loyalty of the army is, of course, advertised on the many coins bearing *fides exercitum* and *fides militum*.[17] The *fides* of individual soldiers is attested on the funerary inscriptions of veterans resettled in Roman Britain, Dacia, Asia Minor, and Greece, and P(ia) F(idelis) became the epigraphic abbreviation for any legion that had proved itself faithful and obedient.[18]

Indeed, early Christian authors after Paul will cast Christians as a kind of divine army, appropriating the imagery and nomenclature of obedient soldiery. In his treatise *On Idolatry*, for example, Tertullian remarks on the sheer incompatibility of this oath of loyalty in the (Roman) army with obedience and loyalty to Christ: "There is no agreement between the divine and the human sacrament, the standard [i.e., the military flag] of Christ and the standard of the devil, the camp of light and the camp of darkness. One soul cannot be due to two masters—God and Caesar" (19.2). Just prior to this passage, Tertullian asks whether a *fidelis* (i.e., a Christian) can commit himself to the military for service and whether an enlisted soldier can be admitted into the (Christian) *fides*.[19] Notably, Tertullian refers to the Christian as the *fidelis*—not the soldier or the military—which suggests a growing tension over who can lay better claim over the virtue of *fides* and the title *fidelis*.[20]

---

17. See Carlos Noreña, "Coins and Communication," in *The Oxford Handbook of Social Relations in the Roman World*, ed. Michael Peachin (Oxford University Press, 2011), 248–68; Lucia Carbone, "The First Italia on Coinage," *American Numismatics Society* (2020): 6–23; Morgan, *Roman Faith*, 82–86.

18. See, for example: CIL 11, 00021; Sanja Ivčević, "Roman Military Gear Depicted on Grave Monuments from the Archaeological Museum in Split," in *Funerary Sculpture of the Western Illyricum and Neighbouring Regions of the Roman Empire*, ed. Nenad Cambi and Guntram Koch (Književni Krug, 2013), 443–79.

19. *On Idolatry* 19.2.

20. For more on early Christians as "soldiers" of Christ, see Korinna Zamfir, "Christians as Soldiers of Christ: Military Metaphors in Basil of Caesarea," *Sacra Scripta* 21 (2023): 181–97; Thomas Noble and Thomas Head, eds., *Soldiers of Christ: Saints and Saints' Lives from Late Antiquity and the Early Middle Ages* (Penn State University Press, 2000). We eventually see the fullest expression of this unwavering *pistis*/*fides* in martyrdom accounts (albeit, equally ideological, propagandistic, and spectacular). In Augustine's sermon on martyrs, for example, he observes, "The materially-minded look on, and think how wretched and unfortunate those martyrs are, thrown to wild beasts, beheaded, burned with fire, and they are filled with detestation and horror. Others, however, look on, as do the holy angels, and don't fix their attention on the mangling of bodies, but instead marvel at the completeness of *fides*."

Martial Imagery in Philosophy

Ancient authors commonly used martial imagery metaphorically to describe certain states of mind, virtues, dispositions, or emotions—especially in the field of philosophy. Abraham Malherbe has suggested that this begins with Greek admiration for Sparta's lack of architectural fortification—on the conviction that an admirable city is fortified not by walls, but by the bravery of its citizens—which became the exemplar for numerous philosophers as early as Gorgias and Socrates.[21] Antisthenes (446–366 BCE), for example, "adopted and elaborated the Spartan view of moral argument." A student of Socrates and later founder of Cynic philosophy, Antisthenes "applied the image of the fortified city to the sage's soul."[22] In one surviving fragment from Diogenes Laertius (*Lives of Eminent Philosophers* 6.16), Antisthenes is said to have taught that "Prudence (*phronēsis*) is a most secure stronghold, for it does not crumble nor is it betrayed. We must build walls of defense with our own impregnable reasonings."[23]

Similarly, in Plato's *Apology*, Socrates likens his life in philosophy to not breaking rank in military formation. Note the way he describes his philosophical life in terms of receiving military orders from someone up the chain of command to occupy a particular station:

> So I should have done a terrible thing, [28e] if, when the commanders whom you chose to command me stationed me, both at Potidaea and at Amphipolis and at Delium, I remained where they stationed me, like anybody else, and ran the risk of death, but when the god gave me a station, as I believed and understood, with orders to spend my life in philosophy and in examining myself and others, [29a] then were I to desert my post through fear of death or anything else whatsoever.

See Augustine of Hippo, in *Sermons 51–94*, vol. III/3, The Works of Saint Augustine: A Translation for the 21st Century, trans. Edmund Hill (New City Press, 1991), semon 51.2. See also Elizabeth Castelli, *Martyrdom and Memory: Early Christian Culture Making* (Columbia University Press, 2007), 105.

21. Malherbe, "Antisthenes and Odysseus."

22. Malherbe, "Antisthenes and Odysseus," 150.

23. Malherbe, "Antisthenes and Odysseus," 150.

> It would be a terrible thing, and truly one might then justly hale me into court, on the charge that I do not believe that there are gods, since I disobey the oracle and fear death and think I am wise when I am not.[24]

In place of disloyalty through disregarding the commands of an officer during a war, Socrates connects disloyalty with disobedience to the god who "stationed" him in philosophy.

Some Stoics, too, used military imagery to describe the sage's life, an association that gains ground in the early Principate. In letter 46 to Lucilius, Seneca states *vivere militare est* ("to live is to serve as a soldier").[25] Elsewhere, Seneca suggests that, through the wisdom cultivated by philosophy, when Fate takes one's fortified walls by storm, "if the inner part (of a person) is safe, a man can be attacked, but cannot be captured" (epistle 74.19, my translation). In discussing the uses of simile and metaphor in Q. Sextius, a Stoic philosopher of Julius Caesar's day, Seneca approves of the likening of the Stoic's practice as a military struggle and the soul a citadel: "But the wise man is fortified against all inroads; he is alert; he will not retreat before the attack of poverty, or of sorrow, or of disgrace, or of pain. He will walk undaunted both against them and among them" (letter 59.8) The feature of wisdom, here, is like the bravery of a city's occupants as mentioned above: It fortifies, defends, and shores up the person against the passions and sufferings of an unvirtuous life. Seneca further clarifies the association between martial imagery and human virtue: "And what is Bravery? It is the impregnable fortress for our mortal weakness; when a man has surrounded himself therewith, he can hold out free from anxiety during life's siege; for he is using his own strength and his own weapons." Seneca then quotes Posidonius: "There are never any occasions when you need think yourself safe because you wield the weapons of Fortune; fight with your own! Fortune does not furnish arms against herself; hence men equipped against their foes are unarmed against Fortune herself" (113.28).[26]

---

24. Plato, *Apology* 28d–29a. Translation from *Plato in Twelve Volumes*, vol. 1, trans. Harold North Fowler, introduction by W. R. M. Lamb (Harvard University Press), 1966.

25. Seneca, *Epistle* 96.5.

26. Seneca, *Epistles*, 113. Trans. Richard M. Gummere, Loeb Classical Library 75 (Harvard University Press, 1917).

Epictetus, for his part, likens the soldier's oath of loyalty to the emperor as "*the* model for the philosophic life dedicated to the god within." Note that the loyalty Epictetus speaks of has less to do with following military orders than with aligning oneself with the will of god:

> To what better and more careful guardian could he have committed each one of us? So that when you have shut your doors, and darkened your room, remember never to say that you are alone; for you are not alone, but God is within, and your genius is within; and what need have they of light to see what you are doing? To this God you likewise ought to swear such an oath as the soldiers do to Caesar. For they, in order to receive their pay, swear to prefer before all things the safety of Caesar; and will you not swear, who have received so many and so great favors; or, if you have sworn, will you not fulfil the oath? And what must you swear? Never to distrust, nor accuse, nor murmur at any of the things appointed by him; nor to shrink from doing or enduring that which is inevitable.[27]

Epictetus describes the cognitive work required to live a life according to nature, which, for the Stoics, meant becoming aware of and fitting into every aspect of divine will. The individual should aspire to inculcate an obedience to god that follows the model of the faithfulness of a soldier to his emperor.

It should not be surprising that scholars have pointed toward the philosophical usage of martial imagery to situate Paul within a rhetorical context—the evidence seems robust. Yet, philosophical uses of martial metaphors tend to emphasize the practicing philosopher's specific conscience more than loyalty as a virtue among and towards a nascent social group and its leader(s). Seneca does not write to Lucilius commending the latter's "breastplate of fidelity" in the face of some perceived persecution of fellow Stoics. Socrates does not exhort Plato's soldier-like obedience toward him. Thus, my interest lies neither in available images that make for good metaphors nor in literary precedent, but in rhetorical usage and purpose. To what end does Paul leverage his martial

27. Epictetus, *Discourses* 1.14. Translation from *Works of Epictetus: His Discourses, in Four Books, the Enchiridion, and Fragments*, trans. Thomas Wentworth Higginson (Thomas Nelson and Sons, 1890).

metaphors? Toward what does he exhort his readers, through the imagery of militarization?

Paul's Use of Martial Imagery and *Pistis*

In 1 Thessalonians, Paul's reliance on martial imagery and metaphors, paired especially with *pistis* language, represents a strategy of group-making, and the manufacture and maintenance of group boundaries. In an Althusserian sense, Paul "interpellates" his ancient audience; that is, he conjures or summons groupness through his language.[28] He calls followers faithful, and, in the calling, he brings into being the idea of a loyal *ekklesia* ("assembly"). More than simply *paraenesis*, or moral exhortation, Paul names his followers in Thessaloniki (and elsewhere) in a way that more resembles an Althusserian act of "hailing."[29] Most studies examining martial imagery in Paul's letters look at Philippians or 1 and 2 Corinthians. Most analyses of *pistis* language have privileged Romans and Galatians.[30] Passing under the radar, however, is the intersection of martial

---

28. See Louis Althusser, "Ideology and Ideological State Apparatuses (Notes towards an Investigation)," in *Lenin and Philosophy and Other Essays*, trans. Ben Brewster (New Left Press, 1971), 127–86; see also Rogers Brubaker, *Ethnicity without Groups* (Harvard University Press, 2004), 7–18. For more on the notion of conjuring groupness, see Erin Roberts, "Introduction: Myth, Our Bloodless Battleground," in *Christian Tourist Attractions, Mythmaking, and Identity Formation*, ed. Erin Roberts and Jennifer Eyl (Bloomsbury, 2018), 17.

29. Although Althusser's essay pertains to the how the modern state constructs subjects, so much of his approach matches what Paul does with rhetoric, *mutatis mutandis*. Althusser's idea of interpellation, or hailing, is such that when a police officer shouts "hey you!"—one either recognizes oneself in that hailing, and is thus turned into a subject, or one does not. But more often than not, one would recognize oneself as being hailed, and in that particular instance, because the police officer represents coercive power of the state, one's subjectivity as controlled by the state materializes.

30. Forms of *pistis* appear forty times in Romans, whereas in 1 Thessalonians we find it only eight times. Thus, it would appear that *pistis* is of much greater concern for Paul when he wrote Romans. However, Romans is almost five times the length of 1 Thessalonians. When we take that into account, the occurrences of *pistis* are almost the same in both letters—one out of every 177 words in Romans, and one out of 185 words in 1 Thessalonians. If 1 Thessalonians is the earliest letter that survives from Paul's letter writing career, and if Romans is the last we hear of him, there does not appear to be significant change in the rate at which he concerns himself with *pistis*. That is, he uses *pistis* as a strategy from the earliest of our evidence. We see roughly the same pattern for the verb form, *pisteuō*—twenty-one occurrences in Romans and five in 1 Thessalonians.

imagery and *pistis* language in 1 Thessalonians. In the first two chapters of the letter, Paul first hails his followers as an *ekklesia*, before proceeding to offer wave after wave of encouraging, warm exhortation. Consider the following statements:

> "[We remember] before our God and Father your work of fidelity [*pistis*] and labor of love and steadfastness of hope" (1:3)
> "He [God] has chosen you" (1:4)
> "You became imitators of us" (1:6)
> ". . . in every place your fidelity [*pistis*] to God has become known" (1:8)
> "Our experience among you was unlike the difficulty and mistreatment in Philippi" (2:1–2)
> "You have become dear to us" (2:8)
> "We are to you as a nurse is to her patients or a father is to his children" (2:8; 11)
> "You have become imitators of the *ekklēsiai* in Judea" (2:14)

Paul showers readers with exhortations and comments intended to compliment, to foster group solidarity and resolve, and to establish a sense of close identification between Paul and his followers. Nevertheless, 1 Thessalonians 3 is largely about his anxiety over whether followers in Thessaloniki have remained faithful to him in his absence. Have they been led astray? Are they obedient and unwavering? In 3:2, he indicates that he sent Timothy to Thessaloniki to help strengthen the resolve of their *pistis* (fidelity) so that no one would be moved by the pushback against them: "We sent Timothy . . . to strengthen you and exhort [*parakaleō*] you with regard to your fidelity [*pistis*], so that no one would be shaken by these pressures." Paul's use of *parakaleō* alludes to the marshalling of an army. Typically translated as "exhort" in this instance, it equally as often means "demand," "appeal to," or "summon." This is the verb for summoning allies, in Herodotus (*Histories* 1.77), and for calling soldiers to battle or giving them commands in Plutarch (*Titus Flaminius*, 5.3; *Tiberius and Gracchus* 9). A quick Boolean search in the *Thesaurus Linguae Graecae* (TLG), an extensive digital library of ancient Greek literature, turns up dozens of examples of pairing *parakaleō* with *stratiōtēs* (soldier) from Xenophon's *Anabasis* to Cassius Dio's *Roman History*, including Aeschines, Polybius, Josephus, Philo, Plutarch, Posidonius, and Diodorus Siculus.

Indeed, Paul continues, "for this reason, when I could bear it no longer, I sent [Timothy] to find out about your loyalty [*pistis*]; in case somehow a tempter had lured you away and that our work had been in vain" (1 Thess 3:5). Thankfully, Timothy returned with "good news"—they remain steadfast and loyal (3:6). To whatever extent they may occasionally vacillate, he seeks to restore their *pistis* face to face. He celebrates the fidelity of followers in Thessaloniki:

> For this reason, brothers, during all our distress and persecution we have been encouraged about you through your faithfulness [*pistis*]. For we now live, if you continue to stand firm in the Lord. How can we thank God enough for you in return for all the joy that we feel before our God because of you? Night and day we pray most earnestly that we may see you face to face and restore whatever is lacking in your fidelity [*pistis*]. (3:7–10)

Promising them that this trust or faithfulness is fully reciprocated, he ends his letter with the reminder: "The one who calls you is *pistos* [faithful]" (5:24).

In between the accolades regarding their stalwart fidelity in the first two chapters and the final promise that God is also *pistos*, we encounter the eschatological prediction of 1 Thessalonians 4, where Paul refers to the cry of command, the archangel's call, and the sound of God's trumpet, at which time the dead will rise and, together with the living (among whom Paul expects to be), will be taken up into the heavens forever. Destruction will rain down on earth and, amid the tumult, Paul's followers will be protected by their breastplate of loyalty (*pistis)* and love (*agapē*), and their helmet of hope: "But since we belong to the day, let us be sober and put on the breastplate of fidelity [*thoraka pisteōs*] and love [*agapē*] and for a helmet the hope of salvation" (5.8).

This evokes the Roman army once (upon a time) organized around *gens* or clan, now organized and fortified by oaths of loyalty to a common superior—in this case, God, Christ, or, perhaps, just Paul. By his words, *pistis* operates as the apotropaic, protective, and salvific virtue defending followers and identifying them as insiders, worn as a body shield. In imagery simultaneously reminiscent of the battle command *and* the triumphal procession after victory, 1 Thessalonians 4 and 5 invite the ancient follower to imagine their own virtue-laden breastplates—so much a part of the iconography of imperial Rome,[31] and, in particular, the nearly ubiquitous cuirass statues.

Such portrait statues, depicting a general or an emperor in military regalia with ornate breastplate, "celebrated the achievements of the elite and powerful whose images provided an ongoing exemplar of civic benefaction and virtue. These virtues included, but were not limited to, *virtus*, *clementia*, *pietas*, and *concordia*."[32] Indeed, such virtues are often personified on the breastplate. David Janssen has observed that cuirass statues were "part of the iconographical program [of Rome], expressing a consistent theme of peace, victory, and salvation."[33] Part of this iconographical program is also the "subduing and pacifying the foreign dangers at the boundaries of the Roman empire."[34] Janssen draws on Vernon Robbins' idea of "rhetography"—that is, "the rhetorical effect of vivid speech (*ekphrasis*)."[35] The term refers to "the dual process of i) using vivid language to excite listeners in order to win them over to a particular agrument, and ii) using speech which conjures visual imagery in the mind, evoking familiar contexts and encouraging listeners to think differently about them."[36] Paul's vivid description of an eschatological event from which his faithful followers will emerge unscathed and divine, paired with an allusion to the virtue-laden cuirass portrait statue, no doubt widely familiar to his ancient listeners, makes for persuasive, galvanizing rhetoric, indeed. The virtues adorning this breastplate are *pistis* and *agapē*.

Conclusion

A longstanding misstep in the study of early Christianity is the scholarly assumption of "groupness" or "communities" among Paul's followers, without evidence. If Paul refers to his auditors as an *ekklesia*, so the assumption goes,

31. David Janssen, "The Roman Cuirass Breastplate Statue and Paul's Use of Armor Language in Romans 13:12 and 1 Thessalonians 5:8," *Colloquium* 46 (2014): 55–85.

32. Janssen, "Cuirass," 58.

33. Janssen, "Cuirass," 58–59.

34. Janssen, "Cuirass," 59.

35. Janssen, "Cuirass," 77.

36. Janssen, "Cuirass," 78.

they must have been an *ekklesia*.[37] Such conjecture hides from view the great labor in inventing groupness. Rather than assume the existence of "groups" or "communities" revealed in Paul's letters, we are better positioned to examine the apostle's variegated strategies for summoning a sense of groupness in his writings, regardless of how strongly or loosely networks or assemblies materialized on the ground in Thessaloniki, Corinth, or anywhere else. Paul's use of martial language, especially when paired with *pistis*, constitutes a significant aspect of this strategy. As he exhorts and commends the fidelity of "his troops," he simultaneously names them as such. The rhetoric endeavors to form a boundary that demarcates insiders from outsiders (who, in other letters, he will designate as the *pistoi* and the *apistoi*).[38] Less than evidence for or description of a social formation that already exists, we find rhetorical efforts at bringing such social formation into being.

We are not equipped with enough reliable evidence to determine whether Paul's endeavors at group formation were successful in his own lifetime.[39] If anything, we have ample evidence that readers or listeners were often unswayed and that they readily disobeyed his calls for obedience and loyalty. Nevertheless, the readily available martial imagery and the demand for a soldier's allegiance and obedience in the Roman army provided Paul with an evocative exemplar for interpellating his gentile followers.

37. For more on this misstep, see Stanley Stowers, "The Concept of Community and the History of Early Christianity," *MTSR* 23 (2011): 238–56.

38. For more on Paul's terminology for insiders and outsiders, see Paul Trebilco, *Outsider Designations and Boundary Construction in the New Testament: Early Christian Communities and the Formation of Group Identity* (Cambridge University Press, 2017); Paul Trebilco, *Self-Designations and Group Identity in the New Testament* (Cambridge University Press, 2012).

39. In not too long later, of course, early Christian authors would propagate the idea of being a soldier of Christ, as in 2 Tim 2:3: "Join with me in suffering, like a good soldier of Christ Jesus."

CHAPTER FOURTEEN

Paul among Pagan Penises

Ryan D. Collman
Westcott House

Introduction: "Foreskin" for the "Uncircumcised"

Paul lived his life among circumcisions and foreskins. While putting it this way may be surprising, it is not a particularly controversial statement.[1] Whereas one might expect to read that Paul lived among Jews and gentiles, for Paul, saying that he lived among circumcisions and foreskins is the same thing: Jews are circumcised and non-Jews are foreskinned. The language of foreskin, however, is often missing from discussions of Paul's writings. When the word *akrobustia* ("foreskin") appears in his writings it is typically translated as "uncircumcised" or "uncircumcision."[2] But the Greek word for "uncircumcision" (*aperitmētos*) does not appear anywhere in the Pauline corpus.[3] This phenomenon is what one scholar refers to as the "invisibility of *akrobustia*": "Foreskin" has been cut out of the text by the translational preference for "uncircumcision."[4]

At first glance, it may seem like an insignificant translation choice to modern readers—after all, what is an uncircumcised penis if not a foreskinned one?—but in the ancient Mediterranean world this is a distinction with a

1. This is, of course, a not-so-subtle nod to the opening of Krister Stendahl's classic essay, "Paul among Jews and Gentiles."

2. This is not merely a translation choice found in English Bibles, but is ubiquitous in standard German, French, Italian, Spanish, Portuguese, and Scandinavian translations.

3. The only use of *aperitmētos* in the NT occurs in Acts 7:51 when Stephen accuses some of his fellow Jews as having uncircumcised hearts and ears (cf. Lev 26:41; Jer 6:10, 9:26; Ezek 44:7, 9).

4. Karin B. Neutel, "Restoring Abraham's Foreskin: The Significance of ἀκροβυστία for Paul's Argument about Circumcision in Romans 4:9–12," *JJMJS* 8 (2021): 53–74, at 41.

difference. As I demonstrate below, foreskin was an important component of the ideal penis (and body) in the dominant culture of Paul's time. Had Paul chosen to highlight the fact that his non-Jewish audiences were uncircumcised, he would have been centering the idea that their penises lacked a particular modification. By recognizing the presence of their foreskins, Paul not only acknowledges their own phallic ideals but also affirms their understanding of their own bodies. They would not have viewed themselves as being uncircumcised, but as possessing a foreskin. Had Paul wished to refer to his non-Jewish audiences as "the uncircumcision" he could have done so; the word existed.[5] But he did not, so we should not.

Given this standard (mis)translation of *akrobustia*, the emphasis in scholarship has been on the place and importance of circumcision in Paul's Judaism. This is valuable in its own right, but it has been to the detriment of portraying the significance of foreskin in Paul's wider cultural context. In this essay, I show why it is a necessity to restore foreskin to our reading of Paul's writings. When foreskin is excised from these texts, we obscure Paul's language and how his original audiences may have understood him. Highlighting the place of foreskin in Paul's letters and in the ancient Mediterranean world allows us to read these texts with a fresh perspective, and to better understand Paul's Judaism within paganism.

Penises in Pauline Perspective

Paul believed that humanity could be broken down into two constituent parts: Jews, and an undifferentiated cluster of non-Jews whom he calls, "the nations" (Rom 3:29; 9:24; Gal 2:14–15).[6] Elsewhere, he crudely substitutes Jews and

5. In contrast to Paul, the Greek translation(s) of the Hebrew Bible does substitute "uncircumcised" (*aperitmētos*) for "foreskin" (Hebrew: *ʿārēl*) when it modifies an individual. Thus, a "foreskinned Philistine" becomes an "uncircumcised Philistine." On this translational tendency, see Karin B. Neutel, "Missing Foreskin in the Septuagint: Circumcision Related Metaphors Lost in Translation," in *Circumcision and Jewish Identity*, ed. Lieve M. Teugels and Karin B. Neutel (Gorgias, 2023), 63–92.

6. For an overview of Paul's division of humanity into Jews and the nations, see Matthew V. Novenson, *Paul and Judaism at the End of History* (Cambridge University Press, 2024), 138–43.

the nations with phallic categories: Circumcisions and foreskins.[7] "Since God is one, he will rightwise the circumcision from trust and the foreskin through the same trust" (Rom 3:30).[8] "Is this blessing, then, only upon the circumcision or also upon the foreskin?" (Rom 4:9). "I had been entrusted with the good news for the foreskin, just as Peter for the circumcision" (Gal 2:7). In these instances Paul uses circumcision and foreskin as ethnic categories. In his mind, the state of one's penis as circumcised or foreskinned correlates to a specific ethnic identity. And for Paul these identities are fixed. Like many ancient people who thought about ethnicity, Paul was an ethnic essentialist, meaning ethnicity is not mutable but a matter of blood and genealogy.[9] Thus, when Paul writes about his and Peter's Jewishness, he says that they are "Jews by nature" (Gal 2:15). And while he does not write about individuals that are "gentiles by nature," he does speak of those who are "the foreskin from nature" (Rom 2:27). For readers from the twenty-first century, to say that someone is "the foreskin from nature" or "naturally foreskinned" is an empirical fact for infant boys (assuming they are not born with a physical anomaly like aposthia). For Paul, however, foreskin was natural only for non-Jews and circumcision was only natural for Jews. Conversely, it was unnatural for a Jew to be foreskinned after eight days of life, and it was equally unnatural for a non-Jew to be circumcised.[10]

Paul's belief that these statuses are doled out by nature is reflective of ancient understandings of what is natural. Ancient Greek and Roman

7. Paul's division of humanity into these two groups is unabashedly androcentric. For a classic treatment of circumcision, gender, and the status of women, see Shaye J. D. Cohen, *Why Aren't Jewish Women Circumcised? Gender and Covenant in Judaism* (University of California Press, 2005).

8. All Bible translations are the author's.

9. Paula Fredriksen, "God Is Jewish, but Gentiles Don't Have to Be: Ethnicity and Eschatology in Paul's Gospel," in *The Message of Paul the Apostle within Second Temple Judaism*, ed. František Ábel (Lexington Books/Fortress Academic, 2020), 3–19, at 5–9.

10. It is commonly assumed that in Paul's day one could become a Jew through circumcision and allegiance to the Jewish god. This perspective, however, was far from universal, nor did Paul subscribe to it. For a detailed examination of texts that portray the impossibility of conversion in the Hebrew Bible and Second Temple Judaism, see Matthew Thiessen, *Contesting Conversion: Genealogy, Circumcision, and Identity in Ancient Judaism and Christianity* (Oxford University Press, 2011).

ethnographers often appealed to an ethnic group's environment and geographic homeland as shaping their nature.[11] Similarly, issues of culture or conventional practice can also be understood in the ancient world as being natural. For example, Philo notes that some customs are so ancient that they become elevated to the status of nature (*On the Special Laws* 2.109).[12] Paul's use of natural phallic categories to describe and represent people groups demonstrates his participation in ancient ethnographic culture in which people groups are conceptualized through a "select description of their social, cultural, or physical features."[13] In this context, circumcision and foreskin function in a way that maintain and assert the "natural" boundaries and differences between people groups. As demonstrated by some of the pagan authors below, phallic features are one of the many characteristics that were highlighted in ancient ethnographic discourse when commenting on the differing practices and ideals of various ethnic groups.

The ethnic dimension of Paul's perspective on circumcision and foreskin has been broadly ignored in scholarship up until recently. Traditionally, Paul has been interpreted as having abandoned Judaism and "converting" to Christianity, which includes abandoning the Jewish law and circumcision.[14] Combine this understanding of Paul's supposed new religious affiliation with the common tendency to universalize Paul's teaching, and the ethnic component of circumcision easily vanishes. This perspective on Paul also promotes the common idea that he replaces physical circumcision with its supposedly

11. Benjamin Isaac, *The Invention of Racism in Classical Antiquity* (Princeton University Press, 2004), 82–102.

12. C.f. Philo, *On Dreams* 2.90, where "nature, race, and custom" are connected. Philo also notes that, over time, customs can overpower nature (*On the Decalogue* 137).

13. Maia Kotrosits, "The Ethnography of Gender," *SLAn* 7 (2023): 5–28, at 6n2. For a helpful understanding of Paul's participation in ancient ethnographic culture, see Philip A. Harland, "Climbing the Ethnic Ladder: Ethnic Hierarchies and Judean Responses," *JBL* 138 (2019): 665–86.

14. The idea that Paul converted from one religion to another has been widely refuted in recent scholarship. On this, see Paula Fredriksen, "Paul the 'Convert'?," in *The Oxford Handbook of Pauline Studies*, ed. Matthew V. Novenson and R. Barry Matlock (Oxford University Press, 2022), 31–53.

superior, universalistic counterpart: Spiritual circumcision.[15] This interpretation, however, is incorrect. Nowhere in Paul's letters does he repudiate the circumcision of Jews—regardless if they are within or outwith the Jesus movement—nor does he argue that Jews should cease circumcising their sons. In Romans 3:1–2, Paul states quite boldly that circumcision continues to have value for Jews. Even the author of Acts confirms that the rumors about Paul abandoning the law and teaching Jews to dispense with circumcision are false (Acts 21:20–25). Every instance where Paul prohibits circumcision is directed at its adoption by non-Jewish men. Rather than being against or indifferent to circumcision, his perspective is actually representative of a strict interpretation of the laws concerning circumcision, where it is understood as only being valid for descendants of Abraham on the eighth day after birth.[16] This strict interpretation of circumcision is why Paul's language is so harsh when he fears that non-Jews in his assemblies are being encouraged to or coerced into removing their foreskins (e.g., Gal 5:2, 12).[17]

Since Paul styles himself as the apostle to the nations (Rom 11:13; Gal 2:2, 7) and wrote his letters to non-Jewish audiences scattered throughout the ancient Mediterranean (1 Thess 1:9; 1 Cor 12:2), it is imperative that we take the wider pagan context of his letters and of his Judaism into account when thinking about circumcision and foreskin. It is to this wider pagan context that I now turn.

Penises in Pagan Perspective

In the ancient Mediterranean world, the paradigmatic penis possessed a foreskin. For centuries before and after Paul's letters, there is ample evidence from physicians, ethnographers, historians, and satirists that there was a shared understanding that foreskin adorns the ideal penis. In addition to our textual sources, the visual culture from this period also attests to the preference for foreskinned penises when visualizing the idealized male form. More

15. Against this perspective on spiritual circumcision in Paul, see Ryan D. Collman, "(Un) Making a Theological Mountain out of a Cardiological Mohel: Heart-Circumcision in Paul's Epistles," *JJMJS* 10 (2023): 89–105.

16. Thiessen, *Contesting Conversion*.

17. On the underlying logic of Paul's ban on circumcision for non-Jews in his assemblies, see Novenson, *Paul and Judaism at the End of History*, 128–32.

specifically, it is not simply the presence of a foreskin that perfects the penis but the foreskin itself must be of sufficient length, fully concealing the glans.[18] As our sources demonstrate, when a penis and its foreskin differ from this idealized conception it is characterized as deviant—something to be scorned, concealed, or in need of repair.

For some, the focus on foreskin began at birth. Ancient physicians and midwives thought that part of their duty was to mold and shape newborns in accordance with nature (Soranus, *Gynecology* 2.14). If a baby was born and something was out of alignment or appeared too swollen it was their job to fix it. Even the protocol for swaddling male and female babies was different because the swaddling set their body's formation on a particular trajectory (*Gynecology* 2.15). While they believed that they were shaping the body according to what was natural, what is "natural" is simply what they deemed to be conventional or ideal. So when an infant's foreskin appeared to be lacking and did not sufficiently cover the glans—a condition they referred to as lipodermos (literally, "lacking skin")—Soranus instructs midwives to gently pull the tip of the foreskin forward or pull it forward and bind it in place with a piece of yarn (*Gynecology* 2.34).[19] If this process is repeated enough, then the foreskin will stretch and achieve a "natural length." The general term used to refer to methods for foreskin elongation or restoration is "epispasm," which comes from the Greek word *epispaō* (used here by Soranus), meaning "to draw/pull over." By diagnosing a congenitally short foreskin as being contrary to nature, Soranus indicates that it was a medical impairment in need of solving. As Isaac Soon argues, an impairment is "a condition that is functionally and/or

18. Frederick M. Hodges, "The Ideal Prepuce in Ancient Greece and Rome: Male Genital Aesthetics and Their Relation to *Lipodermos*, Circumcision, Foreskin Restoration, and the *Kynodesmē*," *Bulletin of the History of Medicine* 75 (2001): 375–405.

19. Whereas Paul and the Greek translations of the Hebrew Bible use the word *akrobustia* for foreskin, the terms used for foreskin in Greek sources are *posthē* and *akroposthion* (and their variant forms). *Akrobustia* likely comes from combining the Greek prefix *akro* (tip) with the Hebrew word *bōshet* (shame) (or the Babylonian *bustu* [pudenda]) meaning "tip of the shame," where shame euphemistically refers to the penis. While *posthē* could refer to the entire structure of the foreskin covering the length of the penis, it primarily refers to the part that covers the glans. *Akroposthion* ("tip of the *posthē*"), on the other hand, specifically refers to the part of the foreskin that goes beyond the glans and tapers to the preputial opening. On this terminology, see Hodges, "The Ideal Prepuce in Ancient Greece and Rome," 377–78.

aesthetically deviant from a socially constructed bodily ideal."[20] Here, the societal ideal (i.e., what is "natural") is a foreskin that completely covers the glans. Anything that deviates from this standard requires medical intervention.

If an individual did not have their deficient foreskin treated shortly after birth and it continued to be insufficient into adolescence and adulthood, medical intervention continued to be an option. Some treatments were minimally invasive, whereas others required surgery and significant healing time. For example, the first century CE physician and pharmacognosist Discorides offered two treatments for a lipodermic foreskin. First, he notes that mixing honey and potassium alum and rubbing in on one's freshly bathed penis for thirty days can restore the foreskin (*On Medical Material* 2.82.2). Alternatively, one could apply the milky juice of the thapsia plant to their foreskin, which would cause it to swell up and appear more natural (*On Medical Material* 4.153.4). Since these treatments are only topical, he notes that these methods only work on a lipodermic penis, not one that has been circumcised. Other treatments, like the ones offered by Celsus (*On Medicine* 7.25.1) and Galen (*Method of Medicine* 14.16), required surgery in order to achieve the desired results. Celsus notes that his procedures work better on boys than men, and on those whose foreskins are congenitally short and not due to circumcision. One procedure entails drawing the foreskin over the glans, securing it with yarn, and then making an incision around the base of the penis so that the foreskin is free to move forward. After some time, the wound heals and the foreskin remains covering the glans. If, however, the foreskin was lacking due to circumcision then a significantly more traumatic procedure was needed. In these instances the skin of the penis—from its base to just underneath the glans—is surgically separated from the shaft and pulled forward over the glans to simulate the look of a foreskin. This required a significant aftercare regiment and lengthy healing time in order for the procedure to be successful. Celsus warns those who undergo this procedure to fast until nearly overwhelmed by hunger, in order to hinder the possibility of "exciting that part" and interfering with the delicate healing process.

Galen's methods for lengthening the foreskin follow those of Discorides and Celsus, but his language about the aesthetics of foreskin is worth noting. In *On*

20. Isaac T. Soon, *A Disabled Apostle: Impairment and Disability in the Letters of Paul* (Oxford University Press, 2023), 9.

the Usefulness of the Parts of the Body, Galen discusses the way that nature—who is personified as a divine, creative being—skillfully and purposefully designed the bodies of humans and animals. And while the parts of the body are functional, nature also makes many of them beautiful ornaments to demonstrate her skill and abundance. When discussing the ornamental nature of the ears, Galen notes that the foreskin—like the flesh of the buttocks—also shows obvious ornamentation (*On the Usefulness of the Parts of the Body* 11.13). It is not simply that foreskin has a purpose and is natural; it is beautiful. When the length of the foreskin deviates from what is in accordance with nature, he refers to this condition as a disease (*Method of Medicine* 14.16). While one could argue that the deficient prepuce was unable to serve its function properly, the major driving factor in these early penile procedures was cosmetic. None of these physicians discuss the function of the foreskin when outlining their foreskin-lengthening procedures; rather, they all focus on culturally normative aesthetics.

The idea that foreskin is ornamental and beautiful is widely attested in ancient Greek and Roman art. Some of the most well-known examples of this are found on Attic red-figure pottery, where penises are typically depicted as dainty and are accompanied by a long tapering foreskin (fig. 1). The foreskin was of specific interest to the artists as it is often exaggerated in form; in some examples it is clearly painted with separate strokes from the penis and sometimes extends well beyond the end of the glans. In one particularly notable depiction of foreskin where a young couple is about to engage in intercourse (fig. 2), the man is seated and the woman is in the process of climbing on top of him. Despite the fact that his penis is erect, his foreskin continues to cover his glans, extends well beyond it, and is roughly 20 percent of the length of his penis. Even though the scene is erotic and the foreskin would normally have been retracted in this scenario, the artist sticks to the ideals of his day and leaves the foreskin prominently on display. Similarly, in a famous fresco found in Pompeii, the god Priapus is depicted with an erection that is the same length as his thigh but his glans is still concealed by his foreskin (fig. 3). While the artist had no problem depicting his absurdly sized erection, he ensured that an equally large foreskin covered his glans.

It is worth noting how the perceived beauty, character, and identity of an individual is often mirrored by their genitals in ancient art; a handsome Greek youth might have a petite penis with foreskin covering his glans, whereas an enslaved foreigner might have a grotesque face and a large penis with his glans on display. An oft-cited example of this convention is a depiction of Heracles

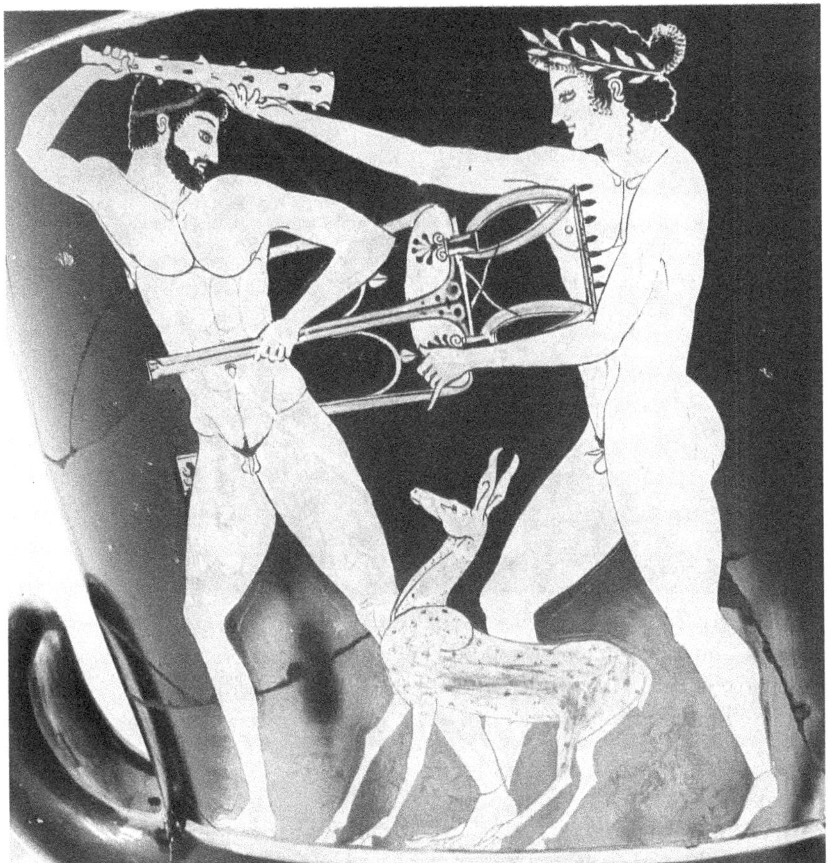

Fig. 1. Apollo and Heracles fight over the Delphic Tripod by Myson. ca. fifth-century BCE. Athens. Attic red-figured calyx-krater. British Museum, GR 1842.8-22.1 (Vase E 458). Photograph © Ryan D. Collman 2024.

and Busiris on a ceramic container (fig. 4). Here, the Greek hero Heracles is depicted as stereotypically handsome with a petite penis and identifiable foreskin. Busiris and two other Egyptians are depicted as having foreign (read: Ugly) facial features and clothing, as well as having their circumcised penises on display. Not only are their glans clearly exposed, but their penises are significantly larger than Heracles's. Part of the idealized form of the petite penis covered by foreskin was that it represented self-control (*sōphrosynē*) and the ability to have sexual restraint. On the other hand, a lack of self-control was represented by a large penis and exposed glans. Timothy McNiven refers to this artistic

Fig. 2. Erotic scene with a young man and courtesan by the Shuvalov Painter. ca. 430 BCE. Locri (Italy). Attic red-figured oinochoe. Altes Museum (Antikensammlung), Berlin F 2414. Image in the public domain courtesy of Wikimedia Commons.

convention as "the unheroic penis," where marginalized individuals—typically foreigners, the enslaved, or satyrs—can often be identified in art by how their penises deviate from the societal ideal.[21] The visual trope of the unheroic penis offers nontextual contributions to the wider ethnographic culture of the time, identifying those whose bodies, character, and genitals strayed from the dominant culture's archetype.

When penises deviated from the foreskinned ideal, they became objects of humor and offense. The exposed glans—whether by erection, circumcision, or lipodermos—was used by comics and satirists to elicit laughter and disgust from their audiences and, in some instances, to identify an individual as Jewish (or *appearing* Jewish). There were even Greek and Latin terms that specifically referred to a penis that has an exposed glans: *Psōlos* (Greek) and

21. Timothy J. McNiven, "The Unheroic Penis: Otherness Exposed," *Source* 15 (1995): 10–16.

Fig. 3. Priapus with phallus on scale. ca. first-century CE. Fresco. House of the Vettii, Pompeii. Photo by Chappsnet (cropped). Image courtesy of Wikimedia Commons and licensed under the Creative Commons Attribution-Share Alike 4.0 International license.

Fig. 4. Herakles and Busiris by the Pan Painter. ca. 470 BCE. Attic red-figured pelike. National Archaeological Museum, Athens 9683. Photo by Marsyas, 2005. Image courtesy of Wikimedia Commons and licensed under the Creative Commons Attribution-Share Alike 2.5 Generic license.

verpus (Latin).[22] For example, on a handful of occasions the comic playwright Aristophanes uses a penis with an exposed glans as the punchline in his comedy. In one instance, when describing the many flaws of a particular character, he writes that he is "useless, filthy, hunched over, wretched, shriveled, bald, toothless, and I think, by heavens, he is even *psōlos*!" (*Wealth*,

22. In contexts where these terms are applied to Jews they are typically used to indicate a circumcised penis (e.g., Martial, *Epigrams* 7.55; 11.94, discussed below).

265–67). If his other flaws were not enough, his permanently exposed glans is the icing on the cake. In another play, a group of foreign mercenaries are revealed as being circumcised, which reflects poorly on their usefulness as soldiers (*Acharnians* 155–74). When told what it will cost the hire them, the protagonist responds incredulously, "Two drachmas? For these docked dicks (*apepsōlēmenois*)!?" Aristophanes is also conscious that vulgar humor about exposed penises is somewhat of a comedic cliché that gets easy laughs. When trying to distinguish one particular work of his from lesser comics, he notes that in his sophistication he has not resorted to using a prop phallus that is "red tipped and thick," which makes children laugh (*Clouds* 537–39). Here, the red tip and thickness indicate that the prop phallus is trying to imitate an erect penis with an exposed glans—a *psōlos*.

By the turn of the first century CE, circumcision had become chiefly associated with Jewish men and there are two instances where an exposed glans is euphemistically referred to as a "Jewish weight" (or "Jewish burden").[23] One is from a comedic discussion of athletics in the gymnasium where a man is introduced as "bearing a Jewish weight," eliciting both laughter and disgust from the audience (*Corpus Papyrorum Judaicarum* 3.519). The speaker notes that the unsightliness of the man's body could possibly lead to his disqualification from athletic competition, but in his case his unsightliness is due to misfortune—likely indicating a lipodermic penis, not a circumcised one—and should not disqualify him. The other instance of this phrase comes from Martial, who discusses a scene in a bathhouse where he describes his slave as possessing a Jewish weight hanging below his lack of (fore)skin (*Epigrams* 7.35). In this sexually charged and vulgar scene, the Jewish weight likely refers not only to a lipodermic penis with a chronically exposed glans, but to its formidable size as well. As noted by Michael Peppard, it is unlikely that these men are themselves Jewish or circumcised, but their lipodermic penises make them *appear* as if they are.[24] Like circumcised Jews, their exposed glans is a burden they bear when nude in public.

---

23. Interestingly, the two instances of this phrase occur in different languages: Greek (*Ioudaikov phortion*) and Latin (*pondus Iudaeum*). For a recent evaluation of these passages, see Michael Peppard, "Bearing a 'Jewish Weight': A New Interpretation of a Greek Comedic Papyrus about Athletics (CPJ 3.519)," *JIBS* 5, no. 2 (2024): 21–41.

24. Peppard, "Bearing a 'Jewish Weight,'" 31.

Because of the wider societal conception of the ideal penis and the social stigma surrounding having an exposed glans in public, men who were circumcised or lipodermic sometimes sought to conceal their glans in situations when public nudity was the norm (e.g., during athletic competition or at public baths). Presumably, many Jewish men did not want to surgically reverse their circumcisions and others probably did not find surgical options appealing for obvious reasons.[25] Thus, there were two temporary options that allowed men to conceal their glans in public: Infibulation or the use of a *kynodesmē*. Infibulation was a practice in which the foreskin—or residual foreskin for the circumcised or lipodermic man—was pierced and secured over the glans with a pin or ring called a fibula. This prevented the glans from being accidentally exposed, but as Celsus also notes, some practiced it "for the sake of the voice or for health" (*On Medicine* 7.25.2). Martial recounts one instance where an infibulated man named Menophilus was exercising and his fibula came out in front of everyone, revealing the embarrassing fact that he had a chronically exposed glans (*verpus erat*; *Epigrams* 7.82). The *kynodesmē* ("dog leash") was a thin strip of leather that was tied around the foreskin (or residual foreskin), which pulled the penis upward, and was then secured around the waist as a way of keeping the glans covered and the penis in place during athletics (figs. 5 and 6).[26] Alternatively, instead of wrapping the strap around the waist in order to secure the penis, it could be secured by being wrapped around the scrotum and base of the penis. It was commonly depicted as being worn by athletes,

25. It is worth noting that despite being described by ancient medical writers, it is unlikely that surgical foreskin restoration was a particularly common procedure. While we do have two accounts that mention Jews "making themselves foreskins" (1 Macc 1:15) or "wearing the Greek hat" (2 Macc 4:12)—a euphemism for a penis that has undergone epispasm—the evidence for the prevalence of surgical epispasm is scant. On the meaning of "wearing the Greek hat," see Sara Parks, "The Greek Hat: 2 Maccabees 4:12 as a Euphemism for Reverse Circumcision," *JIBS* 5, no. 2 (2024): 1–20. Paul also notes that the circumcised should not undergo epispasm in 1 Cor 7:18. In this letter circumcision and epispasm are not central issues and there does not seem to be any particular social situation that indicates that epispasm was prevalent in this community. Rather, Paul's prohibition against epispasm and circumcision in this passage are part of his understanding of the ethnic specificity of circumcision and foreskin.

26. The reason it was called a "dog leash" is because "dog" was a slang term for the penis; Ryan D. Collman, *The Apostle to the Foreskin: Circumcision in the Letters of Paul*, Beihefte Zur Zeitschrift für Die Neutestamentliche Wissenschaft 259 (De Gruyter, 2023), 132–33. On the *kynodesmē*, see Hodges, "The Ideal Prepuce in Ancient Greece and Rome," 381–84.

but it was also likely an accepted means for men with an exposed glans to maintain decorum when nude. For those who wore a *kynodesmē* consistently, the persistent traction applied to the foreskin could lead to a lengthening of it over time.

From a modern perspective, having a permanently exposed glans in the ancient Mediterranean could be considered a disability. While the pathologization of lipodermos indicated that physicians considered it to be an impairment, an impairment is elevated to the level of disability when it "generates negative effects in its social and cultural environment. As impairment depends on a socially constructed ideal, so too does disability rely on an environment's unfavourable reaction to an impairment."[27] This can be easily demonstrated through the repeated marginalization, demonization, and stigmatization of those whose foreskins are lacking or missing. By failing to possess an ideal penis these individuals are not just punchlines in jokes but are also objects of ridicule. In the same way that modern individuals try to "correct" or "fix" their disabilities through the use of prosthetics or other aids in order to conform their bodies to a particular societal norm, so too did these ancient men use the aforementioned methods to conceal their glans when nude to meet societal expectations and thwart negative reactions.

Given that an exposed glans was associated with having an erection, those whose glans were permanently exposed could also be viewed as being in a permanent state of arousal. Thus, one of the insults hurled at Jews is that they are sexually insatiable and possess unruly penises. In one epigram, Martial issues an obscene threat to a man who has not properly reciprocated in gift giving. He says that if he acts unfairly, he will be forced to perform oral sex, and not on Martial's "well-behaved and diminutive" penis, but on a penis from Jerusalem, promoting the hypersexualized stereotype that circumcised Jewish penises are neither well-behaved nor small (*Epigrams* 7.55). Elsewhere, Martial repeatedly describes a poet from Jerusalem as circumcised (*verpe*) and accuses him of sodomizing his servant (*Epigrams* 11.94). His circumcised penis demonstrates that he is exceedingly lustful and results in him committing sexual assault. In his scathing description of the Jews, the historian Tacitus also comments they are prone to lust (*Histories* 5.5). And while he notes that they do not sleep with foreign women, no sexual act is off limits for them otherwise.

27. Soon, *Disabled Apostle*, 9.

Fig. 5. An athlete prepares for competition by putting on a *kynodesmē* by Euphronios. ca. 500 BCE. Athens. Attic red-figured calyx-krater. Altes Museum (Antikensammlung), Berlin F 2180. Photo by ArchaiOptix (cropped). Image courtesy of Wikimedia Commons and licensed under the Creative Commons Attribution-Share Alike 4.0 International license.

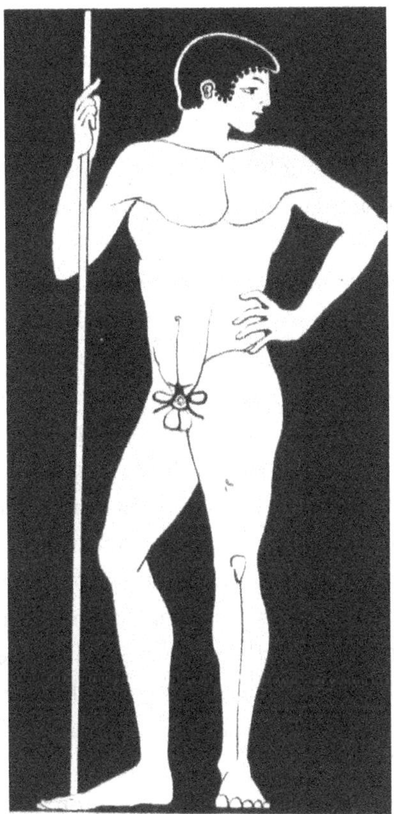

Fig. 6. An athlete wearing a *kynodesmē*. ca. 480 BCE. Vulci (Italy). Attic red-figured amphora. Staatliche Antikensammlungen, Munich 2314. Image in the public domain courtesy of Wikimedia Commons.

In addition to being hypersexualized, Jews were also called various slurs that critiqued their lack of foreskin. Horace refers to them as the "clipped" or "mutilated Jews" (*curtis Iudaeis*; *Satires* 1.9.69–70). Persius refers to the Jewish sabbath as the "skinned sabbath" (*recutitaque sabbata*; *Satires* 5.184). Martial critiques a young Roman woman for providing sexual favors to numerous foreigners while ignoring Roman men. Among those whom she provides favors for are the "skinned Jews" (*recutitorum Iudaeorum*; *Epigrams* 7.30). In a rant against the Jewish people, Juvenal lists the surrendering of their foreskins (*praeputia ponunt*; *Satires*, 14.99) among the many practices of theirs that he rejects. He also critiques them for only showing courtesy to those who are also circumcised (*verpos*; *Satires*, 14.104). While the *Historia Augusta* does not offer a direct insult in the same way as these other authors, it does link the practice of circumcision with mutilation. The author states that the Jews started a war (the Bar Kokhba revolt) because they were forbidden from mutilating their genitals (*mutilare genitalia*; *Historia Augusta*, Hadrian 14.3).[28] Though the author does not refer to the Jews as "the mutilated Jews" or something similar, by critiquing circumcision as a bodily mutilation the effect is the same.

Prior to Jews being singled out for their practice of circumcision, Egyptians and other ethnic groups were also critiqued for practicing circumcision and other types of penile modification. In their accounts of foreign peoples, ethnographers like Herodotus, Strabo, and Diodorus Siculus discussed these types of practices to note how other groups were dissimilar from wider Greek culture. Whereas many might assume that the practice of circumcision has Jewish roots, these three authors prominently connect circumcision to Egypt and note that other nations in the ancient Mediterranean who practiced it learned it from the Egyptians. Herodotus states that the Egyptians practiced circumcision for hygienic reasons because they value cleanliness over good looks (*Histories* 2.37), a clearly negative evaluation of the aesthetics of circumcision. In addition to mentioning that circumcision is practiced by Egyptians and Jews—who he believes are Egyptian in origin—Strabo comments on the penile modifications of the Creophagi and Troglodytes.[29] Concerning the Creophagi, Strabo writes that they "mutilated their acorns" (*koloboi tas balanous*; *Geography* 16.4.9), a reference to some form of cutting on or amputation of the glans.[30] The Troglodytes, on the other hand, are described by

28. This is a reference to Hadrian's supposed ban on circumcision. On this supposed ban, see Collman, *Apostle to the Foreskin*, 114n278.

29. Strabo's language is fairly neutral when discussing Egyptians and circumcision (*Geography* 17.2.5), but when he writes about Jewish circumcision his evaluation is negative. In a section where he paints a positive portrait of Moses, he notes that those who succeeded Moses were tyrannical and overzealous, and were the ones who instituted circumcision amongst the Jews (*Geography* 16.2.37).

30. Strabo also notes that the men in the area of Deirê (located in modern-day Djibouti) also have their "acorns mutilated" (*Geography* 16.4.5). If these are references to circumcision, it could be that the glans is "mutilated" via their permanent exposure.

Strabo as not only being mutilated (*koloboi*) but that some are also circumcised (*Geography* 16.4.17). Diodorus Siculus offers a slightly different account of the Trogodytes,[31] noting that they are circumcised like the Egyptians. There are some among the Trogodytes, however, that are called "colobi" (*kolobōn*) because when they are infants they have "all that part" cut off that is only circumcised by other peoples (*The Library of History* 3.32.4). It isn't entirely clear what procedure Diodorus aims to indicate by this, but it is possible that he has in mind a more severe form of circumcision than was typically practiced or some form of amputation of the glans or penis. Regardless of what this practice was, this form of penile modification sets them apart in a way that has earned them the name "mutilated."

As this discussion has demonstrated, there was a consistent phallic ideal in the dominant culture of Paul's world, an ideal that included a foreskin. Possessing a penis that deviated from this norm brought ridicule and shame upon its owner, and was viewed as defective, hypersexualized, or mutilated. When considering the issue of circumcision in the early years of the Jesus movement, it is critical that we take into account the perspectives explored above. How would non-Jews in Paul's assemblies think about circumcision, foreskin, and the ideal penis, and how would this inform their interpretation of his letters?

Thinking Phallically with Paul and the Pagans

An understanding of the significance of foreskin in the ancient Mediterranean world should inform our interpretation of the phallic language in Paul's letters. By reading his phallic discourse within paganism, new interpretive options arise. While I cannot fully explore circumcision and foreskin in Paul's letters in this section, I want to draw attention to some key aspects of Paul's participation in this discourse that would have been intelligible to non-Jews in his assemblies.[32] Here, I focus on three areas: Paul's phallic ideals, the self-identification of Paul's audiences, and the circumcision controversy related in the letter to the Galatians.

---

31. This group of people is known to Diodorus as the "Trogodytes" not the "Troglodytes."

32. For a recent and comprehensive treatment of circumcision and foreskin in Paul's letters, see Collman, *Apostle to the Foreskin*.

Unlike the authors of the Hebrew Bible and our pagan sources above, Paul's ideal penis was twofold. Whereas the authors of the Hebrew Bible do not seem to entertain the idea of an acceptable foreskin, Paul believes that foreskin was the ideal for pagans. Pagans, on the other hand, could not conceive of an acceptable circumcision, but Paul believes that circumcision was the ideal for Jews. As a circumcised-on-the-eighth-day Jew himself (Phil 3:5), it is clear that circumcision was not an affront to Paul at all, let alone in the way that it was to pagans. But Paul's embrace of pagan foreskin is innovative when compared to our Jewish sources. For Paul, both have their place when belonging to the right body. As I previously argued, this perspective on Jewish and pagan penises is rooted in Paul's understanding of what is "natural" for Jews and non-Jews respectively. While Paul's ideals differ from our pagan sources, he engages in the same type of ethnographic discourse to describe groups of people by their preferred penile aesthetics.

Like the typical pagan understanding, Paul offers a negative evaluation of penises that deviate from the ideal and insists that one's penis must not go against "nature." Given that Paul addresses his letters to non-Jews, there does not seem to be any reason for him to explicitly outline a rejection of epispasm, save his rule in all the assemblies in 1 Corinthians 7:18. However, when a non-Jewish penis deviates from the foreskinned ideal, Paul's language reflects the harsh critique that was common in the ancient Mediterranean; he considers it to be a mutilation. In Philippians 3:2, when describing a group of outsiders who seek to impose circumcision on the men in Philippi, Paul refers to them as "the mutilation" (or "the slashers"; *katatomē*).[33] Traditionally, based on the anti-law and anti-circumcision position often ascribed to Paul, interpreters believed these individuals were Jews and that Paul's reference to mutilation was a harsh critique of Jewish circumcision. But this is incorrect. Paul is not critiquing Jewish circumcision, a mark that he bears on his own body. Rather, Paul is critiquing the circumcision of *non-Jewish* opponents as a genital mutilation.[34] And not only are they mutilated, but they seek to mutilate other

33. While *katatomē* is not normally used to describe cuttings on human bodies, in the Greek translation of the Hebrew Bible the cognate verb *katatemnō* is used to describe ritualized self-harm (Lev 21:5; 3 Kgdms 18:28; Hos 7:14). See Soon, *Disabled Apostle*, 135–36.

34. On the identity of the opponents in Philippians, see Collman, *Apostle to the Foreskin*, 125–42.

non-Jews as well.[35] This is in contrast to the Jewish authors of the letter, Paul and Timothy, who are "the circumcision" (Phil 3:3) and do not improperly impose circumcision on non-Jewish penises. Paul has no misgivings toward circumcision or foreskin, but when the natural order is subverted, he calls it like he sees it.

Paul's use of foreskin also reflects the self-identification of his audiences. In light of the perspective on penile aesthetics that was common among pagans, they would have viewed themselves as foreskinned and not "uncircumcised." By restoring foreskin to our translations of Paul's letters we can better understand how his audiences might have received his words and what his language intended to convey. For example, in Romans 4:9–10, when Paul is discussing Abraham's trust in relationship to his righteousness, the common translation of this text reads, "Is this blessing, then, pronounced only on the circumcised or also on the uncircumcised [*tēn akrobustian*]? We say, 'Faith was reckoned to Abraham as righteousness.' How then was it reckoned to him? Was it before or after he had been circumcised [*en akrobustia*]? It was not after but before he was circumcised [*en akrobustia*]" (NRSVue). As Karin Neutel has observed, this standard translation centers the chronology of when Abraham was reckoned right—was it before or after he was circumcised?—but chronological language is absent from the Greek text.[36] What Paul actually highlights is the fact that Abraham was "in foreskin" when he was reckoned right. For Paul's original audience who may have been aware of the negative disposition toward foreskin in Jewish thought—not to mention their own valorization of foreskin—the focus on the acceptability of foreskin would have been welcome. If they model their trust after Abraham's, it is not a "before being circumcised" trust, but an "in foreskin" trust. It is not about them being faithful despite lacking a circumcision, but them be faithful in their natural state of foreskin. And while this may seem like a trivial distinction, for those whom foreskin was an important component of the ideal body, highlighting

35. Paul also styles these opponents as "dogs," which up until very recently was almost universally understood as an inversion of a supposed Jewish slur about non-Jews that Paul uses ironically against Jewish opponents. But as our pagan sources show, "dog" was a slang term for the penis. Thus, Paul's employment of the term actually reflects wider pagan usage. Here it functions as a vulgar, four-letter word, akin to calling these opponents "dicks."

36. Neutel, "Restoring Abraham's Foreskin," 55–60.

its continued relevance for their identity would have made a difference. Even more so, they were outsiders in a Jewish sect and Paul presents their foreskins as offering them a point of connection to one of the most important figures in Judaism (Rom 4:11).

There are two places in Paul's writings that have been read alongside one another in order to argue that Paul redefines the category of "the circumcision" to include foreskinned non-Jews: Romans 2:28–29 and Philippians 3:3. In Romans 2:28–29, Paul has often been (mis)interpreted as replacing physical circumcision with spiritual circumcision, the so-called true circumcision.[37] This is then read alongside Paul's statement in Phil 3:3, "We are the circumcision . . ." where "we" is read as a reference to all followers of Jesus. The result of this interpretive move is the idea that the only kind of circumcision that matters is circumcision of the heart, and that the title "the circumcision" has been transferred from Jews to the Christian church. While later gentile authors (incorrectly) theologized about how the church's spiritual circumcision usurped the physical circumcision of Jews,[38] how would this have been understood by Paul's foreskinned audiences? Given the negative evaluation of circumcision as mutilation and the stigma surrounding having an exposed glans, it seems unlikely that Paul's earliest readers would have wanted to be identified with circumcision—metaphorical or otherwise. Similarly, when those in Philippi heard Philippians 3:3, they would not have instinctively identified with being a part of "the circumcision." Since they would have identified as being foreskinned, when Paul states, "We are the circumcision," the physical and ethnic element of this would have been intelligible to them: They would have rightly not read Paul as counting them among the circumcised.[39]

37. Against the traditional understanding, see Novenson, *Paul and Judaism at the End of History*, 171–74.

38. On spiritual circumcision in early Christianity, see Everett Ferguson, "Spiritual Circumcision in Early Christianity," *SJT* 41 (1988): 485–97.

39. It is worth noting that Origen of Alexandria, who was a proponent of spiritual circumcision replacing physical circumcision, mirrored the general pagan perspective on physical circumcision. He derides the circumcision of Jews as "ugly, hideous, deformed, and indecent both in manner and appearance," but styles the spiritual circumcision of the church as "holy, honorable, and worthy of God" (*Homilies on Genesis* 3.6). He also writes that it is more appropriate to speak of spiritual circumcision than the "pruning of the flesh" (*carnis obtruncatio*; *Homilies on Genesis* 3.4).

If the general disposition of non-Jews toward circumcision was overwhelmingly negative, how does this shape our understanding of the circumcision controversy in Galatians? When Paul writes about the potential adoption of circumcision by non-Jews in Galatia, he notes that it is being forced upon them. It is not something they are actively seeking out and willfully submitting themselves to, but it is being thrust upon them. In Galatians 6:12 (cf. Gal 2:3), Paul uses the verb *anankazō* ("to compel/force") to demonstrate that this was not voluntary, describing the agitators as "those who are forcing you to be circumcised."[40] While Paul's letter suggests that circumcision was being imposed upon them, its widespread adoption was not yet a reality. Rather than thinking that the Galatians were nearly convinced to be circumcised and that Paul's letter was the eleventh-hour intervention that preserved their foreskins, in all likelihood the vast majority of the Galatians were not seriously considering adopting the practice. After all, if their perspective was aligned with the wider pagan world, it is improbable that they would be interested in disfiguring their penises and actively stigmatizing their bodies. They did not need to be convinced by Paul's strong language and detailed argumentation to reject circumcision, but were likely simply relieved to find that their strong aversion to circumcision had the backing of a prominent apostle. While we know that some non-Jews did get circumcised in antiquity, there were many more who actively resisted it. Even though the zeal of religious converts is well-documented, and this zeal probably led to the circumcision of some converts in Galatia, the barrier to entry in this case was still particularly high. Regarding their resistance to coerced circumcision, Paul's gospel for the foreskin (Gal 2:7) was not actually what the Galatians needed to hear but was exactly what they were hoping to hear.

Conclusion: Pagan Foreskins and the Circumcised Apostle

It is imperative to read Paul's phallic language in light of his ancient Mediterranean context. Paul was a participant in a wider cultural conversation that focused on penile aesthetics and their relationship to one's identity. Like

40. The combination of *anankazō* and the verb "to circumcise" is also used to indicate forced circumcisions in Josephus, *Life* 113.

his pagan contemporaries, Paul appealed to natural order when discussing the ideal penis and this discourse would have been intelligible to his pagan readers. By restoring foreskin to his letters we are not only able to better understand the words of the circumcised apostle, but also the perspectives of his foreskinned readers, and thus, read his Judaism within paganism.

CHAPTER FIFTEEN

Gendering Sin and Salvation in Paul

Stephen L. Young
Appalachian State University

Could Paul's letters present gentile sin as a feminine corruption of masculinity and salvation as a masculine transformation? Is it even possible that his teachings about Christ's significance and human sin are embedded in dominant Greco-Roman ideologies about gender? These questions may sound odd since it has become a truism among many students of Paul that his gospel was liberating for women, countercultural, and subversive of empire. But do such approaches overlook ways that Paul's religious program resonated in Mediterranean antiquity? At a basic level, he would have been recognizable precisely as a Jewish freelance expert in the gods whose divinatory practices, teachings about how to make progress in virtue, mythmaking, facility with sacred texts, and offer of a superior afterlife made him native to the ancient Mediterranean.[1] Since Paul was part of and not essentially separated from Mediterranean religion, we should explore the ways his gospel resonated with dominant ideals of that world.

My goal in this essay is to highlight how Paul's gospel message participated in wider Greek and Roman discourses about gender. His religious program paints gentiles with a feminizing brush and his gospel then offers them access

---

1. For key examples, see Laura Dingeldein, "Gaining Virtue, Gaining Christ: Moral Development in the Letters of Paul" (PhD Diss., Brown University, 2014); Jennifer Eyl, *Signs, Wonders, and Gifts: Divination in the Letters of Paul* (Oxford University Press, 2019); Stanley Stowers *History and the Study of Religion: The Ancient Mediterranean as a Test Case* (Oxford University Press, 2024), 201–336; Heidi Wendt's essay in this volume; Stephen Young, *Paul among the Mythmakers: Sins, Gods, and Scriptures* (Edinburgh University Press, forthcoming). On Paul as a Jewish teacher of gentiles, see Paula Fredriksen, *Paul: The Pagans' Apostle* (Yale University Press, 2017); for a recent more-popular introduction, see Matthew Thiessen, *A Jewish Paul: The Messiah's Herald to the Gentiles* (Baker Academic, 2023).

to a virtuous masculine transformation through the high Jewish god's *Christos*. It is not that Paul's overt message in his letters is the feminization of sin and masculinity of salvation through Christ. Gendered discourses about virtue, vice, piety, divinization, and rulers do not always operate at the surface like that. But Paul's claims about gentile sin and the corresponding relevance of Christ reflect prevailing ideas about femininity and masculinity.[2]

Masculinity and Femininity in Ancient Literature: It's Not Just about Gender

It will be helpful to sample some passages from Greek, Roman, Jewish, and Christian sources that illustrate the assumptions about masculinity and femininity that pervade the literature of Mediterranean antiquity. These passages reveal traits commonly associated with femininity and women versus traits associated with masculinity and men.

> [Womankind] is inclined to be secretive and crafty, because of its weakness. . . . You see, leaving women to do what they like is not just to lose half the battle; a woman's natural potential for virtue is inferior to a man's, so she is proportionately a greater danger, perhaps even twice as great. (Greek philosopher: Plato, *Laws* 781a–c)

> How can one reach agreement with a woman? By recognizing . . . that the female sex is bold, positively acting for something which it desires, easily liable to change its mind because of poor reasoning powers, and of naturally weak constitution. (Jewish writer: *Letter of Aristeas* 250)

> For the character of the females is softer, and quicker to be tamed, and more receptive of handling. . . . For man's nature is the most complete. . . . Hence a wife is more compassionate than a husband and more given to tears, but also more jealous and complaining and more apt to scold and strike. The female is also more dispirited and

2. See Young, *Paul among the Mythmakers*, chapter 2, "Make Gentiles Masculine Again: The Gender of Decline and Salvation."

despondent than the male, more shameless and lying, and is readier to deceive. (Greek philosopher: Aristotle, *History of Animals* 608a–b)

But first and foremost, we must reject pleasures. They render us weak and womanish; they make great demands upon us. . . . What I protest against is not that virtue is placed second to pleasure, but that virtue is associated with pleasure at all, for virtue despises pleasure, is its enemy, and recoils from it as far as it can, being more acquainted with hard work and difficulty, which are manly inconveniences, than with this womanish good of yours. (Roman philosopher: Seneca, *Epistles* 104.34 and *On Benefits* 4.2.4)

Women were born to be penetrated. (Seneca, *Epistles* 95.21)

Because a male is more complete, more dominant than the female, closer akin to causal activity, for the female is incomplete and in subjection and belongs to the category of the passive rather than the active. So too with the two ingredients which constitute our life principle, the rational and the irrational; the rational which belongs to the mind and reason is of the masculine gender, the irrational, the province of sense, is of the feminine. Mind belongs to a genus wholly superior to sense as man is to woman. (Jewish philosopher: Philo, *Special Laws* 1.200–201)

His beard, then, is the badge of a man and shows him unmistakably to be a man. It is older than Eve and is the symbol of the stronger nature. . . . Whatever smoothness or softness there was in him God took from him when he fashioned the delicate Eve from his side to be the receptacle of his seed, his helpmate both in procreation and in the management of the home. What was left (remember, he had lost all traces of hairlessness) was manhood. His characteristic is action; hers, passivity. For, what is hairy is by nature drier and warmer than what is bare; therefore, the male is hairier and more warm-blooded than the female; the uncastrated, than the castrated; the perfect, than the imperfect. (Christian philosopher: Clement of Alexandria, *Christ the Educator* 3.3.19)

Male	**Female**
Active	Passive
Perfect / Complete	Imperfect / Incomplete
Superior	Inferior
Penetrating	Penetrated / Receptive
Dominant	Subordinated
Self-Controlled	Weak Self-Control, or lack of it
Mastering Desire, Pleasures, and Passions	Enslaved to Desire, Pleasures, and Passions
Rational / Strong Reasoning	Irrational / Poor Reasoning Powers
Superior Virtue	Vice and Inferior Virtue
Strong [Physically, Rationally, and Morally]	Weak [Physically, Rationally, and Morally]
Hard [Physically and in Character]	Soft [Physically and in Character]
Discerning and Truthful	Deceivable and Deceptive
Hairy / Warm / Dry	Smooth / Cold / Wet

The gender ideals reflected in these passages define masculinity in terms of domination, self-mastery, activity, penetration, strength, rationality, and virtue versus dominated, passive, penetrated, weak, irrational, and vicious femininity (i.e., vice is the classic opposite of virtue).

There is not just one single or systematically consistent model of masculinity and femininity in Greco-Roman texts. But we may loosely refer to what Meghan Henning labels the "hierarchical understanding of gender" that pervades ancient writings.[3] The study of gender in antiquity attempts to excavate a variety of models from our sources that organize how the usual male and female traits relate to each other. One model is the penetration paradigm:

3. Meghan Henning, *Hell Hath No Fury: Gender, Disability, and the Invention of Damned Bodies in Early Christian Literature* (Yale University Press, 2021), 25.

To be masculine is to penetrate less masculine others and to dominate them. Another model is simply active versus passive: To be masculine is to be active, controlling, and dominant whereas to be feminine is to be passive, suffering, controlled, and receptive. Yet another is to conceptualize masculinity in terms of self-mastery: The ideal man rules over himself as well as over less masculine others (e.g., free women, lower-status men, children, enslaved humans) in his orbit who are not capable of ruling over themselves. Finally, a rubric that many scholars used to think was pervasive is the one-sex model: The idea that ancient texts do not conceive of two separate sexes, but one fluid sex hierarchy in which to be on the masculine end is superior to the feminine. Much in these models overlaps. They all presume a general hierarchy of male over female. But each model configures the relationships between moral, cognitive, and bodily characteristics in different ways that elevate certain traits as avenues for thinking about others.[4]

The lack of a single or rigid gender system is important for reading ancient texts. Yes, most of the bodily, cognitive, and moral characteristics seen in the chart retain their masculine or feminine associations across ancient Greek, Roman, Jewish, or Christian sources. But writers could work with these building blocks in numerous ways, often in disagreement with each other. Pauline literature itself reflects this fluid phenomenon. Paul could envision a divinely created hierarchy of men over women (maybe husband over wife?) in which women still have authoritative agency around men like prophesying (see 1 Cor 11:2–16). But one of the many Pseudo-Pauls could stress the same

4. Publications about the gender ideologies of Greek and Roman era texts are legion. For an accessible introduction, see Sara Parks, Shayna Sheinfeld, and Meredith Warren, *Jewish and Christian Women in the Ancient Mediterranean* (Routledge, 2022), 8–14. For more involved discussion that gets into the complicated histories of scholarship, see Brooke Holmes, *Gender: Antiquity and Its Legacy* (I.B. Tauris, 2012). For a detailed discussion focused on Roman literature, see Craig Williams, *Roman Homosexuality*, 2nd ed. (Oxford University Press, 2010), 13–19, 94–99, 137–202, 258–67. There are criticisms of the models of gender mentioned above. But such criticisms do not so much dispense with active versus passive or the penetration paradigm as destabilize certain aspects or note (as Henning does) ways in which some ancient texts frame matters differently; e.g., Benjamin Dunning, *Specters of Paul: Sexual Difference in Early Christian Thought* (University of Pennsylvania Press, 2011), 13–19, 51–74; Maia Kotrosits, "Penetration and Its Discontents: Greco-Roman Sexuality, the *Acts of Paul, and Thecla*, and Theorizing Eros without the Wound," *Journal of the History of Sexuality* 27 (2018): 343–66. It is noteworthy that the presumed ubiquity of the one-sex model has been widely critiqued (including in the Henning and Holmes publications cited above).

hierarchy of male-over-female in order to deny women any space for teaching or having authority over men (see 1 Tim 2:11–15). The ability to discuss masculinity or femininity via different bodily, cognitive, or character traits also allowed ancient writers to redefine their gender ideals. For example, some civic leaders emphasized the material, militaristic, and victorious aspects of mastery (or ruling over others) for masculinity even if self-mastery over their passions was still an ideal for them. Then other leaders and some philosophers attempted to one-up that image of masculinity by stressing primarily self-mastery of the passions and the ability to attain virtue through suffering as the ideal.[5] The hierarchy of male over female, plus their associated traits, was still presumed by each. As Henning explains, we must "respect the tensions that are present" and "avoid imposing a single theoretical model of gender in antiquity upon the texts" or even upon any individual text since sometimes "multiple ways of talking about gender occur within the same text."[6]

It is also important to clarify that when ancient authors write about masculinity and femininity, they are not just writing about gender. They are also often writing about other topics like ideal kings, moral psychology, progress in piety or virtue, enslaved people, foreigners, or the corruption of society. In the same way, when ancient authors write about these other topics, they are also writing about gender. As Jennifer Knust illustrates in her research on the slandering of political, religious, or philosophical rivals as effeminate in antiquity, male and female were perspectives for thinking about the rest of reality.[7] While gender concerns are not always present in our ancient sources, they are

5. See John Fitzgerald, *Cracks in an Earthen Vessel: An Examination of the Catalogues of Hardships in the Corinthian Correspondence* (SBL, 1988). Revelation (plus Paul to some extent) and then a variety of Christian writings stretching into Late Antiquity redefine masculinity to deprioritize penetration (even if they variously retain a concern over men being penetrated) and families while further emphasizing self-mastery, virtue, and ascetic ideals that even incorporate traits traditionally coded as feminine in ways that further naturalized masculine authority. See Virginia Burrus, *"Begotten Not Made": Conceiving Manhood in Late Antiquity* (Stanford: Stanford University Press, 2000); L. Stephanie Cobb, *Dying to Be Men: Gender and Language in Early Christian Martyr Texts* (Columbia University Press, 2008); Henning, *Hell Hath No Fury*; Lynn Huber, *Thinking and Seeing with Women in Revelation* (Bloomsbury, 2013).

6. Henning, *Hell Hath No Fury*, 16–17.

7. Jennifer Knust, *Abandoned to Lust: Sexual Slander and Ancient Christianity* (Columbia University Press, 2006).

more present than untrained readers appreciate.[8] Writers and audiences of ancient texts thus often looked for masculine and feminine characteristics.

Paul and the Femininity of Gentile Corruption

It is almost a cliché among students of Paul that he writes about sin. Romans 1:18–32 is a classic example. Aside from focusing on "idolatry," foolishness, and sexual transgressions, he ends with an entire vice list: for example, injustice, evil, murder, gossip, slander, and even disobedience to parents (Rom 1:28–31). Modern readers are typically unaware that in this passage Paul reuses mythological plots about the decline of civilization to sketch the corruptions of gentiles.[9] In this view, there was an earlier period when gentiles knew God: See Romans 1:20 and "For though they knew God" in 1:21a (the participle *gnontes* that the NRSV translates as "knew" is an aorist—in other words, a completed action—and is further governed by the aorist finite verbs that follow; e.g., *edoxasan*). But at some point they offended the deity and corrupted proper aniconic worship with iconic (1:21b–23). God then initiates cycles of punishments through which gentiles degenerate further in their impiety, minds, and morality (1:24–32).

Paul's sketch of gentile degeneration in Romans 1:18–32 aligns with his version of Jewish polemical tropes about gentile nations elsewhere in his letters. He often lists gentile vices and specifies fleshly passions, cognitive failures, and perversions in cult or "idolatry."[10] Just as Wisdom 13:1 configures gentiles as foolish "by nature" (*phusei*) and expounds at length on their cultic corruptions

---

8. See Holmes, *Gender*, 24–25 for similar points about how gender works in ancient sources.

9. See Stanley Stowers, *A Rereading of Romans: Justice, Jews, and Gentiles* (Yale University Press, 1994), 83–125. The traditional, and still common, understanding of Rom 1:18–32 is that it concerns the sin of all humanity. But for the view that Paul here focuses on just gentile sin, see Stowers, *Rereading of Romans*, 86–97; more accessibly, Thiessen, *Jewish Paul*, 62–69. For Paul, Jewish and gentile sin have different histories and characteristics; see Stephen L. Young, "Ethnic Ethics: Paul's Eschatological Myth of Jewish Sin," *NTS* 70 (2024): 235–48.

10. See 1 Thess 1:9–10; 4:3–5; Gal 4:8–9, 5:16–26; 1 Cor 5:9–10, 6:9–11; 12:2; see also Eph 4:17–19 for an example from Ps-Paul. For discussion of these features of gentile sin in Paul, plus exploration of how vice lists work, see Frederik Ivarson, "Vice Lists and Deviant Masculinity: The Rhetorical Function of 1 Corinthians 5:10–11 and 6:9–10," in *Mapping Gender in Ancient Religious Discourses*, ed. Todd Penner and C.V. Stichele (Brill, 2007), 163–84; Knust, *Abandoned to Lust*, 19–87.

(Wis 13:1–14:31), for Paul they are "idolatrous" sinners *phusei* (e.g., Gal 2:15): This is their hereditary condition.[11]

Paul's mythmaking about gentile decline was itself intelligible as an iteration of a wider Mediterranean phenomenon. Greek and Roman period sources are full of mythic materials about the corruption of humanity and of civilization.[12] In these schemes, society has declined from an idyllic masculine, rural, and pious past to a corrupt, feminized, urban, and impious present. These ideas about human and societal decay were widespread. Hesiod's myth of the five races of men in *Works and Days* (106–201) provides a classic example. This is fitting since his myth became a reservoir from which later Greek and Roman writers drew when imagining societal history.[13] First came the golden race of men (109–26) who prospered under the reign of Cronos: "Just like the gods, they spent their lives, with a spirit free from care, entirely apart from toil and distress." These men were not immortal, but they died pleasant deaths and the cosmos provided everything in abundance during their lives. It is important to note that there is not a linear decline of humanity in *Works and Days*, in particular given the fourth race of heroes.[14] But things get worse after the golden race with the introduction of shorter lives, women, and a variety of other matters coded as evil or undesirable across the silver, bronze, and iron races. The silver race is "much worse" and "like the golden one neither in body nor in mind" (127–29). They escalate to "wicked outrage against each other"

11. See Sarah Emmanuel, *Wrestling with Paul: The Apostle, His Readers, and the Fate of the Jews* (Fortress Academic, 2025), chapter 4; Brian Rainey elucidates the connections between Paul's depictions of gentile cultic perversions, his ethnic framework for this sketch of gentiles, and the idea that gentiles are thus sinners by nature or heritage (*Religion, Ethnicity, and Xenophobia in the Bible* [Routledge, 2019], 229–35).

12. For a classic discussion of relevant sources, see Arthur Lovejoy and George Boas, *Primitivism and Related Ideas in Antiquity* (Johns Hopkins University Press, 1935). See also Stowers, *Rereading of Romans*, 85–125; Stephen Young, "'Make Rome Great Again' Preceded 'Make America Great Again': The Ancient Romo-Nationalism of Biblical Writers," *Interpretation* 78 (2024): 321–34, at 324–29.

13. On the reuses of Hesiod's myth of the races by later writers, see Stephen Scully, *Hesiod's Theogony: From Near Eastern Creation Myths to Paradise Lost* (Oxford University Press, 2015), 69–159; Helen Van Noorden, *Playing Hesiod: The "Myth of the Races" in Classical Antiquity* (Cambridge University Press, 2015).

14. See Glenn Most, "Hesiod's Myth of the Five (or Three or Four) Races," *Proceedings of the Cambridge Philological Society* 43 (1998): 104–27, at 104–8.

in tandem with their unwillingness to "honor the immortals or to sacrifice upon the holy altars of the blessed ones" (134–37). The iron race has sunk so low that they experience unceasing work during the day and suffering at night, with the gods giving "grievous cares" to them (178–79).

Gender is prominent in these imaginations of history, particularly in how the decline itself upends a proper masculine dominated order. Human corruption is marked by the appearance of women, trouble from women, men becoming (more) effeminate, and sexual deviance (which exemplifies gender disorder for these writers). In *Works and Days*, women do not appear until the silver race (131–32), and it is debatable whether the text classifies them among the race or simply as its caretakers. As Jenny Strauss Clay argues, "The introduction of women in the silver age also marks a fall from an idyllic time when only males existed."[15] The nonexistence of women among the golden race of men is, in fact, crucial to the plot: The golden race no longer exists bodily since they could not procreate given the lack of women. Thus "the earth covered up this race, by the plans of great Zeus" (121–22).

The myths of Pandora in both *Works and Days* and in Hesiod's *Theogony* further encode women as the catalyst of evil. The gods inflict women as a punishment. In *Works and Days*, Pandora is created with "lies and guileful words and a thievish character" (77–80) and is "a woe for men" (82). Before her advent, "the tribes of men used to live upon the earth entirely apart from evils, and without grievous toil and distressful diseases" (90–92). Though Hesiod offers a different myth about Pandora in the *Theogony* (561–616), it also corelates human degeneration with women. In response to Prometheus's deception, "Immediately [Zeus] contrived an evil for human beings in exchange for fire" (570). The full range of evils for men are associated with this woman: "For from her comes the race of female women: for of her is the deadly race and tribe of women, a great woe for mortals, dwelling with men, no companions of baneful poverty but only of luxury" (590–93). In Hesiod's influential mythmaking, the arrival of women marks the end of the idyllic period. Cosmic decline is gendered.

Roman writers adapted themes from ideologies of decline to portray their present as a time of moral, religious, gender, and sexual decay that undermines

15. Jenny Strauss Clay, *Hesiod's Cosmos* (Cambridge University Press, 2003), 88.

the power of Rome.[16] Horace's *Ode* 3.6 is a famous example. It takes up the issue of recent Roman imperial setbacks (3.6.7–16). The poet appeals to an earlier time when Roman men were pious and thus blessed with the divine favor of imperial rule (3.6.5) but were then, along with their descendants, punished by the gods for their impiety (3.6.1–3, 7–8).

Horace's invocation of impiety is simply the appetizer. The main course will taste familiar to anyone who has consumed modern conservative tropes about how the health of the nation depends on the health of the (hetero-patriarchal) family. From this perspective, the supposed decline of society stems from the corruption of marriage and from gender disorder in families.[17] Horace introduces the final two-thirds of *Ode* 3.6 with, "Generations prolific in sin first defiled marriage, the family, and the home. From this source is derived the disaster which has engulfed our fatherland and its folk" (3.6.17–20). He asserts a twofold corruption of the gendered order that has catalyzed national catastrophe. First, corrupted masculinity is evidenced by husbands failing to control their wives.[18] Second, and at greater length, elite women have destabilized their marriages, and thus the Roman state, by transgressing feminine norms through their education in foreign erotic dancing and their "illicit love affairs" with lower-status and even foreign men such as "some salesman or the captain of some Spanish ship" (3.6.19–32). In other words, Horace sermonizes on how women having sex in a way not controlled by their patriarch—a blatant upheaval of the normative gendered order—caused the ruin of the Roman state.

Horace concludes *Ode* 3.6 by further amplifying his claims about the femininity of decline. The Roman men of old who initially conquered the Mediterranean did not come from "parents like these" (i.e., the failed husband and wife). "No, they were the manly children of peasant soldiers, who had been

16. For general discussion, see Catherine Edwards, *The Politics of Immorality in Ancient Rome* (Cambridge University Press, 1993), 42–47, 176–98; Andrew Wallace-Hadrill, "The Golden Age and Sin in Augustan Ideology," *Past and Present* 95 (1982): 19–36; Nancy Shumate, *Nation, Empire, Decline: Studies in Rhetorical Continuity from the Romans to the Modern Era* (Duckworth, 2006), 19–32, 37–61, 67–79.

17. Sara Moslener traces the history of associating national health—or even national security—with conservative Christian norms for families, sexuality, and gender (*Virgin Nation: Sexual Purity and American Adolescence* [Oxford University Press, 2015]).

18. *Ode* 3.6.29–30. See Shumate's discussion in *Nation, Empire, Decline*, 74.

taught to turn the sod with a Sabellian mattock, and on the instructions of their stern mother to cut and carry firewood" (3.6.33–40). Horace similarly decries the loss of past rustic and masculine virtues in *Ode* 3.5: "Once true manliness is gone, it refuses to be put back into men who have become worse" (3.5.29–30). To focus back on *Ode* 3.6, it concludes by asserting that now it is an "iniquitous time.... Our fathers' age, worse than our grandfathers', gave birth to us, an inferior breed, who will in due course produce still more degenerate offspring" (3.6.46–48).

Paul's history of gentile decline in Romans 1 similarly culminates in effeminizing degeneration. Due to gentile impiety and foolishness, the Jewish god hands them over to their desires (*epithumia*, 1:23) and their dishonorable passions (*pathē*, 1:26) such that gentile men burn in their desires (*orexis*, 1:27). This is a myth of complete gentile loss of self-mastery over passions.[19] Whether one understands Paul's moral psychology to be Middle Platonist (i.e., a tripartite soul that is inherently irrational since its lower two parts are seats of desires and passion) or Stoic (i.e., a unitary and inherently rational soul whose passions are the result of false beliefs about what is good), he stresses the total moral failure of gentiles.[20] Cicero's outline of the loss of self-mastery (*intemperantia*) is but one of many examples from Latin and Greek texts that imagine such moral decay: "A revolt from all guidance of the mind and right reason, so completely alien from the control of reason that the cravings of the soul cannot be guided or curbed ... [it] kindles, confounds and agitates the whole condition of the soul, with the result that from it come distress and fear and all other disorders" (*Tusculan Disputations*. 4.9.22). Paul's story of gentile impiety and the resulting divine infliction of domination by passions

---

19. Thus, influentially, Stowers, *Rereading of Romans*, 42–82.

20. On Paul's sketch of gentile total moral failure or soul death, see Emma Wasserman, *The Death of the Soul in Romans 7*, WUNT 2/256 (Mohr Siebeck, 2008). For a brief rundown of Middle Platonist versus Stoic moral psychologies and debates about how to understand where Paul fits, see Stephen L. Young, "So Radically Jewish That He's an Evangelical Christian: N.T. Wright's Judeophobic and Privileged Paul," *Interpretation* 76 (2022): 339–51, at 340–46. For more detail, see Stanley Stowers, "Paul and Self-Mastery," in *Paul in the Greco-Roman World: A Handbook*, vol. 2, ed. J. Paul Sampley (Bloomsbury, 2016), 270–300. Following Stowers, Dingeldein ("Gaining Virtue, Gaining Christ"), and Wasserman, I understand Paul to have a Platonist moral psychology and Stoic physics. But for an influential argument that Paul has a Stoic moral psychology, see Troels Engberg-Pedersen, *Paul and the Stoics* (Westminster John Knox, 2000).

in 1:21b–27 then turns to gentiles' failed minds and proliferation of vices in 1:28–32. In other words, Romans 1 sounds like Paul's version of describing a revolt from all guidance of the mind and right reason, which results in all other disorders.

It is important to note that Paul's history of gentile degeneration has strikingly gendered resonances within Greco-Roman discourses. Like Horace *Ode* 3.6, Romans 1 is a myth of gender trouble, failures in masculinity, and feminine degeneration given the associations of masculinity with rationality, self-mastery, and control over passions versus femininity with weaker reason, lack of self-mastery, and being ruled by passions.[21] When the first-century CE historian Diodorus Siculus wanted to stress that the (fictitious) king Sardanapallus was a failed man and thus a failed king, he feminizes him. Sardanapallus "outdid all his predecessors in luxury" and "lived the life of a woman," covering himself with so many cosmetics that "he rendered [his body] more delicate than any luxury-loving woman" (*Bibliotheca historica* 2.23.1). He "took care to make even his voice to be like a woman's" and pursued excessive sexual pleasures without restraint (2.23.2), causing "the total destruction of the Assyrian empire" (2.23.4) because of his captivity to luxury and "womanish practices" (2.24.4). The early second-century CE philosophical writer Dio Chrysostom describes a man's moral decay as having been changed "to the life and garb of women" and thus becoming "enslaved to pleasure, pleasure-loving, and carnally-minded . . . and [living] a disgraceful and reprehensible life" (*Orations* 4.101–15). Clement of Alexandria's *Christ the Educator* depicts unvirtuous men as unwilling to restrain their "uncontrolled passion" and thus "effeminate" (e.g., 3.2.13, 3.3.15).

But Paul does not leave the effeminate significance of having lost self-mastery implicit at the beginning of Romans. Gentiles' effeminate traits unfold in corruptions of the proper gender-sexual and patriarchal orders similarly to how Horace sermonizes about Roman decline. "Their [i.e., gentile men's] women" (*thēleiai autōn*) exchanged natural "use" (i.e., the sexual use of their bodies) for sex that is *para phusin* or "beyond nature" (Rom 1:26). Gentile men give up the "natural use" of women and both sexually penetrate and are penetrated by each other (1:27). Paul's language resonates with the elite

21. For more detailed discussion of the effeminizing valence of Paul's claims about gentile sin, see Knust, *Abandoned to Lust*, 51–87; Joshua Reno, "Pornographic Desire in the Pauline Corpus," *JBL* 140 (2021): 163–85; Young, "Gender of Decline and Salvation."

gender ideals discussed above. The language of "nature" and what is "natural" in 1:26–27 refers most basically to this patriarchal gender-sexual hierarchy and the idea that each person should behave in accordance with where they exist within it (i.e., free men should penetrate and not be penetrated; women's sexuality is for the sexual use of men).[22]

Paul has thus painted a picture of comprehensive corruption. Gentile women are no longer being sexually used (i.e., penetrated) by their men as they should be in accordance with "nature."[23] Gentile men are mastered by their own passions and have lost sexual control of their women, which is a basic failure in their own masculinity and thus a blow to the patriarchal social order that Paul presumed as normative.[24] The destruction of masculinity then has a double climax: Gentile men are effeminized since they let themselves be penetrated sexually by men, and they effeminize other men by penetrating them. Romans 1's focus on sexual sin reflects the established theme in Greco-Roman discourses wherein the corruption of humanity entails transgression of the patriarchal order. Paul's claims about female sexual dysfunction in Romans 1:26 and male homoeroticism in 1:27 participate in hierarchical Greco-Roman gender norms.

The Jewish philosopher Philo illustrates these gendered cultural logics of Paul's language. Philo describes morally incurable men with a barrage of feminizing evaluations in *Special Laws* 1.325. They are effeminate men afflicted

---

22. Numerous studies explicate these varied Greco-Roman gender-sexual ideologies, rhetoric about what is "natural," and the participation of Jewish writers like Paul in them; e.g., Benjamin Dunning, "Same-Sex Relations," in *The Oxford Handbook of New Testament, Gender, and Sexuality*, ed. Benjamin Dunning (Oxford University Press, 2019), 573–91; Jimmy Hoke, *Feminism, Queerness, Affect, and Romans: Under God?* (SBL, 2021); at a more popular level, Jennifer Knust, *Unprotected Texts: The Bible's Surprising Contradictions about Sex and Desire* (HarperOne, 2011), 79–94.

23. It is debated whether Rom 1:26 has female homoeroticism in view or women engaging in sexual acts with men other than being (vaginally) penetrated. For a classic argument that female homoeroticism is in view, see Bernadette Brooten, *Love between Women: Early Christian Responses to Female Homoeroticism* (University of Chicago Press, 1996), 189–302.

24. See Hoke, *Under God*, 83–86; Joseph Marchal, *Appalling Bodies: Queer Figures before and after Paul's Letters* (Oxford University Press, 2020), 163–64. 1 Corinthians 11:2–16 also reflects Paul's rejections of confusions or transgressions of patriarchal hierarchy; see Ross Kraemer, *Her Share of the Blessings: Women's Religions among Pagans, Jews, and Christians in the Greco-Roman World* (Oxford University Press, 1992), 146–47; also, Knust, *Abandoned to Lust*, 81–84.

with the disease of femaleness (*tōn nosountōn tēn thēleian noson androgunōn*) who falsify the established usage of nature (*to phuseōs nomisma parakoptontes*) and force themselves into the passions and form of uncontrolled women (*eis akolastōn gunaikōn pathē kai morphas eisbiazontai*), remodeling the male shape into a female-type form (*ton arrena tupon metacharattontas eis thēlumorphon idean*). Notably, Philo reprises much of this language later in *Special Laws* when criticizing the moral failures of men who let themselves be sexually penetrated (3.37–38) and the men who penetrate them and thus ruin the masculinity of free males (3.39).[25] Like Paul in Romans 1, Philo invokes men pursuing no-normative sex as an example of how moral decay upends proper gender hierarchies. Philo even makes the effeminacy of vice explicit: "The transformation of the male nature into the female" (*tēn arrena phusin . . . eis thēleian metaballein* - see *Special Laws* 3.37). Philo's discussion of moral failure and Paul's depiction of gentile sexual dysfunction swim in the same Greco-Roman gendered currents. Invoking Philo's language, Diana Swancutt even argues that both writers explicate a "disease of effemination" when describing such losses of virtue.[26]

25. As often noted (and at the risk of overgeneralization), whereas some Greek sources accept a higher-status older free man sexually penetrating a younger free man, Roman writings often reject such an arrangement and condemn the active/penetrating partner since he feminizes a future free Roman male (e.g., Jonathan Walters, "Invading the Roman Body: Manliness and Impenetrability in Roman Thought," in *Roman Sexualities*, ed. Judith Hallett and Marilyn Skinner [Princeton University Press, 1997], 29–43, at 33–35, 41). Some Jewish writers of the Roman period notably expand the condemnation of the active partner in male homoerotic sex to all active partners, not just those who penetrate free men (e.g., Rom 1:27; Josephus, *Against Apion* 2.199; Ps- Phocylides 190–91). Philo elsewhere condemns both active and passive partners (e.g., *Abraham* 133–36) and seems to in *Special Laws* 3.39, in keeping with his commenting on Lev 20:13 where both are punished. But given his stress on the active partner's culpability for ruining the future of the city due to his effeminizing of the man he penetrates, it is possible *Special Laws* 3.39 reflects the more limited condemnation of a man who penetrates a free man. It is important to note that when Ps-Phocylides, Philo, Paul, and Josephus critique male homoeroticism, they all still presume wider Greco-Roman gender hierarchies and active-vs-passive roles in their moral logics, not some exceptional Jewish or Christian interest in rejecting "homosexuality" (there is a massive bibliography; for now, see Dunning, "Same-Sex Relations," 574–78, 584–85).

26. Diana Swancutt, "'The Disease of Effemination': The Charge of Effeminacy and the Verdict of God (Romans 1:18–2:16)," in *New Testament Masculinities*, ed. Stephen Moore and Janice Capel Anderson (SBL, 2003), 193–233.

Given Paul's participation in dominant ideologies about masculinity and femininity when it comes to virtue, it is unsurprising that he lumps effeminacy (*malakos*) into the vice list for gentile sin in 1 Corinthians 6:9–10 as though it requires no further explanation. English translations often obscure the gendered tone of *malakos* by rendering it as an inherently sexual term (e.g., "homosexuals" in NKJV, "male prostitutes" in NRSVue; other translations combine *oute malakoi oute arsenokoitai* as "men who have sex with men" in the NIV or "men who practice homosexuality" in the ESV). But *malakos* is a common Greek word meaning soft or effeminate. Since being sexually penetrated is a feminizing experience in Greco-Roman discourses, ancient sources frequently describe such a man as *malakos* (e.g., Philo, *Special Laws* 3.40). But context must suggest such a specific meaning. The basic valence of the word is softness or effeminacy, often reflected in uncontrolled or excessive desire—not just for sex, but also for luxury or food. A variety of ancient texts thus describe a man who excessively penetrates too many women as *malakos* as well![27] Paul's vice list in 1 Corinthians 6:9–10 accordingly illustrates the feminine valence of gentile sin in an explicit manner: Gentile sin involves effeminacy.[28]

The Masculinity of Salvation in Christ

So why does Paul write his story of gentile degeneration is these specific ways? The answer is surprisingly simple. Paul reuses common ideals about decline to make his religious expertise seem absolutely necessary for the gentiles whom he teaches about Christ. He sketches a catastrophic problem and offers the solution![29] For Paul, gentiles have lost masculine self-mastery and become com-

27. See Dale Martin, *Sex and the Single Savior: Gender and Sexuality in Biblical Interpretation* (Westminster John Knox, 2006), 44–47. For similar points about *effēminātus*, *mollis*, and *muliebris* in Latin literature, see Edwards, *Politics of Immorality*, 67–68, 76–78, 81–86, 130; Amy Richlin, *The Garden of Priapus: Sexuality and Aggression in Roman Humor*, rev. ed. (Oxford University Press, 1992), 3–5, 139, 222; Williams, *Roman Homosexuality*, 156–70.

28. On the gendered rhetoric of vice lists and vice as deprivation of manliness in some contexts, see Ivarson, "Vice Lists and Deviant Masculinity," 164, 166–71, 176, 180.

29. My position may seem to run afoul of E.P. Sanders's influential argument that Paul's thought moves "from solution-to-plight" (*Paul and Palestinian Judaism: A Comparison of Patterns of Religion* [Fortress, 1977], 434–47, 508–11). Sanders's point was related to long running debates about Paul's theology and rightly critiqued prior Protestant understandings of sin and salvation in Paul's letters. But I am interested in the social logic of how Paul's

prehensively sinful. They accordingly face the wrath of Israel's god and fail in every metric for virtue, philosophical prestige, and legitimacy. But Paul offers them access to the god of Israel's *Christos*, whose actions deal with God's wrath against them while making them descendants of Abraham (Rom 3–4; Gal 3–4) and thus recipients of divine *pneuma* ("spirit"). Gentile Christ initiates are thus empowered to master their passions (Romans 6–8; note also the final fruit of the spirit in Gal 5:22–23) and behave in holiness and honor sexually (1 Thess 4:3–5).[30]

But Paul goes beyond simply hinting that the benefits of his gospel resonate with masculine ideals. He makes explicit that gentiles re-attain masculinity through Christ. The context of *malakos* in 1 Corinthians 6:9–11 is a vice list that explains what some of the Corinthian gentiles were like before "you were washed, you were dedicated, you were set right in the name of the Lord Jesus Christ and by the *pneuma* of our God" (6:11). Effeminacy was a trait of these gentiles until its *pneumatic* removal by their participation in Christ. Note how Epictetus similarly associates effeminacy with other vices that proper piety will remove: "Clear away from out of your own mind . . . fear, desire, envy, joy at others' ills; cast out greed, effeminacy, and lack of self-control. These things you cannot cast out in any way other than by looking to God alone, being specially devoted to him only, and consecrated to his commands" (*Discourses* 2.16.45–46).

Paul's gospel of masculinization in Christ in 1 Corinthians 6:9–11 participates in Greco-Roman discourses wherein moral improvement, increased piety, and even divinization are coded as masculine transformations. Think about the dominant Greco-Roman ideals for masculinity and femininity. If being irrational, dominated by one's passions, sexually penetrated, and passive are effeminate conditions, then (re)attaining self-mastery, virtue, and

portrayals of gentile sin relate to the religious practices he offers. From such a social vantage point, Paul's mythmaking about gentile corruption absolutely serves to naturalize and legitimate his gospel.

30. For discussion of the *pneumatic* transformation Paul envisions gentiles gaining via their participation in and divinization like Christ, see Troels Engberg-Pedersen, *Cosmology and the Self in the Apostle Paul: The Material Spirit* (Oxford University Press, 2010); see also the essays by Litwa and Thiessen in this volume; Stanley Stowers, "The Dilemma of Paul's Physics: Features Stoic-Platonist or Platonist-Stoic?," in *From Stoicism to Platonism: The Development of Philosophy, 100 BCE–100 CE*, ed. Troels Engberg-Pedersen (Cambridge University Press, 2017), 231–53, at 240–46.

likeness to the gods are masculine transformations. This situation is why, for example, "conversion" is often imagined as masculinizing in ancient Jewish and Christian sources.[31] Writings that discuss virtuous women likewise conceptualize them as displaying manly traits and behaviors. Valerius Maximus's story about Lucretia as "a model of Roman chastity" describes her virtue in terms of having a "manly spirit" (*virilis animus*) despite having been given a "woman's body" (*muliebre corpus*).[32] While masculinity belonged more naturally, if you will, to those who were born as free men, this gendered economy of virtue resides behind the practices of masculinity—explicated by Maud Gleason—that conceive of masculinity as fragile and requiring constant vigilance to maintain.[33]

When Paul draws 1 Corinthians to a close by commanding his gentiles to be manly, his religious program resonates with such recognizable practices of masculinity. The common translation of *andrizesthe* in 1 Corinthians 16:13 as "be courageous" obscures the gendered mechanics of this text for modern readers. Yes, the Greek verb *andrizō* and related noun *andreia* encompass courage. But courage is a decidedly masculine trait in Greco-Roman discourses—which is why manliness is *andreia*'s basic meaning. The manliness of virtue and courage as reflected in the Greek word *andreia* is not an etymological fallacy to prop up a modern scholarly fantasy. Latin and Greek moral writers make exactly this point.[34] To explain the masculinity of virtue, Cicero exploits how the Latin *virtus* means both virtue and manliness. He writes,

31. See, for example, Willi Braun, "Fugitives from Femininity: Greco-Roman Gender Ideology and the Limits of Early Christian Women's Emancipation," in *Fabrics of Discourse: Essays in Honor of Vernon K. Robbins*, ed. D. B Gowler, L. G. Bloomquist, D. F. Watson (Trinity, 2003), 317–32, at 323–25; Ross Kraemer, "The Other as Woman: An Aspect of Polemic among Pagans, Jews, and Christians in the Greco-Roman World," in *The Other in Jewish Thought and History: Constructions of Jewish Culture and Identity*, ed. L. J. Silberstein & R. L. Cohn (New York University Press, 1994), 121–44, at 131, 135–36; Diane Lipsett, *Desiring Conversion: Hermas, Thecla, Aseneth* (Oxford University Press, 2010), 3–5.

32. Valerius Maximus, *Memorable Deeds and Sayings* 6.1.1. On virtuous women as exhibiting manly traits in appropriate ways (i.e., it was bad manliness for women to penetrate men; see Seneca, *Epistles* 95.21); from works already cited, see Cobb, *Dying to Be Men*, 30–31; Marchal, *Appalling Bodies*, 40–48.

33. Maud Gleason, *Making Men: Sophists and Self-Presentation in Ancient Rome* (Princeton University Press, 1995).

34. See Cobb, *Dying to Be Men*, 30.

"For it is from the word man (*vir*) that the word virtue (*virtus*) is derived" and "These [virtues] we must exercise if we wish to prove possessors of virtue, or, rather, since the word for virtue (*virtus*) is borrowed from the word for man (*vir*), if we wish to be men" (*Tusculan Disputations* 2.18.43). To focus on a Greek author, when discussing the ability to avoid pleasure, "to which they gave the names self-mastery (*enkrateian*), justice (*dikaiosunēn*), and manliness (*andreian*)," Plutarch adduces how Romans have the same word for manliness and virtue (*Coriolanus* 1.4). The masculinizing effect of Christ's *pneuma* for gentiles thus bubbles to the surface in the middle of 1 Corinthians and then again in Paul's concluding commands for his gentiles in 16:13.

Galatians 3:28's "no male and female" since "you are all one in Christ Jesus" is perhaps the clearest and yet most misunderstood example of Paul clarifying the masculine valence of initiation into Christ. Up through Galatians 3 Paul has been laying out his ethnic understanding of how gentiles have access to the eschatological blessings of the Jewish deity by becoming descendants (or, sons) of Abraham through Christ and receiving divine *pneuma* (e.g., Gal 3:14, 24–26).[35] In Galatians 3:27 Paul attributes this meaning to baptism: "For as many of you as were baptized into Christ have put on Christ." Then comes his famous language in 3:28, "There is neither Jew nor Greek, neither enslaved person nor free, no male and female. For you all are one in Christ Jesus."

Since the middle of the twentieth century, it has been common for interpreters to understand Galatians 3:28 as a statement (whether pre-Pauline and redeployed by Paul, or initially by Paul himself) of gender equality. But this approach severs the verse's rhetoric from the gendered Greco-Roman discourses that shaped Paul. Galatians 3:28's language introduces three hierarchical polarities—Jew/Greek, enslaved/free, and male/female—in the midst of Paul's repeated assertions that gentiles undergo transformation into higher status existences.[36] By participation in Christ they become descendants of Abraham and thus heirs to God's promise (Gal 3) and they also become free instead of enslaved (Gal 4–5). As Sarah Emmanuel emphasizes, Paul's

35. On Paul's participatory, ethnic, and *pneumatic* logics in Gal 3–4, see Caroline Johnson Hodge, *If Sons, Then Hiers: A Study of Kinship and Ethnicity in the Letters of Paul* (Oxford University Press, 2007), 67–107.

36. So, Colleen Conway, *Behold the Man: Jesus and Greco-Roman Masculinity* (Oxford University Press, 2008), 79.

ethnocentric hierarchy of Jew over Greek is the premise of his rhetoric. That hierarchy is not leveled in Christ, but amplified.[37] The logic of Galatians 3:28 is precisely that in Christ gentiles undergo assimilation from their lower places in the polarities (Greek, enslaved, female) to the benefits of the higher status (Jew, free, male). At no point in Galatians 3:27–29 does Paul introduce language of equality, which he is capable of using (e.g., *isotēs* in 2 Cor 8:13–14). His language in Galatians 3:27–29 is instead of oneness in Christ Jesus, which includes hierarchy here just as when Paul elsewhere writes about unified hierarchy in the body of Christ in 1 Corinthians 12:12–30. Paul even deploys the polarities of Jews or Greeks and enslaved or free there in 12:12–13 in conjunction with baptism, *pneuma*, and participation in Christ.

When re-placed in its literary and ancient Mediterranean settings, Galatians 3:28 emerges for modern readers of Paul in the same ways it plausibly resonated for various ancient hearers: Gentiles (re)attain masculinity in Christ. The verse is not just an assertion of "neither Jew nor Greek, neither enslaved person nor free, no male and female." Paul's claim is that, in Christ, gentile initiates no longer exist across the polarities because "you are all one in Christ Jesus." It is an argument of assimilation to "one," and the one that gentiles are in Christ is emphatically (and grammatically) a masculine one.[38] In Paul's letters, the resurrected and divinized Christ is the last Adam and the man from heaven who now has a *pneumatic* body characterized by incorruption, glory, and power instead of deterioration, dishonor, and weakness.[39] Christ, the man from heaven, has a hypermasculine body whose traits all signal masculinity.[40] Just as Paul explains that through participation in Christ gentiles undergo the *pneumatic* transformation Christ underwent (with their souls prior to resurrection and then in a complete bodily manner after their own resurrection), so they too they will bear the image of the man of heaven (1 Cor 15:49) and their humiliated bodies will be transformed by Christ to

37. Emmanuel, *Wrestling with Paul*, chapter 4.

38. As in, the word for "one" in Gal 3:28 is *heis*, which is a masculine singular form.

39. See 1 Cor 15:42–47; see also Phil 3:21. On Christ's resurrected *pneumatic* heavenly body for Paul, Engberg-Pederson, *Cosmology and the Self*, 8–38; Stowers, "Dilemma of Paul's Physics."

40. For a sustained discussion of the masculinity of Christ in Paul's letters, see Conway, *Behold the Man*, 67–82.

be in the same form as his body of glory (Phil 3:21).[41] In Galatians 3:28 Paul expresses this gendered understanding of participation in Christ by writing that gentiles who are faithful in the right way (i.e., Paul's way) undergo baptism to become one in Christ.

Greco-Roman era writings include many examples of idealizing some kind of effacing of gender. In place of engaging with the diverse details of these texts, it suffices to note that they are generally not disruptions of gender hierarchies but reaffirmations.[42] The Gospel of Thomas is a famous example. This text includes passages about assimilating various polarities, including gender, into one; for example, "Jesus said to them, 'When you make the two into one, and when you make the inner like the outer and the outer like the inner . . . and when you make the male and female into a single one, so that the male will not be male nor the female be female'" (22). The final section of the Gospel of Thomas then clarifies the gendered situation. Peter asks Jesus to send Mary away since "females are not worthy of life." Jesus replies, "Look, I shall guide her to make her male, so that she too may become a living spirit resembling you males. For every female who makes herself male will enter the kingdom of heaven" (114). This saying shows, as Melissa Harl Sellew explains, that for the writer of the Gospel of Thomas "the whole matter of subsuming two genders into one, or of replacing duality with singularity, involves a precisely androcentric process."[43] There is no longer male and female because all are a masculine one. Galatians 3:28 reflects similar Greco-Roman sensitivities about the femininity of undesirable traits or statuses and the masculinity of moral and pious improvement. In this passage Paul is clear that his religious program offers male and female gentiles masculinization in Christ. The *pneuma* Paul writes of gentiles receiving through Christ in Galatians 3 then empowers their disentanglement from vices ("the works of the flesh") in Galatians 5:18–21 and

---

41. Ronald Charles argues Phil 3:21 is at the nexus of an argument that Christ's conquering, heroic, and male body transforms the feminine and conquered bodies of Christ followers into masculine bodies that will then likewise exercise authority and power (*The Silencing of Slaves in Early Jewish and Christian Texts* [Routledge, 2019], 96–97n67).

42. For example, Marchal, *Appalling Bodies*, 34–45; Kari Vogt, "'Becoming Male': A Gnostic and Early Christian Metaphor," in *The Image of God: Gender Models in Judaeo-Christian Tradition*, ed. Kari Elisabeth Børresen (Fortress, 1995), 170–86.

43. Melissa Harl Sellew, "Reading the *Gospel of Thomas* from Here: A Trans-centered Hermeneutic," *JIBS* 1 (2020): 61–96, at 81.

attainment of virtue in 5:22–23, with the culminating fruit of the *pneuma* being self-mastery.

Paul's depiction of gentile decline denied them any share in the masculine ideals that mark virtue, power, or favor. But their pious restoration in Christ (Rom 12:1–2; 1 Thess 1:9–10) entails their exceptional attainment of masculine traits like self-mastery, glory or honor, power, and authority. Now they are coheirs and brothers with Christ atop the hierarchies of authority, understand the high god's secret plans, and help rule his empire.[44] In other words, Paul's religious program participates in the dominant ideals of masculinity and femininity in the ancient Mediterranean by monopolizing those ideals for Christ, himself, and his gentiles.

44. For example, see Rom 8:17, 29–30; 1 Cor 2:7–16, 6:2–3. On gentiles as pneumatically transformed and divinized to such positions alongside Christ, see Litwa's essay in this volume; Stowers, "Dilemma of Paul's Physics," 240–49.

Response

From Paul Beyond the Judaism/"Paganism" Divide to Paul as an Ancient Eastern Mediterranean Jew in the Early Roman Imperial Period

Troels Engberg-Pedersen
University of Copenhagen

In this concluding essay, I will try to assess how far scholarship has come in its attempt to locate Paul in his ethnic, social, and cultural milieu. There will be a number of casualties, some of which I have myself been involved in: "Paul in His Hellenistic Context," "Paul beyond the Judaism/Hellenism Divide," "Paul within Judaism"—and also the title of the present volume: "Paul within Paganism." I was asked to entitle this essay "Paul beyond the Judaism/'Paganism' Divide." But that formulation will be among the casualties, too.

In the second half of the essay, I will first focus on some methodological rules that I propose should be followed once we have reached an agreement on the first issue. Then I will address and situate two specific issues in Paul within "the whole of Paul" as reflecting the overall ethnic, social, and cultural space that was his. The aim here is not finally to solve those issues, but rather to indicate that once one has considered the particularities on which one will invariably focus, there remains the task of showing how what one has discovered in a single place coheres with all the rest of Paul.

This essay is not meant as a review of what the reader will have encountered in this volume. I have myself learned a whole lot from these essays (think of people's having the Pauline *pneuma* as a form of possession! think of the role of the moon! of Paul's martial imagery! of the pagan foreskin! of the effeminacy of sin and the masculinity of salvation!) and I applaud the overall direction of it all. More generally, however, I aim to bring all the methodological reflections in the essays to a hopefully valid conclusion that will provide a solid base for further work.[1]

Paul Beyond and Within and . . .

Paul and Hellenism: Context and Beyond

In 1994, I edited a collection of essays that was titled *Paul in His Hellenistic Context*.[2] It arose from a conference titled "Paul on His Hellenistic Background." It soon became clear during the conference—not least, through the efforts of Abraham J. Malherbe—that speaking of Paul's "background" was quite wrong. Paul should be seen not *against* whatever else one might point to in his contemporary ethnic, social, and cultural milieu, but as participating *in* it. Speaking of a "background" against which he "stood out" was just a bad reflection of seeing him as unique and a hero of "early Christianity." Here, then, the notion of context proved healthy. This is actually reflected (though not directly theorized) in a number of essays in the present volume. Thus, "contextualization" of Paul may stand as one adequate way of describing what we are after.[3]

Seen from hindsight, however, speaking of Paul's "Hellenistic" context remained unsatisfactory in another respect. It implied that one should see Paul in two more or less opposing ways: In relation to "Hellenism" to be understood as being different from and in opposition to (his) "Judaism." Here, then, "Hellenism" and "Judaism" were implicitly understood as standing—once more—*against* one another. That did not, perhaps, matter so much if one looked at what was actually said in the essays of that volume. But the sense that there was some basic contrast between the two -isms remained as an

1. In what follows, I will refer to the essays of this volume by second name and page only, e.g., Chantziantoniou, p. 3.

2. Troels Engberg-Pedersen, ed., *Paul in His Hellenistic Context* (T&T Clark/Fortress, 1994).

3. For "contextualization," see explicitly, e.g., Chantziantoniou, p. 16 and Sharp, p. 146. For "participation" and "sharing in," see, e.g., Gruen, p. 40, Sharp, pp. 149–50, Young, pp. 259 and 273–76. For "nonuniqueness," see, e.g., Chantziantoniou, pp. 13–16, Bazzana, pp. 121–22, and Rollens, pp. 199–202. Here, too, belongs the concerned effort on the part of almost all contributors to provide a "redescription" of the Pauline material in terms derived from his wider world that will make it "comprehensible," "intelligible," and "legible," both to his contemporaries and to us, see, e.g., Chantziantoniou, pp. 13–16, Wendt, pp. 43 and 46, Novenson, pp. 60 and 73, Fredriksen, p. 84n15, Sharp, p. 149, Collman, pp. 253, 256, 258, and Young, p. 266.

undercurrent to the whole project. That no doubt went back to the impact of Martin Hengel's very influential book, whose title one must have in German: *Judentum und Hellenismus*.[4] Here the two -isms stand out in heavily reified form with a history of an intrinsic opposition that goes the whole way back—via Gustav Droysen's work in the German tradition, *Geschichte des Hellenismus* (English translation: *History of Hellenism*, 1836–43)—to Tertullian's talk of "Athens and Jerusalem."[5] The weight of this tradition is enormous and the present volume is one huge attempt to shake it off our shoulders.[6]

Back in the 1990s, that led to another follow-up conference that came to be called *Paul beyond the Judaism/Hellenism Divide*.[7] The idea behind that title was precisely that: To shake off Hengel. By considering Paul *beyond* his divide, would it not be possible to see the whole of Paul without being bothered by any -isms? The sad answer is: No! Even though we said "beyond," we still carried with us an underlying *distinction* between "Judaism" and "Hellenism" as categories that were in some form of opposition to one another.[8] Thus we did not in fact manage—in the title itself—to shake off Hengel, including all those normative connotations that had always been involved in speaking of "Greek culture" (and from the nineteenth century onward, "Hellenism") versus "Judaism"—and vice versa. But these normative connotations are pernicious. We want to find a way understanding the "Hellenistic," "Greek," and "Roman" features of Paul as well as the "Jewish" ones *without* operating, first, with any normative connotations at all and, second, with any intrinsic opposition

4. Martin Hengel, *Judentum und Hellenismus* [English translation: *Judaism and Hellenism*], WUNT 10 (J.C.B. Mohr [Paul Siebeck], 1969 and later).

5. "What has Athens to do with Jerusalem?" Tertullian, *The Prescriptions against the Heretics* 7.

6. For this, see, e.g., Chantziantoniou, pp. 6–8 when speaking of the idea that "that Jews would need to 'assimilate,' 'acculturate,' or 'accommodate' to dominant Greek culture": "It essentializes what counts as 'Judaism' and 'Hellenism,' despite the irreducible diversity of both, and subtly reinforces an implicit dichotomy between them as self-contained rival entities that can resist or subsume one another." See also Bazzana, p. 122, speaking against a traditional Christian "exceptionalism via rehabilitating the old Judaism versus Hellenism dichotomy."

7. Troels Engberg-Pedersen, ed., *Paul beyond the Judaism/Hellenism Divide* (Westminster John Knox, 2001).

8. However, for a strong argument against this, see chapter 2 of the book, which is Dale B. Martin's splendid essay, "Paul and the Judaism/Hellenism Dichotomy: Toward a Social History of the Question," in Engberg-Pedersen, *Paul beyond the Judaism/Hellenism Divide*, 29–61.

between them. And in both respects, we want to be able to articulate both similarities and differences. It is only once we have achieved these goals that we may feel reasonably sure that we have actually reached the historical Paul himself, as it were on the other side of our own taxonomies.[9]

Another way of saying this is that we should constantly attempt to apply the perspective on Paul that belongs to the discipline of religious studies. This is explicitly reflected in many of the essays of this volume. Drawing not least on the work of Jonathan Z. Smith, they repeatedly object to the traditional, theological approach to Paul that more or less takes it for granted that Paul is, basically, *right* in his understanding of God and the world. This attitude reflects the approach that is called an "emic" one within social anthropology, in that it adopts Paul's own view on the matter (his "I" or "me"), but now also as the scholar's own view (his or her "I" and "me"). Of course, for the understanding of Paul one certainly cannot dispense with the emic perspective even in the scholarly effort. Rather, one must always attempt to gather the meaning of any Pauline phenomenon the way Paul saw it. But one must *also* apply an "etic" perspective (with a *t* indicating the third-person) even on Paul himself. By contrast, with regard to the scholar's own perspective, the emic perspective should be banned. That is what distinguishes religious studies as a scholarly discipline from theology. What we want is that Paul becomes directly comparable with other contemporary phenomena that are both similar to and also different from his. In that way he will become fully "legible" within his overall context—and so also to us.

It is worth noting here the huge extent to which these theoretical considerations are all primarily about—us! It is *our* ways of looking at the material that are up for discussion.[10] In the religious studies approach, we do not as scholars wish to favor any particular viewpoint that might be in line with our own, nonscholarly ones. We just want to understand. Then somebody might ask the following question: If the whole issue is primarily about us, will a theological approach to Paul then not also be valid, one that more directly reflects the reader's own interests? I will respond to this briefly in the epilogue to this essay.

---

9. See Chantziantoniou, p. 5 for this as an "historicizing project of defamiliarization."

10. Here belongs a topic in many of the essays that I unfortunately cannot address here: Skepticism toward a metaphorical reading of Paul. See, for instance, the illuminating essay by Eyl.

So far, then, we may conclude that neither the title of "Paul in His Hellenistic Context" nor that of "Paul beyond the Judaism/Hellenism Divide" will quite do the trick.

Paul, Judaism, and Paganism: Within and Beyond

Since the appearance of these two books, Pauline studies have taken a marked turn that can hardly be taken back. Paul is now distinctly seen not as a founder of the new religion of Christianity but rather as one Jew among many others, albeit with an understanding of Judaism post–Jesus-the-Messiah that at one and the same time remained through and through Jewish, which also had features that made it possible for later Christ believers to understand Paul—wrongly—as having left Judaism behind. So, Paul himself belongs wholly "within Judaism," both "emically" and "etically" seen.[11]

That perspective has been celebrated in a companion volume to the present one from 2015: *Paul within Judaism*.[12] But then, surely, there is every reason not to forget that Paul, and Judaism as a whole, *also* stood in an intimate relationship with the broader political and cultural world of Paul's own time. So, should we not also speak of *Paul within Paganism*?

This, however, is where things become complicated—and partly for reasons that also plagued both "Paul in His Hellenistic Context" and "Paul beyond the Judaism/Hellenism Divide." One problem is new: That of speaking of "paganism." As is duly noted in several essays of the present volume, the notion itself is anachronistic, derived, as it is, from fourth-century Christian use.[13] It is also strongly normative in a manner that fits neither the normal

11. I believe that Paul himself saw the risk of the later understanding and addressed it in Rom 9–11. Here he insists that, as non-Jews, his Roman addressees have only been grafted in "to share the rich root of the olive tree" (11:17), which is Judaism. If they therefore "boast over the branches" that they themselves have become to the denigration of the Jewish branches, they must "remember that it is not you that support the root, but the root that supports you" (11:18). Translations from Paul in this essay are basically my own, though often relying substantially on the NRSV.

12. *Paul within Judaism: Restoring the First-Century Context to the Apostle*, ed. Mark D. Nanos and Magnus Zetterholm (Fortress, 2015).

13. For discussion, see Chantziantoniou, pp. 17–18, who on p. 5n15 has already said this: "For now, I note that the category itself is anachronistic and irreparably broken. No attempt is made here, or anywhere else in this volume, to defend it, reclaim it, or make light of its troubling history. Quite to the contrary, by applying 'paganism' to Paul, it can be seen for what

usage of Jews more generally nor of Paul himself. The latter repeatedly speaks of either *ta ethnē* ("the nations or gentiles") or "the Greeks."[14] These are clearly implied to be different from "the Jews." Moreover, the difference between them matters enormously. But they are not described with the derogatory tone that came to be part of the term "pagan."

A further problem with "Paul within Paganism" is that it is self-contradictory![15] If Paul *was* a Jew and if "paganism" means "non-Judaism," then Paul the Jew cannot belong *within* it! Here we meet the fact that what the essays presented here are after is not features in Paul that fall outside his Judaism. Instead, it is features of Judaism (and of Paul) that belong—together with similar features from other cultural segments—within an overarching culture that must not be called "non-Judaism" (or even "paganism") since it precisely contains Judaism alongside those other segments. It is *this* understanding of Paul and his Judaism that we are after. But how can we get there?

One suggestion might repeat the idea behind "Paul beyond the Judaism/Hellenism Divide." Should we not just say "Paul *beyond* the Judaism/'Paganism' Divide"? However, quite apart from the negative, normative connotations of "paganism" that continue to be there, we would still be operating with -isms

it is: a colonialist category that simply does not and cannot work, even on its own terms. For the very practices it labels as 'non-Jewish' or 'non-Christian' can in fact be found among Jews and Christians themselves." Gruen concurs, p. 21: "There was no such animal as 'paganism.' The word 'pagan' simply served as a label applied by Christians to non-Christians, a pejorative designation signifying 'rustic' or 'country bumpkin.' There was no pagan entity, no pagan religion that converts would be expected to join, no uniform set of beliefs to which they would be expected to conform. And if there was nothing to convert to, what was there to assimilate to? The idea is a nonstarter." Bazzana, p. 122n1, articulates where I will myself end: "In itself, the very label 'paganism' is an anachronistic misnomer and should probably be abandoned, as it inappropriately conflates a mass of diverse and often at odds religious practices and beliefs. In addition, the very term 'pagan' emerged in Latin-speaking Christianity (*paganus*) only much later than the period examined here, and it was employed almost exclusively in a derogatory sense. *Adopting 'ancient Mediterranean' instead* allows for a more appropriate comparative exercise that also has the advantage of sidestepping and redescribing the outdated opposition of Judaism and Paganism" (my italics). See also Nasrallah, pp. 166–68, and Rollens, p. 199n1.

14. See, e.g., Rom 1:5 (*ethnē*) and 1:14 ("Greeks"). Also Collman, p. 236: "Paul believed that humanity could be broken down into two constituent parts: Jews, and an undifferentiated cluster of non-Jews whom he calls, 'the nations' (Rom 3:29, 9:24; Gal 2:14–15)."

15. This is well brought out by Chantziantoniou, p. 18, who speaks of it as "self-contradictory," but then also wishes to exploit it as part of "strategic anachronism," "pitched with tongue planted firmly in cheek."

and hence with an implied opposition that we would rather be without. It is true that "beyond" points away from it, but only negatively so. It does not state in positive terms what the resulting picture looks like.

Another suggestion that is made in several essays of the present volume is therefore that we should just speak of the "ancient Mediterranean."[16] This has the huge advantage that it is only a matter of space and hence avoids the various normative connotations, the opposition of reified -isms, and more. Perhaps we might even narrow it by speaking of the "ancient Eastern Mediterranean." There are two drawbacks, however. One is that it may seem too vague. Instead, we might speak of the "ancient Eastern Mediterranean in the early Roman imperial period." This adds a dimension of time, but is otherwise fairly innocuous. In particular, it should be understood as identifying a particular time or period in terms that are strictly political. In the case of the term *Hellenistic*, it seems best to understand it similarly as identifying, not so much a certain "culture," but rather a *political* state in the Eastern Mediterranean that began with Alexander the Great and continued until the Roman takeover, first of the Macedonian kingdom (Greece), then of the Attalid kingdom and the Seleucid empire and then (by 31 BCE) of the Ptolemaic kingdom. Similarly, the term *Roman* should primarily be understood as standing for the various periods of time when the Romans had politically established themselves in the eastern parts of the Mediterranean. Paul therefore belongs squarely to the "early Roman imperial period."[17]

16. See, e.g., Chantziantoniou referring to "what historians have called '*Mediterraneanism*.' This larger category refers to a set of globalizing cultural processes that pervaded the ancient Mediterranean basin, intelligible and recognizable among Jews and Greeks, *no less than Romans, Persians, Egyptians, Gauls, Germans, Phoenicians, and a host of others*, notwithstanding their regional variations" (p. 8, my italics). Novenson, too, says this: "Within ancient Mediterranean religion, or 'paganism,' more generally" (p. 61n7; here, as I see it, "or 'paganism'" should be deleted). Fredriksen refers to the Jews living "within their natal Mediterranean cultural context" (p. 89). Thiessen, too, speaks of "the ancient Mediterranean world" (p. 95). And Bazzana concurs: ". . . within their broader context of ancient Mediterranean culture and society. The goal is to understand the apostle historically both as *wholly* part of the Judaism of his time and as *fully* part of *the ancient Mediterranean socio-cultural space*" (p. 122, my italics). Sharp, too, wishes to "contextualize Paul within his broader pagan environment, *in the ancient Mediterranean world*" (p. 122, my italics; here the use of "pagan" is salvaged by means of "broader," meaning so as to include Judaism within it). Finally, Young just speaks of "Mediterranean" (p. 259 and passim).

17. Wendt rightly speaks of "the early imperial period" (p. 44).

So far, then, what we have is this: "Paul as an ancient Eastern Mediterranean Jew in the early Roman imperial period." But then there also is a second possible drawback. As is clear from many essays in this volume, there *is* something more to be said about that period. That has to do with the language that was spoken everywhere in the Eastern Mediterranean (including by Paul), the literary culture that flourished there, the political system in the form of "city-states" and their organization, the gymnasium, and much more.[18] All of this was present in the whole area where Paul was operating and continued to be so even after the Romans took over politically. And it was all (originally) Greek. In some way, we would like to bring in the fact that this particular culture in the overall mix was also especially important in that Paul, for instance, and significant parts of contemporary Judaism, too, interacted particularly with that culture in the overall mix. To solve that problem, should we then speak, for instance, of "the early Roman imperial period of Greco-Roman culture"?

That is extremely tempting. However, I believe that we should resist the temptation. It is certainly true that much of what we find in Judaism from this particular period does interact with what we call Greek culture in its various forms, but it seems better to see this as an interaction between two social and cultural entities at the *same* level and *locally* understood than seeing one of them (say, "Hellenistic culture") as an overarching or global entity into or under which these forms of Judaism would then be subsumed.[19]

There are two reasons for this decision. The most important is that by subsuming Judaisms under something called "Hellenistic culture," one strongly risks falling back on reifying both entities with the concomitant normative understandings that have caused so much trouble. Another is that speaking of "Hellenistic culture" as a superordinate phenomenon is an abstraction that does not do justice to the differences on the ground. Thus, it seems highly likely that

18. For this—and its close connection with Jews—see, in particular, the essays by Gruen and Fredriksen.

19. I am thus somewhat skeptical about speaking (with Fredriksen) of forms of Judaism (and Paul) sitting within their "broader, and native first-century context" of "Mediterranean *Graeco-Roman* culture" (p. 88, my italics) and even of the same as a "*majority* culture" (p. 83). Similarly, Gruen speaks of "the majority culture" (p. 21) and of Jews living in "scattered communities *dominated by Greek culture* and Roman power" (p. 27, my italics). We may well, with Benjamin G. Wright III as quoted by Chantziantoniou (p. 8), speak of a "larger cultural 'container,'" but that will then be an abstraction that includes within and under it Greek, Jewish, Roman, etc. local communities and cultures. The "container" itself is not Greek.

the "Hellenism" with which Philo the Jew was acquainted in Alexandria (with its heavy, Ptolemaic heritage, its library, its translation of the Tanak into the Septuagint, etc.) was very different from the "Hellenism" that Paul knew from Tarsus—and indeed, from the various places in Asia Minor and Greece that he visited. With a view to understanding *what actually went on* on the ground in all the local places, it seems much better to drop the "colonizing" abstraction of "Hellenistic culture" and instead to consider whatever originally Greek features will have been present in the various local groupings in each their individual place. But the overarching *political* category (of "Hellenistic" and "Roman") that we employed above is perfectly acceptable. If we accept this proposal and see "Greeks" and "Jews" (and everybody else) as interacting at the same level, then the emphasis found in several essays on the porosity of any group boundaries is exactly right.[20]

From Within and Beyond to a Place without Abstractions

The conclusion to all this is that we should stay with this formulation of our topic: "Paul as an ancient Eastern Mediterranean Jew in the early Roman imperial period." This has a genuinely liberating effect. What we will now be looking for is the interaction and similarities and differences of cultural input on the ground and at the same, horizontal level between local social groupings, without any of them being seen as superordinate and overarching. They *all* belong within the overarching entity of "the ancient Eastern Mediterranean in the early Roman imperial period," but that category is precisely only one of place and time. Within that overarching entity, we may look entirely dispassionately in the customary "emic" *cum* "etic" manner and with a comparative gaze at whatever cultural or social features strike us as noteworthy. Here "Hellenism" has at long last been downsized from its overarching, colonizing dimension to being just one social grouping among others, just as "Judaism" is.

20. E.g., Fredriksen on "mixing" and "interpenetration" (p. 78). Also, Benjamin G. Wright III as quoted by Chantziantoniou (p. 8), who speaks of the "cultures" of Jews and Greeks (as distinct groups) as "permeable and porous." Nasrallah similarly warns against thinking that communities were "sealed off from each other" (p. 166).

Three Methodological Rules

It is at this new, normatively neutral level that all the essays of the present volume are in fact operating. They do so by extensively engaging in comparison of features in the various social and cultural groupings that appear similar. If, however, as is also the case, the aim is to add to the elucidation of Paul, then there are a number of further rules to be adopted.

One such rule follows directly from our attempt to situate the various social and cultural groupings "horizontally" on the same level. I call it the *Lex Malherbe.* It says that in comparing some feature in Paul with a similar feature in some other social and cultural entity within the overall mix, one should always give each feature the benefit of the doubt in the sense of trying to understand—emically—what it meant to say on its own within its own social context. When one then turns, etically, to the actual comparison, one may avoid skewing either comparandum as part of the comparison. And that will be to the gain of the comparison by allowing one to see both similarities and also differences. Let that sense of equity in the approach be the core of the *Lex Malherbe.*

This law is in fact followed in the essays of the present volume, not least when they rehabilitate ideas and practices in the non-Jewish part of the overall mix and try to make Paul intelligible by comparing him with that material. If there is a danger here, it is perhaps that any *differences* in Paul may escape notice, or not be sufficiently emphasized. Here the burden of previous scholarship on Paul may still be weighing too heavily on us and prevent us from admitting any differences where there are any.[21] I will give one example of this later.

There is a second law to be followed, which I call the *Lex Meeks.* It insists that as part of Pauline scholarship the whole business of comparison should be conducted with a view to understanding *Paul* better, not just to point out similarities and differences at a general level in the overall field. This may seem different from the practice enjoined by the *Lex Malherbe*, but in fact is not. It rather presupposes the equitable analysis stipulated in that law and then insists that *if* it is Paul whom we want to understand better, then we should also *use* the similarities and differences that we have discovered to *elucidate* Paul and

21. Allow me, however, to quote this excellent formulation from Chantziantoniou (p. 13): "As a Jewish religious expert promoting the Jewish god to nonnatives, Paul's letters exhibit a highly original concoction of social, ethical, and cultic features distinct to his own group-making project, clustering together to form a social *novum*."

understand *him* better. What lies behind this law (never articulated as such by Meeks himself) is the whole query of the productiveness of "comparisons" famously raised by Samuel Sandmel.[22] But note that the *Lex Meeks* is not a theological one—as if it were Paul alone who matters. On the contrary, use as much as you can from Paul's wider context—but *use* it![23]

To these two rules, I will myself add one that lies on the same line. What it says is that in applying all the machinery discussed so far to the analysis of Paul, one should never restrict oneself to elucidating a single feature in Paul, namely, the one that is up for comparison. Instead, one should always try to connect that feature with as much as one possibly can that goes into Paul's overall thought and practice. This is not just because one may in general want to understand as much as possible in Paul and its inner connections, but also because there is a constant risk that by focusing on a single feature one may skew its overall importance within Paul's thought and practice. Here the aim of trying to keep in mind the whole of Paul helps to generate the required balance between all the relevant features.

Enough about these generalities. What I now want to do is to pick up two issues that are discussed in the volume and to see how they will come out in the light of the generalities.

Two Specific Issues

Paul and the Gods

Four essays in the volume—by Novenson, Fredriksen, Thiessen, and Litwa—discuss Paul's understanding of divine beings other than the Jewish god. They all agree—quite rightly—that Paul was a "polytheist" and then consider in detail his understanding of the various figures that fall under the category "other divine beings." Novenson presents an *interpretatio Iudaica et Paulina* of the Greeco-Roman gods. Fredriksen considers Paul's view of the same gods as possibly *daimonia*, which she terms "godlings," insisting that "gods they were" (p. 76). Similarly, Thiessen admits that to Paul, "Israel's god is the Supreme God," but he is one who "reign[s] over all other gods who necessarily must exist if Israel's god is to reign over them" (p. 96). Thiessen then considers the divine

22. Samuel Sandmel, "Parallelomania," *JBL* 81 (1962): 1–13.

23. I am happy to note that this rule is in fact followed throughout the volume, e.g., in the essays by Walsh, Rollens, and Eyl.

status of Christ and Christ followers as "*sons* of God," while also speaking of their *theōsis* and "deification" (p. 100n27). And Litwa follows suit by spelling out how such "deification" should be understood.

All of this situates the Jewish Paul (and, indeed, Judaism as such) as one player among others in a closely comparable field of talk about divine beings. And that is entirely appropriate. My concern is that as these scholars themselves *also* show there are distinctions to be drawn in Paul's handling of the divine beings that to some extent remove him from *just* being similar to all the others. In other words, there also is a (vital) difference!

What matters here is Paul's use of the term *theos* ("a god" or "God"). At one point, Thiessen states this: "The terminology differs—*gods*, sons of God, angels, even *daimonia*, but the genus remains the same: divine beings" (p. 96, my italics). But he also adds that to Paul "there was only one supreme divinity, the God of Israel." As I see it, however, to Paul the God of Israel was not just the "supreme" divinity: He was the only *god*, whom we may therefore call "God." For Paul specifically reserves the term *theos* for the God of Israel alone.[24] Christ, for one, is not a *theos* in Paul. He is certainly a "divine being," but no *theos*. Romans 9:5 is relevant here. On this, I agree with Michael Wolter, who concludes from a cogent excursus that 9:5b speaks of God, not Christ.[25] Philippians 2:6 is relevant, too, where Paul says this of Christ Jesus (basically NRSV): "Who, though he was in the form of God [*morphē theou*], did not regard equality with [*to einai isa*] God [*theōi*] as something to be exploited." Whatever Paul may have in mind here, he does not *identify* Christ with God, but rather says that Christ was in some way very *close* to God before his appearance on earth. Still, Christ both was and is the *son* of God (as Thiessen shows).

The same is certainly true of Christ's followers, those whom Paul is directly addressing. Both now and later they are "sons of God." This is because they have already received within them God's own *pneuma*, which by Romans

24. What, then, about 2 Cor 4:4 (on "the god [*theos*] of this world," who has "blinded the minds of the unbelievers")? (Thanks to Paula Fredriksen for reminding me of this text.) To understand this, compare the equally odd phrase "the *pneuma* of the (or this) world" in 1 Cor 2:12, which is there opposed to "the *pneuma* that is from God."

25. M. Wolter, *Der Brief an die Römer, Teilband 2: Röm 9–16* [English: *The Letter to the Romans*, vol. 2, *Rom 9–16*], EKK VI/2 (Patmos/Vandenhoeck & Ruprecht, 2019), 37–42.

8:9–10 is also Christ's *pneuma*, and, indeed, Christ himself. And this will become even clearer when, at their resurrection, their "sarkic" bodies of flesh and blood will be completely transformed into bodies of *pneuma*. Sons (and "children," Rom 8:16–17) of God they certainly and already are. But neither they nor Christ himself are *theoi*, gods. How one will combine this streak of "monotheism" with Paul's evident "polytheism" (taken more broadly) is a question that must be further addressed. Perhaps the best approach is—once more—to give up altogether talking of those -isms!

But what about the various divine beings like angels and *daimonia* below those higher up in the divine hierarchy? Are they not *theoi*, after all? Relevant here are 1 Corinthians 8:4–6 and 10:19–22.[26] Here is the former passage (NRSV, parentheses and italics mine):

> Hence, as to the eating of food offered to idols, *we know* that "no idol in the world really exists," and that "there is no God but one [*oudeis theos ei mē heis*]." Indeed, even though there may be *so-called gods* [*legomenoi theoi*] in heaven or on earth—as in fact there are many gods [*theoi*] and many lords [*kyrioi*]—yet *for us there is one God* [*heis theos*], the Father, from whom are all things and for whom we exist, *and one Lord,* Jesus Christ, through whom are all things and through whom we exist.

When Paul here says that "there are" many gods and lords, does he retract his earlier determination of them as only "so-called" gods? Not at all. "For us there is (only) *heis theos*, a single God," and here the "for us" does not, of course, just mean "as we see it—and others may have their own legitimate views." No, as we *know* (compare "we know," the strong *oidamen*, in 8:4), there only *is* a single God, the Father. The others of course *speak* of their "gods" (the *so-called* ones) *as* (precisely) *theoi*. But they are wrong.

10:19–22 then makes it clear how one should in fact understand those "so-called gods" who are certainly there (as divine beings), but not as *theoi*. They are *daimonia*, that is, lower divine beings, precisely Paula Fredriksen's

26. In what follows, I am reacting to the analyses of these two passages in Novenson and Fredriksen.

"godlings." In 10:19–22, Paul begins in a manner that explicitly refers back to 8:4 (my translation):

> What am I saying, then? That food sacrificed to idols is in fact something, or that an idol is in fact something? No, I am saying that what they sacrifice, they sacrifice to *daimonia*, not to a god (*or* to God!). . . .

Here Paul almost explicitly says that the gentiles' "so-called gods" are in fact *daimonia*. And *these* do exist! Do not mingle with *them*: "I do not want you to be partners of *daimonia*."

The conclusion should be clear. Paul certainly recognized the existence of divine powers in the cosmos below Christ and the Jewish God (and also, as Thiessen and Litwa show, below the Christ followers when they have been resurrected). He also recognized them as *so-called theoi* (and *kyrioi*)—the "godlings," who are actually there, but as no more than *daimonia*. But in fact ("for us"!), there is only *one theos*, only one *God*. It seems difficult to get around the sense that viewed as a (religious) reinterpretation of the usual Greco-Roman kind, this particular *interpretatio (Iudaica et) Paulina* is a quite ironic one.

The lesson is of course that a starting point that looks for similarities across the whole field should never miss any differences where they are relevant and revealing. Whereas an *interpretatio* of foreign divine beings of the usual Greco-Roman kind is in principle equitable and positive, Paul's is distinctly different: Much more hierarchical and negative to the effect that there is in fact only one true *theos*, the God of Israel.

Pneuma and Ethics: The Issues

An intriguing observation for one who, like myself, has focused on Paul and philosophy is the extent to which many of the essays end up speaking of "knowledge," even where their topics have been quite different. That seems to me exactly right and a good example of how—by my third methodological rule—one must always try to ask about "the whole Paul." Among the essays that progress like this are those by Wendt, Litwa, Sharp, Nasrallah, and Eyl.[27]

---

27. Wendt, pp. 45–47, Litwa passim, Sharp, pp. 155–58, Nasrallah, p. 175, and Eyl, pp. 229–32. By contrast, I miss this turn in Bazzana's essay.

But are they right in also connecting the idea of knowledge with Platonism?[28] Seen from my own perspective, this position runs the distinct risk of reading into Paul himself Platonizing ways of understanding him that belong to the period after 100 CE when Platonism was gradually becoming the dominant philosophy.[29]

I raise this issue here since it is present in those essays and touches directly on two central concerns of the whole volume: We must retain all contextual oddities in Paul even when they remove him from his traditional role as a founding father of Christianity; and correspondingly, we must not anachronistically read him in the light of the later developments (here: Christian Platonism). I cannot argue my case here properly. Instead, the aim is to give an ultrashort presentation of the overall structure of the argument so that we can at least all agree on where we may disagree. The issue concerns the relationship of Paul's cosmology (physics), his anthropology (and moral psychology), and his ethics (and *paraenesis* or moral exhortation). How do these various features of his thought cohere?

On Paul's cosmology, there is almost universal agreement in the present volume on the importance and role of the *pneuma* ("spirit"). I have myself argued for a basically Stoic, material, and monistic understanding of the *pneuma* in Paul. Several essays in the present volume concur, and Litwa puts

28. For this, see Wendt, p. 55, on "the Stoic-Platonic Paul," though with emphasis on Plato. Also Litwa, pp. 111–12, claiming to find "a basic analogy between Paul's anthropology and the anthropology of popular Platonism" (p. 112). Sharp, pp. 155–58, is an interesting comparison with Plato in the *Timaeus*, Posidonius, and Plutarch. Finally, Walsh passim, including p. 181 on "what Stanley Stowers has called the 'new terrain [of philosophy]' for thinkers of the imperial period like Paul, Philo, and Plutarch, which combines elements from Pythagoreanism with Platonism, 'mixed with elements of Stoic thought.'" Wendt, in particular (pp. 54–56), explicitly introduces "the *afterlife* of Paul's letters" (p. 56, my italics) into the analysis of Paul himself, which yields clearly Platonizing readings of him. But notice Litwa's splendid remark, p. 108: "Christian notions of a fully transcendent God—an unmoved mover beyond the limits of thought and being—developed centuries after Paul. Paul believed that the Father was immensely powerful, but that he still resided in this cosmos, not outside of it."

29. On the development of philosophy, see Troels Engberg-Pedersen, ed., *From Stoicism to Platonism. The Development of Philosophy, 100 BCE–100 CE* (Cambridge University Press, 2017). The rise of Platonism began in Alexandria with Eudorus already in the first century BCE. Philo is an early witness to this development. But Paul was not "an Alexandrian Jew."

it very well in one place.[30] Against this stands a much more Platonic, dualistic, and material/immaterial interpretation of Paul's cosmology that has been developed by Stanley Stowers and is accepted in several essays of this volume.[31] Here Paul is found to be rather similar to Philo of Alexandria.

Then there is Paul's anthropology and moral psychology, focusing on his understanding of *nous* ("reason"). Is Paul here inspired in Romans 7 by Plato's famous account of the dualistic struggle between the horses in his psychic chariot in the *Phaedrus* (246A–E)?[32] Or if not Plato, perhaps it is Aristotle here? He remained a dualist in his moral psychology. Thus, in his *Ethics* he distinguished between a "desiderative" part of soul and a "logistic" part (alias the *nous*). In "weakness of will" (*akrasia*), the former was not controlled by the latter, whereas in "strength of will" or "self-control" (*enkrateia*) it is; still, there are also remaining desires in the desiderative part.[33] Or, finally, should we rather understand Paul along Stoic, monistic lines? Here we may note that the Stoics, too, spoke of something like "weakness of will." In fact, they understood the "passions" *as* just that, namely as cases where the *nous* itself runs, as we may say, "out of control" in a kind of "blackout" since it is apparently not itself strong enough (in the sense of sufficiently widely based) to insist on its own insights.[34] So, should we in this place Paul together with Plato and Aristotle, or with the Stoics?

30. Litwa, p. 113: "Scholars and exegetes are increasingly realizing that pneuma does not mean a Platonic, immaterial 'spirit.' It is more suitably translated by 'breath' or 'wind.' Among ancient philosophers and medical professionals, it was thought of as a corporeal substance, though not a solid, earthly substance like soil and water. It was more like air. Air, however, was thought to be naturally cold and misty, whereas pneuma was hot, fiery, refined, or subtle. Stoics described pneuma as a fine mixture of air and fire, and identified it with the substance of aether, or the fiery air thought to exist in the upper reaches of the universe." See also chapter 1 of my *Cosmology and Self in the Apostle Paul: The Material Spirit* (Oxford University Press, 2010).

31. See Stanley Stowers, "The Dilemma of Paul's Physics: Features Stoic-Platonist or Platonist Stoic?" in Engberg-Pedersen, *From Stoicism to Platonism*, 231–53.

32. For the whole issue, see Emma Wasserman, *The Death of the Soul in Romans 7: Sin, Death, and the Law in Light of Hellenistic Psychology*, WUNT 2/256 (Mohr Siebeck, 2008).

33. For all this, see Aristotle, *Nicomachean Ethics* 7.1–10.

34. For this see none other than Plutarch, the "Middle Platonist" (!), who says this of the Stoic understanding of the passions: "It is the *same* part of the soul, the one they call thought (*dianoia*) and the *hegemonikon*, which becomes vice or virtue by turning over all through and

Finally, there is Paul's ethics, in particular this: Did Paul allow, dualistically, for continuing desires in the Christ believer who had received the *pneuma*, only they would now be *controlled* by this person's *nous*? Or did he take it, monistically, that with the empowerment of a Christ believer's *nous* by the *pneuma*, the potentially opposing desires would be altogether eradicated? In the former case, the central idea of Paul's ethics will be that of *enkrateia*. In the latter case, it will be something else: Full moral virtue where there are no longer any contravening desires.

Here too Aristotle is relevant. For in addition to the two states of character we noted, he also worked with a moral state in which there are no longer any remains of the faulty desires at all. This is what Aristotle called "full virtue" or "virtue proper" (*hē kyria aretē*), where the person both does and wills only one thing: What is good.[35] This is also the state that the Stoics were after, but now monistically understood as the state of full virtue had by the rare person who was genuinely and fully wise. Here there is no longer anything to control. For the wise person sees, knows, wants, and does only what is right. In this person, the *nous* has become all-powerful. Is this also the state that Paul was after? Did he go for *enkrateia* to be understood in the Aristotelian, dualistic way? Or did he go for full virtue, but now to be understood in the monistic, Stoic way?

---

changing when it undergoes the changes of the passions and the (underlying) states and dispositions: *it has nothing irrational in itself.* It is *called* irrational, however, when the *horme* (impulse) exceeds, having become strong and so as to govern, and when as a consequence of this it (i.e. reason) is *carried away* towards some scandalous object against (the directions of) rational choice. For passion, they say, is reason (that has become) vicious and intemperate (or uncontrolled), resulting from a wrong and faulty judgement that has *acquired additional strength and power*" (*On Moral Virtue* 441C–D; *SVF* 3.459). Young also quotes from Cicero (*Tusculan Disputations*, 4.9.22) an account of lack of self-mastery (*intemperantia*) that sounds very Stoic: "A *revolt* from all *guidance* of the mind and right reason, so completely alien from the control of reason that the cravings of the soul cannot be guided or curbed . . . [it] kindles, confounds and agitates the *whole* condition of the soul, with the result that from it come distress and fear and all other disorders" (p. 269, my italics). For the whole issue, see chapter 8, "Intention and Passion: Desire as Belief," in my *The Stoic Theory of Oikeiosis: Moral Development and Social Interaction in Early Stoic Philosophy* (Aarhus University Press, 1990), 170–206.

35. For the notion of "full" virtue, see Aristotle, *Nicomachean Ethics* 1144b4 and 17. However, note that Aristotle remained a dualist. The central theme of his *Ethics* is how the "desiderative" and "logistic" parts of the soul may come to *agree* completely. For this, see my *Aristotle's Theory of Moral Insight* (Clarendon Press, 1983).

Still on Paul's ethics, how should we understand his constant practice of engaging in *paraenesis*? If he actually thought that by receiving the *pneuma* his addressees had been completely removed from the area of sin, if they were now totally virtuous and had *no* contravening desires, then why does he constantly engage in moral exhortation? Does this not indicate that they still had some contravening desires in the Platonic and Aristotelian way to be subdued by the by now powerful *nous*?

These questions show the direct relevance of the issue of Paul's supposed Platonism (or Aristotelianism) to the overall profile of the present volume: The willingness, indeed almost the obsession, to make Paul *different* (by the contextualizing move that we have discussed) from the way he has appeared in the post-Pauline, Christian theological tradition. Concretely: A Paul who thought that his Christ-believing addressees had become completely wise and good, as in Stoicism, is a distinct oddity. By contrast, if we adopt a Platonizing solution, he will be much more in line with the later tradition. Indeed, one can almost hear a sigh of relief among theologians. Here the passions will not be eradicated, only *checked* in Christian self-control. And so "we" may all continue to be Pauline Christians!

How, then, should we read *together* Paul's cosmology, his anthropology and moral psychology, and his ethics and *paraenesis*?

Pneuma and Ethics: The Solution

For Paul's cosmology—partly overlapping with his anthropology—the texts are well known: 1 Thessalonians 4:13–18, Philippians 2:15, 1 Corinthians 15:12–28 and 35–55, 2 Corinthians 4:7–5:10, and (possibly) 12:1–10. As I see it, there is no indication in these texts of anything like a material/immaterial cosmology of the type Stanley Stowers has tried to develop for Philo—and then for Paul. On the contrary, a wholly material and monistic understanding looks much more obvious and fits Paul's relatively unsophisticated thought in this area best.[36] It also fits the fact that Paul was a Jew. Although the much more sophisticated (and Platonic) Philo of Alexandria was also a Jew, a Stoicizing,

---

36. Think, for instance, of the "pneumatic *body* [*sōma*]," that will be raised after a full "transformation" (1 Cor 15:44 and 51) and make the raised ones be "caught up in the clouds" to "meet the Lord in the air" (1 Thess 4:17).

monistic cosmology sits much better with Paul's Jewish apocalypticism than anything like what one finds in Philo, the nonapocalypticist.

Then there is more directly Paul's anthropology and moral psychology, leading into his ethics. Two sets of texts point in a Stoicizing direction. The first consists of three texts on *nous* in Romans.[37] In its first appearance (1:28), Paul speaks of an "undiscerning" (*adokimos*) *nous* in gentiles. They lack a proper knowledge of God and so act wrongly. In its third appearance (12:2), Paul (again!) speaks of a "transformation" of believers and a "renewal of the *nous*"—and (again!) connects both with their *bodies* (12:1). How has this change come about? The second appearance of *nous* (7:23 and 25) gives the answer by showing (8:1–13) that once a person has received the *pneuma*, the problem of the passions from 7:7–25 is solved. The shift from 7:7–25 to 8:1–13 is one from being "under sin" to being altogether "*free*" from sin (8:2). Here, having God's *pneuma*, Christ's *pneuma*, and, indeed, Christ himself *in* one (8:9–10a) means that "the body is *dead* [*nekron*] vis-à-vis sin" (8:10b). There is no longer any risk of acting from a passion since the *nous* has now become *all*-powerful.

Thus understood, the *pneuma* gives *full* knowledge and "renews the *nous*" "so that you may discern [*dokimazein*] what is the will of God—what is good and acceptable and perfect" (12:2). If we contrast this with the "undiscerning" *nous* of 1:28, we should conclude that Paul basically saw the soul as one of *cognition* and hence with the monistic shape found in Stoicism. What the *pneuma* then does is to *prevent* the proper understanding of "God's law" (7:22) that one has in one's *nous* from "running out of control" in the "blackout" of having a passion. Instead, there is *only* the full knowledge that goes with "discerning the will of God."

The second hint at this understanding is given by Paul in Galatians 5:13–26. Here (5:22–23) we find a list of what are clearly full virtues, which are explicitly generated by the *pneuma*. They belong to Christ believers since "those who belong to Christ Jesus have (already!) *crucified* the flesh *with* its

37. See my "Pauline Epistemology: *Nous* and *Pneuma* in Stoicism and Paul," in *Der* Nous *bei Paulus und in seiner Umwelt*, ed. Jörg Frey and Manuel Nägele, WUNT 464 (Mohr Siebeck, 2021), 21–41. Reprinted in Troels Engberg-Pedersen, *Paul and Philosophy*, WUNT 509 (Mohr Siebeck, 2023), 365–85.

passions and desires" (5:24). They *have* crucified the passions. They are no longer there![38]

Then, of course, the problem of *paraenesis* raises its head. Why should Paul also engage in *paraenesis* in both Galatians 5:13–26 and Romans 8:12–13 (concluding 7:7–8:11)? I have suggested an answer elsewhere. By receiving the *pneuma*, a person enters what Fredriksen in this volume calls "a *zone*, a single kinetic arc of eschatological divine empowerment and redemption," and I have myself called "the Christ *circle*."[39] Within this zone and circle, "sin" and its consequence, death, have been left altogether behind. It is an either-or: Inside or outside the circle. However, Paul also operates (e.g., in Phil 3:15–16) with the possibility of *differences within* the circle. He himself has not yet reached the circle's center (3:12–14). And so, in his *paraenesis* he appeals to his addressees' knowledge (as obtained through the *pneuma*) of what the center is like and urges them to move even further towards it. They already *are* inside the circle but need to be *reminded* of it in order to get closer to its center.

In summary, Paul was a "faith fanatic" (Paula Fredriksen) and an apocalypticist (Fredriksen, too).[40] In bringing out his own message, he used a number of contextual ideas and practices that appear strange to us. One was his idea that the Christ faith (which led to receiving the *pneuma*) had solved the problem of sin and death already now.[41] They had gone: Christ believers

---

38. Note here that the state of *enkrateia* mentioned by Paul in 5:23 will not be the technical, Aristotelian one of control of desires that continue to be present. Aristotle himself allows that we may "speak by likeness [or resemblance, *kath' homoiotēta*] of the 'continence' (*enkrateia*) of the *temperate* man (*tou sōphronos*)," who is the fully virtuous person; "for both the continent man and the temperate man are such as to *do* nothing [and so are "similar"] contrary to the rule for the sake of the bodily pleasures, but the former has and the latter has not bad appetites, and the latter is such as not to feel pleasure contrary to the rule, while the former is such as to feel pleasure but not to be led by it." *Nicomachean Ethics* 1151b33–1152a3.

39. Fredriksen, pp. 85–86, and myself in the introduction to *Paul and Philosophy*, "Speaking within the Christ Circle," 1–36, at 24–34.

40. The first phrase is one of Fredriksen's wonderful off-hand formulations (during discussion at an SBL Annual Meeting). The other claim pervades her scholarship on Paul.

41. On the present power of the *pneuma*, see Thiessen, pp. 96–100 and this (p. 103, my italics): "Those in the Messiah have taken on a divine identity *already*, but it is one that is, for the most part, hidden. . . . This hidden identity *should* both *dictate* and *enable* how those in the Messiah behave morally here and now." Should the "should" here be "*does*"? Also Bazzana, p. 127 (my italics): "As in many instances of possession attested in ethnographic literature,

were already sons of God. Exploring all the particular topics that bind him to his historical context and seeing their inner connection should never make us vacillate when it makes Paul look distinctly odd (to us). Least of all should we let us be influenced by later, Platonizing readings of him in the Christian tradition that made him more palatable.

Epilogue

If the aim of Pauline scholarship should be to make him strange where he *is* strange, does this mean that this scholarship becomes altogether irrelevant to theologians, who presumably wish to be able to use something in and from Paul more or less directly? My own answer is: No! We cannot, anyway, use *all* of Paul, so we are constantly referred back on ourselves for any use we may want to make. But then, surely, it is better to know *what Paul was really like* taken on his own, historical premises, which, as this volume shows, are those of his many contexts. Understood in this way, the present volume may even be said to make a contribution to theology.

---

in the case of Paul as well the *pneuma* (who is Christ) *controls completely* his agency, and Paul is quite straightforward in making this clear in his surviving letters." This will also have ethical implications.

CONTRIBUTORS

Giovanni B. Bazzana (PhD, International School of Modena, Italy, 2003) is Professor of New Testament at Harvard Divinity School.

Alexander Chantziantoniou (PhD, University of Cambridge, 2024) is Assistant Professor of Religious Studies at Crandall University.

Ryan D. Collman (PhD, University of Edinburgh, 2021) is Associate Supervisor at Westcott House, Cambridge, UK.

Troels Engberg-Pedersen (DPhil, University of Copenhagen, 1982; DTheol, University of Copenhagen, 2000) is Professor Emeritus of the New Testament at the University of Copenhagen.

Jennifer Eyl (PhD, Brown University, 2012) is Associate Professor in the Department of Religious Studies at Tufts University.

Paula Fredriksen (PhD, Princeton University, 1979) is Aurelio Professor Emerita at Boston University and Distinguished Visiting Professor Emerita at the Hebrew University of Jerusalem.

Erich S. Gruen (PhD, Harvard University, 1964) is Wood Professor Emeritus at the University of California, Berkeley.

M. David Litwa (PhD, University of Virginia, 2013) is an independent scholar.

Laura Salah Nasrallah (PhD, Harvard Divinity School, 2002) is Buckingham Professor of New Testament Criticism and Interpretation at Yale University.

Matthew V. Novenson (PhD, Princeton Theological Seminary, 2010) is Helen H. P. Manson Professor of New Testament at Princeton Theological Seminary.

Sarah E. Rollens (PhD, University of Toronto, 2013) is R. W. Webb Associate Professor of Religious Studies at Rhodes College.

Matthew T. Sharp (PhD, University of Edinburgh, 2021) is Lecturer in New Testament Studies at the University of St Andrews.

Matthew Thiessen (PhD, Duke University, 2010) is Associate Professor at McMaster University.

Robyn Faith Walsh (PhD, Brown University, 2014) is Associate Professor of the New Testament and Early Christianity at the University of Miami.

Heidi Wendt (PhD, Brown University, 2013) is Associate Professor of Religions of the Greco-Roman World at McGill University.

Stephen L. Young (PhD, Brown University, 2016) is Senior Lecturer in the Department of Languages, Literatures, and Cultures at Appalachian State University.

BIBLIOGRAPHY

Ábel, František. *The Message of Paul the Apostle within Second Temple Judaism.* Lexington, 2020.

Ademollo, Francesco. "Cosmic and Individual Soul in Early Stoicism." In *Body and Soul in Hellenistic Philosophy.* Edited by Brad Inwood and James Warren. Cambridge University Press, 2020.

Ahearne-Kroll, Stephen. *The Origins of the Corinthian Christ-Group: Paul's Chord of Gods.* ESRA. Edinburgh: Edinburgh University Press, 2024.

Ahuvia, Mika. "An Ancient Jewess Invoking Goddesses." *Ancient Jew Review* 2019.

Aitken, James K. "Hengel's *Judentum und Hellenismus.*" *Journal of Biblical Literature* 123 (2004): 331–41.

Alexander, Philip. "Hellenism and Hellenization as Problematic Historiographical Categories." In *Paul beyond the Judaism/Hellenism Divide.* Edited by Troels Engberg-Pedersen. Westminster John Knox, 2001.

Algra, Keimpe. "Stoics on Souls and Demons: Reconstructing Stoic Demonology." In *Demons and the Devil in Ancient and Medieval Christianity.* Edited by N. Vos and W. Otten. Brill, 2011.

Allison, Dale. *Constructing Jesus.* Baker Academic, 2010.

Allo, P. E.-B. *Saint Paul Première Épitre aux Corinthiens.* J. Balada, 1956.

Althusser, Louis. "Ideology and Ideological State Apparatuses (Notes towards an Investigation)." Translated by Ben Brewster. In *Lenin and Philosophy and Other Essays.* New Left Press, 1971.

Ando, Clifford. "*Interpretatio Romana.*" *Classical Philology* 100 (2005): 41–51.

Arnal, William E. *The Symbolic Jesus: Historical Scholarhsip, Judaism, and the Construction of Contemporary Identity.* Equinox, 2005.

Arzt-Grabner, Peter and Michael Ernst. *1 Korinther.* Vol. 2 of *Papyrologische Kommentare zum Neuen Testament.* Vandenhoeck & Ruprecht, 2006.

Asad, Talal. *Formations of the Secular: Christianity, Islam, Modernity.* Stanford University Press, 2003.

Ascough, Richard S. "Reimagining the Size of Pauline Christ Groups in Light of Association Meeting Places." In *Scribal Practices and Social Structures among Jesus Adherents: Essays in Honour of John S. Kloppenborg.* BETL 285. Edited by William E. Arnal et al. Peeters, 2016.

Ascough, Richard S. "Translocal Relationships among Voluntary Associations and Early Christianity." *Journal of Early Christian Studies* 5 (1997): 223–41.

Ascough, Richard S., Philip Harland, and John S. Kloppenborg. *Associations in the Greco-Roman World: A Sourcebook*. Baylor University Press, 2012.

Ashton, John. *The Religion of Paul the Apostle*. Yale University Press, 2000.

Athanassiadi, Polymnia, and Michael Frede, eds. *Pagan Monotheism in Late Antiquity*. Oxford University Press, 1999.

Atkinson, Kenneth. *A History of the Hasmonean State*. Bloomsbury, 2016.

Au, Wing Yi. *Paul's Designations of God in Romans*. WUNT 2/590. Mohr Siebeck, 2023.

Audollent, Auguste. *Defixionum Tabellae*. Fontemoing, 1904.

Babcock, William. *The City of God (de Civitate dei) (Books 1–10)*. The Works of Saint Augustine: A Translation for the 21st Century. New City Press, 2012.

Bailliot, Magali. "Rome and the Roman Empire." In *Guide to the Study of Ancient Magic*. Edited by David Frankfurter. Brill, 2019.

Barclay, John M.G. *Jews in the Mediterranean Diaspora from Alexander to Trajan*. T&T Clark, 1996.

Bartlett, John R. *Jews in the Hellenistic and Roman Cities*. Routledge, 2002.

Barton, Carlin A., and Daniel Boyarin. *Imagine No Religion: How Modern Abstractions Hide Ancient Realities*. Fordham University Press, 2016.

Bauckham, Richard. *Jesus and the God of Israel: God Crucified and Other Studies on the New Testament's Christology of Divine Identity*. Eerdmans, 2008.

Bazzana, Giovanni. *Having the Spirit of Christ: Spirit Possession and Exorcism in the Early Christ Groups*. Yale University Press, 2020.

Bazzana, Giovanni. "Negotiating the Experience of Possession in Hermas's *Shepherd*." In *Experiencing the Shepherd of Hermas*. Edited by Angela Kim Harkins and Harry O. Meier. De Gruyter, 2022.

Beentjes, Pancratius C. *The Book of Ben Sira in Hebrew: A Text Edition of All Extant Hebrew Manuscripts and a Synopsis of All Parallel Hebrew Ben Sira Texts*. VTSup 68. Brill, 1997.

Belayche, Nicole. "*Kyrios* and *Despotes*: Addresses to Deities and Religious Experiences." In *Lived Religion in the Ancient Mediterranean World: Approaching Religious Transformations from Archaeology, History and Classics*. Edited by Valentino Gasparini, Maik Patzelt, Rubina Raja, Anna-Katharina Rieger, Jörg Rüpke, and Emiliano Urciuoli. De Gruyter, 2020.

Bell, Brigidda. "The Cost of Baptism? The Case for Paul's Ritual Compensation." *Journal for the Study of the New Testament* 42 (2020): 431–52.

Bélyácz, Katalin, Kata Endreffy, and Árpád M. Nagy, eds. *Campbell Bonner Magical Gems Database (CBd)*. Museum of Fine Arts, Budapest. http://cbd.mfab.hu/.

Berger, David. "Three Typological Themes in Early Jewish Messianism: Messiah Son of Joseph, Rabbinic Calculations, and the Figure of Armilus." *AJS Review* 10 (1985): 141–64.

Bernhardt, Johann Christian. *Die Jüdische Revolution*. De Gruyter, 2017.

Berthelot, Katell. "The Notion of Anathema in Ancient Jewish Literature Written in Greek." In *The Reception of Septuagint Words in Jewish-Hellenistic and Christian Literature*. Edited by Eberhard Bons, Ralph Brucker, and Jan Joosten. WUNT 2/367. Mohr Siebeck, 2014.

Betz, Hans Dieter. "2 Cor 6:14–7:1: An Anti-Pauline Fragment?" *Journal of Biblical Literature* 92 (1973): 88–108.

Beyer, Barbara. *Determined by Christ: The Pauline Metaphor "Being in Christ"*. NovTSup 191. Brill, 2024.

Binder, Donald. *Into the Temple Courts: The Place of the Synagogues in the Second Temple Period*. Society of Biblical Literature, 1999.

Blackwell, Ben. *Christosis: Pauline Soteriology in Light of Deification in Irenaeus and Cyril of Alexandria*. WUNT 2/314. Mohr Siebeck, 2011.

Blackwell, Ben. *Pauline Soteriology in Light of Deification in Irenaeus and Cyril of Alexandria*. WUNT 2/314. Mohr Siebeck, 2011.

Blau, Ludwig, and Kaufmann Kohler. "Angelology." In *Jewish Encyclopedia*. Vol. 1. Edited by Isidore Singer. Funk & Wagnalls, 1906.

Blum, Jason N. "What Is the Difference between a Religion and a Cult?" In *Religion in 5 Minutes*. Edited by Aaron W. Hughes and Russell T. McCutcheon. Equinox, 2017.

Boccaccini, Gabriele, and Carlos A. Segovia, eds. *Paul the Jew: Rereading the Apostle as a Figure of Second Temple Judaism*. Fortress, 2016.

Boddy, Janice P. *Wombs and Alien Spirits: Women, Men, and the Zar Cults in Northern Sudan*. Wisconsin University Press, 1989.

Bohak, Gideon. *Ancient Jewish Magic: A History*. Cambridge University Press, 2011.

Bonner, Campbell. *Studies in Magical Amulets: Chiefly Graeco-Egyptian*. University of Michigan Press, 1950.

Bookidis, Nancy, and Ronald S. Stroud. *The Sanctuary of Demeter and Kore: Topography and Architecture*. Corinth XVIII.3. Princeton University Press, 1997.

Boys-Stone, G. R. *Post-Hellenistic Philosophy: A Study of Its Development from the Stoics to Origen*. Oxford University Press, 2001.

Brakke, David. "Valentinians and their Demons: Fate, Seduction, and Deception in the Quest for Virtue." In *From Gnostics to Monastics*. Edited by D. Brakke, S. J. Davis, and S. Emmel. Peeters, 2017.

Bremmer, Jan N. *Initiation into the Mysteries of the Ancient World*. De Gruyter, 2014.

Braudel, Fernand. *La Méditerranée et la Monde Méditerranéen à l'Époque de Philippe II*. Colin, 1949.

Braudel, Fernand. *The Mediterranean and the Mediterranean World in the Age of Philip II*. Translated by Siân Reynolds. 2 vols. Collins, 1972–1973.

Braun, Willi. "Fugitives from Femininity: Greco-Roman Gender Ideology and the Limits of Early Christian Women's Emancipation." In *Fabrics of Discourse: Essays in Honor of Vernon K. Robbins*. Edited by D. B Gowler, L. G. Bloomquist, D. F. Watson. Trinity, 2003.

Braun, Willi. *Jesus and Addiction to Origins: Toward an Anthropocentric Study of Religion*. Edited by Russell T. McCutcheon. Equinox, 2020.

Brooten, Bernadette. *Love between Women: Early Christian Responses to Female Homoeroticism*. Chicago: University of Chicago Press, 1996.

Brubaker, Rogers. *Ethnicity without Groups*. Harvard University Press, 2004.

Bucur, Bogdan. *Angelomorphic Pneumatology: Clement of Alexandria and Other Early Christian Witnesses*. Brill, 2009.

Buell, Denise Kimber. "The Microbes and Pneuma That Therefore I Am." In *Divinanimality: Animal Theory, Creaturely Theology*. Edited by Stephen D. Moore. Fordham University Press, 2014.

Buell, Denise Kimber, and Caroline Johnson Hodge. "The Politics of Interpretation: The Rhetoric of Race and Ethnicity in Paul." *Journal of Biblical Literature* 123 (2004): 235–511.

Bunta, Silviu. *The Lord God of Gods: Divinity and Deification in Early Judaism*. Perspectives on Hebrew Scriptures and its Contexts 35. Gorgias Press, 2021.

Burrus, Virginia. *"Begotten Not Made": Conceiving Manhood in Late Antiquity*. Stanford University Press, 2000.

Byrne, Brendan. *Sons of God: Seed of Abraham: A Study of the Idea of the Sonship of All Christians in Paul against the Jewish Background*. Analecta biblica 83. Biblical Institute, 1979.

Cameron, Ron, and Merril P. Miller. "Redescribing Paul and the Corinthians." In *Redescribing Paul and the Corinthians*. ECL. Edited by Ron Cameron and Merril P. Miller. Society of Biblical Literature, 2011.

Capes, David. *Old Testament Yahweh Texts in Paul's Christology*. WUNT 2/47. Mohr-Siebeck, 1992.

Carbone, Lucia. "The First Italia on Coinage." *American Numismatics Society* (2020): 6–23.

Castelli, Elizabeth. *Martyrdom and Memory: Early Christian Culture Making*. Columbia University Press, 2007.

Chantziantoniou, Alexander. "Paul and the Politics of Idolatry." PhD diss., University of Cambridge, 2023.

Chantziantoniou, Alexander. "Paul's Iconic Christ among Mediterranean Cult Statues: A Comparison of Divine Images." *Journal for the Study of the New Testament*. Forthcoming.

Chantziantoniou, Alexander. "The Politics of Paul's Image Parodies: Material Epiphany, Human-Divine Reciprocity, and Social Power." *New Testament Studies*. Forthcoming.

Charles, Ronald. *The Silencing of Slaves in Early Jewish and Christian Texts*. Routledge, 2019.

Cheyne, T. K. "The Origin and Meaning of Belial." *Expository Times* 8 (1897): 423–24.

Clark, Ernest P. *Weak Elements, Weak Flesh: Reading Galatians in Conversation with Philo and Greek Medical Discourse*. Lexington/Fortress, 2023.

Cobb, L. Stephanie. *Dying to Be Men: Gender and Language in Early Christian Martyr Texts*. Columbia University Press, 2008.

Cohen, Adam, Joel Siegel, and Paul Rozin. "Faith versus Practice: Different Bases for Religiosity Judgments by Jews and Protestants." *European Journal of Social Psychology* 33 (2003): 287–95.

Cohen, Shaye J. D. *Why Aren't Jewish Women Circumcised? Gender and Covenant in Judaism*. University of California Press, 2005.

Cole, Spencer. *Cicero and the Rise of Deification at Rome*. Cambridge University Press, 2013.

Collar, Anna. *Religious Networks in the Roman Empire: The Spread of New Ideas*. Cambridge University Press, 2013.

Collins, John J. *Between Athens and Jerusalem: Jewish Identity in the Hellenistic Diaspora*. Crossroad, 1986.

Collins, John J. "Cult and Culture: The Limits of Hellenization in Judea." In *Jewish Cult and Hellenistic Culture: Essays on the Jewish Encounter with Hellenism and Roman Rule*. Brill, 2005.

Collman, Ryan D. *The Apostle to the Foreskin: Circumcision in the Letters of Paul*. Beihefte Zur Zeitschrift für Die Neutestamentliche Wissenschaft 259. De Gruyter, 2023.

Collman, Ryan D. "Beware the Dogs! The Phallic Epithet in Phil 3.2." *New Testament Studies* 67 (2021): 105–20.

Collman, Ryan D. "(Un)Making a Theological Mountain out of a Cardiological Mohel: Heart-Circumcision in Paul's Epistles." *Journal of the Jesus Movement in its Jewish Setting* 10 (2023): 89–105.

Concannon, Cavan W. *"When You Were Gentiles": Specters of Ethnicity in Roman Corinth and Paul's Corinthian Correspondence*. Synkrisis. Yale University Press, 2014.

Concannon, Cavan, and Lindsay A. Mazurek. *Across the Corrupting Sea: Post-Braudelian Approaches to the Ancient Eastern Mediterranean*. Routledge, 2016.

Conway, Colleen. *Behold the Man: Jesus and Greco-Roman Masculinity*. Oxford University Press, 2008.

Conzelmann, Hans. *1 Corinthians: A Commentary on the First Epistle to the Corinthians*. Fortress, 1975.

Cornell, Collin. "*Interpretatio* among Levantines in Hellenistic Egypt." In *What's in a Divine Name? Religious Systems and Human Agency in the Ancient Mediterranean*. Edited by Alaya Palamidis and Corinne Bonnet. De Gruyter, 2024.

Cowey, James M. S., and Klaus Maresch. *Urkunden des Polituema der Juden von Herakleopolis*. Wiesbaden, 2001.

Crafer, Thomas Wilfrid, trans. *The Apocriticus of Macarius Magnes*. SPCK, 1919.

Craffert, Pieter. "Altered States of Consciousness: Visions, Spirit Possession, Sky Journeys." In *Understanding the Social World of the New Testament*. Edited by Richard DeMaris and Dietmar Neufeld. Routledge, 2009.

Cranfield, C. E. B. *A Critical and Exegetical Commentary on the Epistle to the Romans*. 6th ed. Clark, 1975.

Crook, Zeba. *Reconceptualising Conversion: Patronage, Loyalty, and Conversion in the Religions of the Ancient Mediterranean.* De Gruyter, 2004.

Davies, John A. "The Heavenly Access of the Holy Ones." *Reformed Theological Review* 68 (2009): 3–11.

De Bruyn, Theodore S. *Making Amulets Christian: Artefacts, Scribes, and Contexts.* Oxford Early Christian Studies. Oxford University Press, 2017.

Deissmann, Adolf. *Light From the Ancient East: The New Testament Illustrated by Recently Discovered Texts of the Graeco-Roman World.* Translated by Lionel R. M. Strachan. Hodder & Stoughton, 1910.

Denzey, Nicola Frances. "Under a Pitiless Sky: Conversion, Cosmology and the Rhetoric of 'Enslavement to Fate' in Second-Century Christian Sources." PhD diss., Princeton University, 1998.

Dillon, John. *The Platonic Heritage: Further Studies in the History of Platonism and Early Christianity.* Routledge, 2012.

Dimant, Devorah. "Men as Angels: The Self-Image of the Qumran Community." In *Religion and Politics in the Ancient Near East.* Edited by Adele Berlin. University Press of America, 1996.

Dingeldein, Laura. "Gaining Virtue, Gaining Christ: Moral Development in the Letters of Paul." PhD diss., Brown University, 2014.

Donaldson, Terence L. *Judaism and the Gentiles: Jewish Patterns of Universalism (to 135 CE).* Baylor University Press, 2007.

Dosoo, Korshi, Markéta Preininger, Julia Schwarzer et al., eds. *Kyprianos Database.* Julius Maximilian University Würzburg. https://www.coptic-magic.phil.uni-wuerzburg.de/.

Dunning, Benjamin. "Same-Sex Relations." In *The Oxford Handbook of New Testament, Gender, and Sexuality.* Edited by Benjamin Dunning. Oxford University Press, 2019.

Dunning, Benjamin. *Specters of Paul: Sexual Difference in Early Christian Thought.* University of Pennsylvania Press, 2011.

Dzwiza, Kirsten. *Schriftverwendung in antiker Ritualpraxis.* Heidelberg: Erfurt, 2013.

Edmonds, Radcliffe G., III. *Drawing down the Moon: Magic in the Ancient Greco-Roman World.* Princeton University Press, 2019.

Edwards, Catherine. *The Politics of Immorality in Ancient Rome.* Cambridge University Press, 1993.

Eliav, Yaron Z. *A Jew in the Roman Bathhouse: Cultural Interaction in the Ancient Mediterranean.* Princeton University Press, 2023.

Emmanuel, Sarah. *Wrestling with Paul: The Apostle, His Readers, and the Fate of the Jews.* Fortress Academic, 2025.

Engberg-Pedersen, Troels. *Aristotle's Theory of Moral Insight.* Clarendon Press, 1983.

Engberg-Pedersen, Troels. *Cosmology and the Self in the Apostle Paul: The Material Spirit.* Oxford University Press, 2010.

Engberg-Pedersen, Troels. "Paul, Virtues, and Vices." In *Paul and the Graeco-Roman World: A Handbook*. Edited by J. Paul Sampley. Trinity Press, 2003.

Engberg-Pedersen, Troels. *Paul and the Stoics*. Westminster John Knox, 2000.

Engberg-Pedersen, Troels. "Pauline Epistemology: *Nous* and *Pneuma* in Stoicism and Paul." In *Der* Nous *bei Paulus und in seiner Umwelt*. Edited by Jörg Frey and Manuel Nägele. WUNT 464. Mohr Siebeck, 2021.

Engberg-Pedersen, Troels. *Paul on Identity*. Fortress Press, 2021.

Engberg-Pedersen, Troels. *The Stoic Theory of Oikeiosis: Moral Development and Social Interaction in Early Stoic Philosophy*. Aarhus University Press, 1990.

Engberg-Pedersen, Troels, ed. *From Stoicism to Platonism: The Development of Philosophy, 100 BCE–100 CE*. Cambridge University Press, 2017.

Engberg-Pedersen, Troels, ed. *Paul beyond the Judaism/Hellenism Divide*. Westminster John Knox, 2001.

Eyl, Jennifer. "'I Myself Am an Israelite': Paul, Authenticity, and Authority." *Journal for the Study of the New Testament* 40 (2017): 148–68.

Eyl, Jennifer. "Putting the End Back into the Beginning: Paula Fredriksen, Eschatology, and Paul: The Pagans' Apostle." syndicate.network, https://syndicate.network/symposia/theology/paul-the-pagans-apostle/.

Eyl, Jennifer. "A Reexamination of *Pistis* in the Letters of Paul." Paper presented at the Boston Area Patristics Group. Harvard University, April 2019.

Eyl, Jennifer. "Semantic Voids, New Testament Translation, and Anachronism: The Case of Paul's Use of *Ekklēsia*." *Method and Theory in the Study of Religion* 26 (2014): 315–39.

Eyl, Jennifer. *Signs, Wonders, and Gifts: Divination in the Letters of Paul*. Oxford University Press, 2019.

Faraone, Christopher A. *The Transformation of Greek Amulets in Roman Imperial Times*. University of Pennsylvania Press, 2018.

Faraone, Christopher A., and Sofía Torallas Tovar, eds. *Greek and Egyptian Magical Formularies: Text and Translation*. California Classical Studies. University of California, 2022.

Faraone, Christopher A., and Sofía Torallas Tovar, eds. *The Greco-Egyptian Magical Formularies: Libraries, Books, and Individual Recipes*. University of Michigan Press, 2022.

Fee, Gordon. *The First and Second Letters to the Thessalonians*. NICNT. Eerdmans, 2009.

Fee, Gordon. *The First Epistle to the Corinthians*. NICNT. Eerdmans, 1987.

Feldman, Louis. *Jew and Gentile in the Ancient World*. Princeton University Press, 1993.

Ferguson, Everett. "Spiritual Circumcision in Early Christianity." *Scottish Journal of Theology* 41 (1988): 485–97.

Finlan, Stephen. "Can We Speak of Theosis in Paul?" In *Partakers of the Divine Nature: The History and Development of Deification in the Christian*

Traditions. Edited by Michael J. Christensen and Jeffery A. Wittung. Baker Academic, 2007.

Fitzgerald, John T. *Cracks in an Earthen Vessel: An Examination of the Catalogues of Hardships in the Corinthian Correspondence*. Society of Biblical Literature, 1988.

Fitzmyer, Joseph A. "Qumran and the Interpolated Paragraph in 2 Cor 6:14–7:1." *Catholic Biblical Quarterly* 23 (1961): 271–280.

Flower, Michael Attyah. *The Seer in Ancient Greece*. University of California Press, 2008.

Forbes, Christopher. *Prophecy and Inspired Speech in Early Christianity and its Hellenistic Environment*. WUNT 2/75. Mohr Siebeck, 1995.

Fotopoulos, John. "Paul's Curse of Corinthians: Restraining Rivals with Fear and *Voces Mysticae* (1 Cor 16:22)." *Novum Testamentum* 56 (2014): 275–309.

Frankfurter, David. "Ancient Magic in a New Key: Refining an Exotic Discipline in the History of Religions." In *Guide to the Study of Ancient Magic*. Edited by David Frankfurter. Brill, 2019.

Frankfurter, David. "Preface." In *Guide to the Study of Ancient Magic*. Edited by David Frankfurter. Brill, 2019.

Frankfurter, David. "Spell and Speech Act: The Magic of the Spoken World." In *Guide to the Study of Ancient Magic*. Edited by David Frankfurter. Brill, 2019.

Fredriksen, Paula. "God Is Jewish, but Gentiles Don't Have to Be: Ethnicity and Eschatology in Paul's Gospel." In *The Message of Paul the Apostle within Second Temple Judaism*. Edited by František Ábel. Lexington Books/Fortress Academic, 2020.

Fredriksen, Paula. "How High Can Early High Christology Be?" In *Monotheism and Christology in Greco-Roman Antiquity*. Edited by Matthew V. Novenson. NovTSup 180. Brill, 2020.

Fredriksen, Paula. "How Jewish Is God? Divine Ethnicity in Paul's Theology." *Journal of Biblical Literature* 137 (2018): 193–212.

Fredriksen, Paula. "If It *Looks* Like a Duck, and It *Quacks* Like a Duck . . .: On *Not* Giving Up the Godfears." In *A Most Reliable Witness: Essays in Honor of Ross Shepard Kraemer*. Edited by Susan Ashbrook Harvey. BJS 358. Brown Judaic Studies, 2016.

Fredriksen, Paula. "Judaizing the Nations: The Ritual Demands of Paul's Gospel." *New Testament Studies* 56 (2010): 232–52.

Fredriksen, Paula. "Mandatory Retirement: Ideas in the Study of Christian Origins Whose Time Has Come to Go." *Studies in Religion/Sciences Religieuses* 35 (2006): 231–46.

Fredriksen, Paula. *Paul: The Pagans' Apostle*. Yale University Press, 2018.

Fredriksen, Paula. "Paul the 'Convert'?" In *The Oxford Handbook of Pauline Studies*. Edited by Matthew V. Novenson and R. Barry Matlock. Oxford University Press, 2022.

Fredriksen, Paula. "Philo, Herod, Paul, and the Many Gods of Ancient Jewish 'Monotheism.'" *Harvard Theological Review* 115 (2022): 23–45.

Fredriksen, Paula. "What Does It Mean to See Paul 'within Judaism'?" *Journal of Biblical Literature* 141, no. 2 (2022): 359–80.

Fredriksen, Paula, and Oded Irshai. "'Include Me Out': Tertullian, the Rabbis, and the Graeco-Roman City." In *L'identité à travers l'éthique: nouvelles perspectives sur la formation des identités collectives dans le monde gréco-romain*. Edited by K. Berthelot et al. Brepols, 2015.

Gaca, Kathy L. *The Making of Fornication: Eros, Ethics, and Political Reform in Greek Philosophy and Early Christianity*. University of California Press, 2017.

Gager, John G. *Curse Tablets and Binding Spells from the Ancient World*. Oxford University Press, 1992.

Gager, John G. *Reinventing Paul*. Oxford University Press, 2002.

Gambetti, Sandra. *The Alexandrian Riots of 38 CE and the Persecution of the Jews: A Historical Reconstruction*. Brill, 2009.

Gill, Christopher. *The Structured Self in Hellenistic and Roman Thought*. Oxford University Press, 2006.

Gleason, Maud. *Making Men: Sophists and Self-Presentation in Ancient Rome*. Princeton University Press, 1995.

Glissant, Édouard. *Poetics of Relation*. University of Michigan Press, 1997.

Glover, Daniel B. *Patterns of Deification in the Acts of the Apostles*. WUNT 2/576. Mohr Siebeck, 2022.

Goodenough, Erwin R. *Jewish Symbols in the Greco-Roman Period*. 13 vols. Princeton University Press, 1953–68.

Goodman, Martin. "Galatians 6.12 on Circumcision and Persecution." In *From Strength to Strength: Essays in Appreciation of Shaye J. D. Cohen*. Edited by Michael L. Satlow. Brown Judaic Studies, 2018.

Goodman, Martin. *Herod the Great: Jewish King in a Roman World*. Yale University Press, 2024.

Goodman, Martin. "Jews, Greeks, and Romans." In *Jews in a Graeco-Roman World*. Edited by Martin Goodman. Oxford University Press, 1998.

Gordon, Richard. "Charaktêres between Antiquity and Renaissance: Transmission and Re-invention." In *Les savoirs magiques et leur transmission de l'Antiquité à la Renaissance*. Edited by V. Dasen and J.-M. Spieser. SISMEL/Edizioni del Galluzzo, 2014.

Gordon, Richard. "Compiling P. Lond I 121 = PGM VII in a Transcultural Context." In *Cultural Plurality in Ancient Magical Texts and Practices: Graeco-Egyptian Handbooks and Related Traditions*. Edited by Ljuba M. Bortolani, William Furley, Svenja Nagel, and Joachim F. Quack. Orientalische Religionen in der Antike 32. Mohr Siebeck, 2019.

Gordon, Richard. "The Healing Event in Greco-Roman Folk Medicine." In *Ancient medicine in Its Socio-Cultural Context*. Volume 2, *Papers Read at the Congress Held at Leiden University, 13–15 April 1992*. Edited by H. F. J. Horstmanshoff, Philip J. van der Eijk, and P. H. Schrijvers. Clio Medica 28. Brill, 1995.

Gordon, Richard. "Queering Their Pitch: The Curse Tablets from Mainz, with Some Thoughts on Practising 'Magic.'" *Journal of Roman Archaeology* 27 (2014): 774–84.

Gorman, Michael. "Romans: The First Christian Treatise on Theosis." *Journal of Theological Interpretation* 5 (2011): 13–34.

Grainger, John D. *The Seleucid Empire of Antiochus III (323–287 BC).* Pen and Sword Books Limited, 2015.

Gross, Simcha, and Avigail Manekin-Bamberger. "Babylonian Jewish Society: The Evidence of the Incantation Bowls." *Jewish Quarterly Review* 112 (2022): 1–30.

Gruen, Erich S. "Contingency and Context: The Origins of the Jewish War against Rome." In *Empire and Religion in the Roman World.* Edited by Harriet Flower. Cambridge University Press, 2021.

Gruen, Erich S. *Diaspora: Jews amidst Greeks and Romans.* Harvard University Press, 2002.

Gruen, Erich S. *Heritage and Hellenism: The Reinvention of Jewish Tradition.* University of California, 1998.

Gruen, Erich S. "Herod, Rome, and the Diaspora." In *Herod and Augustus.* Edited by David M. Jacobson and Nikos Kpkkinos. Brill, 2009.

Gupta, Nijay. "Fighting the Good Fight: The Good Life in Paul and the Giants of Philosophy." In *Paul and the Giants of Philosophy: Reading the Apostle in Greco-Roman Context.* Edited by Joseph R. Dodson and David E. Briones. InterVarsity Press, 2019.

Halbwachs, Maurice. *On Collective Memory.* Edited and translated by Lewis Coser. 1925. Repr., University of Chicago Press, 1992.

Hanson, J. S. "Dreams and Visions in the Greco-Roman World and Early Christianity." *ANRW* 23, no. 2 (1980): 1395–1427.

Harker, Christina. *The Colonizers' Idols: Paul, Galatia, and Empire in New Testament Studies.* Mohr Siebeck, 2018.

Harl Sellew, Melissa. "Reading the *Gospel of Thomas* From Here: A Trans-centered Hermeneutic." *Journal of Interdisciplinary Biblical Studies* 1 (2020): 61–96.

Harland, Philip A. "Climbing the Ethnic Ladder: Ethnic Hierarchies and Judean Responses." *Journal of Biblical Literature* 138 (2019): 665–86.

Harland, Philip A. *Greco-Roman Associations: Texts, Translations and Commentary II North Coast of the Black Sea, Asia Minor.* BZNW 204. De Gruyter, 2014.

Harland, Philip A. "Familial Dimensions of Group Identity: 'Brothers' (ἀδελφοί) in Associations of the Greek East." *Journal of Biblical Literature* 124 (2005): 491–513.

Harland, Philip A. "Familial Dimensions of Group Identity (II): 'Mothers' and 'Fathers' in Associations and Synagogues of the Greek World," *Journal for the Study of Judaism* 38 (2007): 57–79.

Harrill, J. Albert. *Paul the Apostle.* Cambridge University Press 2012.

Harris, W. V., ed. *Rethinking the Mediterranean*. Oxford University Press, 2005.

Harrisson, Juliette. *Dreams and Dreaming in the Roman Empire: Cultural Memory and Imagination*. Bloomsbury, 2013.

Hart, Patrick. *A Prolegomenon to the Study of Paul*. Brill, 2020.

Hay, David H. *Glory at the Right Hand: Psalm 110 in Early Christianity*. Abingdon Press, 1973.

Hayman, Peter. "Monotheism—a Misused Word in Jewish Studies?" *Journal of Jewish Studies* 42 (1991): 1–13.

Hays, Richard B. *Echoes of Scripture in the Letters of Paul*. Yale University Press, 1989.

Heiser, Michael S. "Monotheism, Polytheism, Monolatry, or Henotheism? Toward an Assessment of Divine Plurality in the Hebrew Bible." *Bulletin for Biblical Research* 18 (2008): 1–30.

Hengel, Martin. *Judentum und Hellenismus: Studien zu ihrer Begegnung unter Berücksichtigung Palästinas bis zur Mitte des 2 Jh.s v. Chr.* Mohr Siebeck, 1969.

Hengel, Martin. *Judaism and Hellenism: Studies in Their Encounter in Palestine during the Early Hellenistic Period*. Translated by John Bowden. 2 vols. Fortress, 1974.

Henning, Meghan. *Hell Hath No Fury: Gender, Disability, and the Invention of Damned Bodies in Early Christian Literature*. Yale University Press, 2021.

Heschel, Abraham J. *The Prophets*. Harper & Row, 1962.

Hezser, Catherine. "Ancient 'Science Fiction': Journeys into Space and Visions of the World in Jewish, Christian, and Greco-Roman Literature of Antiquity." In *Christian Origins and Hellenistic Judaism: Social and Literary Contexts for the New Testament*. Edited by Stanley E. Porter et al. Brill, 2013.

Hicks-Keeton, Jill. *Arguing with Aseneth: Gentile Access to Israel's Living God in Jewish Antiquity*. Oxford University Press, 2018.

Hodge, Caroline Johnson. *If Sons, Then Heirs: A Study of Kindship and Ethnicity in the Letters of Paul*. Oxford University Press, 2007.

Hodges, Frederick M. "The Ideal Prepuce in Ancient Greece and Rome: Male Genital Aesthetics and Their Relation to *Lipodermos*, Circumcision, Foreskin Restoration, and the *Kynodesmē*." *Bulletin of the History of Medicine* 75 (2001): 375–405.

Hoke, Jimmy. *Feminism, Queerness, Affect, and Romans: Under God?* SBL, 2021.

Holladay, Carl R. *Fragments from Hellenistic Jewish Authors*, I. Scholars Press, 1983.

Holladay, Carl R. *Fragments from Hellenistic Jewish Authors*, II. Scholars Press, 1989.

Holladay, Carl R. *Fragments from Hellenistic Jewish Authors*, III. Scholars Press, 1995.

Holmes, Brooke. *Gender: Antiquity and Its Legacy*. I.B. Tauris, 2012.

Hooker, Morna D. "Interchange in Christ." *Journal of Theological Studies* 21 (1971): 349–61.

Horbury, William, and David Noy. *Jewish Inscriptions of Graeco-Roman Egypt*. Cambridge University Press, 1992.

Horden, Peregrine and Nicholas Purcell. *The Corrupting Sea: A Study of Mediterranean History*. Blackwell, 2000.

Horky, Phillip Sidney. "Cosmic Spiritualism among the Pythagoreans, Stoics, Jews and Early Christians." In *Cosmos in the Ancient World*. Edited by Phillip Sidney Horky. Cambridge University Press, 2019.

Hoskins, Paul M. "The Use of Biblical and Extrabiblical Parallels in the Interpretation of First Corinthians 6:2–3." *Catholic Biblical Quarterly* 63 (2001): 287–97.

Howley, Joseph A. *Aulus Gellius and Roman Reading Culture: Text, Presence and Imperial Knowledge in the 'Noctes Atticae'*. Cambridge University Press, 2018.

Huber, Konrad. "Verhext—verflucht—am Leib gezeichnet. Aspekte von Magie im Galaterbrief?" In *Antike Fluchtafeln und das Neue Testament: Materialität—Ritualpraxis—Texte*. Edited by Michael Hölscher, Markus Lau, and Susanne Luther. WUNT 474. Mohr Siebeck, 2021.

Huber, Lynn. *Thinking and Seeing with Women in Revelation*. Bloomsbury, 2013.

Hurtado, Larry W. "'Ancient Jewish Monotheism' in the Hellenistic and Roman Periods." *Journal of Ancient Judaism* 4 (2013): 379–400.

Hurtado, Larry W. *Lord Jesus Christ: Devotion to Jesus in Earliest Christianity*. Eerdmans, 2003.

Isaac, Benjamin. *The Invention of Racism in Classical Antiquity*. Princeton University Press, 2004.

Ivarson, Frederik. "Vice Lists and Deviant Masculinity: The Rhetorical Function of 1 Corinthians 5:10–11 and 6:9–10." In *Mapping Gender in Ancient Religious Discourses*. Edited by Todd Penner and C. V. Stichele. Brill, 2007.

Ivčević, Sanja. "Roman Military Gear Depicted on Grave Monuments from the Archaeological Museum in Split." In *Funerary Sculpture of the Western Illyricum and Neighbouring Regions of the Roman Empire*. Edited by Nenad Cambi and Guntram Koch. Književni Krug, 2013.

Janssen, David. "The Roman Cuirass Breastplate Statue and Paul's Use of Armor Language in Romans 13:12 and 1 Thessalonians 5:8." *Colloquium* 46 (2014): 55–85.

Jastrow, Morris. *The Religion of Babylonia and Assyria*. Athenaeum, 1898.

Jipp, Joshua W. "Ancient, Modern, and Future Interpretations of Romans 1:3–4: Reception History and Biblical Interpretation." *Journal of Theological Interpretation* 3 (2009): 241–59.

Johnson, Luke Timothy. "Review of Richard H. Bell, No One Seeks for God." *Review of Biblical Literature* (1999).

Johnson, Paul Christopher. "Toward an Atlantic Genealogy of 'Spirit Possession.'" In *Spirited Things: The Work of "Spirit Possession" in Afro-Atlantic Religions*. Edited by Paul Christopher Johnson. University of Chicago Press, 2014.

Johnson-DeBaufre, Melanie and Laura S. Nasrallah. "Beyond the Heroic Paul: Toward a Feminist and Decolonizing Approach to the Letters of Paul." In *The Colonized Apostle: Paul through Postcolonial Eyes*. Edited by Christopher D. Stanley. Fortress, 2011.

Johnston, Sarah Iles. *Ancient Greek Divination*. Wiley-Blackwell, 2008.

Johnston, Sarah Iles. *Restless Dead: Encounters between the Living and the Dead in Ancient Greece.* University of California Press, 1999.

Jones, Brice C. *New Testament Texts on Greek Amulets from Late Antiquity.* LNTS 554. Bloomsbury T&T Clark, 2016.

Kahlos, Maijastina. "'A Christian Cannot Employ Magic': Rhetorical Self-Fashioning of the Magicless Christianity of Late Antiquity." In *Rhetoric and Religious Identity in Late Antiquity.* Edited by Richard Flower and Morwenna Ludlow. Oxford University Press, 2020.

Kahlos, Maijastina. "*Artis heu magicis*: The Label of Magic in the Fourth-Century Disputes and Conflicts." In *Pagans and Christians in Late Antique Rome: Conflict, Competition, and Coexistence in the Fourth Century.* Edited by Michele Salzman, Marianne Sághy, and Rita Lizzi Testa. Cambridge University Press, 2015.

Kahlos, Maijastina. *Debate and Dialogue: Christian and Pagan Cultures, c. 380–430.* Taylor & Francis, 2007.

Kahlos, Maijastina. *Religious Dissent in Late Antiquity, 350–450.* Oxford University Press, 2020.

Kahlos, Maijastina. "The Shadow of the Shadow: Examining Christian Fourth and Fifth Century Depictions of Pagans." In *The Faces of the Other: Religious Rivalry and Ethnic Encounters in the Later Roman World.* Edited by Maijastina Kahlos. Brepols, 2011.

Kasher, Aryeh. *The Jews in Hellenistic and Roman Egypt: The Struggle for Equal Rights.* Mohr Siebeck, 1985.

Keener, Craig S. *Acts: An Exegetical Commentary.* 4 vols. Baker Academic, 2012–2015.

Kelhoffer, James A. Persecution, *Persuasion and Power: Readiness to Withstand Hardship as a Corroboration of Legitimacy in the New Testament.* WUNT 270. Mohr Siebeck, 2010.

Kent, Benedict H. M. "Curses in Acts: Hearing the Apostles' Words of Judgment alongside 'Magical' Spell Texts." *Journal for the Study of the New Testament* 39 (2017): 412–40.

Kim, Seon Yong. *Curse Motifs in Galatians: An Investigation into Paul's Rhetorical Strategies.* WUNT 2/531. Mohr Siebeck, 2020.

King, Justin D. "Paul, Zechariah, and the Identity of the 'Holy Ones' in 1 Thessalonians 3:13: Correcting an Un'Fee'sible Approach." *Perspectives in the Study of Religion* 39 (2012): 25–38.

Kloppenborg, John S. *Christ Associations: Connecting and Belonging in the Ancient City.* Yale University Press, 2019.

Kloppenborg, John S. "Cursing in the Corinthian Christ Assembly." In *Antike Fluchtafeln und das Neue Testament: Materialität—Ritualpraxis—Texte.* Edited by Michael Hölscher, Markus Lau, and Susanne Luther. WUNT 474. Mohr Siebeck, 2021.

Kloppenborg, John S. "Greco-Roman *Thiasoi*, the *Ekklêsia* at Corinth, and Conflict Management." In *Redescribing Paul and the Corinthians*. ECL. Edited by Ron Cameron and Merrill Miller. Society of Biblical Literature, 2011.

Knust, Jennifer. *Abandoned to Lust: Sexual Slander and Ancient Christianity*. Columbia University Press, 2006.

Knust, Jennifer. *Unprotected Texts: The Bible's Surprising Contradictions about Sex and Desire*. HarperOne, 2011.

Kohler, Kaufmann, and Lous Ginzberg. "Asmodeus, or Ashemedai." In *Jewish Encyclopedia*. Vol. 2. Edited by Isidore Singer. Funk & Wagnalls, 1906.

Kotansky, Roy. "Greek Exorcistic Amulets." In *Ancient Magic and Ritual Power*. Edited by Paul Mirecki and Marvin Meyer. Brill, 1995.

Kotansky, Roy. *Greek Magical Amulets*. Wiesbaden: Springer Fachmedien, 1994.

Kotrosits, Maia. "The Ethnography of Gender." *Studies in Late Antiquity* 7 (2023): 5–28.

Kotrosits, Maia. "Penetration and Its Discontents: Greco-Roman Sexuality, the *Acts of Paul, and Thecla*, and Theorizing Eros without the Wound." *Journal of the History of Sexuality* 27 (2018): 343–66.

Kraemer, Ross. *Her Share of the Blessings: Women's Religions among Pagans, Jews, and Christians in the Greco-Roman World*. Oxford University Press, 1992.

Kraemer, Ross. "The Other as Woman: An Aspect of Polemic among Pagans, Jews, and Christians in the Greco-Roman World." In *The Other in Jewish Thought and History: Constructions of Jewish Culture and Identity*. Edited by L. J. Silberstein and R. L. Cohn. New York University Press, 1994.

Krentz, Edgar. "Military Langauge and Metaphors in Philippians." In *Origins and Method--towards a New Understanding of Judaism and Christianity: Essays in Honour of John C. Hurd*. Edited by Bradley McLean. Sheffield Academic Press, 1993.

Lambek, Michael. *Human Spirits: A Cultural Account of Trance in Mayotte*. Cambridge University Press, 1981.

Lamont, Jessica L. *In Blood and Ashes: Curse Tablets and Binding Spells in Ancient Greece*. Oxford University Press, 2023.

Lamont, Jessica L. "A New Commercial Curse Tablet from Classical Athens." *Zeitschrift Für Papyrologie Und Epigraphik* 196 (2015): 159–74.

Larsson, Stefan. "Just an Ordinary Jew: A Case for Why Paul Should Be Studied within Jewish Studies." *Nordisk judaistik/Scandinavian Jewish Studies* 29, no. 2 (2018): 2–16.

Last, Richard. *The Pauline Church and the Corinthian Ekklēsia: Greco-Roman Associations in Comparative Context*. SNTS Monograph Series 164. Cambridge University Press, 2015.

Last, Richard. "What Purpose Did Paul Understand His Mission to Serve?" *Harvard Theological Review* 104 (2011): 299–324.

Last, Richard and Sarah Rollens. "Accounting Practices in P.Tebt. III/2 894 and Pauline Groups." *Early Christianity* 5 (2014): 441–74.

Lee, Max J. *Moral Transformation in Greco-Roman Philosophy of Mind: Mapping the Moral Milieu of the Apostle Paul and His Diaspora Jewish Contemporaries.* WUNT 2/515. Mohr Siebeck, 2020.

Lee, Michelle V. *Paul, the Stoics, and the Body of Christ.* SNTS Monograph Series 137. Cambridge University Press, 2006.

Leon, Harry J. *The Jews of Ancient Roma.* Hendrickson, 1960.

Levine, Lee I. *The Ancient Synagogue.* Yale University Press, 2000.

Levine, Lee I. *Judaism and Hellenism in Antiquity: Conflict or Confluence?* University of Washington Press, 1998.

Levinskaya, Irina. *The Book of Acts in Its Diaspora Setting.* Eerdmans, 1996.

Leyerle, Blake. "John Chrysostom on the Gaze." *Journal of Early Christian Studies* 1 (1993): 159–74.

Lieu, Judith M. *Marcion and the Making of a Heretic: God and Scripture in the Second Century.* Cambridge University Press, 2015.

Lipsett, Diane. *Desiring Conversion: Hermas, Thecla, Aseneth.* Oxford University Press, 2010.

Litwa, M. David. "The Deification of Moses in Philo of Alexandria." *Studia Philonica Annual* 26 (2014): 1–27.

Litwa, M. David. *Iesus Deus: The Early Christian Depiction of Jesus as a Mediterranean God.* Fortress, 2014.

Litwa, M. David. *We Are Being Transformed: Deification in Paul's Soteriology.* De Gruyter, 2012.

Lovejoy, Arthur, and George Boas. *Primitivism and Related Ideas in Antiquity.* Johns Hopkins University Press, 1935.

Luckritz Marquis, Timothy. *Transient Apostle: Paul, Travel, and the Rhetoric of Empire.* Synkrisis. Yale University Press, 2013.

Lum, Kathryn Gin. *Heathen: Religion and Race in American History.* Harvard University Press, 2022.

Luther, Susanne. "Neutestamentliche 'Bindeformeln'? Eine Spurensuche in der paulinischen Korintherbriefkorrespondenz." In *Antike Fluchtafeln und das Neue Testament: Materialität—Ritualpraxis—Texte.* Edited by M. Hölscher, M. Lau, and S. Luther. WUNT 474. Mohr Siebeck, 2021.

MacDonald, Nathan. *Deuteronomy and the Meaning of "Monotheism".* FAT 2/1. Mohr Siebeck, 2003.

Mach, Michael. *Entwicklungsstadien des jüdischen Engelglaubens in vorrabinischer Zeit.* TSAJ 34. Mohr, 1992.

MacRae, Duncan. *Legible Religion: Books, Gods, and Rituals in Roman Culture.* Harvard University Press, 2016.

Malherbe, Abraham J. "Antisthenes and Odysseus, and Paul at War." *Harvard Theological Review* 76 (1983): 143–73.

Malherbe, Abraham J. "'Gentle as a Nurse': The Lyric Background to I Thessalonians ii." *Novum Testamentum* 12 (1970): 203–17.

Malherbe, Abraham J. *Paul and the Popular Philosophers*. Fortress Press, 1989.

Malkin, Irad, ed. *Mediterranean Paradigms and Classical Antiquity*. Routledge, 2005.

Manekin-Bamberger, Avigail. "The Vow-Curse in Ancient Jewish Texts." *Harvard Theological Review* 112 (2019): 340–57.

Masuzawa, Tomoko. *The Invention of World Religions: Or, How European Universalism Was Preserved in the Language of Pluralism*. University of Chicago Press, 2005.

Majercik, Ruth Dorothy. *The Chaldean Oracles: Text, Translation, and Commentary*. Studies in Greek and Roman Religion 5. Brill, 1989.

Marchal, Joseph. *Appalling Bodies: Queer Figures before and after Paul's Letters*. Oxford University Press, 2020.

Marshak, Adam Kolman. *The Many Faces of Herod the Great*. Eerdmans, 2015.

Martin, Dale. *Sex and the Single Savior: Gender and Sexuality in Biblical Interpretation*. Westminster John Knox, 2006.

Marx-Wolf, Heidi. *Spiritual Taxonomies and Ritual Authority: Platonists, Priests, and Gnostics in the Third Century C.E.* Divinations. University of Pennsylvania Press, 2016.

Mason, Steve. *A History of the Jewish War, A.D. 66–74*. Cambridge University Press, 2016.

Mason, Steve. "Paul's Announcement (τὸ εὐαγγέλιον): 'Good News' and Its Detractors in Earliest Christianity." In *Josephus, Judea, and Christian Origins: Methods and Categories*. Hendrickson, 2009.

Mason, Steve. "Stranger Danger! Judaean Non-mixing (*Amixia*) in Graeco-Roman Context." In *Jews and Christians in the Roman World: From Historical Method to Cases*. AJEC. Brill, 2023.

Mastrocinque, Attilio, Joseph E. Sanzo, and Marianna Scapini, eds. *Ancient Magic: Then and Now*. Stuttgart: Franz Steiner Verlag, 2020.

McMurray, Patrick. *Sacrifice, Brotherhood, and the Body: Abraham and the Nations in Romans*. Fortress Academic, 2021.

McNiven, Timothy J. "The Unheroic Penis: Otherness Exposed." *Source* 15 (1995): 10–16.

Méleze-Modrzejewski, Joseph. *The Jews of Egypt from Ramses II to Emperor Hadrian*. Jewish Publication Society, 1995.

Meyers, Carol L., and Eric M. Meyers, *Zechariah 9–14: A New Translation with Introduction and Commentary*. AB 25C. Doubleday, 1993.

Minets, Yuliya. *The Slow Fall of Babel: Languages and Identities in Late Antique Christianity*. Cambridge University Press, 2021.

Mitchell, Stephen, and Peter van Nuffelen, eds. *One God: Pagan Monotheism in the Roman Empire*. Cambridge University Press, 2010.

More, Henry. *An Explanation of the Grand Mystery of Godliness*. Flesher, 1660.

Morgan, Teresa. *Roman Faith and Christian Faith: Pistis and Fides in the Early Roman Empire and Early Churches*. Oxford University Press, 2015.

Moses, Robert Ewusie. *Practices of Power: Revisiting the Principalities and Powers in the Pauline Letters*. Fortress, 2014.

Moslener, Sara. *Virgin Nation: Sexual Purity and American Adolescence*. Oxford University Press, 2015.

Moss, Candida. *God's Ghostwriters: Enslaved Christians and the Making of the Bible*. Little, Brown, and Company, 2024.

Most, Glenn. "Hesiod's Myth of the Five (or Three or Four) Races." *Proceedings of the Cambridge Philological Society* 43 (1998): 104–27.

Mount, Christopher. "1 Corinthians 11:3–16: Spirit Possession and Authority in a Non-Pauline Interpolation." *Journal of Biblical Literature* 124 (2005): 313–34.

Mouritsen, Henrik. *The Freedman in the Roman World*. Cambridge University Press, 2011.

Mussies, Gerard. "The *Interpretatio Judaica* of Sarapis." In *Studies in Hellenistic Religions*. Edited by M. J. Vermaseren. Brill, 1979.

Mussies, Gerard. "The *Interpretatio Judaica* of Thot-Hermes." In *Studies in Egyptian Religion*. Edited by M. Heerma Van Voss, E. J. Sharpe, and R. J. Z. Werblowsky. Brill, 1982.

Myers, Jason. *Paul, the Apostle of Obedience*. T&T Clark, 2023.

Nanos, Nanos D. "Paul and Judaism: Why Not Paul's Judaism?" In *Paul Unbound: Other Perspectives on the Apostle*. Edited by Mark D. Given. 2nd ed. Society of Biblical Literature, 2022.

Nanos, Mark D., and Heidi Wendt. "Galatians." In *T&T Clark Handbook to the Historical Paul*. Edited by Ryan S. Schellenberg and Heidi Wendt. T&T Clark, 2022.

Nanos, Mark D., and Magnus Zetterholm, eds. *Paul within Judaism: Restoring the First-Century Context to the Apostle*. Fortress, 2015.

Nasrallah, Laura Salah. *Ancient Christians and the Power of Curses: Magic, Aesthetics, and Justice*. Cambridge University Press, 2024.

Nasrallah, Laura Salah. *Archaeology and the Letters of Paul*. Oxford University Press, 2019.

Nasrallah, Laura Salah. "Judgment, Justice, and Destruction: Defixiones and 1 Corinthians." *Journal of Biblical Literature* 140 (2021): 347–67.

Nasrallah, Laura Salah. "Making Justice: Justin Martyr and a Curse from Amathous, Cyprus." *Zeitschrift für Antikes Christentum* 28 (2024): 76–99.

Neutel, Karin B. "Missing Foreskin in the Septuagint: Circumcision Related Metaphors Lost in Translation." In *Circumcision and Jewish Identity*. Edited by Lieve M. Teugels and Karin B. Neutel. Gorgias, 2023.

Neutel, Karin B. "Restoring Abraham's Foreskin: The Significance of ἀκροβυστία for Paul's Argument about Circumcision in Romans 4:9–12." *Journal for the Study of the Jesus Movement in Its Jewish Setting* 8 (2021): 53–74.

Newman, Carey C. *Paul's Glory Christology: Tradition and Rhetoric*. Brill, 1992.

ní Mheallaigh, Karen. *The Moon in the Greek and Roman Imagination: Myth, Literature, Science and Philosophy*. Cambridge University Press, 2020.

ní Mheallaigh, Karen. *Reading Fiction with Lucian: Fakes, Freaks and Hyperreality.* Cambridge University Press, 2014.

Niehoff, Maren R. *Philo of Alexandria: An Intellectual Biography.* Yale University Press, 2018.

Nielsen, Inge. *Housing the Chosen: The Architectural Context of Mystery Groups and Religious Associations in the Ancient World.* Contextualizing the Sacred. Brepols, 2014.

Noble, Thomas and Thomas Head, eds. *Soldiers of Christ: Saints and Saints' Lives from Late Antiquity and the Early Middle Ages.* Penn State University Press, 2000.

Nongbri, Brent. *Before Religion: A History of a Modern Concept.* Yale University Press, 2013.

Novenson, Matthew V. "Beyond Compare, or: Some Recent Strategies for How Not to Compare Early Christianity with Other Things." In *The New Testament in Comparison: Validity, Method, and Purpose in Comparing Traditions.* Edited by John M. G. Barclay and Benjamin G. White. T&T Clark, 2020.

Novenson, Matthew V. *Christ among the Messiahs: Christ Language in Paul and Messiah Language in Ancient Judaism.* Oxford University Press, 2012.

Novenson, Matthew V. "Did Paul Abandon either Judaism or Monotheism?" In *The New Cambridge Companion to St. Paul.* Edited by Bruce W. Longenecker. Cambridge University Press, 2020.

Novenson, Matthew V. *The Grammar of Messianism: An Ancient Jewish Political Idiom and Its Users.* Oxford University Press, 2017.

Novenson, Matthew V. "The Messiah ben Abraham in Galatians: A Response to Joel Willitts." *Journal for the Study of Paul and his Letters* 2 (2012): 163–69.

Novenson, Matthew V. "Messiahs and Their Messengers." *Svensk Teologisk Kvartalskrift* 95 (2019): 3–16.

Novenson, Matthew V. *Paul, Then and Now.* Eerdmans, 2022.

Novenson, Matthew V. *Paul and Judaism at the End of History.* Cambridge University Press, 2024.

Novenson, Matthew V. "The Universal Polytheism and the Case of the Jews." In *Monotheism and in Greco-Roman Antiquity.* Edited by Matthew V. Novenson. NovTSup 180. Brill, 2020.

Noreña, Carlos. "Coins and Communication." In *The Oxford Handbook of Social Relations in the Roman World.* Edited by Michael Peachin. Oxford University Press, 2011.

O'Meara, Dominic J. *Platonopolis: Platonic Political Philosophy in Late Antiquity.* Clarendon, 2003.

Ogden, Daniel. *Drakōn: Dragon Myth and Serpent Cult in the Greek and Roman Worlds.* Oxford University Press, 2013.

Økland, Jorunn. *Women in Their Place: Paul and the Corinthian Discourse of Gender and Sanctuary Space.* JSNTSup 269. T&T Clark, 2004.

Olender, Maurice. *The Languages of Paradise: Race, Religion, and Philology*. Translated by Arthur Goldhammer. Harvard University Press, 2009.

Olley, John W. "A Precursor of the NRSV? 'Sons and Daughters in 2 Cor 6.18." *New Testament Studies* 44 (1998): 204–12.

Orlin, Eric M. *Foreign Cults in Rome: Creating a Roman Empire*. Oxford University Press, 2010.

Parker, Robert. *Greek Gods Abroad: Names, Natures, and Transformations*. University of California Press, 2017.

Parker, Robert. *On Greek Religion*. Cornell University Press, 2011.

Parks, Sara. "The Greek Hat: 2 Maccabees 4:12 as a Euphemism for Reverse Circumcision." *Journal of Interdisciplinary Biblical Studies* 5 (2024): 1–20.

Parks, Sarah, Shayna Sheinfeld, and Meredith Warren. *Jewish and Christian Women in the Ancient Mediterranean*. Routledge, 2022.

Patel, Shaily Shashikant. "Magical Practices and Discourses of Magic in Early Christian Traditions: Jesus, Peter, and Paul." PhD diss., University of North Carolina at Chapel Hill, 2017.

Patel, Shaily Shashikant. "Rehabilitating 'Magic' in the Study of Early Christian Literature." *Religion Compass* 15, no. 10 (2021): 1–12.

Peppard, Michael. "Adopted and Begotten Sons of God: Paul and John on Divine Sonship." *Catholic Biblical Quarterly* 73 (2011): 92–110.

Peppard, Michael. "Bearing a 'Jewish Weight': A New Interpretation of a Greek Comedic Papyrus about Athletics (CPJ 3.519)." *Journal for Interdisciplinary Biblical Studies* 5 (2024): 21–41.

Peters, Janelle. "Creation, Angels, and Gender in Paul, Philo, and the Dead Sea Scrolls." *Open Theology* 7 (2021): 248–55.

Petrey, Taylor. *Resurrecting Parts: Early Christians on Desire, Reproduction, and Sexual Difference*. Routledge, 2015.

Petridou, Georgia. *Divine Epiphany in Greek Literature and Culture*. Oxford University Press, 2015.

Porten, Bezalel. *The Elephantine Papyri in English: Three Millenia of Cross-Cultural Continuity and Change*. 2nd ed. Brill, 2011.

Preller, L. "Das Zwölfgötterssystem der Greichen." In *Verhandlungen der neunten Versammlung deutscher Philologen, Schulmänner und Orientalisten zu Jena*. Jena, 1846.

Punt, Jeremy. "Paul, Military Imagery, and Social Disadvantage." *Acta Theologica* 23 (2016): 201–24.

Rainey, Brian. *Religion, Ethnicity and Xenophobia in the Bible: A Theoretical, Exegetical and Theological Survey*. Routledge, 2019.

Rajak, Tessa. *The Jewish Dialogue with Greece and Rome*. Brill, 2002.

Reed, Annette Yoshiko. "When Did *Daimones* Become Demons? Revisiting Septuagintal Data for Ancient Jewish Demonology." *Harvard Theological Review* 116 (2023): 340–75.

Reed, Annette Yoshiko. "Writing Jewish Astronomy in the Early Hellenistic Age: The Enochic Astronomical Book as Aramaic Wisdom and Archival Impulse." *Dead Sea Discoveries* 24 (2017): 1–37.

Regev, Eval. *The Hasmoneans: Ideology, Archaeology, History*. Vandenhoeck & Ruprecht, 2013.

Renberg, Gil H. *Where Dreams May Come: Incubation Sanctuaries in the Greco-Roman World*. 2 vols. RGRW 184. Brill, 2017.

Reno, Joshua. "Pornographic Desire in the Pauline Corpus." *Journal of Biblical Literature* 140 (2021): 163–85.

Richlin, Amy. *The Garden of Priapus: Sexuality and Aggression in Roman Humor*. Rev. ed. Oxford University Press, 1992.

Ripat, Pauline. "Expelling Misconceptions: Astrologers at Rome." *Classical Philology* 106 (2011): 115–54.

Ritter, Bradley. *Judaeans in the Greek Cities of the Roman Empire*. Brill, 2015.

Rives, James B. *Animal Sacrifice in the Roman Empire (31 BCE–395 CE)*. Oxford University Press, 2024.

Rives, James B. "Magic in Roman Law: The Reconstruction of a Crime." *Classical Antiquity* 22 (2003): 312–39.

Roberts, Erin. "Introduction: Myth, Our Bloodless Battleground." In *Christian Tourist Attractions, Mythmaking, and Identity Formation*. Edited by Erin Roberts and Jennifer Eyl. Bloomsbury, 2018.

Robertson, A., and Plummer, A. *A Critical and Exegetical Commentary on the First Epistle of St. Paul to the Corinthians*. 2nd ed. International Critical Commentary 33. T&T Clark, 1914.

Roediger, Henry L. "Three Facets of Collective Memory." *The American Psychologist* 76 (2021): 1388–1400.

Rogers, Guy Maclean. *For the Freedom of Zion: The Great Revolt of Jews against Romans, 66–74 CE*. Yale University Press, 2021.

Rollens, Sarah E. "The Anachronism of 'Early Christian Communities.'" In *Theorizing "Religion" in Antiquity*. Edited by Nickolas Roubekas. Studies in Ancient Religion and Culture. Equinox, 2018.

Rollens, Sarah E. "The God Came to Me in a Dream: Epiphanies in Voluntary Associations as a Context for Paul's Vision of Christ." *Harvard Theological Review* 111 (2018): 41–65.

Römer, Thomas. *The Invention of God*. Translated by Raymond Geuss. Harvard University Press, 2015.

Rothschild, Clare K. *Paul in Athens: The Popular Religious Context of Acts 17*. Mohr Siebeck, 2014.

Roubekas, Nickolas P. *An Ancient Theory of Religion: Euhemerism from Antiquity to the Present*. Routledge, 2016.

Runesson, Anders, in collaboration with Rebecca Runesson. *Judaism for Gentiles: Reading Paul beyond the Parting of the Ways Paradigm*. WUNT 494. Mohr Siebeck, 2022.

Runia, David T. *Philo of Alexandria and the Timaeus of Plato*. PhA 44. Brill, 1986.
Rüpke, Jörg. "'Historicizing Religion': Varro's *Antiquitates* and History of Religion in the Late Roman Republic." *History of Religions* 53 (2014): 246–68.
Rüpke, Jörg. *The Roman Calendar from Numa to Constantine: Time, History, and the* Fasti. Translated by David M. B. Richardson. John Wiley & Sons, 2011.
Rutgers, Leonard V. *The Hidden Heritage of Diaspora Judaism*. Peeters, 1998.
Salinero, Raúl Gonzáles. *Military Service and the Integration of Jews into the Roman Empire*. Brill, 2022.
Sanders, E. P. *Paul and Palestinian Judaism: A Comparison of Patterns of Religion*. Fortress, 1977.
Sandmel, Samuel. "Parallelomania." *Journal of Biblical Literature* 81 (1962): 1–13.
Sandnes, Karl Olav. *The Challenge of Homer: School, Pagan Poets and Early Christianity*. LNTS 400. T&T Clark, 2009.
Sanfridson, Martin. *Paul and Sacrifice in Corinth: Rethinking Paul's View on Gentile Cults in 1 Corinthians 8 and 10*. WUNT 2/623. Mohr Siebeck, 2025.
Sanzo, Joseph E. "Deconstructing the Deconstructionists: A Response to Recent Criticisms of the Rubric 'Ancient Magic.'" In *Ancient Magic: Then and Now*. Edited by Attilio Mastrocinque, Joseph Sanzo, and Marianna Scapini. Franz Steiner, 2020.
Sanzo, Joseph E. *Ritual Boundaries: Magic and Differentiation in Late Antique Christianity*. University of California Press, 2024.
Sanzo, Joseph E. *Scriptural Incipits on Amulets from Late Antique Egypt: Text, Typology, and Theory*. Mohr Siebeck, 2014.
Satlow, Michael L. "A History of the Jews or Judaism? On Seth Schwartz's Imperialism and Jewish Society, 200 BCE to 630 CE." *Jewish Quarterly Review* 95 (2005): 151–62.
Schäfer, Peter. "Communion with the Angels: Qumran and the Origins of Jewish Mysticism." In *Wege mystischer Gotteserfahrung: Judentum, Christentum und Islam: Mystical Approaches to God: Judaism, Christianity, and Islam*. Edited by Peter Schäfer et al. Oldenbourg Wissenschaftsverlag, 2009.
Schäfer, Peter. *Judeophobia*. Harvard University Press, 1997.
Schäfer, Peter. *Two Gods in Heaven: Jewish Concepts of God in Antiquity*. Translated by Allison Brown. Princeton University Press, 2020.
Schalit, Abraham. *König Herodes: der Mann und sein Werk*. Rev. ed. De Gruyter, 2001.
Schellenberg, Ryan S. *Abject Joy: Paul, Prison, and the Art of Making Do*. Oxford University Press, 2021.
Schellenberg, Ryan S. *Rethinking Paul's Rhetorical Education: Comparative Rhetoric and 2 Corinthians 10–13*. ECL 10. Society of Biblical Literature, 2013.
Schnelle, Udo. *The Human Condition: Anthropology in the Teachings of Jesus, Paul, and John*. Translated by O. C. Dean Jr. T&T Clark, 1996.
Schrage, Wolfgang. *Unterwegs zur Einzigkeit und Einheit Gottes: Zum "Monotheismus" des Paulus und seiner alttestamentlich-frühjudischen Tradition*. Neukirchener Verlag, 2002.

Schwartz, Joshua. "Methodological Remarks on 'Jewish' Identity: Jews, Jewish Christians, and Prolegomena on Pauline Judaism." In *Second Corinthians in the Perspective of Late Second Temple Judaism*. Edited by Reimund Bieringer et al. Brill, 2014.

Schwartz, Seth. *Imperialism and Jewish Society, 200 BCE to 640 CE*. Princeton University Press, 2001.

Schwartz, Seth. *Were the Jews a Mediterranean Society? Reciprocity and Solidarity in Ancient Judaism*. Princeton University Press, 2009.

Schweitzer, Albert. *The Mysticism of Paul the Apostle*. Translated by William Montgomery. Johns Hopkins University Press, 1953.

Schweitzer, Albert. *The Quest of the Historical Jesus*. 1906. Repr., Fortress Press, 2001.

Schumacher, Thomas. "Feurige Kohlen und die Macht der Feindesliebe: Überlegungen zum Fluchmotiv in Röm 12, 14–21." In *Antike Fluchtafeln und das Neue Testament: Materialität—Ritualpraxis—Texte*. Edited by M. Hölscher, M. Lau, and S. Luther. WUNT 474. Mohr Siebeck, 2021.

Scott, James M. "The Use of Scripture in 2 Corinthians 6.16c–18 and Paul's Restoration Theology." *Journal for the Study of the New Testament* 56 (1994): 73–99.

Scully, Stephen. *Hesiod's Theogony: From Near Eastern Creation Myths to Paradise Lost*. Oxford University Press, 2015.

Segal, Alan. "Heavenly Ascent in Hellenistic Judaism, Early Christianity and their Environment." *ANRW* 2: 23, no. 2 (1980): 1333–94.

Senft, Christophe. *La première épitre de saint Paul aux Corinthiens*. 2nd ed. Labor et Fides, 1990.

Sharp, Matthew T. "Courting Daimons in Corinth: Daimonic Partnerships, Cosmic Hierarchies, and Divine Jealousy in 1 Corinthians 8–10." In *Demons in Early Judaism and Christianity*. Edited by H. M. Patmore and J. Lössl. Brill, 2022.

Sharp, Matthew T. *Divination and Philosophy in the Letters of Paul*. ESRA. Edinburgh University Press, 2022.

Shumate, Nancy. *Nation, Empire, Decline: Studies in Rhetorical Continuity from the Romans to the Modern Era*. Duckworth, 2006.

Smith, David R. *"Hand This Man over to Satan": Curse, Exclusion and Salvation in 1 Corinthians 5*. T&T Clark, 2008.

Smith, Jonathan Z. *Drudgery Divine: On the Comparison of Early Christianities and the Religions of the Late Antiquity*. School of Oriental and African Studies, 1990.

Smith, Jonathan Z. "The 'End' of Comparison: Redescription and Rectification." In *A Magic Still Dwells: Comparative Religion in the Postmodern Age*. Edited by Kimberley C. Patton and Benjamin C. Ray. University of California Press, 2000.

Smith, Jonathan Z. *Map Is Not Territory*. University of Chicago Press, 1978.

Smith, Jonathan Z. "Religion, Religions, Religious." In *Critical Terms for Religious Studies*. Edited by Mark C. Taylor. University of Chicago Press, 1998.

Smith, Mark S. *God in Translation: Cross-cultural Recognition of Deities in the Biblical World*. FAT 57. Mohr Siebeck, 2008.

Smith, Mark S. *The Origins of Biblical Monotheism: Israel's Polytheistic Background and the Ugaritic Texts*. Oxford University Press, 2003.

Smith, Morton. "Pauline Worship as Seen by Pagans." *Harvard Theological Review* 73 (1980): 241–49.

Soon, Isaac T. *A Disabled Apostle: Impairment and Disability in the Letters of Paul*. Oxford University Press, 2023.

South, James. "A Critique of the 'Curse/Death' Interpretation of 1 Corinthians 5.1–8." *New Testament Studies* 39 (1993): 539–61.

Sprinkle, Preston. "The Afterlife in Romans: Understanding Paul's Glory Motif in Light of the Apocalypse of Moses and 2 Baruch." In *Lebendige Hoffnung—ewiger Tod?! Jenseitsvorstellungen im Hellenismus, Judentum und Christentum*. Edited by Michael Labahn and Manfred Lang. Evangelische Verlagsanstalt, 2007.

Ste Croix, G.E.M de. "Why Were the Early Christians Persecuted?—a Rejoinder." *Past and Present* 27 (1964): 28–33.

Stern, Menahem, ed. *Greek and Latin Authors on Jews and Judaism*. 3 vols. Israel Academy of Sciences and Humanities, 1984.

Stowers, Stanley. *Christian Beginnings: A Study in Ancient Mediterranean Religion*. ESRA. Edinburgh University Press, 2024.

Stowers, Stanley. "The Concept of Community and the History of Early Christianity." *Method and Theory in the Study of Religion* 23 (2011): 238–56.

Stowers, Stanley. "The Dilemma of Paul's Physics: Features Stoic-Platonist or Platonist-Stoic?" In *From Stoicism to Platonism: The Development of Philosophy, 100 BCE–100 CE*. Edited by Troels Engberg-Pedersen. Cambridge University Press, 2018.

Stowers, Stanley. *History and the Study of Religion: The Ancient Mediterranean as a Test Case*. Oxford University Press, 2024.

Stowers, Stanley. "Jesus the Teacher and Stoic Ethics in the Gospel of Matthew." In *Stoicism in Early Christianity*. Edited by Tuomus Rasimus, Troels Engberg-Pedersen, and Ismo Dunderberg. Baker Academic, 2010.

Stowers, Stanley. "Kinds of Myth, Meals, and Power: Paul and the Corinthians." In *Redescribing Paul and the Corinthians*. ECL. Edited by Ron Cameron and Merrill Miller. Society of Biblical Literature, 2011.

Stowers, Stanley. "Matter and Spirit, or What Is Pauline Participation in Christ?" In *The Holy Spirit: Classic and Contemporary Readings*. Edited by Eugene Rogers. Wiley-Blackwell, 2009.

Stowers, Stanley. "The Ontology of Religion." In *Introducing Religion: Essays in Honor of Jonathan Z. Smith*. Edited by Willi Braun and Russell T. McCutcheon. Equinox, 2008.

Stowers, Stanley. "Paul and Self-Mastery." In *Paul in the Greco-Roman World: A Handbook*. Vol. 2. Edited by J. Paul Sampley. Bloomsbury, 2016.

Stowers, Stanley. *A Rereading of Romans: Justice, Jews, and Gentiles*. Yale University Press, 1994.

Stowers, Stanley. "What Is 'Pauline Participation in Christ'?" In *Redefining First-Century Jewish and Christian Identities: Essays in Honor of Ed Parish Sanders.* Edited by Fabian E. Udoh et al. Christianity and Judaism in Antiquity 16. University of Notre Dame Press, 2008.

Stowers, Stanley. "Why 'Common Judaism' Does Not Look Like Mediterranean Religion." In *From Strength to Strength: Essays in Appreciation of Shaye J. D. Cohen.* Edited Michael L. Satlow. Brown Judaic Studies, 2018.

Stratton, Kimberly B., and Dayna S. Kalleres, eds. *Daughters of Hecate: Women and Magic in the Ancient World.* Oxford University Press, 2014.

Strauss Clay, Jenny. *Hesiod's Cosmos.* Cambridge University Press, 2003.

Strauss Clay, Jenny. *The Wrath of Athena: Gods and Men in the Odyssey.* Rowman & Littlefield, 1997.

Stroud, Ronald S. *The Sanctuary of Demeter and Kore: The Inscriptions.* Corinth XVIII.6. American School of Classical Studies at Corinth, 2013.

Struck, Peter T. *Divination and Human Nature: A Cognitive History of Intuition in Classical Antiquity.* Princeton University Press, 2016.

Stuckenbruck, Loren T. "'Angels' and 'God': Exploring the Limits of Early Jewish Monotheism." In *Early Jewish and Christian Monotheism.* Edited by Loren T. Stuckenbruck and Wendy E. S. North. JSNTSup 263. T&T Clark, 2005.

Swancutt, Diana. "'The Disease of Effemination': The Charge of Effeminacy and the Verdict of God (Romans 1:18–2:16)." In *New Testament Masculinities.* Edited by Stephen Moore and Janice Capel Anderson. SBL, 2003.

Tabor, James. "Paul's Notion of Many 'Sons of God' and Its Hellenistic Contexts." *Helios* 13 (1986): 87–97.

Tabor, James. *Things Unutterable: Paul's Ascent to Paradise in Its Greco-Roman, Judaic, and Early Christian Contexts.* Studies in Judaism. University Press of America, 1986.

Tanner, Kathryn. *Christ the Key.* Current Issues in Theology. Cambridge University Press, 2010.

Taylor, Tristan. "The Roman Military Oath: The *Sacramentum Militiae.*" In *Religion and Classical Warare: The Roman Empire.* Edited by Matthew Dillon and Christopher Matthew. Philadelphia: Penn & Sword, 2022.

Teixidor, Javier. *The Pagan God: Popular Religion in the Graeco-Roman Near East.* Princeton University, 1977.

Thiessen, Matthew. *Contesting Conversion: Genealogy, Circumcision, and Identity in Ancient Judaism and Christianity.* Oxford University Press, 2011.

Thiessen, Matthew. *A Jewish Paul: The Messiah's Herald to the Gentiles.* Baker Academic, 2023.

Thiessen, Matthew. *Paul and the Gentile Problem.* Oxford University Press, 2016.

Thiselton, Anthony C. *The First Epistle to the Corinthians: A Commentary on the Greek Text.* Eerdmans, 2000.

Thorndike, Lynn. *A History of Magic and Experimental Science: During the First Thirteen Centuries of Our Era.* Vol. 1. Columbia University Press, 1923.

Tilling, Chris. *Paul's Divine Christology*. WUNT 2/323. Mohr Siebeck, 2012.

Trebilco, Paul. *Outsider Designations and Boundary Construction in the New Testament: Early Christian Communities and the Formation of Group Identity*. Cambridge University Press, 2017.

Trebilco, Paul. *Self-Designations and Group Identity in the New Testament*. Cambridge University Press, 2012.

Tupamahu, Ekaputra. *Contesting Languages: Heteroglossia and the Politics of Languages in the Early Church*. Oxford University Press, 2023.

University of Hamburg. "Thesaurus Defixionum (TheDefix)." https://thedefix.uni-hamburg.de/.

Urbanová, Daniela. *Latin Curse Tablets of the Roman Empire*. Innsbrucker Beiträger zur Kulturwissenschaft, 2018.

Urbanová, Daniela. "Latin Curse Texts: Mediterranean Tradition and Local Diversity." *Acta Antiqua Academiae Scientiarum Hungaricae* 57 (2017): 57–82.

van der Horst, Pieter. "'The God Who Drowned the King of Egypt': A Short Note on an Exorcistic Formula." In *Wisdom of Egypt: Jewish, Early Christian, and Gnostic Essays in Honor of Gerard P. Luttikhuizen*. Edited by Anthony Hilhorst and George H. van Kooten. Brill, 2005.

van der Horst, Pieter. *Saxa iudaica loquuntur*. Leiden, 2014.

van der Kooij, Arie. "The Ending of the Song of Moses: On the Pre-Masoretic Version of Deut 32:43." In *Studies in Deuteronomy in Honor of C. J. Labuschagne on the Occasion of His 65th Birthday*. Edited by F. García Martínez, A. Hilhorst, J. T. A. G. M. van Ruiten, and A. S. van der Woude. VTSup 53. Brill, 1994.

van Kooten, George H. "Moses/Musaeus/Mochos and His God Yahweh, Iao, and Sabaoth, Seen from a Graeco-Roman Perspective." In *The Revelation of the Name YHWH to Moses*. Edited by George H. van Kooten. TBN 9. Brill, 2006.

van Kooten, George H. *Paul's Anthropology in Context: The Image of God, Assimilation to God, and Tripartite Man in Ancient Judaism*. WUNT 232. Mohr Siebeck, 2008.

van Kooten, George H. "St. Paul on Soul, Spirit, and the Inner Man." In *The Afterlife of the Platonic Soul: Reflections of Platonic Psychology in Monotheistic Religions*. Edited by Maha Elkaisy-Friemuth and John Dillon. Leiden & Boston: Brill, 2009.

Van Noorden, Helen. *Playing Hesiod: The "Myth of the Races" in Classical Antiquity*. Cambridge University Press, 2015.

Visintin, Monica. *La vergine e l'eroe: Temesa e la leggenda di Euthymos di Locri*. Edipuglia, 1992.

Versnel, H. S. "Beyond Cursing: The Appeal to Justice in Judicial Prayers." In *Magika Hiera: Ancient Greek Magic and Religion*. Edited by Christopher A. Faraone and Dirk Obbink. Oxford University Press, 1991.

Versnel, H. S. "The Poetics of the Magical Charm: An Essay in the Power of Words." In *Magic and Ritual in the Ancient World*. Edited by Paul Mirecki and Marvin Meyer. Brill, 2002.

Versnel, H. S. "Prayers for Justice, East and West: New Finds and Publications since 1990." In *Magical Practice in the Latin West: Papers from the International Conference Held at the University of Zaragoza, 30 Sept.—1 Oct. 2005*. Edited by Robert L. Gordon and F. Marco Simón. Brill, 2010.

Vogt, Kari. "'Becoming Male': A Gnostic and Early Christian Metaphor." In *The Image of God: Gender Models in Judaeo-Christian Tradition*. Edited by Kari Elisabeth Børresen. Fortress, 1995.

Wade, Nicholas, *The Faith Instinct: How Religion Evolved and Why It Endures*. Penguin, 2009.

Wallace-Hadrill, Andrew. "The Golden Age and Sin in Augustan Ideology." *Past and Present* 95 (1982): 19–36.

Wallace-Hadrill, Andrew. "*Mutatas Formas:* The Augustan Transformation of Roman Knowledge." In *The Cambridge Companion to the Age of Augustus*. Edited by Karl Galinsky. Cambridge University Press, 2005.

Wallace-Hadrill, Andrew. *Rome's Cultural Revolution*. Cambridge University Press, 2008.

Walsh, Matthew L. *Angels Associated with Israel in the Dead Sea Scrolls: Angelology and Sectarian Identity at Qumran*. WUNT 2/509. Mohr Siebeck, 2019.

Walsh, Robyn Faith. "*Argumentum ad lunam*: Pauline Discourse, 'Double Death,' and Competition on the Moon," *Harvard Theological Review*, 117, no. 4 (2024): 720–43.

Walsh, Robyn Faith. *Origins of Early Christian Literature: Contextualizing the New Testament within Greco-Roman Literary Culture*. Cambridge University Press, 2021.

Walters, Jonathan. "Invading the Roman Body: Manliness and Impenetrability in Roman Thought." In *Roman Sexualities*. Edited by Judith Hallett and Marilyn Skinner. Princeton University Press, 1997.

Wasserman, Emma. *Apocalypse as Holy War: Divine Politics and Polemics in the Letters of Paul*. AYBRL. Yale University Press, 2018.

Wasserman, Emma. *The Death of the Soul in Romans 7: Sin, Death, and the Law in Light of Hellenistic Moral Psychology*. WUNT 2/256. Mohr Siebeck, 2008.

Wasserman, Emma. "Gentile Gods at the Eschaton: A Reconsideration of Paul's 'Principalities and Powers' in 1 Corinthians 15." *Journal of Biblical Literature* 136 (2017): 727–46.

Wasserman, Emma. "'An Idol Is Nothing in the World' (1 Cor 8.4): The Metaphysical Contradictions of 1 Corinthians 8.1–11.1 in the Context of Jewish Idolatry Polemics." In *Portraits of Jesus: Studies in Christology*. Edited by Susan E. Myers. WUNT 2/321. Mohr Siebeck, 2012.

Wasserman, Emma. "Paul and Religion." In *The Oxford Handbook of Pauline Studies*. Oxford University Press, 2022.

Watson, Francis. "The Triune Divine Identity: Reflections on Pauline God-Language, in Disagreement with J. D. G. Dunn." *Journal for the Study of the New Testament* 80 (2000): 90–124.

Weiss, Johannes. *Der erste Korintherbrief.* 2nd ed. Göttingen: Vandenhoeck & Ruprecht, 1977.

Wendt, Heidi. *At the Temple Gates: The Religion of Freelance Experts in the Roman Empire.* Oxford University Press, 2016.

Wendt, Heidi. "*Ea Superstitione:* Christian Martyrdom and the Religion of Freelance Experts." *Journal of Roman Studies* 105 (2015): 183–202.

Wendt, Heidi. "Galatians 3:1 as an Allusion to Textual Prophecy." *Journal of Biblical Literature* 135 (2016): 369–89.

Wendt, Heidi. "Mythmaking and Exegesis." Iin *T&T Clark Handbook to the Historical Paul.* Edited by Ryan S. Schellenberg and Heidi Wendt. T&T Clark, 2022.

Whitmarsh, Tim. *The Second Sophistic.* Greece & Rome 35. Oxford University Press, 2005.

Wilburn, Andrew T. "Building Ritual Agency: Foundations, Floors, Doors, and Walls." In *Guide to the Study of Ancient Magic.* Edited by David Frankfurter. Brill, 2019.

Wilburn, Andrew T. *Materia Magica: The Archaeology of Magic in Roman Egypt, Cyprus, and Spain.* University of Michigan Press, 2012.

Williams, Craig. *Roman Homosexuality.* 2nd ed. Oxford University Press, 2010.

Williams, Margaret H. *Jews among Greeks and Romans: A Diasporan Sourcebook.* Johns Hopkins University Press, 1998.

Wolter, Michael. *The Letter to the Romans.* EKK. Vanderhoeck and Ruprecht, 2019.

Wright, Benjamin G., III. "Globalization and the 'Hellenization' of Jews in the Second Temple Period." *Journal for the Study of Judaism* 53 (2022): 1–20.

Yarbro Collins, Adela. "The Function of 'Excommunication' in Paul." *Harvard Theological Review* 72 (1980): 251–63.

Young, Stephen L. "Ethnic Ethics: Paul's Eschatological Myth of Jewish Sin." *New Testament Studies* 70 (2024): 235–48.

Young, Stephen L. "'Let's Take the Text Seriously': The Protectionist Doxa of Mainline New Testament Studies." *Method and Theory in the Study of Religion* 32 (2020): 328–63.

Young, Stephen L. "'Make Rome Great Again' Preceded 'Make America Great Again': The Ancient Romo-Nationalism of Biblical Writers." *Interpretation* 78 (2024): 321–34.

Young, Stephen L. *Paul among the Mythmakers: Sins, Gods, and Scriptures.* ESRA. Edinburgh University Press, 2025.

Young, Stephen L. "Paul the Mythmaker." PhD diss., Brown University, 2016.

Young, Stephen L. "Paul's Ethnic Discourse on 'Faith': Christ's Faithfulness and Gentile Access to the Judean God in Romans 3:21–5:1." *Harvard Theological Review* 108 (2015): 30–51.

Young, Stephen L. "So Radically Jewish That He's an Evangelical Christian: N. T. Wright's Judeophobic and Privileged Paul." *Interpretation* 76 (2022): 339–51.

Zamfir, Korinna. "Christians as Soldiers of Christ: Military Metaphors in Basil of Caesarea." *Sacra Scripta* 21 (2023): 181–97.

Zawadzki, Konrad. "Die Anfänge des, Anathema' in der Urkirche. Teil 1: Status quaestionis." *Vox Patrum* 28 (2008): 1323–43.

Zawadzki, Konrad. "Teil 2: Anhaltspunkte für das Anathem im Neuen Testament." *Vox Patrum* 29 (2009): 495–520.

Zimmermann, Christiane. "Anathema und Übergabe an den Satan als Aktualisierungen des göttlichen Gerichts in den paulinischen Gemeinden." *Novum Testamentum* 63 (2021): 360–89.

Zuckerman, Phil. *Faith No More: Why People Reject Religion.* Oxford University Press, 2012.

INDEX OF SUBJECTS

adoption, 85, 87n22, 97n16, 133n21
angels
  and possession, 130, 137
  angelic tongues, 176–77
  as divine beings, 68–70, 77n5, 80, 93, 96, 101, 103–4, 108, 167, 292, 293
  human judgment over, 118, 119, 195
  human transformation into, 102–3
  in martial imagery, 86–87, 225n20, 231
  opposite of demons, 89n27, 130
apocalyptic eschatology, 53, 79, 82–83, 85–87, 188, 232
associations, 56, 186n29, 186n31, 200–11, 213, 214, 215, 216–17
astrology, 42, 43, 44, 45n10, 181, 182

body, 84, 107 115, 119, 120, 183, 190, 194, 195–96, 278, 299
  and aesthetics/ideals, 236, 240–42, 244, 247, 249, 254, 255, 257
  of Christ 84, 109, 113–15, 136, 277
  and curses, 169, 171n32, 174
  and divination, 150–51, 153, 154, 155–56, 158
  fleshly/corruptible, 112, 115, 293
  heavenly, 72, 114–15, 136, 179–80, 187, 191n42, 193
  pneumatic, 53, 84, 87, 113–15, 116, 187, 188, 189–90, 193, 194, 195, 277, 293, 298n36
  and possession, 133n20
  terrestrial, 114–15, 179

Christianity
  and pagan/paganism, 17, 121n1, 199n1, 282
  and Paul's religion, 46, 51, 238, 282, 285, 295
circumcision, 22, 48–49, 51, 66, 78, 83, 85n16, 235–39, 253–58
  and ethnicity, 237–39, 254–56
  pagan critiques, 243–53
  and Pauline ideals, 254–55
cosmos/cosmology, 71, 86, 87, 115, 116, 152–54, 179–82, 187, 188, 193, 194, 295–96, 298–99
  cosmic forces, 80, 86–87, 117, 119
  populated by divine beings, 67, 70, 71, 77, 80, 108, 116–19, 131, 294, 295n28
  spirit of, 150, 155–56
curses, 131, 161–78
  and tablet (*defixio*), 163, 164, 167, 168, 171, 172n37, 174, 176, 177–78
  and "evil eye," 162

daimon/daimones
  and divination, 145, 150, 158–59, 185, 195
  as divine beings (lesser divinities), 9, 68, 71, 73, 76, 80, 89n27, 96, 108–9, 291, 292, 293–94
  as evil powers, 167
  and possession, 130–31, 132–33, 135, 144

death
  and astrology, 182
  as a force/power, 69, 70, 86, 117, 119, 193
  and the law, 191
  and mortality/immortality, 55, 93, 107, 112–13, 116, 120, 194–95, 196, 266, 300
  and the soul, 180–81, 183, 185, 188
  and union with Christ, 109
deification/divinization, 14, 100, 104, 107, 108, 109–10, 120, 279n44, 292
  and gender, 260, 274, 277
divination, 14, 18–19, 54, 84, 141–48, 158–59, 172, 184, 185, 193
  and daimons, 68n39, 137
  and possession 126, 129, 130, 137
  physics of, 149–58
dreams, 51–52, 142, 146, 152, 153, 203, 204, 208

Ephebes 36–37, 76
epiphany, 146–48, 199–200, 202–11, 216–17
  and Paul, 211–16
epispasm, 240–42, 248–49, 254
ethics, 84–85, 294–300
ethnicity
  and associations, 200, 208
  and ethics 85n16, 265–66
  ethnic reasoning, 15
  and foreskin/circumcision, 237–38, 248n25, 252, 256
  and religion, 9, 12, 16n63, 33, 35, 43, 49, 50, 52–53, 82, 276
exorcism, 50, 84, 85, 125–26, 132–34, 145

femininity, 260–65, 274, 278, 279
  and corruption 265–73
foreskin, 235–58
  and ethnicity 237–39, 254–56
  not "uncircumcised," 235–36, 255
  and pagan ideals, 239–53
  and Pauline ideals, 254–55
  restoration. See *epispasm*

gender, 128, 180, 196, 237n7, 259–60, 267–68, 270–73
  traits and ideals, 260–65, 270, 275, 277, 278, 279
God-fearers 35, 78, 82, 83
gymnasium 34, 36–37, 40, 76, 88, 247, 288

Hellenism, 17, 40, 286
  and Judaism, 5, 7–8, 10–11, 122, 149, 281, 282, 285

idol/idolatry/images, 9, 10, 18, 63, 67, 70, 72–73, 79, 80, 82, 85, 97n15, 105n41, 108–9, 265–66, 293, 294
inscriptions
  concerning associations, 201, 204–11, 215
  concerning synagogue s, 28
  of curses, 169
  as evidence of Jewish life, 31, 32, 33–34, 37, 78, 87, 88
  of military *fides*, 225

lineage (genealogy), 185, 193
  and ethnicity, 237
  and Abraham, 37, 39, 85, 167

magic, 14, 18, 19, 133, 162–68, 170–71, 178, 181
  magical voices 174, 175–78
  magicians, 45–46
masculinity, 259–65, 271–79
  and virtue, 262, 264, 269, 270
Mediterraneanism, 8, 9–10, 11, 287n16
monotheism, 4, 10, 76–77, 89, 94, 96, 108, 293

moon, 72, 87, 114, 115, 179–87, 188, 193, 194–96
mythmaking, 14, 50, 259, 266, 267, 273n29

paganism 5–6, 10–11, 17–19, 21, 83, 89, 121, 253, 285, 287n16
  Judaism within, 3–4, 236, 258
  Paul within, x–xii, 13, 17–19, 61n7, 145, 166, 181, 285–86
pax deorum (peace of the gods), 43, 70
physics, 72, 85, 116n19, 179, 180, 188, 193, 269n20, 295
  and divination, 149–58
Platonism, 53–55, 110, 113, 190, 192, 196, 295–296, 298, 301
  and anthropology, 112
  and cosmology, 179–82, 187, 193
  and divination, 150–51, 153–54, 157, 158
  and divine beings, 68, 93, 108, 120
  and moral psychology, 53, 269, 296
pneuma, 53, 55, 84–86, 98, 105, 111–12, 117n21, 150, 152–54, 156n30, 157, 180–81, 185n25, 187–88, 191, 192, 194, 274, 276, 277, 278–79, 292–93, 295, 297, 298–300
  and baptism, 50, 53, 54, 55, 276
  and bodies. See *body, pneumatic*
  as divine being(s), 49, 52, 64, 77n5, 80n10, 130, 131, 138
  material, 85, 113–16, 136–37, 190, 295n30
  and possession, 99, 127–29, 134–35, 136–37, 143, 125n7
polytheism, 14, 18–19, 60, 73, 94, 293
prophecy 49, 51, 84, 130, 135, 141–43, 149, 203n12

reciprocity, 35, 77n5, 84n15, 231, 249
religion
  category of, ix, 9–12, 15–16
resurrection, 70, 81, 85, 86n19, 97, 103, 109, 113, 114, 186, 193, 194, 277, 293
  of Jesus, 82, 86n19, 98

salvation, 107, 112, 144
  and martial imagery, 219, 231, 232
  as masculine transformation, 259, 260, 273–79
soul, 269, 277, 296, 299
  and cosmology, 180–81, 182–185, 187–90, 194–96
  and curses 163, 169, 173, 174, 175
  and divination, 151–59
  and martial imagery, 225, 226, 227
  and *pneuma*, 116n19, 190
stars, 72, 80, 87n23, 88, 103n37, 104, 114–16, 179–84, 186–90, 194–95, 196n54
stoicheia (cosmic elements) 71–72, 80, 108
Stoics/Stoicism 54, 55, 295–98, 299
  cosmology/cosmogony 67n33, 108, 180, 181, 187, 190, 295
  and divination, 143, 152–57
  and martial imagery, 227–28
  and moral psychology, 269
  and *pneuma*, 53, 113, 116n19, 136–37, 138, 190, 192, 295
synagogue, 26, 27, 28–29, 34, 36, 76, 77–78, 82, 83, 88

INDEX OF SCRIPTURE AND ANCIENT SOURCES

Old Testament

Genesis
- 1 — 150, 202
- 1:26, 28 — 119
- 1:26–27 — 112
- 2:7 — 155
- 3 — 112
- 3:15 — 103
- 5:1–3 — 110
- 6:2–4 — 96
- 10 — 69
- 11 — 69
- 14:22 — 62

Exodus
- 3 — 199
- 12:12 — 75, 95
- 15:11 — 75, 95, 100, 105
- 18:11 — 95
- 22:28 LXX — 76
- 34:29–35 — 191

Leviticus
- 18:8 — 170
- 20:11 — 170
- 20:13 — 272
- 21:5 — 254
- 26:41 — 235

Numbers
- 22–24 — 65

Deuteronomy
- 4:19 — 76
- 6:4 — 66, 97
- 10:17 — 95
- 18 — 145
- 18:9–14 — 142
- 18:10 — 142, 143
- 18:11 — 144
- 18:14–19 — 142
- 27:20 — 170
- 27:26 LXX — 162
- 32 — 68–69
- 32:8 — 76, 83, 95
- 32:8–9 — 62, 69
- 32:17 — 68
- 32:19 — 99
- 32:34 — 75
- 32:36 — 118
- 33:2–3 — 100–101

Judges
- 3:10, 30 — 118
- 4:4 — 118
- 10:2–3 — 118
- 12:7–9, 11, 13–14 — 118
- 15:20 — 118
- 16:31 — 118

Ruth
- 1:1 — 118

2 Chronicles
26:21 118

Job
1:6 96
1:6–9, 12 65
2:1 96
2:1–7 65
5:1 101
38:7 96

Psalms
2:7 97
2:10 118
8:6 103
9:9 118
15:3 101
29:1 [28:1 LXX] 96
31:23 100
33:10 101
66:5 [67:5 MT] 118
71:2, 4 118
82:1 75, 96
88:6, 8 101
89:7 [88:7 LXX] 96
95:3 62, 96
95:5 76
95:10, 13 118
96:4 96
96:13 118
97:7 87, 96
97:9 118
109:1 LXX 103
110:1 87, 119
113:4 62
134:14 118

Proverbs
21:22 220
29:14 118

Isaiah
2:2–4 82
19:20 118
25:6 82
43:6 99
51:22 118
61:3 191

Jeremiah
6:10 235
9:26 235
43:12 75
46:25 75
49:3 75

Ezekiel
44:7, 9 235

Daniel
10:10–21 69

Hosea
2:1 LXX 98
7:14 254
13:10 118

Micah
4:3 118
4:5 76, 83

Zechariah
8:23 82
12:8 103
14:5 101, 102

OT Apocrypha/Deuterocanonical Books

1 Maccabees
1:15 248
9:73 118
12.6–23, 14.16–23 39

2 Maccabees
3:3 23
4:12 248
4.7–15 37

3 Maccabees
3:2, 21 101

4 Ezra
7.28–29 86

Sirach
4:15 118
21:27 65
36:17 82
45:26 118

Tobit
3:2 118
13:11 82
14:5–6 82

Wisdom
1:1 118
3:8 118
5:5 100, 102
12:13, 18 118
13:1 265–66
13:1–14:31 266
13:10 79
18:9 100

OT Pseudepigrapha
1 Enoch
1:9 101
6 96
9–10 118
89:59 69
90:20–27 118
91.14 82

Jubilees
5 96

Letter of Aristeas
9–11, 295–321 36
250 260

Pseudo-Phocylides
190–91 272

Psalms of Solomon
17:29 118
17:31 82

Sibylline Oracles
3.110–55 40
3.110–58, 199–201 38
3.616 82
3.715–24 82
3.772 82
3.809–29 40

New Testament
Matthew
2:1–12 200

Mark
1:10 125
1:10–12 86
1:15 RSV 81
1:24 102
3:22 127
5 134
5:2 127
14:71 169

Luke
4:33, 41 144
4:34 102
8:28 144

9:39 144
22:30 118

John
1:32–33 86
6:69 102

Acts
2 125
3:14 102
4 170
7:51 235
9 199
9:3–19 212
10:9–15 204
10:22 78
13:35 102
16 146
16:16 143
16:16, 19 145
16:17 143–44
16:18 144, 145
17:18 96
17:22–24, 30–31 63
17:28 63
21:20–25 239

Romans
1:1 144
1:1–7 144
1:2 147
1:3 81
1:3, 4, 9 97
1:3–4 86, 97
1:4 86, 107, 110, 112
1:5 222, 224, 286
1:7 100
1:8 222
1:14 286
1:16 144
1:18 148
1:18–32 265
1:19–20 63
1:20 265
1:21–23 63
1:21a 265
1:21b–23 265
1:21b–27 270
1:23 269
1:24–32 265
1:26 269, 270, 271
1:26–27 271
1:27 269, 270, 271, 272
1:28 299
1:28–31 265
1:28–32 270
1:29 111
2:21–22 48
2:27 237
2:28–29 256
3–4 274
3:1–2 239
3:2 46, 147
3:6 118
3:29 62, 236, 286
3:30 66, 97, 237
4–5 62
4:9 237
4:9–10 255
4:11 256
4:13 103
5:10 97
5:17 118
5:19 222
6–8 274
6:4 109, 113
6:5 109
6:6 109
6:8 109
6:12, 16a, 16b, 16c 222

6:22 144
7 296
7:7–8:11 300
7:7–25 299
7:14 192
7:22 299
7:23 111
7:23, 25 299
7:24 119
8 69, 87
8:1–13 299
8:2 299
8:3, 29, 32 97
8:5 159
8:9 127, 128, 146
8:9–10 292–93
8:9–10a 299
8:10b 299
8:12–13 300
8:14 110, 112
8:14, 19 98
8:14–16 146
8:15 133, 144
8:15, 23 97
8:15–16 133
8:15–16, 19, 23 112
8:16–17 293
8:16–17, 21 99
8:17 109, 117, 120
8:17, 19, 29 120
8:17, 29–30 279
8:17–18, 21, 30 112
8:23 112
8:23b 112
8:26 55
8:27 100
8:29 84, 85, 99, 110, 118
8:29–30 115
8:32 118
8:38 80, 103, 117
8:38–39 69, 70
9–11 285
9:3 161
9:4 97
9:5 107, 292
9:5b 292
9:8 99
9:24 236, 286
9:26 98, 110
9:27 144
11:13 239
11:17 285
11:18 285
11:25 146
11:25–26 87
11:26 81
11:36 118
12:1 299
12:1–2 279
12:2 112, 159, 299
12:13 100
12:14–21 161
13:8–10 85
15:4 147
15:6 61
15:12 81
15:18 222
15:19 148
15:25, 26, 31 100
16:2, 15 100
16:19 222
16:19, 26 222
16:20 65, 79, 103, 119
16:20, 26 85
16:22 161
16:25–26 51
16:26 222

1 Corinthians
1–3 155
1:1 96
1:2 100

1:9 97
1:11–17 46
1:18 149
1:18–3:4 145, 149
1:22 149
2:4 148
2:6 108, 149
2:6–10 146
2:7–16 279
2:8 80, 113
2:9 155
2:10 155
2:10–13 149–50
2:11 156
2:11–12 156
2:12 292
2:13–15 157
2:14 155–56
2:16 112, 159
3:1–4 157
3:4 117
3:6 46
3:21 116, 117
3:22 117
4:8 117
4:9 118
5 171
5:1–5 170, 172
5:3 172
5:4a 170
5:5 65, 79, 161, 175
5:5a 170
5:9–10 265
6:1, 2 100
6:2 118
6:2–3 104, 118, 279
6:3 104, 108
6:9–10 273
6:9–11 265, 274
6:11 274
6:15 109
6:15–17 84
6:17 109
7 196
7:5 65
7:7 79
7:12 146
7:14 100
7:18 248, 254
7:19 85
7:40 146
8 67, 71
8–10 61
8:4 97, 294
8:4–6 66, 79, 293
8:5 80, 97, 108
8:6 66, 80, 97, 108, 118
9:1 84
9:11–18 48
10 62
10:1–4 50
10:2–4 216
10:11 85, 117
10:19–21 67
10:19–22 293
10:20 80, 108
10:20–21 80, 130–31
10:20–22 97
11:2–16 263, 271
11:12 118
11:23 146
11:23–26 50
11:25, 26 55
11:27–32 148
11:28 55
11:30 55
12 131
12–14 123, 130, 133
12:2 239, 265
12:3 131, 156, 161

12:4–11 53, 129
12:4–13 156
12:8 146
12:10 131, 176
12:12–13 277
12:12–14, 27 84
12:12–30 277
12:25 109
13:1 176
14 157
14:6–19 129
14:14 146
14:14–15 55
14:23 135–36
14:26 176
14:33 100
14:33b–35 176
15 71, 215
15:3 212, 215
15:3–7 212, 215
15:5–8 84
15:8 213
15:12–21 86
15:12–28, 35–55 298
15:20 109
15:24 70, 87, 119, 195
15:24–26 86
15:25 87, 195
15:25–27 117
15:26 119
15:27 118, 119
15:27–28 118
15:30, 24 195
15:32 47
15:35 113
15:35–38 190
15:35–49 194
15:35–53 113
15:39 115
15:39–49 115
15:39–52 113–14
15:39–53 113
15:40 115, 193
15:40–41 115
15:41 115
15:42–43 114
15:42–47 277
15:44 84, 189
15:44, 51 298
15:44–46 156
15:45 112, 113, 114, 115, 155
15:47 84, 114, 115
15:47–49 194
15:48–49 113, 114, 116
15:49 113, 115–16, 277
15:50 84, 114
15:50–52 116
15:50–57 53
15:50–58 194
15:51 146
15:51–52 86
15:53–56 119
15:57 193
16:1, 15 100
16:13 275, 276
16:21–22 161–62
16:22 176

2 Corinthians
1:1 100
1:5 109
1:8–9 47
1:19 97
1:22 156
2:11 65, 79
3:1–18 191
3:2 191
3:3 191
3:7 191
3:11 192
3:12–18 46

3:13 191
3:14 191
3:15 51, 191
3:17 112, 113, 192
3:18 86, 109, 110, 113, 116, 119, 192, 195
4:1–5:10 179
4:4 66, 79, 81, 108, 110, 113, 119, 292
4:6 113
4:7–5:10 298
4:10 109
4:13 146
4:16 110–11
4:17 115
4:18 191
5:1–5 190–91
5:7 85
5:10 118
6:7 219
6:15 65
6:18 99
7:15 222
8:4 100
8:13–14 277
9:1, 12 100
10:3–6 219
10:5, 6 222
11–12 215
11:1–15 214
11:2 214
11:7–9 48
11:8 48
11:14 65, 79
11:16–33 214
11:23–25 47
11:24–29 83
11:32–33 47
12 179, 214
12:1 147, 213
12:1–4 116
12:1–10 298
12:1–14 212
12:7 65, 79
12:8 147
12:9 147
12:10 83
12:11–21 214
12:12 148
13:5 55
13:12 100
15 179

Galatians
1:1 61
1:8–9 162
1:10 144
1:11–12 52, 147
1:12 212
1:13–14 51
1:13–17 213
1:15 166, 213
1:15–16 212
1:16 84, 97, 213
1:17–22 213
2:2, 7 239
2:2–5 46
2:3 257
2:7 237, 257
2:9 215
2:14–15 236, 286
2:15 237, 266
2:19 109
2:19–20 109
2:20 97, 98, 127
3 62, 276
3–4 274
3:1 147, 162
3:5 148
3:8 147
3:10–14 162
3:14, 24–26 276

3:16 54
3:16, 29 85
3:19 108
3:20 66
3:26 98, 110, 120
3:27 276
3:27–29 277
3:28 276, 277, 278
4–5 276
4:1–11 71
4:3–9 81
4:4 97, 98, 107
4:5 97
4:6 98, 105, 108, 110, 133, 144, 146, 156
4:8–9 71, 99, 265
4:9 108
4:19 109
4:24 54
5:2, 12 239
5:13–26 299, 300
5:14 85
5:16–26 111, 265
5:18–21 278–79
5:22 112, 221
5:22–23 111, 274, 279, 299
5:23 300
5:24 111, 300
6:12 257
6:16 85

Ephesians
1:1, 15, 18 100
1:5 97
2:6 109
2:19 100
3:6 109
3:8, 18 100
3:10 87
4:12 100
4:13 97
4:17–19 265
4:27 65
5:3 100
6:11 65
6:12 80
6:12–13 87
6:18 100

Philippians
1:1 100, 144
1:12–13 47
1:14 47
1:16b 47
2 71, 87, 98
2:3 48
2:6 292
2:6–7 84
2:6–9 107
2:9–11 71
2:10 86, 87
2:10–11 80, 117, 119
2:15 99, 116, 298
3:2 254
3:3 255, 256
3:5 254
3:10 109
3:12–14 300
3:15–16 300
3:19 66, 189
3:19–21 179, 189
3:20 116, 189
3:20–21 87
3:21 113, 115, 116, 118, 277, 278
4:8 112
4:15–19 48
4:22 100

Colossians
1:2, 4, 12, 26 100
1:13 97
1:15 113
1:16 108
1:24 109
2:12 109
2:16 179
2:20 109
3:1 109

1 Thessalonians
1:3 230
1:4 230
1:5 148
1:6 230
1:8 230
1:9 82, 144, 239
1:9–10 72, 265, 279
1:10 97
2:1–2 230
2:2, 15 47
2:8 230
2:8, 11 230
2:13 215
2:14 230
2:18 65, 79
3:2 230
3:5 79, 231
3:6 231
3:7–10 231
3:10 55
3:13 102
4–5 193, 231–32
4:3–5 265, 274
4:5 63
4:13 188
4:13–5:11 194
4:13–18 188, 298
4:15–17 146
4:16 86, 87, 188
4:17 116, 188, 298
5:2 188
5:3 188
5:8 219, 231
5:24 231
5:25 55

2 Thessalonians
1:10 100
2:9 65
2:14 109

1 Timothy
1:20 65
2:11–15 264
3:6, 11 65
5:10 100
5:15 65

2 Timothy
2:3 233
2:11 109
2:12 109
2:26 65
3:3 65

Titus
2:3 65

Philemon
5, 7 100
21 222

Hebrews
7:11–17 86

Jude
14 102

Revelation
1:18 70
6:8 70
20:13 70

Testaments of the Twelve Patriarchs
Testament of Solomon
5:3 96

Dead Sea Scrolls
1QH[2] XI
19–23 177
1 QS IX, 11 86
4QDeut 95

Jewish Sources
Josephus
Antiquities of the Jews
18.261–309 88
Against Apion
2.23–29 30
2.39 30
2.199 272
Jewish Antiquities
1.239–41 37
8.44–49 50
12.119 30
12.138–46 23
14.117 29
14.223–28, 234, 240 31
14.235, 260–61 29
19:281 30
24.235, 14.259 30
Jewish War
3.352 52
3.353–54 52
6.47 189
Judean Antiquities
13.189 222–23
Life
9–11 52
113 257

Philo of Alexandria
On Abraham
133–36 272
205–6 183
Against Flaccus
53 30
On the Creation of the Universe
7.27 80
On the Decalogue
137 238
On Dreams
2.90 238
On the Embassy to Gaius
150, 183, 194 30
150, 193–94, 349, 363, 371 30
158 31
162, 188 88
On the Giants
31.266–267 196
Special Laws
1.200–201 261
1.325 271–72
2.42–45 181
2.109 238
3.37 272
3.37–38 272
3.39 272
3.40 273

Rabbinic Sources
b. Avodah Zarah
43a 65
b. Sanh
93b 86
m. Avodah Zara
3:4 89

NT Apocrypha and Pseudepigrapha
Gospel of Thomas
22 278
114 278
Artifacts, Inscriptions, Papyri
IG X/2.1 255 206, 209, 216

SEG
15, 637 207, 210
SIG[2] 663 209–10
SIG[3] 985 205, 208–9, 210–11

Early Christian Sources
Aelian
Historical Miscellany
12.35 51

Athanasius
Letter to Serapion
2.4.4 105
Life of Anthony
78 17

Augustine
City of God
7.6 183
9.23 93
On the Trinity
4.3 180

Clement of Alexandria
Christ the Educator
3.2.13 270
3.3.15 270
3.3.19 261–62

Eusebius
Church History
9.20.2–4 37
9.27.3–4 38
Preparation for the Gospel
9.17 65
9.27 65

John Chrysostom
Homilies on the Acts of the Apostles
38 164

Justin Martyr
1 Apology
5.1–2 68

Origen of Alexandria
Against Celsus
7.3 51
Commentary on John
2.3 105
2.21.138 117
Contra Celsum
4.33–34 167
7.9 177
First Principles
1.1.2 113
Homilies on Exodus
6.5 105
Homilies on Genesis
3.4 256
3.6 256

Tertullian
On Idolatry
19.2 225
On Modesty
13–14 171
The Prescriptions against the Heretics
7 283

Greco-Roman Sources
Aratus
Phaenomena
5 63

Aristophanes
Acharnians
155–74 247
Clouds
537–39 247
Wealth
265–267 246–47

Aristotle
The Generation of Animals
737a 25–30 196
History of Animals
608a–b 261
Nicomachean Ethics
7.1–10 296
1151b33–1152a3 300
1444b4 and 17 297
Soul
1.411a8 108

Cicero
Divination
1.1 141
1.5 143
1.12 142
1.38, 80, 114 153
1.64 152
1.66 153
1.79 153
1.110 152–53
1.110–13 153
1.115 155
1.127 157
Pro Cluentio
5.14–6.15 170
On the Republic
6.16 184
Tusculan Disputations
1.43 188
1.44 189
2.18.43 275–76
4.9.22 269, 297

Dio Cassius
Roman History
57.18.4–5 148
62.14.3 153
62.18.3–5 148

Dio Chrysostom
Orations
4.101–15 270

Diodorus Siculus
Bibliotheca historica
2.23.1 270
2.23.2 270
2.23.4 270
2.24.4 270
Library of History
3.32.4 253
34/35.1–2 22

Diogenes Laertius
Lives of Eminent Philosophers
6.16 226
7.156 190
7.157 152

Epictetus
Discourses
1.14 228
2.16.45–46 274
4.1.127 48

Herodotus
Histories
1.77 230
2.37 252

Hesiod
Theogony
561–616 267
570 267
590–93 267
Works and Days
77–80 267
82 267
90–92 267
106–201 266
109–26 266

121–22 267
127–29 266
131–32 267
134–37 267
178–79 267

Homer
Iliad
1.70 142–43
5.342 115

Horace
Odes
3.5 269
3.5.29–30 269
3.6 268–69, 270
3.6.1–3, 7–8 268
3.6.5 268
3.6.7–16 268
3.6.17–20 268
3.6.19–32 268
3.6.29–30 268
3.6.33–40 269
3.6.46–48 269
Satires
1.9.69–70 251

Iamblichus
Life of Pythagoras
6.30 185

Julian
Suda
nos. 433–34 55

Juvenal
Satires
6.542–47 50
14.96–105 78
14.99 252
14.104 252
14.104–105 22

Lucian
Alexander the False Prophet
8–17 186
26–40, esp. 35 186
The Lover of Lies
16 133
Passing of Peregrinus
12.1–4 45
12.5–13.7 45
13.6–7 45

Martial
Epigrams
7.30 251
7.35 247
7.55 246, 249
7.82 248
11.94 246, 249

Maximus of Tyre
Philosophical Orations
11.5 95, 97

Pausanias
Description of Greece
2.4.7 172
10.12.9 51

Philostratus
Life of Apollonius of Tyana
4.20 132

Plato
Apology
28d–29a 226–27
28e 226
29a 226
Laws
781a–c 260
899b 108
Phaedrus
244b–d 142, 143

244c–d 143
246A–E 296
265b 151
Republic
462a9–e3 196
462b4–d3 196
462b8–c5 196
Symposium
202e–203a 68
Theaetetus
176a–b 110
176B 104
Timaeus
40a 93
70d–72b 150
71d 151
71e 151
71e–72b 142
90a 150

Pliny the Elder
Letters
10,96.1–2, 9 44
10.97.1 44
Natural History
2, 6 184
18.5, 57, 69 184
18.211 43
37, 59 184

Plutarch
Coriolanus
1.4 276
On the Decline of Oracles
432c 154, 155
432d 154
432d–e 154
On the Face of the Moon
927C 194
928B 194
943A 194
943B 194
943B–C 195
943C 195
943D 185, 194, 195
944D 185
945A 195
945B 195
Life of Caesar
59.5 43
Moralia
41F 173
149a 103
165F–166A 177
782e 103
On Moral Virtue
441C–D 297
Roman Questions
282A 185
Socrates' Sign
591d–e 158
592c 158
Tiberius and Gracchus
9 230
Titus Flaminius
5.3 230

Polybius
Histories
5.2.10 223

Seneca
On Benefits
4.2.4 261
Epistles
95.21 261, 275
96.5 227
104.34 261
113 227

Strabo
Geography
9.3.5 153
16.2.35 67

16.2.37 252
16.4.5 252
16.4.9 252
16.4.17 253

Suetonius
Life of Augustus
31.1 163
The Lives of the Caesars
[Vespasian]
5.5–7 203–4

Tacitus
Annals
2.69 163
Germania
43.4 59
Histories
5.5 249
5.5.1–2 22

Thucydides
History of the Peloponnesian War
2.8.3 148
2.21.3 148
2.54.2 148
5.26.3–4 148

Valerius Maximus
Memorable Deeds and Sayings
6.1.1 275

INDEX OF AUTHORS

Ademollo, Francesco, 152
Aelian, 51
Aeschines, 230
Aeschylus, 38, 134
Ahearne-Kroll, Stephen, 64
Ahuvia, Mika, 77
Aitken, James K., 6, 7
Alexander, Philip, 9
Algra, Keimpe, 137
Allison, Dale, 81
Allo, P. E.-B., 170, 172
Althusser, Louis, 229
Ando, Clifford, 59, 60
Antisthenes, 226
Apollonios, 215
Aratus, 63
Aristobulus, 39
Aristophanes, 246–47
Aristotle, 108, 181–82, 196, 261, 296, 297, 300
Arnal, William E., 122
Artapanus, 37, 39
Arzt-Grabner, Peter, 171
Asad, Talal, 162
Ascough, Richard S., 201
Ashton, John, 127, 136
Athanasius, 17, 105
Atkins, Christopher, 168
Atkinson, Kenneth, 24
Au, Wing Yi, 61
Audollent, Auguste, 168
Augustine, 93, 179, 183, 188
Babcock, William, 93
Bailliot, Magali, 163
Barclay, John M. G., 7, 23, 27, 76
Bartlett, John R., 27
Barton, Carlin A., 11
Bauckham, Richard, 98
Bazzana, Giovanni, x, xi, 14, 84, 86, 99, 121–38, 146, 282, 283, 286, 287, 294, 300
Beentjes, Pancratius C., 101
Belayche, Nicole, 80
Bell, Brigidda, 48
Berger, David, 65
Berthelot, Katell, 168–69
Betz, Hans Dieter, 65
Beyer, Barbara, 99
Binder, Donald D., 28
Blackwell, Ben C., 100, 120
Blau, Ludwig, 69
Bloch, René, 76
Blum, Jason N., 207
Boas, George, 266
Boccaccini, Gabriele, x, 6
Boddy, Janice P., 126
Bohak, Gideon, 169
Bonner, Campbell, 165
Bookidis, Nancy, 172, 173
Bowie, David, 194
Boyarin, Daniel, 11
Boys-Stone, G. R., 54
Brakke, David, 89

Braudel, Fernand, 8
Braun, Willi, 14, 275
Bremmer, Jan N., 168
Brooten, Bernadette, 271
Brubaker, Rogers, 13, 229
Bruyn, Theodore S. De, 165
Bucur, Bogdan, 130
Buell, Denise Kimber, 15, 124
Bunta, Silviu, 96
Burrus, Virginia, 264
Byrne, Brendan, 98

Cameron, Alan, 17, 18
Cameron, Ron, 11
Capes, David, 98
Carbone, Lucia, 225
Cassius Dio, 230
Celsus, 241, 248
Chantziantoniou, Alexander, ix–xiii, xi, 3–19, 67, 72, 282, 283, 284, 285–86, 287, 288, 290
Cheyne, T. K., 66
Cicero, 80, 141, 142, 143, 152–53, 155, 157, 170, 184, 188, 190, 269, 275–76, 297
Clark, Ernest P., 72
Clay, Jenny Strauss, 267
Clement of Alexandria, 261–62, 270
Cleodemus Malchus, 37
Cobb, L. Stephanie, 264, 275
Cohen, Adam, 221
Cohen, Shaye J. D., 237
Cole, Spencer, 104
Collar, Anna, 42
Collins, Adela Yarbro, 171
Collins, John J., 7, 10
Collman, Ryan D., xiii, 66, 235–58, 282, 286
Concannon, Cavan, 8, 12, 15
Conway, Colleen, 276, 277
Conzelmann, Hans, 54, 170, 172
Cornell, Collin, 60
Cowey, James M. S., 29
Cox Miller, Patricia, 174, 176, 177
Crafer, Thomas Wilfrid, 93
Craffert, Pieter, 203
Cranfield, C. E. B., 120
Crook, Zeba, 221, 222

Dante, 188
Davies, John A., 101
Deissmann, Adolf, 147, 171
Denzey, Nicola Frances, 103
Dijkstra, Jitse H. F., 165
Dillon, John, 192
Dimant, Devorah, 103
Dingeldein, Laura B., 5, 259
Dio Cassius, 148, 153
Dio Chrysostom, 270
Diodorus Siculus, 22, 230, 252, 253, 270
Diogenes Laertius, 152, 190, 226
Dionysios, 215
Dionysus, 135
Discorides, 241
Donaldson, Terence L., 82
Droysen, Gustav, 283
Dunn, James D. G., 118
Dunning, Benjamin, 271, 272
Dzwiza, Kirsten, 176

Edmonds, Radcliffe G., III, 164
Edwards, Catherine, 268, 273
Emmanuel, Sarah, 266, 276–77
Engberg-Pedersen, Troels, xiii, 7, 87, 111, 115, 136, 155, 187, 192, 269, 274, 277, 281–301
Epictetus, 48, 228, 274
Erinyes of Clytemnestra, 134
Ernst, Michael, 171
Eudorus, 295
Eusebius, 37, 38, 65
Evagrius of Antioch, 17

Eyl, Jennifer, x, xi, xiii, 4, 14, 15, 44, 49, 84, 122, 145, 162, 172, 187, 192, 219–33, 259, 284, 291, 294
Ezekiel, 38

Faraone, Christopher A., 165, 185
Fee, Gordon, 102, 171
Feldman, Louis, 22, 36
Ferguson, Everett, 256
Finlan, Stephen, 100
Fitzgerald, John T., 47, 264
Fitzmyer, Joseph A., 65
Flower, Michael Attyah, 142, 157
Forbes, Christopher, 141
Fotopoulos, John, 170, 171, 176
Frankfurter, David, 163, 164, 168
Fredriksen, Paula, ix–xiii, xi, xii, 3–4, 5–6, 15, 49, 62, 70, 75–89, 96, 98, 108, 122, 202, 221, 237, 238, 259, 282, 287, 288, 289, 291, 292, 293–94, 300

Gaca, Kathy L., 196
Gager, John G., 49, 168, 169
Galen, 155, 241–42
Gambetti, Sandra, 26
Gill, Christopher, 190
Ginzberg, Louis, 64
Gleason, Maud, 275
Glover, Daniel B., 104
Goodenough, Erwin, 6, 11
Goodman, Martin, 16, 83
Goodman, Mertin, 25
Gordon, Richard, 165, 175, 176, 178
Gorman, Michael, 100
Grainger, John D., 23
Gross, Simcha, 165
Gruen, Erich S., xii, 7, 21–40, 282, 286, 288
Gupta, Nijay, 220

Hadrian, 252
Halbwachs, Maurice, 211
Hanson, J. S., 203
Harker, Christina, 72
Harland, Philip A., 201, 205, 207, 238
Harrill, J. Albert, 79, 80
Harris, W. V., 8
Harrison, Juliette, 208
Hart, Patrick, 3
Hay, David H., 117
Hayman, Peter, 94
Hays, Richard B., 62
Head, Thomas, 225
Heiser, Michael S., 94
Hengel, Martin, 6, 7, 11, 283
Henning, Meghan, 262, 264
Heraclitus, 183
Herodian, 223
Herodotus, 230, 252
Heschel, Abraham J., 141
Hesiod, 38, 266–67
Hezser, Catherine, 184
Hicks-Keeton, Jill, 98
Hippolytus, 184
Hodge, Caroline Johnson, 15, 49, 98, 276
Hodges, Frederick M., 240, 248
Hoke, Jimmy, 271
Holladay, Carl R., 38, 39
Holmes, Brooke, 263, 265
Hölscher, Michael, 171, 172
Homer, 40, 115, 142
Hooker, Morna D., 99
Horace, 251, 268–69, 270
Horbury, William, 32
Horden, Peregrine, 8
Horky, Phillip Sidney, 155
Hoskins, Paul M., 118
Howard, Bart, 181
Howley, Joseph A., 180
Huber, Konrad, 171
Huber, Lynn, 264
Hurtado, Larry W., 88, 98

Iamblichus, 185
Iles Johnston, Sarah, 134, 142, 147
Irshai, Oded, 89
Isaac, Benjamin, 22, 89, 238
Ivarson, Frederik, 265, 273
Ivčević, Sanja, 225

Janssen, David, 232
Jastrow, Morris, 66
Jipp, Joshua W., 97
John Chrysostom, 164
Johnson-DeBaufre, Melanie, 12
Johnson, Luke Timothy, 5
Johnson, Paul Christopher, 123
Johnston, Sarah Iles, 134, 142, 147
Jones, Brice C., 165
Josephus, 23, 29, 30, 31, 37, 38, 50, 51–52, 88, 189, 222–23, 230, 257, 272
Julian, 55
Justin Martyr, 68
Juvenal, 50, 78, 252

Kahlos, Maijastina, 17
Kalleres, Dayna S., 164
Kasher, Aryeh, 23
Keener, Craig S., 141, 145
Kelhoffer, James A., 214
Kent, Benedict H. M., 170
Kim, Seon Yong, 171
King, Justin D., 102
Kloppenborg, John S., 16, 172, 186, 201
Knust, Jennifer, 164, 264, 265, 270, 271
Kohler, Kaufmann, 64, 69
Kotansky, Roy, 77, 132
Kotrosits, Maia, 238, 263
Kraemer, Ross, 271, 275
Krentz, Edgar, 220

Lactantius, 163
Lambek, Michael, 126
Lamont, Jessica L., 164, 174
Larsson, Stefan, 4
Last, Richard, 13, 201
Lau, Markus, 171, 172
Le Bohec, Yann, 33
Lee, Max J., 104
Lee, Michelle V., 156
Leibniz, Gottfried Wilhelm, 124
Lennon, John, 186
Leon, Harry J., 28
Levine, Lee I., 7, 27, 28
Levinskaya, Irina, 78
Lieu, Judith M., 61
Lipsett, Diane, 275
Litwa, M. David, xi, xii, 14, 15, 53, 81, 100, 104, 107–20, 182, 184, 189, 190, 274, 279, 291, 294, 295–96
Locke, John, 124, 137
Lovejoy, Arthur, 266
Lucian, 45, 133, 186, 195–96
Luckritz Marquis, Timothy, 42, 49
Lum, Kathryn Gin, 18
Luther, Susanne, 168, 171–72

Macarius Magnes, 93
MacDonald, Nathan, 96
Mach, Michael, 94
MacRae, Duncan, 43
Macrobius, 183
Majercik, Ruth Dorothy, 54
Makin, Irad, 8
Malherbe, Abraham J., 187, 220, 226, 282
Manekin-Bamberger, Avigail, 165, 178
Marchal, Joseph, 271, 275, 278
Marcion of Sinope, 61
Maresch, Klaus, 29
Marquis, Timothy Luckritz, 42, 49
Marshak, Adam Kolman, 25
Martial, 246, 247, 248, 249, 251
Martin, Dale, 273, 283

Marx-Wolf, Heidi, 130
Mason, Steve, 26, 46
Masuzawa, Tomoko, 18
Maximus of Tyre, 94–95, 97
Mazurek, Lindsay A., 8
McMurray, Patrick, 15
McNiven, Timothy, 243–44
Meyers, Carol L., 102
Meyers, Eric M., 102
Mheallaigh, Karen ní, 179, 180, 182, 183, 184, 186, 193
Miller, Merril P., 11
Miller, Patricia Cox, 174, 176, 177
Minets, Yuliya, 177
Modrzejewski, Joseph Mélèze, 23
More, Henry, 94
Morgan, Theresa, 221, 225
Moses, Robert Ewuise, 171
Moses, Robert Ewusie, 69
Moslener, Sara, 268
Moss, Candida, 161
Most, Glenn, 266
Mount, Christopher, 14, 127
Mouritsen, Henrik, 161
Mussies, Gerard, 65
Myers, Jason, 222

Nanos, Mark, ix, 4, 6, 51
Nasrallah, Laura Salah, xi, xii, 12, 14, 161–78, 286, 289, 294
Neutel, Karin B., 235, 236, 255
Newman, Carey C., 115
Niehoff, Maren R., 52
Nielsen, Inge, 201
Noble, Thomas, 225
Nongbri, Brent, 11, 162
Noreña, Carlos, 225
Novenson, Matthew, x, xii, 3, 4, 13, 14, 46, 59–73, 86, 87, 236, 239, 256, 282, 287, 291, 293
Noy, David, 32

O'Meara, Dominic J., 104
Ocellus, 179
Ogden, Daniel, 144
Økland, Jorunn, 172
Olender, Maurice, 177
Oliver, Isaac W., x
Olley, John W., 99
Ono, Yoko, 186
Origen of Alexandria, 51, 105, 113, 117, 167, 177, 256
Orlin, Eric M., 43

Parker, Robert, 60, 64, 73
Parks, Sara, 248, 263
Parmenides, 183
Patel, Shaily Shashikant, 14
Pausanias, 51, 172
Pearson, Birger A., 177
Peppard, Michael, 99, 247
Persius, 251
Peters, Janelle, 177
Petrey, Taylor, 196
Petridou, Georgia, 146
Philo of Alexandria, 4, 30, 31, 37, 52, 80, 88, 150, 181, 183, 188, 196, 230, 238, 261, 271–72, 273, 289, 295, 296, 298–99
Philostratus, 132
Plato, 39, 54, 55, 68, 93, 104, 108, 110, 112, 120, 142, 143, 150, 151, 153, 154, 158, 177, 181–82, 196, 226, 260, 295, 296
Pliny the Elder, 43, 44, 182, 184
Plummer, Alfred, 117
Plutarch, 43, 103, 144, 154, 155, 156, 158, 173, 177, 179, 183, 185, 188, 193, 194, 195, 230, 276, 295, 296–97
Polybius, 223, 230
Porten, Bezalel, 28
Posidonius, 152, 153–54, 155, 156, 230, 295

Preller, L., 64
Punt, Jeremey, 220
Purcell, Nicholas, 8
Pythagoras, 39

Rainey, Brian, 266
Rajak, Tessa, 77
Reed, Annette Yoshiko, 5, 96
Regev, Eyal, 24
Renberg, Gil H., 147
Reno, Joshua, 270
Richlin, Amy, 273
Ripat, Pauline, 44
Rives, James, 68, 163
Roberts, Erin, 229
Robertson, Archibald, 117
Rocca, Samuele, 25
Roediger, Henry L., 211
Rogers, Guy Maclean, 26
Rollens, Sarah E., xii, 146, 199–217, 286, 291
Römer, Thomas, 62
Rothschild, Clare K., 63
Roubekas, Nickolas P., 72
Rozin, Paul, 221
Runesson, Anders, x, 4
Runia, David T., 150
Rüpke, Jörg, 43
Rutgers, Leonard V., 28

Salinero, Raúl González, 76
Sanders, E. P., 273
Sandmel, Samuel, 291
Sandnes, Karl Olav, 111, 112
Sanfridson, Martin, 97
Sanzo, Joseph E., 164, 165, 167
Sappho, 184
Satlow, Michael L., 10, 83
Schäfer, Peter, 22, 96, 177
Schalit, Abraham, 25
Schellenberg, Ryan S., 44, 48, 51
Schnelle, Udo, 110
Schrage, Wolfgang, 97
Schumacher, Thomas, 161
Schürer, Emil, 78
Schwartz, Joshua, 4
Schwartz, Seth, 7, 9–10
Schweitzer, Albert, 81, 99, 125
Scott, M., 100
Scully, Stephen, 266
Segal, Alan, 189
Segovia, Carlos A., x, 6
Sellew, Melissa Harl, 278
Seneca, 227, 261, 275
Senft, Christophe, 172
Sharp, Matthew, x, xii, 52, 67, 141–59, 282, 287, 294, 295
Sheinfeld, Shayna, 263
Shumate, Nancy, 268
Siculus, Diodorus, 22
Siegel, Joel, 221
Smith, David R., 171, 178
Smith, Jonathan Z., 5, 11, 13, 15, 16, 18, 19, 284
Smith, Mark S., 62, 96
Smith, Morton, 14
Socrates, 39
Soon, Isaac, 240–41, 249, 254
Soranus, 240
South, James, 171
Spinoza, Baruch, 137
Sprinkle, Preston, 115
Ste Croix, G. E. M. de, 83
Stendahl, Krister, 235
Stern, Menahem, 63
Stowers, Stanley K., ix, x, 11, 12, 14, 54, 77, 98, 111, 136, 155, 181, 187, 189–90, 195, 233, 259, 265, 266, 269, 274, 277, 279, 295, 296, 298
Strabo, 29, 67, 73, 153, 252, 253
Stratton, Kimberly B., 164
Stroud, Ronald S., 172, 173, 174, 175, 176
Struck, Peter T., 142, 151, 153, 154
Stuckenbruck, Loren T., 103

Suetonius, 163, 203–4
Swancutt, Diana, 272

Tabor, James, 100, 119
Tacitus, 59, 73, 163, 249
Tanner, Kathryn, 105
Taylor, Charles, 124
Taylor, Tristan, 224
Teixidor, Javier, 94
Tertullian, 171, 225, 283
Thales, 108
Theodotus, 38
Thieselton, Anthony C., 170
Thiessen, Matthew, x, 3, 84, 85, 87, 93–105, 156, 237, 239, 259, 265, 274, 287, 291, 292, 294, 300
Thiselton, Anthony C., 172
Thorndike, Lynn, 182, 184
Thucydides, 148
Tilling, Chris, 98
Tovra, Sofia Torallas, 165
Trebilco, Paul, 33, 233
Tupamahu, Ekaputra, 123

Urbanová, Daniela, 164, 165

Valentinus, 54
Valerius Maximus, 275
van der Horst, Pieter Willem, 77, 178
van der Kooij, Arie, 95
van Kooten, George H., 63, 104, 110
Van Noorden, Helen, 266
Varro, 183
Vermes, G., 78
Versnel, Henk S., 164, 169, 173, 174, 176, 177
Vettius Valens, 103
Visintin, Monica, 135
Vogt, Kari, 278

Wade, Nicholas, 221
Wallace-Hadrill, Andrew, 42, 268
Waller, Daniel James, 176
Walsh, Matthew L., 103, 291, 295
Walsh, Robyn Faith, xii, 16, 179–96
Walters, Jonathan, 272
Warren, Meredith, 263
Wasserman, Emma, 13, 14, 53, 69, 70, 71, 97, 181, 192, 269, 296
Watson, Francis, 61
Weiss, Johannes, 117
Welcker, F. G., 64
Wendt, Heidi, x, xi, xii, 12, 14, 15, 16, 41–56, 147, 172, 203, 214, 216, 259, 282, 287, 294, 295
Whitmarsh, Tim, 44
Wilburn, Andrew, 163, 178
Williams, Craig, 263, 273
Williams, Margaret H., 76, 77
Wolter, Michael, 292
Wright, Benjamin G., III, 8, 288, 289
Wright, N. T., 269

Xenaitenos, 215
Xenophanes, 183
Xenophon, 230

Young, Stephen L., ix–xiii, x, xi, xiii, 5, 12, 13, 15, 64, 85, 259–79, 282, 287

Zamfir, Korinna, 225
Zawadzki, Konrad, 162
Zetterholm, Karin Hedner, x
Zetterholm, Magnus, ix, 6
Zimmerman, Christiane, 171
Zmith, Jonathan Z., ix
Zuckerman, Phil, 221